The Sacred Writings of Leo the Great

LEO THE GREAT

The Sacred Writings of Leo the Great
Jazzybee Verlag Jürgen Beck
86450 Altenmünster, Loschberg 9
Deutschland

ISBN: 9783849671754

Translated by Charles Lett Feltoe (1857 - 1926)

Cover Design: © Sue Colvil - Fotolia.com

www.jazzybee-verlag.de
admin@jazzybee-verlag.de

Printed by Createspace, North Charleston, SC, USA

CONTENTS:

Prefatory Note 1
Introduction 2
Letters 13
Letter I. To the Bishop of Aquileia. 13
Letter II. To Septimus, Bishop of Altinum. 14
Letter III. From Paschasinus, Bishop of Lilybaeum. 15
Letter IV. To the Bishops Appointed in Campania, Picenum,
Etruria, and All the Provinces. 15
Letter V. To the Metropolitan Bishops of Illyricum. 16
Letter VI. To Anastasius, Bishop of Thessalonica. 17
Letter VII. To the Bishops Throughout Italy. 19
Letter VIII. The Ordinance of Valentinian III. Concerning the Manichaeans. 20
Letter IX. To Dioscorus, Bishop of Alexandria. 20
Letter X. To the Bishops of the Province of Vienne.
In the Matter of Hilary, Bishop of Arles 22
Letter XI. An Ordinance of Valentinianus III. 27
Letter XII. 27
Letter XIII. To the Metropolitan Bishops in the Provinces of Illyricum. 31
Letter XIV. To Anastasius, Bishop of Thessalonica. 32
Letter XV. To Turribius, Bishop of Asturia,
Upon the Errors of the Priscillianists. 36
Letter XVI. To the Bishops of Sicily. 45
Letter XVII 49
Letter XVIII. To Januarius, Bishop of Aquileia 49
Letter XIX. To Dorus, Bishop of Beneventum. 50
Letter XX. To Eutyches, an Abbot of Constantinople. 52
Letter XXI. From Eutyches to Leo 52
Letter XXII . The First from Flavian, Bp. Of Constantinople to Pope Leo. 54
Letter XXIII. To Flavian, Bishop of Constantinople. 55
Letter XXIV. To Theodosius Augustus II. 56
Letter XXV. From Peter Chrysologus, Bishop of Ravenna, to Eutyches, the
Presbyter. 57

Letter XXVI. A Second One from Flavian to Leo. 57
Letter XXVII. To Flavian, Bishop of Constantinople. 59
Letter XXVIII. To Flavian Commonly Called "The Tome" 59
Letter XXIX. To Theodosius Augustus. 65
Letter XXX. To Pulcheria Augusta. 65
Letter XXXI. To Pulcheria Augusta 65
Letter XXXII. To the Archimandrites of Constantinople 68
Letter XXXIII. To the Synod of Ephesus 69
Letter XXXIV. To Julian, Bishop of Cos. 70
Letter XXXV.to Julian, Bishop of Cos 70
Letter XXXVI. To Flavlan, Bishop of Constantinople. 73
Letter XXXVII . To Theodoslus Augustus. 73
Letter XXXVIII . To Flavian, Bishop of Constantinople. 73
Letter XXXIX. To Flavian, Bishop of Constantinople. 74
Letter XL.to the Bishops of the Province of Arles in Gaul. 74
Letter XLI. To Ravennius, Bishop of Arles. 75
Letter XLII. To Ravennius, Bishop of Arles. 75
Letter XLIII . To Theodosius Augustus. 75
Letter XLIV. To Theodosius Augustus. 76
Letter XLV. To Pulcheria Augusta. 78
Letter XLVI. From Hilary, Then Deacon (Afterwards Bishop of Rome) to
Pulcheria Augusta. 79
Letter XLVII. To Anastasius, Bishop of Thessalonica. 79
Letter XLVIII. To Julian, Bishop of Cos. 80
Letter XLIX. To Flavian, Bishop of Constantinople 80
Letter L. To the People of Constantinople, by the Hand of Epiphanius and
Dionysius, Notary of the Church of Rome. 80
Letter LI. To Faustus and Other Presbyters and
Archimandrites in Constantinople. 80
Letter LII. From Theodoret, Bishop of Cyrus, to Leo. (See Vol. III. Of This Series,
P. 293.) 80
Letter LIII. A Fragment of a Letter from Anatolius,
Bishop of Constantinople, to Leo 83
Letter LIV. To Theodosius Augustus 83
Letters LV to LVIII. 83

Letter LVI. (from Galla Placidia Augusta to Theodosius). 83
Letter LIX. To the Clergy and People of the City of Constantinople. 84
Letter LX. To Pulcheria Augusta. 87
Letter LXI. To Martinus and Faustus, Presbyters. 87
Letter LXV. From the Bishops of the Province of Arles. 87
Letter LXVI. Leo's Reply to Letter LXV. 87
Letter LXVII. To Ravennius, Bishop of Arles. 88
Letter LXVIII. From Three Gallic Bishops to St. Leo. 89
Letter LXIX. (to Theodosius Augustus.) 90
Letter LXX. To Pulcheria Augusta. 91
Letter LXXI. To the Archimandrites of Constantinople. 91
Letter LXXII. To Faustus, One of the Archimandrites at Constantinople. 91
Letter LXXIII. From Valentinian and Marcian. 92
Letter LXXIV. To Martinus, Another of the Archimandrites at Constantinople. ... 92
Letter LXXV. To Faustus and Martinus Together. 92
Letter LXXVI. From Marcianus Augustus to Leo. 92
Letter LXXVII. From Pulcheria Augusta to Leo. 92
Letter LXXVIII. Leo's Answer to Marcianus. 92
Letter LXXIX. To Pulcheria Augusta. 92
Letter LXXX. (to Anatolius, Bishop of Constantinople.) 93
Letter LXXXI. To Bishop Julian. 95
Letter LXXXII. To Marcian Augustus. 95
Letter LXXXIII. To the Same Marcian. 96
Letter LXXXIV. To Pulcheria Augusta. 96
Letter LXXXV. To Anatolius, Bishop of Constantinople. 96
Letter LXXXVI. To Julian, Bishop of Cos. 97
Letter LXXXVII. To Anatolius, Bishop of Constantinople. 97
Letter LXXXVIII. To Paschasinus, Bishop of Lilybaeum. 98
Letter LXXXIX. To Marcian Augustus. 99
Letter XC. To Marcian Augustus. 99
Letter XCI. To Anatolius, Bishop of Constantinople. 99
Letter XCII. To Julian, Bishop of Cos. 99
Letter XCIII. To the Synod of Chalcedon. 100

Letter XCIV. To Marcian Augustus. 101

Letter XCV. To Pulcheria Augusta by the Hand of Theoctistus the Magistrian .. 101

Letter XCVI. To Ravennius, Bishop of Arles. 102

Letter XCVII. From Eusebius, Bishop of Milan, to Leo. 102

Letter XCVIII. From the Synod of Chalcedon to Leo. 102

Letter XCIX. From Ravennus and Other Gallic Bishops. 105

Letter C. From the Emperor Marcian. 105

Letter CI. From Anatolius, Bishop of Constantinople, to Leo. 105

Letter CII. To the Gallic Bishops. 106

Letter CIII. To the Gallic Bishops. 106

Letter CIV. Leo, the Bishop, to Marcian Augustus. 106

Letter CV. (to Pulcheria Augusta About the Self-Seeking of Anatolius.) 108

Letter CVI. To Anatolius, Bishop of Constantinople, in Rebuke of His Self-Seeking. 110

Letter CVII. To Julian, Bishop of Cos. 113

Letter CVIII. To Theodore, Bishop of Forum Julii. 113

Letter CIX. To Julian, Bishop of Cos. 115

Letter CX. From Marcian Augustus. 116

Letter CXI. To Marcian Augustus. 116

Letter CXII. To Pulcheria Augusta. 116

Letter CXIII. To Julian, Bishop of Cos. 117

Letter CXIV. To the Bishops Assembled in Synod at Chalcedon. 119

Letter CXV. To Marcian Augustus. 119

Letter CXV. To Pulcheria Augusta. 119

Letter CXVII. To Julian, Bishop of Cos. 119

Letter CXVIII. To the Same Julian, Bishop of Cos. 121

Letter CXIX. To Maximus, Bishop of Antioch, by the Hand of Marian the Presbyter, and Olympius the Deacon. 121

Letter CXX. To Theodoret, Bishop of Cyrus, on Perseverance in the Faith. 123

Letters CXXI. And CXXII. The Former to Marcian Augustus, and the Other to Julian the Bishop. 127

Letter CXXIII. To Eudocia Augusta, About the Monksof Palestine 127

Letter CXXIV. To the Monks of Palestine. 128

Letter CXXV. To Julian, the Bishop, by Count Rodanus. 133

Letter CXXVI. To Marcian Augustus. 133
Letter CXXVII. To Julian, Bishop of Cos. 133
Letter CXXVII. To Marcian Augustus. 133
Letter CXXIX. To Proterius, Bishop of Alexandria. 134
Letter CXXX. To Marcian Augustus. 135
Letter CXXXI. To Julian, Bishop of Cos. 136
Letter CXXXII. From Anatolius, Bishop of Constantinople, to Leo. 136
Letter CXXXIII. From Proterius, Bishop of Alexandria, to Leo. 136
Letter CXXXIV. To Marcian Augustus. 136
Letter CXXXV.to Anatolius. 136
Letter CXXXVI. To Marcian Augustus. 136
Letter CXXXVII. To the Same, and on the Same Day. 136
Letter CXXXVIII. To the Bishops of Gaul and Spain.(on Easter.) 136
Letter CXL. To Julian, Bishop of Cos. 138
Letter CXLI. To the Same. 138
Letter CXLIII. To Anatolius, Bishop of Constantinople. 138
Letter CXLIV. To Julian, Bishop of Cos. 139
Letter CXLV.to Leo Augustus 139
Letter CXLVI. To Anatolius, Bishop of Constantinople. 139
Letter CXLVIII. To Leo Augustus. 139
Letter CXLIX. To Basil, Bishop of Antioch. 139
Letter CL to Euxitheus, Bishop of Thessalonica (and Others) 139
Letter CLII. To Julian, Bishop of Cos. 139
Letter CLIII. To Aetius, Presbyter ,of Constantinople. 140
Letter CLIV. To the Egyptian Bishops. 140
Letter CLV. To Anatolius, Bishop of Constantinople. 140
Letter CLVI. To Leo Augustus. 140
Letter CLVII. To Anatolius, Bishop of Constantinople. 143
Letter CLVIII . To the Catholic Bishops of Egypt Sojourning in Constantinople.
.... 143
Letter CLIX. To Nicaetas, Bishop of Aquileia 144
Letter CLX. 145
Letter CLXI. To the Presbyters, Deacons and Clergy of the Church of
Constantinople. 146

Letter CLXII. To Leo Augustus. 146

Letter CLXIII. To Anatolius, Bishop of Constantinople. By Patritius the Deacon the Deacon. 148

Letter CLXIV To Leo Augustus. 148

Letter CLXV. To Leo Augustus. 151

Letter CLXVI. To Neo, Bishop of Ravenna. 151

Letter CLXVII . To Rusticus, Bishop of Gallia Narbonensis, with the Replies to His Questions on Various Points. 152

Letter CLXVIII. To All the Bishops of Campania, Samnium and Picenum. 157

Letter CLXIX. To Leo Augustus. 157

Letter CLXX. To Gennadius, Bishop of Constantinople 158

Letter CLXXI. To Timothy, Bishop of Alexandria. 158

Letter CLXXII. To the Presbyters and Deacons of the Church of Alexandria. 159

Letter CLXXIII. To Certain Egyptian Bishops. 159

Sermons. **160**

Sermon I. Preached on His Birthday , or Day of Ordination. 160

Sermon II. On His Birthday, II.: Delivered on the Anniversary Of His Consecration.) 160

Sermon III. On His Birthday, III: Delivered on the Anniversary of His Elevation to the Pontificate. 161

Sermon IX. Upon the Collections , IV. 164

Sermon X. On the Collections, V. 166

Sermon XII. On the Fast of The, Tenth Month, I. 168

Sermon XVI. On the Fast of the Tenth Month. 170

Sermon XVII. On the Fast of the Tenth Month, VI. 173

Sermon XIX. On the Fast of the Ten Month, VIII. 175

Sermon XXI. On the Feast of the Nativity, I. 177

Sermon XXII. On the Feast of the Nativity, II. 178

Sermon XXIII. On the Feast of the Nativity, III. 181

Sermon XXIV. On the Feast of the Nativity, IV. 184

Sermon XXVI. On the Feast of the Nativity, VI. 187

Sermon XXVII. On the Feast of the Nativity, VII. 190

Sermon XXVIII. On the Festival of the Nativity, VIII. 193

Sermon XXXI. On the Feast of the Epiphany, I. 196

Sermon XXXIII. On the Feast of the Epiphany, III. 198

Sermon XXXIV. On the Feast of the Epiphany, IV. 200

Sermon XXXVI. On the Feast of the Epiphany, VI. 204

Sermon XXXIX. On Lent, I. 206

Sermon XL. On Lent, II. 209

Sermon XLII. On Lent, IV. 211

Sermon XLVI. On Lent, VIII. 214

Sermon XLIX. On Lent, XI. 216

Sermon LI. A Homily Delivered on the Saturday Before the Second Sunday in Lent—On the Transfiguration, *S. Matt.* XVII. 1–13. 219

Sermon LIV. On the Passion, III.; Delivered on the Sunday Before Easter. 223

Sermon LV. On the Lord's Passion IV., Delivered on Wednesday in Holy Week. 225

Sermon LVIII. (on the Passion, VII.) 227

Sermon LIX. (on the Passion, VIII.: on Wednesday in Holy Week.) 230

Sermon LXII. (on the Passion, XI.) 234

Sermon LXIII. (on the Passion, XII.: Preached on Wednesday.) 236

Sermon LXVII. (on the Passion, XVI.: Delivered on the Sunday.) 239

Sermon LXVIII. (on the Passion, XVII.: Delivered on the Wednesday.) 242

Sermon LXXI. (on the Lord's Resurrection, I.; Delivered on Holy Saturday in the Vigil of Easter.) 244

Sermon LXXII. (on the Lord's Resurrection, II.) 247

Sermon LXXIII. (on the Lord's Ascension, I.) 250

Sermon LXXIV. (on the Lord's Ascension, II.) 252

Sermon LXXV. (on Whitsuntide, I.) 254

Sermon LXXVII. (on Whitsuntide, III.) 257

Sermon LXXVIII. (on the Whidsuntide Fast, I.) 259

Sermon LXXXII. On the Feast Of the Apostles Peter and Paul (June 29). 260

Sermon LXXXIV. Concerning the Neglect of the Commemoration. 263

Sermon LXXXV. On the Feast of S. Laurence the Martyr (Aug. 10). 264

Sermon LXXXVIII. On the Fast of the Seventh Month, III 265

Sermon XC. (on the Fast of Seventh Month, V.) 267

Sermon XCI on the Fast of the Seventh Month, .VI. 269

Sermon XCV A Homily on the Beatitudes, St. Matt. V. 1–9. 270

PREFATORY NOTE

Except such valuable help-chiefly however in the way of comment and explanation-as Canon Bright's volume (S. Leo on the Incarnation) has supplied, both the selection and the translation of the Letters and Sermons of Leo Magnus are practically original. It is even more difficult to feel satisfied oneself, than to satisfy others either with a selection from a great man's works or with a translation of them. The powers of Leo as a preacher both of doctrine and of practice are very remarkable, and in my anxiety to keep within the limits imposed by the publishers, I have erred in presenting too few rather than too many of the Sermons to the English reader. Only those that are generally held genuine are represented, though several of the doubtful ones are fine sermons, and those translated are in most cases no better than those omitted. Even when the same thought is repeated again and again (as is often the case), it is almost always clothed in such different language, and surrounded with so many other thoughts of value, that every sermon has an almost equal claim to be selected.

With regard to the Letters, the series connected wit; the Eutychian controversy-the chief occupation of Leo's episcopate-is given nearly complete, whereas only specimens of his mode of dealing with other matters have been selected for presentation. With one or two exceptions, however, I feel more confident about the Letters than about the Sermons that the omitted are less important than the included. I wish I could make even a similar boast about the merits of the translation.

The text rendered is for the most part that of the Ballerinii as given by Migne (Patrologie, Vol. LIV.), though a more critical edition is much to be desired.

Charles Lett Feltoe.
Fornham All Saints,
Eastertide, 1894.

INTRODUCTION

Life

The details of Leo's early life are extremely scanty and uncertain. It is probable that he was born between 390 and 400a.d.There is a tradition that his father was a Tuscan named Quintian, and that Volaterrae , a town in the north of Etruria, was his birthplace. Of his youth we know nothing: his writings contain no allusions to that or to any other part of his personal history. One may reasonably infer from the essentially Roman character of his literary style, from the absence of quotations out of pagan literature, and from his self-confessed ignorance of Greek, that his education was, though thorough after its kind, limited to Christian and Latin culture. A reference to the pages of any secular history of the Roman empire will give the reader an idea of the scenes amidst which, and no doubt by the aid of which, Leo the boy was formed and moulded into Leo Magnus, the first great Latin-speaking pope and bishop of Rome, the first great Italian theologian, "the final defender of the truth of our Lord's Person against both its assailants " (i.e. Nestorius and Eutyches), whom it pleased God in His providence to raise up in the Western (and not as oftenest hitherto in the Eastern) portion of His Church. Politically, intellectually, and theologically the period in which this great character grew up, lived and worked, was one of transition: the Roman Empire, learning and thought, paganism were each alike at the last gasp, and neither in Church nor State was there any other at all of Leo's calibre, This consideration will account for the wonderful influence, partly for good and partly for bad, which his master-mind and will was permitted to exercise on the after-ages of Christendom.

During his early manhood the Pelagian controversy was raging, and it is thought that the acolyte named Leo, whom Augustine mentions in his letters on this subject as employed by pope Zosimus to carry communications between Rome and the African church, is the future pope. Under Celestine, who was pope from 422 to 433, he was archdeacon of Rome, and he seems already to have made a name for himself: for Cassian, the Gallican writer whom he had urged to write a work on the Incarnation, in yielding to his suggestion, calls him "the ornament of the Roman church and of the Divine ministry," and S. Cyril (in 431, the date of the Council of Ephesus) appeals to Leo (as Leo has himself recorded in Letter CXIX., chap. 4) to procure the pope's support in stopping the ambitious designs of Juvenal, bishop of Jerusalem. Under the next pope, Sixtus (432–440), we hear of him in Prosper's *Chronicon* (under the year 439) again in connexion with Pelagianism : he seems to have stirred up the vigilance of the pope against the crafty designs of one Julius of Eclanum, who, having been deprived of his bishopric for holding that heresy, was attempting to be restored without full proof of orthodoxy.

Next year (440) was a momentous one in the life of Leo, and in the history of the papacy. Leo was away on one of those political missions, which bear out our estimate of him as perhaps the most conspicuous and popular figure of his times . The powerful general Aetius Placidia, the queen-regent's chief adviser and *aide-de-camp*, was quarrelling (a not unusual occurrence at this stage of the empire) with Albinus, a rival general in Gaul. Leo was sent to bring about a reconciliation, and apparently with success. In his absence Sixtus died, and it is not surprising that without any hesitation clergy and people should have elected Leo into his place. A deputation was sent after him to hasten his return, and after an interval of forty days he arrived. The whole church received him with acclamation, and on Sept. 29 he was ordained both priest and 47th bishop of Rome. His brief sermon on the occasion is the earliest in the collection, and will be found translated on p. 115 of our selection. His earliest extant letter belongs likewise to the first year of his episcopate, which we have also included in our selection: it is addressed to the bishop of Aquileia in reproof of his and his fellow-bishops' remissness in dealing with Pelagianism in that province. Thus early did he give proof of his conception of his office, as investing him with an authority which extended over the whole of Christendom as the successor of S. Peter. Still clearer proofs were soon forthcoming. Not to speak of a letter in a similarly dictatorial strain to the bishops of the home provinces of Campania, Picenum, and Etruria, which belongs to the year 443, we find him in 444 interfering, though more guardedly, with the province of Illyricum, which was then debatable ground between the East and West; in 445 dictating church regulations to S. Cyril's new successor at Alexandria, Dioscorus, his future adversary; and in 446 and 447 asserting his authority on various pretexts, now in Africa, now in Spain, now in Sicily; while in 444 also occurred his famous and not very creditable encounter with Hilary, bishop of Arles in Gaul. The incidents in this quarrel are briefly these: Hilary in a provincial synod had deposed a bishop, Celidonius, for technical irregularities in accordance with the Gallican canons. Celidonius appealed to Rome. Thereupon Hilary set out in the depth of winter on foot to Rome, but, after an ineffectual statement of his case and some rough treatment from Leo, returned to Gaul. Leo gave orders that Celidonius was to be restored, and Hilary deprived of all his metropolitical rights in the province of Vienne. How far the sentence was carried out is not clear. In a later letter he desires that the bishop of Vienne should be regarded as metropolitan, and yet he seems to recognize Hilary's successor, Ravennius, as still metropolitan in Letter XL., while in 450 the bishops of the one district addressed a formal petition for the restoration of Arles to its old rank, and the bishops of the other a counter-petition in favour of Vienne; whereupon Leo effected a temporary *modus vivendi* by dividing the jurisdiction between the two sees.

Returning to the year 444, besides consulting S. Cyril and Paschasinus, bishop of Lilybaeum, on the right day for keeping Easter that year (a moot point which recurred in other years) we find Leo still taking active measures against heresy, this time that of the Manichaeans . The followers of this sect had since 439 greatly increased at Rome, owing to the number of refugees who came over from Carthage after its capture by Genseric and his Vandal hosts (see Sermon XVI. 5). They were an universally abhorred body, and deservedly so, if all we read about them be really true. In 444, therefore, it was determined, if possible, to stamp them out. By Leo's order a strict search was instituted throughout the city, and the large number of those who were discovered, were brought up for trial before a combined bench of civil and ecclesiastical judges. The most heinous crimes were revealed Those who refused to recant were banished for life and suffered various other penalties by the emperor Valentinian's decree, while Leo used all his influence to obtain similar treatment for them in other parts of Christendom. Three years later the spread of Priscillianism, a heresy which in some points was akin to Manichaeism among other heresies, and a long account of which will be found in Letter XV., was the occasion to which we have referred as giving a pretext for his interference in the affairs of the Spanish church.

We now reach the famous Eutychian controversy, on which Leo's chief claim to our thanks and praise rests: for to his action in it the Church owes the final and complete definition of the cardinal doctrine of the Incarnation. The heresy of Eutyches, as was the case with so many other heresies, sprang from the reaction against a counter heresy. Most of the controversies which have again and again imperilled the cause of Christianity, have been due to human frailty, which has been unable to keep the proportion of the Faith. Over-statement on the one side leads to over-statement on the other, and thus the golden mean is lost sight of. Eutyches, an archimandrite (or head of a monastery) at Constantinople, had distinguished himself for zeal during the years 428 to 431 in combating the heresy of Nestorius, who had denied the perfect union of the Godhead and the Manhood in the one Person, Christ Jesus. He had objected to the Virgin being called *Theotokos* (God-bearing), and said that *Christotokos* (Christ-bearing) would be more correct. This position, as involving two persons as well as two natures in our Lord, was condemned by the 3rd General Council, which met at Ephesus in 431, S. Cyril being its chief opponent. But Eutyches in his eagerness to proclaim the Unity of the Person of Christ fell into the opposite extreme, and asserted that though the two natures of Christ were originally distinct, yet after the union they became but one nature, the human being changed into the Divine. Eutyches appears to have been a highly virtuous person, but possessed of a dull, narrow mind, unfit for the subtleties of theological discussion, and therefore unable to grasp the conception of two Natures in one Person: and nothing worse than stupidity and obstinacy is brought against him by his stern but clear-headed opponent Leo.

The person, however, who first brought the poor recluse's heretical statements prominently into notice was much more reckless and intemperate in his language. This was Eusebius, bishop of Dorylaeum, who took the opportunity of a local synod held in Constantinople under the presidency of the gentle Flavian, in November, 448, for other business, to petition against his former friend and ally as a blasphemer and a madman. The synod, after expostulating with the accuser for his violence, at last reluctantly consented to summon Eutyches to an account. The summons was at least twice repeated and disobeyed under the pretext first that he might not leave the monastery, then that he was ill. At last Eutyches yielded, and appeared accompanied by a crowd of monks and soldiers and by Florentius, a patrician for whom the weak Emperor (Theodosius II.) had been influenced by the eunuch Chrysaphius, Eutyches' godson, to demand a seat at the council. After a long conversation, in which Eutyches tried to evade a definite statement, he was at last forced to confess that our Lord was of two natures before the union, but that after the union there was but one nature (see Letter XXVIII. (Tome), chap vi.). As he persisted in maintaining this position, he was condemned and thrust out of the priesthood and Church-communion. During the reading of the condemnation and the breaking up of the conclave, Eutyches is alleged to have told Florentius that he appealed to the bishops of Rome, Alexandria, and Jerusalem. Flavian, as president of the council, thought it his duty to acquaint the bishops of Rome and other Sees of the first rank with what had taken place. For some unknown reason his letter to Leo was delayed, and the appeal of Eutyches and a letter from the Emperor was the first information that he received. As might be expected from Leo's conception of his office, he was much incensed at this apparent neglect, and wrote to the Emperor explaining his ignorance of the facts, and to Flavian, complaining of being kept in ignorance, and *prima facie* of Eutyches' treatment. Meanwhile the delayed epistle arrived from Flavian, and the account given was enough to satisfy Leo, who thereupon (May, 449) replied briefly expressing his approval and promising a fuller treatment of the question. This promise was fulfilled next month in the shape of the world-famous "Tome," which forms Letter XXVIII. in the Leonine collection. The proper significance of this document is well expressed by Mr. Gore : it is, he says, "still more remarkable for its contents than for the circumstances which produced it," though "in itself it is a sign of the times: for here we have a Latin bishop, ignorant of Greek, defining the faith for Greek-speaking bishops, in view of certain false opinions of Oriental origin." Without reviewing in detail the further correspondence that Leo carried on with the various civil and ecclesiastical authorities at Constantinople (among them being the influential and orthodox Pulcheria the Emperor's sister), we pass on to the events connected with the second council of Ephesus. Through the influence of Chrysaphius, as we have already seen, the Emperor was all along on the side of Eutyches, and it was apparently at his instigation and in spite of Leo's guarded dissuasion that the council was now convened and met in August, 449. The bishop of Rome excused himself from personal attendance on the score of pressing business at homeland sent three legates with instructions to represent hisviews, viz. Julius, bishop of Puteoli, Renatus, a presbyter, and Hilary, a deacon, together with Dulcitius, a notary . They started about the middle of June, and the Synod opened on the 8th of August, in the church of the B.V.M. By the Emperor's order Dioscorus, patriarch of Alexandria, was president, Leo's chief representative sat next him, and Flavian was placed only 5th, the bishop of Antioch and Jerusalem being set above him: 130 bishops in all were admitted, those who had condemned Eutyches being excluded. Owing partly to the presence of the soldiery and a number of turbulent monks under the Syrian archimandrite Barsubas, the proceedings soon became riotous and disorderly. The "Tome" was not read at all, though that was the purpose of its composition. Eutyches was admitted to make his defence, which was received as completely satisfactory. The acts of the Synod of Constantinople on being read excited great indignation. Amid tremendous uproar Eutyches was formally restored to communion and his former position, and the president pronounced deposition upon Flavian and Eusebius. Flavian appealed, and Hilary , after uttering a monosyllabic protest, "*contradicitur,*" managed to make good his escape and carry the lamentable tidings to his anxiously-expectant chief at Rome. The other bishops all more or less reluctantly subscribed the restoration of Eutyches and the deposition of Flavian and Eusebius. The end of Flavian is variously recorded, but the most accurate version appears to be that amid many blows and rough usage he was cast into prison, then driven into exile, and that within a few days he died of the bodily and mental injuries he had received at Epypa, a village in Lydia. These calamitous proceedings Leo afterwards stigmatized as *Latrocinium* (brigandage), and the council is generally known as the Robber council of Ephesus.

At the time when the disastrous news arrived at Rome, Leo was presiding over a council which he had convened; in violent indignation he immediately dispatched letters right and left in his own and his colleagues' name. There is a letter to Flavian, of whose death of course he was not yet aware; there are others to the archimandrites and the whole church of Constantinople, to Julian, bishop of Cos, and to Anastasius, bishop of Thessalonica. He used all his influence to prevail on the Emperor to summon a fresh council, this time in Italy, writing to him himself, and getting Pulcheria on the spot, and Valentinian, his mother Placidia and his wife Eudoxia, by letters from Rome, to assist his cause. As yet, however, the very stars in their courses seemed to fight against him, and the outlook grew yet darker. In the spring of 450 Dioscorus' predominance in the East had become so great that ten bishops were found to join with him in actually excommunicating the bishop of Rome. At the Court, though Pulcheria remained true to the Faith, Chrysaphius still seems to have swayed the Emperor, and to have obtained from him the edict which was issuer confirming the acts of the Ephesine council The fact, too, that Flavian's successor, Anatolius, had in the past been associated with Dioscorus caused him not unnatural anxiety, and this feeling turned to one of actual offence on receiving a letter from Anatolius, in which he simply announces his consecration without asking his consent. Thereupon Leo demanded of the Emperor that Anatolius should make some public proof and profession of his orthodoxy on the lines of the Tome and other catholic statements, and in the month of July sent legates to support this demand.

At this moment the horizon suddenly brightened Before the arrival of the legates, Theodosius was killed by a fall from his horse, and to the triumph of the orthodox cause, his sister, Pulcheria (the first Roman Empress), succeeded him. The whole aspect of things was soon changed. Chrysaphius was almost at once executed, and shortly afterwards Pulcheria married and shared the Eastern empire with Marcian, who was for bravery, wisdom and orthodoxy an altogether suitable partner of her throne.

Leo's petition for a new Synod was now granted, but the place of meeting was to be in the East, not in the West, as more convenient for the Emperor. In the interval S. Flavian's body was brought by reverent hands to Constantinople and buried in the church of the Apostles, and a still more hopeful sign of the times-Anatolius and many other bishops signed the Tome. Hitherto Leo had asked that both councils (that which had condemned and that which had acquitted Eutyches of heresy) should be treated as null and void, and that the matter should be discussed *de nova*. Now, however, he shows a significant change of front: the Faith, he maintains, is decided: nothing needs now to be done but to reject the heretics and to use proper caution in re-admitting the penitents: there is no occasion for a general council. And consequently he semis bishop Lucentius and Basil a presbyter as legates to assist Anatolius in this matter of rejection and re-admission. But, as the Emperor adhered to his determination, Leo was obliged to give way, and though still declining to attend in person, sent bishop Paschasinus of Sicily and Boniface a presbyter with written instructions to act with the former two as his representatives; Julian of Cos, who from his knowledge of Greek and Eastern affairs was a most useful addition, was also asked to be of the number. Nicaea in Bithynia had been fixed upon as the rendezvous, and there on Sept. 1, 451, 520 bishops assembled . The Emperor, however, was too busy and too anxious over his military operations against Attila and the Huns to meet them there, and therefore invites them to Chalcedon, which being on the Bosporus was much nearer to Constantinople. There accordingly on

Oct. 8, in the church of S. Euphemia the Martyr, the council was at last opened. The Emperor himself was still absent, but he was well represented by a goodly number of state officials. In accordance with Leo's request, Paschasinus, with his brother legates, presided: next sat Anatolius, Dioscorus, Maximus of Antioch and Juvenal of Jerusalem, with a copy of the Gospels in the midst Leo's representatives began by trying to have Dioscorus ejected: they only succeeded in getting him deposed from his seat of honour and placed in the middle of the room together with Eusebius of Dorylaeum, his accuser, and Theodoret of Cyrus, the eminent theologian, who was suspected of Nestorianizing language. The remainder of the first day was spent in reading the acts of the Ephesine council, which in the midst of much uproar were provisionally condemned.

At the second session (Oct. 13), the Tome was read by the Imperial secretary, Veronician, and enthusiastically received: "Peter has spoken by Leo," they said. But objections being raised by the bishops of Palestine and Illyria that the twofold Nature was over-stated, its final acceptance was postponed for a few days, that a committee which was nominated might reason with the dissentients.

At the third Session (Oct. 13), Dioscorus, who refused to appear, was accused by Eusebius and by general consent condemned, being deprived of his rank and office as bishop, and the Emperor having confirmed the sentence, he was banished to Gangra in Paphlagonia, and there three years later (in 454) died. His successor at Alexandria was the orthodox Proterius, who was however never recognized by a large portion of the Egyptian Church: even in the Synod of Chalcedon many of the Egyptian bishops refused to sign the "Tome" at the fourth session, on the plea that the custom of their church forbade them to act without the consent of the archbishop, who was not yet appointed, and the still surviving "Jacobite" schism originated with the deposition of Dioscorus.

The fourth session was held on the 17th, and the misgivings of the Palestinian and Illyrian bishops having been quieted in the interval, the Tome was adopted.

In the fifth session (Oct. 24), a difficulty arose over a definition of the Faith which had been composed, but did not satisfy the Roman legates with regard to Eutychianism. However a committee, which was appointed, took it in hand again, and the result of their labours was accepted as fully guarding against the errors both of Nestorius and Eutyches. The remaining sessions were occupied with less important matters, and with drawing up the canons of the Council, of which one-the 28th-was designed to settle the precedence of the patriarch of Constantinople ("New Rome" as it was called), and to give him a place second to the bishop of old Rome. Against this audacious innovation the Roman legates in vain protested; the bitter pill, enwrapped in much sugar, was conveyed to Leo in the synodal letter, and produced the most lamentable results.

The last meeting of the Council on Nov. 1 was graced by the attendance in full state of Marcian and Pulcheria. The Emperor delivered an address, and at its conclusion he and the Empress were vociferously applauded, Marcian being styled the "second Constantine."

To return to Leo, we have letters from Marcian, Anatolius, and Julian, all trying to carry off the difficulty of the 28th Canon under the triumph of the Roman views in other respects. But Leo refused to be conciliated. The canon, he maintains, is in direct violation of the decrees of Nicaea (in which statement he makes an unpardonable confusion between the Nicene canons and those of Sardica, which were often appended to them). With Anatolius he was especially displeased, considering that his doubtful precedents ought to have made him extremely careful not to offend. He therefore ceased all communication with him, eagerly seizing at pretexts of complaint against him, and appointing Julian his *apocrisiarius* or resident representative and correspondent. All this time Marcian continued pleading and Leo inflexible, until Anatolius at last yielded, and the matter for the time is satisfactorily settled, though it must not be imagined that the disputed canon was ever annulled.

Eutychianism still lingered on and caused disturbances in various parts of the East, especially among the monks. In Palestine, Juvenal, the bishop of Jerusalem, was deposed, and the Empress Eudocia, Theodosius II.'s widow, who was living in retirement in that city, was suspected of favouring the rioters. Leo therefore wrote letters to her and to others, in which he restates the doctrine of the Incarnation, endeavouring to clear up any misconceptions which the inaccuracy of the Greek version of the Tome may possibly have caused. Eventually he was able to congratulate the Emperor on the restoration of peace and order in that quarter of their empire.

Similar riots were reported in Cappadocia, where the monks were led by one of their number named George, in Constantinople itself, where the ringleaders were Carosus and Dorotheus, and in Egypt.

But before we narrate the final victory of the orthodox cause throughout Christendom against the Eutychians, there are two events in the political world, belonging one to the year 452 and the other to 455, to which reference must be made, as showing the remarkable prestige which Leo's character had gained for him among all classes of society. When he was made pope we found him absent in Gaul mediating between rival generals. We now find him employed on still harder missions. Leo himself makes none, but the slightest indirect allusion to either of these later incidents, but this silence is only characteristic of the man, in whom there is no trace of vain-boasting, and who consistently sank the personality of himself as well as of others in the principles and causes which absorbed him. There seems no reason, however, to doubt the substantial truth of what Prosper and others have related. In 452 Attila and the Huns, notwithstanding the defeat they had sustained from Aetius at Chalons, continued their devastating inroad into Italy. The whole city of Rome was paralysed with terror, and at last sent Leo with the Consular Avienus and the Prefect Tregetius to intercede with them. The meeting took place on lake Benacus, and Leo's arguments, aided, it is thought, by rumours of threatened invasion at home, persuaded Attila to retire beyond the Danube, on condition of receiving Honoria with a rich dowry as his wife. This was the last time that Attila troubled the Romans: for he died the next year.

Less than three years after this successful encounter with the barbarian, in 455 Leo's powerful services were again brought into requisition by the State. That year the licentious Valentinian was murdered at the instigation of an enraged husband, Maximus, who subsequently compelled the widow, Eudoxia, to marry him. Eudoxia, however, discovering the part Maximus had taken in Valentinian's death, invited the Vandals under Genseric to invade Italy. Maximus himself was put to death before the invaders reached Rome: but, when they did arrive, the panic-stricken citizens again threw themselves into the hands of Leo, who at the head of the clergy went forth to meet the foe outside the city. Once more his intercessions in some measure prevailed, but not sufficiently to prevent the city being pillaged fourteen days.

We now return to more purely religious matters. In 457 Marcian died (his wife having pre-deceased him four years), and was succeeded by a Thracian, named Leo. Fresh outbreaks immediately took place both at Constantinople and at Alexandria: at the former place they were soon stopped, but at Alexandria they were more serious and prolonged. The disaffected monks set up one of their number, Timothy Aelurus (or the Cat) in opposition to Proterius, who was soon after foully murdered in the baptistery, to which he had fled. This flagrant outrage at once aroused the bishop of Rome to fresh energy in every direction: by his promptitude the new Emperor was stirred to action, among the other means employed being a re-statement of the Faith in a long epistle with a catena of patristic authority, sometimes called "the Second Tome." Aelurus was deposed and banished, and another Timothy, surnamed Solophaciolus, of well-approved orthodoxy, elected into his place. This satisfactory consummation was effected in 460, while a no less orthodox successor, named Gennadius, had been found two years before, when Anatolius died, for the See of Constantinople. Thus Leo's joy was full at last, as his latest letters testify. Late in the year 461 he died, after a rule of twenty-one years, during which he had won at least one great victory for the Faith, and had given the See of Rome a prestige, which may be said to have lasted even to the present day.

His body was buried in the church of S. Peter's, since which time it has been thrice moved to different positions, once towards the end of the 7th century by Pope Sergius, again in 1607, after the re-building of the church in its present form, and lastly in 1715. As "saint" and "confessor" from the earliest times, as "doctor of the church" since 1754, he is commemorated in the East on Feb. 18, in the West on April 11.

"It will not be wholly out of place," says Mr. Gore, "to mention that tradition looks back to Leo as the benefactor of many of the Roman churches: he is said to have restored their silver ornaments after the ravages of the Vandals, and to have repaired the basilicas of S. Peter and S. Paul, placing a mosaic in the latter, which represented the adoration of the four and twenty elders: we are told also that he built a church of S. Cornelius, established some monks at S. Peter's, instituted guardians for the tombs of the Apostles, and erected a fountain before S. Paul's, where the people might wash before entering the church."

The only writings of Leo which are usually accepted as authentic are his numerous Sermons and Letters. (certain anti-Pelagian treatises and a long tract upon Humility in the form of a letter to Demetrias, a virgin, have been ascribed to him; but the most important work of all the doubtful ones is a "Sacramentary," which is one of the earliest extant of the Roman church, and is sometimes held to be Leo's composition or compilation. Many of the collects and prayers which it contains bear a remarkable resemblance to his teaching, and may well have come from his pen: there is indeed good reason for the opinion that the Collect proper, which is a distinct feature of the Western Church, owes its origin to Leo.

As a theologian Leo is thoroughly Western in type, being not speculative but dogmatic: no one was better suited in God's Providence to give the final completeness to the Church's Doctrine of the Incarnation than this clear-sighted, unimaginative, and persistent bishop of Rome. His theological position on the cardinal doctrines of the Faith is identical with that of the Athanasian symbol, to the language of which his own language often bears a close resemblance. With his theory of the Pope as universal Ruler of the Church in virtue of his being the successor of S. Peter' the vast majority of English-speaking people will have but little sympathy: and yet it can but be admired from an objective standpoint as a bold, grand, and almost original conception. And there are no doubt many smaller points of detail in his writings connected more with discipline than with doctrine, which will now be reckoned if not as actually objectionable, at least as arising from forgotten needs or belonging to a byegone system: among these may be instanced his objection to slaves as clergy and to the celebration of the Eucharist more than once in one day except on festivals, where the church is too small to hold all the worshippers at once: his advocacy of the innovation of private instead of public confession for ordinary penitents, and on the other hand his insisting on the old rule that baptism should be administered only twice a year (at Easter and at Whitsuntide): and again the somewhat undue prominence that he gives to fasting and almsgiving as being on a level with prayer for Lenten or Ember exercises, and to the intercessions of the saints-particularly of the patron saints of Rome, SS. Peter, Paul, and Lawrence. And yet at the same time there is very much more to be thankful for as instructive than to object to as obsolete or dangerous. For on the negative side we have no trace after all of the later direct invocation of tile paints, nor of the modern *cultus* of the B. V. M. and of relics, while among the many positive good points in his teaching must be reckoned his most proper theory of a bishop as not only the channel of divine grace in virtue of ordination (*sacerdos*) but also the overseer of the flock (*episcopus*), in virtue of the people's choice and approval, which is essential to his office; his strong condemnation of the practice of usury in laity as well as clergy; his high appreciation of corporate even more than individual action among the faithful; the thoroughly practical view he always puts before us of the Christian life; and above all the "singularly Christian" character of all his sermons, in which Christ is the Alpha and Omega of all his thoughts anti of all his exhortations. These are some Of the benefits which Leo has conferred Upon the Church, and which have rightfully earned for him the title "Great."

Manuscripts.

I. At the *Vatican.* (a) *Of the Sermons.* (1) Codd. 3835 and 6 are two volumes in Roman Character of a Lectionary of about the 8th century; the second volume contains the "Tome" (which in the 8th and 9th centuries used to be read in the Church offices before Christmas): (2) 3828, a parchment (10th century), also a lectionary: (3) 1195, a parchment folio (11th century), a lectionary containing *inter alia* some of Leo's homilies: (4) 1267, 8 and 9 of the same character (11th century): (5) 1270 contains the Sermon *de Festo Petri cathedroe*, (now xiv. in Migne's Appendix), from which Cacciari restored Quesnel's imperfect edition of it to its present state: (6) 1271 and 2 are also lectionaries: (7) 4222 in Lombardic characters (9th century), a lectionary: (8) 5451 in Roman characters (12th century), a lectionary: (9) 6450 parchment (12th century): a lectionary containing the sermon *de Festo Petri cathedroe* in the form found and printed by Quesnel: (10) 6451 similar: it contains sermons *de Quadragesima* and others: (11) 6454 similar.

(b) Of the *Letters*: these are mostly rather later (i.e. about 12th or 13th century): but (1) 1322 is of an older date, and contains besides the epistles, all the acts of the

Council of Chalcedon: (2) 5759 is earlier than the 9th century; it used to belong to the monastery of S. Columban at Bobbio, and contains 31 letters: (3) 5845 is very ancient, and according to Cacciari, Lombardic: it contains 24 letters

(g) *Letters and Sermons together*: of these there are nine collections in the Vatican, of which 548 and 9 contain the sermon *de Absalom* which is condemned by Cacciari. the *Regio-Vaticanus codex* 139 is a fine collection of Leo's works (12th century).

II. *At other places*: (1) The codex *Urbinas* 65 is thought to be a copy of the Regio-Vaticanus 139 made in the 14th century.

(2) Codex *Grimanicus* is a ms. on which Quesnel lays great stress: Quesnel assigns it to the ninth century; it contains 107 letters, of which 28 had never been printed before Quesnel.

(3) The *Thuanei*; (a) 129 contains 123 letters: (b) 780 contains the Tome: (g) 729 contains the spurious *de vocatione gentium* and some epistles.

(4) The *Corbienses* are old.

(5) The *Taurinensis* 29 D. iv. is a fine 13th-century ms. containing 52 letters.

(6) The *Florentinus codex* belongs to the 13th century also.

(7) *Ratisbonensis* 113 DD. AA., in the monastery of S. Emeramus, contains 72 letters: it is said to date from about 750a.d.

(8) The two *Bergonenses* are of 12th century, and contain 12 sermons.

(9) Two *Chigiani* also of 12th century contain 4 sermons.

(10) The *Padilironenses* contain 9 sermons and the Tome.

(11) There are three *Patavini*, of which two contain the Tome.

(12) *Vallicellani*: these are a number of 11th or 12th-century codices.

There are also the *Veneti*, the *Vercellenses*, the *Veronenses*, &c.

N.B. The foregoing account is taken from Schönemann's *Notitia Historico-Literaria* (1794), and the translator has no means of knowing whether it is still correct (1890).

Editions.

1. The earliest important edition is P. *Quesnel's* (*prêtre de l'oratoire*), Paris, 1675, Lyons, 1700, of which *Migne's Dict. de Bibliogr. catholique* says, '*on reproche aux éditions du P. Quesnel un grand nombre de falsifications, par lesqelles le P. Quesnel se proposait notamment d'affaiblir l'autorité pontificale .... L'edition que l'on doit aujourd'hui préférer, est* (naturally enough!) *celle qui a été publiée par M. l'abbé Migne sous le titre d'*

2. *Oeuvres très complètes de Saint Leon le Grand publièes d'après l'édition des frères Ballerinii et celle de Paschase Quesnel enrichées de préfaces, d'avertissements et de commentaires, suivies des exercices de Cacciari sur toutes les oeuvres du saint docteur. Paris 1846.*

3. P. *Cacciari* (a carmelite) brought out editions at Rome, 1751 and 1753–5, the latter with dissertations.

4. The edition of the brothers P. and H. Ballerinii (Jesuists), Venice, 1753–7, was a recension of Quesnel's second edition with copious dissertations and notes.

5. *H. Hurter*, S. J., has published selections of Sermons and Letters in vols. xiv., xxv. and xxvi. of his *SS. PP. opuscula selecta*, 1871–4

Translations.

1. Bright's Leo on the Incarnation, London, 1862 (2nd edn. enlarged, 1886, in which the Tome is translated), consists of xviii. sermons translated and the Tome in Latin, with many valuable notes.

2. *Reithmayr's Bibliothek* (1869) contains a German translation.

3. Dr. Neale's *History of the Alexandrian Patriarchate* embodies a translation of the Tome.

4. Dr. Heurtley published a version of the Tome in 1886.

Authorities and Materials.

The chief ancient and medieval authorities for the life and times of Leo the Great are such works as *Prosper's*, and *Idatius' Chronicles, Iiornandes de rebus Geticis, Anastasius Bibliothecarius Historia de vitis Romanorum Pontificum* (9th cent.), the *Historia Miscella* (10th cent), &c.

Among *lives* may be mentioned the following:-(1) La vie et religion de deux bons papes Léon premier et Gregoire premier par Pierre DU Moulin (the younger: a protestant theologian), Sedan, 1650. 12mo. (2) Quesnel's valuable *Dissertatio de vita et rebus gestis S. Leonis Magni*, originally included in his edition of Leo and re-printed by Migne in Vol. ii. of his edition with the Ballerinii's annotations and critical remarks, *Paris*, 1675, *Lyons*, 1700. (3) *Histoire du Pontificat de Saint Léon le Grand par Monsr L. Maimbourg La Haye*, 1687. (4) *The Bollandists' Life by Canisius (Acta Sanctorum)*, *April*, vol. ii. pp. 14–22. (5) Alphonsi Ciaconii *Vitoe Pontificum (Tom* 1, pp. 303–314), *Rome*, 1677, 4*to*. (6) LE Nain DE Tillemont, *Memoires pour servir à l'hitoire Ecclesiastique* (vol. xv. pp. 414–832, 885–934), *Paris*, 1711. (7) *Breve Descrizione deila vita di S. Leone Primo di* Gabrielle Bertazzolo: *Mantova*, 1727. (8) *Memoire istoriche di Sa. Leone Papa da* Teofilo Pacifico: *Brescia*, 1791, 8*vo*. (9) DU Pin, L. E., *History of Ecc. writers* (Eng Edn. vol. 1, pp. 464–480), *Dublin*, 1722. (10) C. Oudinus, *de Scriptoribus Ecclesioe* (vol. 1, pp. 1271–5), *Leipzig*, 1722. (11) Wilhelm Amadeus Arendt *(Roman Catholic)*, *Leo der Grosse und seine Zeit, Mainz*, 1835, 8*vo*. (12) Eduard Perthel, *Papst Leo's I. Leben und Lehren, Jena*, 1843, 8*vo*. (a counterblast to No. 11, and no less exaggerated and prejudiced in statement). (13) A. DE Saint-Chron, *Histoire du pontificat de Saint Léon le Grand, Paris*, 1846. (14) F. BÖHringer, *die Kirche Xti und ihre Zeugen* (vol. 1 part 4, pp. 170 - 309), *Zürich*, 1845. (15) Charles Gore's *Life of Leo the Great* (S.P.C.K.); also his article in Smith's *Dict. of Christian Biogr*. (16) The article in Herzog's *Real-Encyklopädie* of which a condensed English edition was edited by Dr. Philip Schaff at New York in 1883. Other more general accounts of his times will be found in (1) l'abbé Fleury, *Histoire du Xtianisme* (vol. ii. pp.384 - 480), *Paris*, 1836. (2) Brights *History of the Church from* 313–451 (chaps. xiv., xv.), *Oxford and London*, 1860. (3) Milman's *Latin Christianity* (Book ii. chap. 4), *London*, 1864. (4) R. J. Rohrbachers *Histoire Universelle de l'Eglise catholique* (15th edn., vol. 4, pp. 461–575), *Paris*, 1868.A short account of Leo's writings is given in Alzog's *Grundriss der Patrologie*, § 78, pp.368- 375: a most exhaustive one in Ceillier's *Histoire générale des Auteurs sacrés* (new edition) (vol. X., pp. 169–276), 1858–1869. BÄHr's *Geschichte der Römischer Literatur-Supplement band II. Abtheilung* (pp. 354–362), *im Abendland*, vol. 1, p.448, may also be consulted; and Ebert's *Allgemeine Geschichte der Literatur des Mittelalters*.

LETTERS

LETTER I. TO THE BISHOP OF AQUILEIA.

I. Through the Negligence of the Authorities the Pelagian Heresy Has Been Spreading in His Province.

From the account of our holy brother and fellow-bishop Septimus which is contained in the subjoined letter , we have understood that certain priests and deacons and clergy of various orders in your province who have been drawn in by the Pelagian or Caelestian heresy, have attained to catholic communion without any recantation of their peculiar error being required of them; and that, whilst the shepherds set to watch were fast asleep, wolves clothed in sheep-skins but without laying aside their bestial minds have entered into the Lord's sheep-fold: and that they make a practice of what is not allowed even to non-offenders by the injunctions of our canons and decrees : to wit that they should leave the churches in which they received or regained their office and carry their uncertainty in all directions, loving to continue wandering and never to remain on the foundations of the Apostles. For without being sifted by any test or bound by any previous confession of faith, they make a great point of their right to the privilege of going to one house after another under cover of their being in communion with the Church, and corrupting the hearts of many through men's ignorance of their false name. And yet I am sure they could not do this, if the rulers of the churches had exercised their rightful diligence in the matter of receiving such, and had not allowed any of them to wander from place to place.

II. He Orders a Provincial Synod to Be Convened to Receive the Recantation of the Heretics in Express Terms.

Accordingly, lest this should be attempted any further, and lest this pernicious habit, which owes its introduction to certain persons' negligence, should result in the overthrow of many souls, by this our authoritative injunction we charge you, brother, to give diligence that a synod of the clergy of your province be convened, and all, whether priests or deacons or clerics of any rank who have been re-admitted from their alliance with the Pelagians and the Caelestians into catholic communion with such precipitation that they were not first constrained to recant their error, be now at least forced to a true correction, which can advantage themselves and hurt no one, since their deceitfulness has in part been disclosed. Let them by their public confession condemn the authors of this presumptuous error and renounce all that the universal Church has repudiated in their doctrine: and let them announce by full and open statements, signed by their own hand, that they embrace and entirely approve of all the synodal decrees which the authority of the Apostolic See has ratified to the rooting out of this heresy. Let nothing obscure, nothing ambiguous be found in their words. For we know that their cunning is such that they reckon that the meaning of any particular clause of their execrable doctrine can be defended if they only keep it distinct from the main body of their damnable views .

III. The Pelagian View of God's Grace is Unscriptural.

And when they pretend to disapprove of and give up all their definitions to facilitate evasion through their complete art of deception, unless their meaning is detected, they make exception of the dogma that the grace of God is given according to the merits of the recipient. And yet surely, unless it is given freely, it is not a gift, but a price and compensation for merits: for the blessed Apostle says, "by grace ye have been saved through faith, and that not of yourselves but it is the gift of God; not of works lest any should perchance be exalted. For we are His workmanship created in Christ Jesus in good works, which God prepared that we should walk in them ." Thus every bestowal of good works is of God's preparing: because a man is justified by grace rather than by his own excellence: for grace is to every one the source of righteousness, the source of good and the fountain of merit. But these heretics say it is anticipated by men's natural goodness for this reason, that that nature which (in their view) is before grace conspicuous for good desires of its own, may not seem marred by any stain of original sin, and that what the Truth says may be falsified: "For the Son of Man came to seek and to save that which was lost ."

IV. Prompt Measures are Essential.

You must take heed, therefore, beloved, and with great diligence make provision that offences which have long been removed be not set up again through such men and that no seed of the same evil spring up in your province from a doctrine which has once been uprooted: for not only will it take root and grow, but also will taint the future generations of the Church with its poisonous exhalations. Those who wish to appear corrected must purge themselves of all suspicion: and by obeying us, prove themselves ours. And if any of them decline to satisfy our wholesome injunctions, be he cleric or layman, he must be driven from the society of the Church lest he deal treacherously by others' safety as well as forfeit his own soul.

V. the Canons Must Be Enforced Against Clerics Who Wonder from One Church to Another.

We admonish you also to restore to full working that part of the discipline of the Church whereby the holy Fathers and we have often in former times decreed that neither in the grade of the priesthood nor in the order of the diaconate nor in the lower ranks of the clergy, is any one at liberty to migrate from church to church: to the end that each one may persevere where he was ordained without being enticed by ambition, or led astray by greed, or corrupted by men's evil beliefs: and thus that if any one, seeking his own interests, not those of Jesus Christ , neglect to return to his own people and church, he may be reckoned out of the pale both in respect of promotion and of the bond of communion. But do not doubt, beloved, that we must be somewhat sorely moved if, as we think not, our decrees for the maintenance of the canons and the integrity of the faith be neglected: because the short-comings of the lower orders are to be laid at the door of none so much as of those slothful and remiss rulers who often foster much pestilence by shrinking from the application of a stringent remedy.

LETTER II. TO SEPTIMUS, BISHOP OF ALTINUM.

(Caution must be observed in receiving Pelagians back, and clergy must stay in the church of their ordination.)

LETTER III. FROM PASCHASINUS, BISHOP OF LILYBAEUM.

(About the keeping of Easter in 444; recommending the Alexandrine calculation.)

LETTER IV. TO THE BISHOPS APPOINTED IN CAMPANIA, PICENUM, ETRURIA, AND ALL THE PROVINCES.

Leo, bishop of the city of Rome, to all the bishops appointed in Campania, Picenum, Etruria, and all the provinces, greeting in the Lord.

I. Introduction.

As the peaceful settlement of the churches causes us satisfaction, so are we saddened with no slight sorrow whenever we learn that anything has been taken for granted or done contrary to the ordinances of the canons and the discipline of the Church: and if we do not repress such things with the vigilance we ought, we cannot excuse ourselves to Him who intended us to be watchmen , for permitting the pure body of the Church, which we ought to keep clean from every stain, to be defiled by contact with wicked schemers, since the framework of the members loses its harmony by such dissimulation.

II. Slaves and Serfs (Coloni) are Not to Be Ordained.

Men are admitted commonly to the Sacred Order who are not qualified by any dignity of birth or character: even some who have failed to obtain their liberty from their masters are raised to the rank of the priesthood , as if sorry slaves were fit for that honour; and it is believed that a man can be approved of God who has not yet been able to approve himself to his master. And so the cause for complaint is twofold in this matter, because both the sacred ministry is polluted by such poor partners in it, and the rights of masters are infringed so far as unlawful possession is rashly taken of them . From these men, therefore, beloved brethren, let all the priests of your province keep aloof; and not only from them, but from others also, we wish you to keep, who are under the bond of origin or other condition of service : unless perchance the request or consent be intimated of those who claim some authority over them. For he who is to be enrolled on the divine service ought to be exempt from others, that he be not drawn away from the Lord's camp in which his name is entered, by any other bonds of duty.

III. A Man Who Has Married Twice or a Widow is Not Eligible as a Priest.

Again, when each man's respectability of birth and conduct has been established, what sort of person should be associated with the ministry of the Sacred Altar we have learnt both from the teaching of the Apostle and the Divine precepts and the regulations of the canons, from which we find very many of the brethren have turned aside and quite gone out of the way. For it is well known that the husbands of widows have attained to the priesthood: certain, too, who have had several wives, and have led a life given up to all licentiousness, have had all facilities put in their way, and been admitted to the Sacred Order, contrary to that utterance of the blessed Apostle, in which he proclaims and says to such, "the husband of one wife ," and contrary to that precept of the ancient law which says by way of caution: "Let the priest take a virgin to wife, not a widow, not a divorced woman ." All such persons, therefore, who have been admitted we order to be put out of their offices in the church and from the title of priest by the authority of the Apostolic See: for they will have no claim to that for which they were not eligible, on account of the obstacle in question: and we specially claim for ourselves the duty of settling this, that if any of these irregularities have been committed, they may be corrected and may not be allowed to occur again, and that no excuse may arise from ignorance: although it has never been allowed a priest to be ignorant of what has been laid down by the rules of the canons. These writings, therefore, we have addressed to your provinces by the hand of Innocent, Legitimus and Segetius, our brothers and fellow-bishops: that the evil shoots which are known to have sprung up may be torn out by the roots, and no tares may spoil the Lord's harvest. For thus all that is genuine will bear much fruit, if that which has been wont to kill the growing crop be carefully cleared away.

IV. Usurious Practices Forbidden for Clergy and for Laity .

This point, too, we have thought must not be passed over, that certain possessed with the love of base gain lay out their money at in terest, and wish to enrich themselves asusurers. For we are grieved that this is practised not only by those who belong to the clergy, but also by laymen who desire to be called Christians. And we decree that those who have been convicted be punished sharply, that all occasion of sinning be removed.

V. A Cleric May Not Make Money in Another's Name Any More Than in His Own.

The following warning, also, we have thought fit to give, that no cleric should attempt to make money in another's name any more than in his own: for it is unbecoming to shield one's crime under another man's gains . Nay, we ought to look at and aim at only that usury whereby what we bestow in mercy here we may recover from the Lord, who will restore a thousand fold what will last for ever.

VI. Any Bishop Who Refuses Consent to These Rules Must Be Deposed.

This admonition of ours, therefore, proclaims that if any of our brethren endeavour to contravene these rules and dare to do what is forbidden by them, he may know that he is liable to deposition from his office, and that he will not be a sharer in our communion who refuses to be a sharer of our discipline. But lest there be anything which may possibly be thought to be omitted by us, we bid you, beloved, to keep all the decretal rules of Innocent of blessed memory , and also of all our predecessors, which have been promulgated about the orders of the Church and the discipline of the canons, and to keep them in such wise that if any have transgressed them he may know at once that all indulgence is denied him.

Dated 10th of October, in the consulship of the illustrious Maximus(a second time) and Paterius(a.d. 443).

LETTER V. TO THE METROPOLITAN BISHOPS OF ILLYRICUM.

(Appointing Anastasius of Thessalonica his Vicar in the province, and expressing his wishes about its government, for which see Letter VI.)

LETTER VI. TO ANASTASIUS, BISHOP OF THESSALONICA.

Leo to his beloved brother Anastasius.

I. He is Pleased to Have Been Consulted by the Bishops Illyricum an Important Questions.

The brotherly love of our colleagues makes us read with grateful mind the letters of all priests ; for in them we embrace one another in the spirit as if we were face to face, and by the intercourse of such epistles we are associated in mutual converse . But in this present letter the affection displayed seems to us greater than usual: for it informs us of the state of the churches , and urges us to a vigilant exercise of care by a consideration of our office, so that being placed, as it were, on a watch-tower, according to the will of the Lord, we should both lend our approval to things when they run in accordance with our wishes, and correct, by applying the remedies of compulsion, what we observe gone wrong through any aggression: hoping that abundant fruit will be the result of our sowing the seed, if we do not allow those things to increase which have begun to spring up to the spoiling of the harvest.

II. Following the Examples of His Predecessors He Nominates Anastasius Metropolitan of Illyricum.

Now therefore, dear brother, that your request has been made known to us through our son Nicolaus the priest, that you, too, like your predecessors, might receive from us in our turn authority over Illyricum for the observance of the rules, we give our consent and earnestly exhort that no concealment and no negligence may be allowed in the management of the churches situated throughout Illyricum, which we commit to you in our stead, following the precedent of Siricius of blessed remembrance, who then, for the first time, acting on a fixed method, entrusted them to your last predecessor but one , Anysius of holy memory, who had at the time well deserved of the Apostolic See, and was approved by after events: that he might render assistance to the churches situated in that province whom he wished kept up to discipline. Noble precedents must be followed with eagerness that we may show ourselves in all things like those whose privileges we wish to enjoy. We wish you to imitate your last predecessor but one as well as of your immediate predecessor who is known equally with the former to have both deserved and employed this privilege: so that we may rejoice in the progress of the churches which we commit to you in our stead. For as the conduct of matters progresses creditably when committed to one who acts well and carries out skilfully the duties of the priestly position, so it is found to be only a burden to him who, when power is entrusted to him, uses not the moderation that is due.

III. Ordinees Must Be Carefully Selected with Especial Reference to Thecanons of the Church.

And so, dear brother, hold with vigilance the helm entrusted to you, and direct your mind's gaze around on all which you see put in your charge, guarding what will conduce to your reward and resisting those who strive to upset the discipline of the canons. The sanction of God's law must be respected, and the decrees of the canons should be more especially kept. Throughout the provinces committed to thee let such priests be consecrated to the Lord as are commended only by their deserving life and position among the clergy. Permit no licence to personal favour, nor to canvassing, nor to purchased votes. Let the cases of those who are to be ordained be investigated carefully and let them be trained in the discipline of the Church through a considerable period of their life. But if all the requirements of the holy Fathers are found in them, and if they have observed all that we read the blessed Apostle Paul to have enjoined on such, viz., that he be the husband of one wife, and that she was a virgin when he married her, as the authority of God's law requires,[then ordain them]. And this we are extremely anxious should be observed, so as to do away with all place for excuses, lest any one should believe himself able to attain to the priesthood who has taken a wife before he obtained the grace of Christ, and on her decease joinedhimself to another after baptism. Seeing that the former wife cannot be ignored, nor the previous marriage put out of the reckoning, and that he is as much the father of the children whom he begot by that wife before baptism as he is of those whom he is known to have begotten by the second after baptism. For as sins and things which are known to be unlawful are washed away in the font of baptism, so what are allowedor lawful are not done away.

IV. The Metropolitans Must Not Ordain Hastily Nor Without Consultingtheir Primate.

Let one be ordained a priest throughout these churches inconsiderately; for by this means ripe judgments will be formed about those to be elected, if your scrutiny, brother, is dreaded. But let any bishop who, contrary to our command, is ordained by his metropolitan without your knowledge, know that he has no assured position with us, and that those who have taken on themselves so to do must render an account of their presumption . But as to each metropolitan is committed such power that he has the right of ordaining in his province, so we wish those metropolitans to be ordained, but not without ripe and well-considered judgment. For although it is seemly that all who are consecrated priests should be approved and well-pleasing to God, yet we wish those to have peculiar excellence whom we know are going to preside over the fellow-priests who are assigned to them. And we admonish you, beloved, to see to this the more diligently and carefully, that you may be proved to keep that precept of the Apostles which runs, "lay hands suddenly on no man ."

V. Points Which Cannot Be Settled at the Provincial Synod are to Be Referred to Rome.

Any of the brethren who has been summoned to a synod should attend and not deny himself to the holy congregation: for there especially he should know that what will conduce to the good discipline of the Church must be settled. For all faults will be better avoided if more frequent conferences take place between the priests of the Lord, and intimate association is the greatest help alike to improvement and to brotherly love. There, if any questions arise, under the Lord's guidance they will be able to be determined, so that no bad feeling remains, and only a firmer love exists among the brethren. But if any more important question spring up, such as cannot be settled there under your presidency, brother, send your report and consult us, so that we may write back under the revelation of the Lord, of whose mercy it is that we can do ought, because He has breathed favourably upon us : that by our decision we may vindicate our right of cognizance in accordance with old-established tradition and the respect that is due to the Apostolic See: for as we wish you to exercise your authority in our stead, so we reserve to ourselves points which cannot be decided on the spot and persons who have made appeal to us.

VI. Priests and Deacons May Not Be Ordained on Weekdays Any More Than Bishops.

You shall take order that this letter reach the knowledge of all the brethren, so that no one hereafter find an opportunity to excuse himself through ignorance in observing these things which we command. We have directed our letter of admonition to the metropolitans themselves also of the several provinces, that they may know that they must obey the Apostolic injunctions, and that they obey us in beginning to obey you, brother, our delegate according to what we have written. We hear, indeed, and we cannot pass it over in silence, that only bishops are ordained by certain brethren on Sundays only; but presbyters and deacons, whose consecration should be equally solemn , receive the dignity of the priestly office indiscriminately on any day, which is a reprehensible practice contrary to the canons and tradition of the Fathers , since the custom ought by all means to be kept by those who have received it with respect to all the sacred orders: so that after a proper lapse of time he who is to be ordained a priest or deacon may be advanced through all the ranks of the clerical office, and thus a man may have time to learn that of which he himself also is one day to be a teacher. Dated the 12th of January, in the consulship of Theodosius(18th time) and Albinus(444).

LETTER VII. TO THE BISHOPS THROUGHOUT ITALY.

Leo to all the bishops set over the provinces of Italy greeting.
I. Many Manichaeans Have Been Discovered in Rome.

We call you to a share in our anxiety, that with the diligence of shepherds you may take more careful heed to your flocks entrusted to you that no craft of the devil's be permitted: lest that p ague, which by the revealing mercy of the Lord is driven off from our flocks through our care, should spread among your churches before you are forewarned, and are still ignorant of what is happening, and should find means of stealthily burrowing into your midst, and thus what we are checking in the City should take hidden root among you and grow up. Our search has discovered in the City a great many followers and teachers of the Manichaean impiety, our watchfulness has proclaimed them, and our authority and censure has checked them: those whom we could reform we have corrected and driven to condemn Manichaeus with his preachings and teachings by public confession in church, and by the subscription of their own hand, and thus we have lifted those who have acknowledged their fault from the pit of their iniquity by granting them room for repentance . A good many, however, who had so deeply involved themselves that no remedy could assist them, have been subjected to the laws in accordance with the constitutions of our Christian princes, and lest they should pollute the holy flock by their contagion; have been banished into perpetual exile by public judges. And all the profaneand disgraceful things which are found as well in their writings as in their secret traditions, we have disclosed and clearly proved to the eyes of the Christian laity that the people might know what to shrink from or avoid: so that he that was called their bishop was himself tried by us, and betrayed the criminal views which he held in his mystic religion, as the record of our proceedings can show you. For this, too, we have sent you for instruction: and after reading them you will be in a position to understand all the discoveries we have made.

II. The Bishops of Italy Rarest Not Allow Those Manichaeans Who Have Quitted the City to Escape or Lie Concealed.

And because we know that a good many of those who are involved here in too close an accusation for them to clear themselves have escaped, we have sent this letter to you, beloved, by our acolyth: that your holiness, dear brothers, may be informed of this, and see fit to act with diligence and caution, lest the men of the Manichaean error be able to find opportunity of hurting your people and of teaching their impious doctrines. For we cannot otherwise rule those entrusted to us unless we pursue with the zeal of faith in the Lord those who are destroyers and destroyed: and with what severity we can bring to bear, cut them off from intercourse with sound minds, lest this pestilence spread much wider. Wherefore I exhort you, beloved, I beseech and warn you to use such watchful diligence as you ought and can employ in tracking them out, lest they find opportunity of concealment anywhere. For as he will have a due recompense of reward from God, who carries out what conduces to the health of the people committed to him; so before the Lord's judgment-seat no one will be able to excuse himself from a charge of carelessness who has not been willing to guard his people against the propagators of an impious misbelief. Dated 30 January, in the consulship of the illustrious Theodosius Augustus (18th time) and Albinus (444).

LETTER VIII. THE ORDINANCE OF VALENTINIAN III. CONCERNING THE MANICHAEANS.

(The Manichaeans are to be turned out of the army and the City, and to lose all their rights as citizens.)

LETTER IX. TO DIOSCORUS, BISHOP OF ALEXANDRIA.

Leo, the bishop, to Dioscorus, bishop of Alexandria, greeting.

I. The Churches of Rome and Alexandria Should Be at One in Everything.

How much of the divine love we feel for you, beloved, you will be able to estimate from this, that we are anxious to establish your beginnings on a surer basis, lest anything should seem lacking to the perfection of your love, since your meritorious acts of spiritual grace, as we have proved, are already in your favour. Fatherly and brotherly conference, therefore, ought to be most grateful to you, holy brother, and received by you in thesame spirit as you know it is offered by us. For you and we ought to be at one in thought and act, so that as we read , in us also there may be proved to be one heart and one mind. For since the most blessed Peter received the headship of the Apostles from the Lord, and the church of Rome still abides by His institutions, it is wicked to believe that His holy disciple Mark, who was the first to govern the church of Alexandria , formed his decrees on a different line of tradition: seeing that without doubt both disciple and master drew but one Spirit from the same fount of grace, and the ordained could not hand on aught else than what he had received from his ordainer. We do not therefore allow it that we should differ in anything, since we confess ourselves to be of one body and faith, nor that the institutions of the teacher should seem different to those of the taught.

II. Fixed Days Should Be Observed for Ordaining Priests and Deacons.

That therefore which we know to have been very carefully observed by our fathers, we wish kept by you also, viz. that the ordination of priests or deacons should not be performed at random on any day: but after Saturday, the commencement of that night which precedes the dawn of the first day of the week should be chosen on which the sacred benediction should be bestowed on those who are to be consecrated, ordainer and ordained alike fasting. This observance will not be violated, if actually on the morning of the Lord's day it be celebrated without breaking the Saturday fast: for the beginning of the preceding night forms part of that period, and undoubtedly belongs to the day of resurrection as is clearly laid down with regard to the feast of Easter . For besides the weight of custom which we know rests upon the Apostles' teaching, Holy Writ also makes this clear, because when the Apostles sent Paul and Barnabas at the bidding of the Holy Ghost to preach the gospel to the nations, they laid hands on them fasting and praying: that we may know with what devoutness both giver and receiver must be on their guard lest so blessed a sacrament should seem to be carelessly performed. And therefore you will piously and laudably follow Apostolic precedents if you yourself also maintain this form of ordaining priests throughout the churches over which the Lord has called you to preside: viz. that those who are to be consecrated should never receive the blessing except on the day of the Lord's resurrection, which is commonly held to begin on the evening of Saturday, and which has been so often hallower in the mysterious dispensations of God that all the more notable institutions of the Lord were accomplished on that high day. On it the world took its beginning. On it through the resurrection of Christ death received its destruction, and life its commencement. On it the apostles take from the Lord's hands the trumpet of the gospel which is to be preached to all nations, and receive the sacrament of regeneration which they are to bear to the whole world. On it, as blessed John the Evangelist bears witness when all the disciples were gathered together in one place, and when, the doors being shut, the Lord entered to them, He breathed on them and said: "Receive the Holy Ghost: whose sins ye have remitted they are remitted to them: and whose ye have retained, they shall be retained ." On it lastly the Holy Spirit that had been promised to the Apostles by the Lord came: and so we know it to have been suggested and handed down by a kind of heavenly rule, that on that day we ought to celebrate the mysteries of the blessing of priests on which all these gracious gifts were conferred.

III. The Repetition of the Holy Eucharist on the Great Festivals is Not Undesirable.

Again, that our usage may coincide at all points, we wish this thing also to be observed, viz. that when any of the greater festivals has brought together a larger congregation than usual, and too great a crowd of the faithful has assembled for one church to hold them all at once, there should be no hesitation about repeating the oblation of the sacrifice: lest, if those only are admitted to this service who come first, those who flock in afterwards, should seem to be rejected: for it is fully in accordance with piety and reason, that as often as a fresh congregation has filled the church where service is going on, the sacrifice should be offered as a matter of course. Whereas a certain portion of the people must be deprived of their worship, if the custom of only one celebration be kept, and only those who come early in the day can offer the sacrifice . We admonish you, therefore, beloved, earnestly and affectionately that your carefulness also should not neglect what has become a part of our own usage on the pattern of our fathers' tradition, so that in all things we may agree together in our beliefs and in our performances. Consequently, we have given this letter to our son Possidonius, a presbyter, on his return, that he may bear it to you, brother; he has so often taken part in our ceremonials and ordinations, and has been sent to us so many times that he knows quite well what Apostolic authority we possess in all things.Dated 21June (? 445).

LETTER X. TO THE BISHOPS OF THE PROVINCE OF VIENNE. IN THE MATTER OF HILARY, BISHOP OF ARLES .

To the beloved brothers, the whole body of bishops of the province of Vienne, Leo, bishop of Rome.

I. The Solidarity of the Church Built Upon the Rack of S. Peter Must Be Everywhere Maintained.

Our Lord Jesus Christ, Saviour of mankind, instituted the observance of the Divine religion which He wished by the grace of God to shed its brightness upon all nations and all peoples in such a way that the Truth, which before was confined to the announcements of the Law and the Prophets, might through the Apostles' trumpet blast go out for the salvation of all men , as it is written: "Their sound has gone out into every land,and their words into the ends of the world ." But this mysterious function the Lord wished to be indeed the concern of all the apostles, but in such a way that He has placed the principal charge on the blessed Peter, chief of all the Apostles : and from him as from the Head wishes His gifts to flow to all the body: so that any one who dares to secede from Peter's solid rock may understand that he has no part or lot in the divine mystery. For He wished him who had been received into partnership in His undivided unity to be named what He Himself was, when He said: "Thou art Peter, and upon this rock I will build My Church :" that the building of the eternal temple by the wondrous gift of God's grace might rest on Peter's solid rock: strengthening His Church so surely that neither could human rashness assail it nor the gates of hell prevail against it. But this most holy firmness of the rock, reared, as we have said, by the building hand of God, a man must wish to destroy in over-weaning wickedness when he tries to break down its power, by favouring his own desires, and not following what he received from men of old: for he believes himself subject to no law, and held in check by no rules of God's ordinances and breaks away, in his eagerness for novelty, from your use and ours, by adopting illegal practices, and letting what he ought to keep fall into abeyance.

II. Hilary is Disturbing the Peace of the Church by His Insubordination.

But with the approval, as we believe, of God, and retaining towards you the fulness of our love which the Apostolic See always, as you remember, expends upon you, holy brethren we are striving to correct these things by mature counsel, and to share with you the task of setting your churches in order, not by innovations but by restoration of the old; that we may persevere in the accustomed state which our fathers handed down to us, and please our God through the ministry of a good work by removing the scandals of disturbances. And so we would have you recollect, brethren, as we do, that the Apostolic See, such is the reverence in which it is held, has times out of number been referred to and consulted by the priests of your province as well as others, and in the various matters of appeal, as the old usage demanded, it has reversed or confirmed decisions: and in this way "the unity of the spirit in the bond of peace " has been kept, and by the interchange of letters, our honourable proceedings have promoted a lasting affection: for "seeking not our own but the things of Christ ," we have been careful not to do despite to the dignity which God has given both to the churches and their priests. But this path which with our fathers has been always so well kept to and wisely maintained, Hilary has quilted, and is likely to disturb the position and agreement of the priests by his novel arrogance: desiring to subject you to his power in such a way as not to suffer himself to be subject to the blessed Apostle Peter, claiming for himself the ordinations of all the churches throughout the provinces of Gaul, and transferring to himself the dignity which is due to metropolitan priests; he diminishes even the reverence that is paid to the blessed Peter himself with his proud words: for not only was the power of loosing and binding given to Peter before the others, but also to Peter more especially was entrusted the care of feeding the sheep . Yet any one who holds that the headship must be denied to Peter, cannot really diminish his dignity: but is puffed up with the breath of his pride, and plunges himself into the lowest depth.

III. Celidonius Has Been Restored to His Bishopric, the Charges Against Him Having Been Found False.

Accordingly the written record of our proceedings shows what action we have taken in the matter of Celidonius , the bishop, andwhat Hilary said in the presence and hearing of the aforesaid bishop. For when Hilary had no reasonable answer to give in the council of the holy priests, "the secrets of his heart " gave vent to utterances such as no layman could make and no priest listen to. We were grieved, I acknowledge, brothers, and endeavoured to appease the tumult of his mind by patient treatment. For we did not wish to exasperate those wounds which he was inflicting on his soul by his insolent retorts, and strove rather to pacify him whom we had taken up as a brother, although it was he who was entangling himself by his replies, than to cause him pain by our remarks. Celidonius, the bishop, was therefore acquitted, for he had proved himself wrongfully deposed from the priesthood, by the clear replies of his witnesses made in his own presence: so that Hilary, who remained with us, had no opposition to offer. The judgment, therefore, was rescinded, which was brought forward and read to the effect that, as the husband of a widow , he could not hold the priesthood. Now this rule we, maintaining the legal constitutions , have wished scrupulously adhered to, not only in respect of priests but also of clergy of the lower ranks: that those who have contracted such a marriage, or those who are proved not to be the husbands of only one wife contrary to the apostle's discipline, should not be suffered to enter the sacred service . But though we decree that those, whom their own acts condemn, must either not be admitted at all, or, if they have, must be removed, so those who are falsely so accused we are bound to clear after examination held, and not allow to lose their office. For the sentence pronounced would have remained against him, if the truth of the charge had been proved. And so Celidonius, our fellow-bishop, was restored to his church and to that dignity which he ought not to have lost, as the course of our proceedings, and the sentence which was pronounced by us after holding the inquiry testifies.

IV. Hilary's Treatment of Projectus Does Not Redound to His Credit.

When this business was so concluded, the complaint of our brother and fellow-bishop, Projectus , next came before us: who addressed us in a tearful and piteous letter, about the ordaining of a bishop over his head. A letter was also brought to us from his own fellow-citizens, corroborated by a great many individual signatures, and full of the most unpleasant complaints against Hilary: to the effect that Projectus, their bishop, was not allowed to be ill, but his priesthood had been transferred to another without their knowledge, and the heir brought into possession by Hilary, the intruder as if to fill up a vacancy, though the possessor was still alive . We should like to hear what you, brothers, think on the point: although we ought not to entertain any doubt about your feelings, when you picture to yourselves a brother lying on a sick-bed and tortured, not so much by his bodily weakness as by pains of another kind. What hope in life is left a man who is visited with despair about his priesthood whilst another is set up in his place? Hilary gives a clear proof of his gentle heart when he believed that the tardiness of a brother's death is but a hindrance to his own ambitious designs. For, as far as in him lay, he quenched the light for him; he robbed him of life by setting up another in his room, and thus causing him such pain as to hinder his recovery. And supposing that his brother's passage from this world was brief, but after the common course of men, what does Hilary seek for himself in another's province, and why does he claim that which none of his predecessors before Patroclus possessed? whereas that very position which seemed to have been temporarily granted to Patroclus by the Apostolic See was afterwards withdrawn by a wiser decision . At least the wishes of the citizens should have been waited for, and the testimony of the people : the opinion of those held in honour should have been asked, and the choice of the clergy—things which those who know the rules of the fathers are wont to observe in the ordination of priests: that the rule of the Apostle's authority might in all things be kept, which enjoins that one who is to be the priest of a church should be fortified, not only by theattestation of the faithful but also by the testimony of "those who are without ," and that no occasion for offence be left, when, in peace and in God-pleasing harmony with the full approval of all, one who will be a teacher of peace is ordained.

V. Hilary's Action Was Very Reprehensible Throughout, and We Have Restored Projectus.

But Hilary came upon them unawares and departed no less suddenly, accomplishing many journeys with great speed, as we have ascertained, and traversing distant provinces with such haste that he seems to have coveted a reputation for the swiftness of a courier rather than for the sobriety of a priest . For these are the words of the citizens in the letter that has been addressed to us:—"He departed before we knew he had come." This is not to return but to flee, not to exercise a shepherd's wholesome care, but to employ the violence of a thief and a robber, as saith the Lord: "he that entereth not by the door into the sheep-fold , but climbeth up some other way, is a thief and a robber." Hilary, therefore, was anxious not so much to consecrate a bishop as to kill him who was sick, and to mislead the man whom he set over his head by wrongful ordination. We, however, have done what, as God is our Judge, we believe you will approve: after holding counsel with all the brethren we have decreed that the wrongfully ordained man should be deposed and the Bishop Projectus abide in his priesthood: with the further provision that when any of our brethren in whatsoever province shall decease, he who has been agreed upon to be metropolitan of that province shall claim for himself the ordination of his successor.

These two matters, as we see, have been settled, though there are many other points in them which seem to have violated the principles of the Church, and ought to be visited with just censure and judgment. But we cannot linger on them any further, for we are called off to other matters on which we must carefully confer with you, holy brethren.

VI. Hilary's Practice of Using Armed Violence Must Be Suppressed.

A band of soldiers, as we have learnt follows the priest through the provinces and helps him who relies upon their armed support in turbulently invading churches, which have lost their own priests. Before this court are dragged for ordination men who are quite unknown to the cities over which they are to be set. For as one who is well known and approved is sought out in peace, so must one who is unknown, when brought forward, beestablished by violence. I beg and entreat and beseech you in God's name prevent such things, brethren, and remove all occasion for discord from your provinces. At all events we acquit ourselves before God in beseeching you not to allow this to proceed further. In peace and quietness should they be asked for who are to be priests. The consent of the clergy, the testimony of those held in honour the approval of the orders and the laity should be required . He who is to govern all, should be chosen by all . As we said before, each metropolitan should keep in his own hands the ordinations that occur in his own province, acting in concert with those who precede the rest in seniority of priesthood, a privilege restored to him through us. No man should claim for himself another's rights. Each should keep within his own limits and boundaries, and should understand that he cannot pass on to another a privilege that belongs to himself. But if any one neglecting the Apostle's prohibitions and paying too much heed to personal favour, wishes to give up his precedence, thinking he can pass his rights on to another, not he to whom he has yielded, but he who ranks before the rest of the priests within the province in episcopal seniority, should claim to himself the power of ordaining. The ordination should be performed not at random but on the proper day: and it should be known that any one who has not been ordained on the evening of Saturday, which precedes the dawn of the first day of the week , or actually on the Lord's day cannot be sure of his status. For our forefathers judged the day of the Lord's resurrection as aloneworthy of the honour of being the occasion on which those who are to be made priests are given to God.

VII. Hilary is Deposed Not Only from His Usurped Jurisdiction, But Also from What of Right Belongs to Him, and is Restricted to His Own Single Bishopric.

Let each province be content with its own councils. and let not Hilary dare to summon synodal meetings besides, and by his interference disturb the judgments of the Lord's priests. And let him know that he is not only deposed from another's rights, but also deprived of his power over the province of Vienne which he had wrongfully assumed. For it is but fair, brethren, that the ordinances of antiquity should be restored, seeing that he who claimed for himself the ordinations of a province for which he was not responsible, has been shown in a similar way in the present case also to have acted so that, as he has on more than one occasion brought on himself sentence of condemnation by hisrash and insolent words, he may now be kept by our command in accordance with the clemency of the Apostolic See to the priesthood of his own city alone. He is not to be present then at any ordination: he is not to ordain because, conscious of his deserts, when he was required to answer for his action, be trusted to make good his escape by disgraceful flight, and has put himself out of Apostolic communion, of which he did not deserve to be a partaker : and we believe this was by God's providence, who brought him to our court, though we did not expect him, and caused him to retire by stealth in the midst of holding the inquiry, that he should not be a partner in our communion .

VIII. Excommunication Should Be Inflicted Only on Those Who are Guilty of Some Great Crime, and Even Then Not Hastily.

No Christian should lightly be denied communion , nor should that be done at the will of an angry priest which the judge's mind ought to a certain extent unwillingly and regretfully to carry out for the punishment of a great crime. For we have ascertained that some have been cut off from the grace of communion for trivial deeds and words, and that the soul for which Christ's blood was shed has been exposed to the devil's attacks and wounded, disarmed, so to say, and stript of all defence by the infliction of so savage a punishment as to fall an easy prey to him. Of course if ever a case has arisen of such a kind as in due proportion to the nature of the crime committed to deprive a man of communion, he only who is involved in the accusation must be subjected to punishment: and he who is not shown to be a partner in its commission ought not to share in the penalty. But what wonder that one who is wont to exult over the condemnation of priests, should show himself in the same light towards laymen.

IX. Leontius is Appointed in Hilary's Room.

Wherefore, because our desire seems very different to this (for we are anxious that the settled state of all the Churches and the harmony of the priests should be maintained,) exhorting you to unity in the bond of love, we both entreat, and consistently with our affection admonish you, in the interests of your peace and dignity, to keep what has been decreed by us at the inspiration of God and the most blessed Apostle Peter, after sifting and testing all the matters at issue, being assured that what we are known to have decided in this way is not so much to our own advantage as to yours. For we are not keeping in our own hands the ordinations of your provinces, as perhaps Hilary, with his usual untruthfulness, may suggest in order to mislead your minds, holy brethren: but in our anxiety we are claiming for you that no further innovations should be allowed, and that for the future no opportunity should be given for the usurper to infringe your privileges. For we acknowledge that it can only redound to our credit, if the diligence of the Apostolic See be kept unimpaired among you, and if in our maintenance of Apostolic discipline we do not allow what belongs to your position to fall to the ground through unscrupulous aggressions. And since seniority is always to be respected, we wish Leontius , our brother and fellow-bishop, a priest well approved among you, to be promoted to this dignity, if it please you that without his consent no further council be summoned by you, holy brethren, and that he may be honoured by you all as his age and good fame demands, the metropolitans being secured in their own dignity and rights. For it is but fair, and no injury seems to accrue to any of the brethren, if those who come first in seniority of the priesthood should, as their age deserves, have deference paid to them by the rest of the priests in their own provinces, God keep you safe, beloved brethren.

LETTER XI. AN ORDINANCE OF VALENTINIANUS III.

(Confirming Leo's sentence upon Hilary.)

LETTER XII.

Leo, bishop of the city of Rome, to all the bishops of Mauritania Caesariensis in Africa greeting the Lord.

I. The Disorderly Appointments of Bishops Which Have Been Made in the Province are Reprehensible.

Inasmuch as the frequent accounts of those who visited us made mention of certain unlawful practices among you with regard to the ordination of priests, the demands of religion required that we should strive to arrive at the exact state of the case in accordance with that solicitude which by the Divine command we bestow on the whole Church: and so we delegated the charge of this to our brother and fellow-priest, Potentius. who was setting out from us: and who, according to what we wrote and addressed to you by him, was to make inquiry as to the facts about the bishops whose election was said to be faulty, and to report everything faithfully to us. Wherefore, because the same Potentius has most fully disclosed all to our knowledge, and has by his truthful account made clear to us, under what and what manner of governors some of Christ's congregations are placed in certain parts of the province of (Mauritania) Caesariensis, we have found it necessary to open out the grief wherewith our hearts are vexed for the dangers of the Lord's flocks, by sending this letter also to you beloved: for we are surprised that either the over-bearing conduct of intriguers or the rioting of the people had so much weight with you in a time of disorder, that the chief pastorate and governance of the Church was handed over to the unworthiest persons, and such as were farthest removed from the priestly standard. This is not to consult but harm the peoples' interests: and not to enforce discipline but to increase differences. For the integrity of the rulers is the safeguard of those who are under them: and where there is complete obedience, there the form of doctrine is sound. But an appointment which has either been made by sedition or seized by intrigue, even though it offend not in morals or in practice, is nevertheless pernicious from the mere example of its beginning: and it is hard for things to be carried to a good issue which were started with a bad beginning.

II. In No Case Ought Bishops to Be Ordained Hastily.

But if in every grade of the Church great forethought and knowledge has to be employed, lest there be any thing disorderly or out of place in the house of the Lord: how much more carefully must we strive to prevent mistakes in the election of him who is set over all the grades? For the peace and order of the Lord's whole household will be shaken, if what is required in the body be not found in the head. Where is that precept of the blessed Apostle Paul uttered through the Spirit of God, whereby in the person of Timothy the whole number of Christ's priests are instructed, and to each one of us is said: "Lay hands hastily on no one, and do not share in other men's sins ?" What is to lay on hands hastily but to confer the priestly dignity on unproved men before the proper age , before there has been time to test them, before they have deserved it by their obedience, before they have been tried by discipline? And what is to share in other men's sins but for the ordainer to become such as is he who ought not to have been ordained by him? For just as a man stores up for himself the fruit of his good work, if he maintains a right judgment in choosing a priest: so one who receives an unworthy priest into the number of his colleagues, inflicts grievous loss upon himself. We must not then pass over in the case of any one that which is laid down in the general ordinances: nor is that advancement to be reckoned lawful which has been made contrary to the precepts of God's law.

III. The Apostolic Precept About the Marriage of the Clergy Based Upon the Marriage of Christ with the Church of Which It is a Figure.

For as the Apostle says that among other rules for election he shall be ordained bishop who is known to have been or to be "the husband of one wife," this command was always held so sacred that the same condition was understood as necessary to be observed even in the wife of the priest-elect: lest she should happen to have been married to another man before she entered into wedlock with him, even though he himself had had no other wife. Who then would dare to allow this injury to be perpetrated upon so great a sacrament , seeing that this great and venerable mystery is not without the support of the statutes of God's law as well, whereby it is clearly laid down that a priest is to marry a virgin, and that she who is to be the wife of a priest is not to know another husband? For even then in the priests was prefigured the Spiritual marriage of Christ and His Church: so that since "the man is the head of the woman ," the spouse of the Word may learn to know no other man but Christ, who did rightly choose her only, loves her only, and takes none but her into His alliance. If then even in the Old Testament this kind of marriage among priests is adhered to, how much more ought we who are placed under the grace of the Gospel to conform to the Apostle's precepts: so that though a man be found endowed with good character, and furnished with holy works, he may nevertheless in no wise ascend either to the grade of deacon, or the dignity of the presbytery, or to the highest rank of the bishopric, if it has been spread abroad either that he himself is not the husband of one wife, or that his wife is not the wife of one husband.

IV. Premature Promotions are to Be Avoided.

But when the Apostle warns and says: "and let these also first be proved, and so let them minister ," what else do we think must be understood but that in these promotions we should consider not only the chastity of their marriages, but also the deserts of their labours, lest the pastoral office be entrusted to men who are either fresh from baptism, or suddenly diverted from worldly pursuits? for through all the ranks of the Christian army in the matter of promotions it ought to be considered whether a man can manage a greater charge. Rightly did the venerable opinions of the blessed Fathers in speaking of the election of priests reckon those men fit for the administration of sacred things who had been slowly advanced through the various grades of office, and had given such good proof of themselves therein that in each one of them the character of their practices bore witness to their lives . For if it is improper to attain to the world's dignities without the help of time and without the merit of having toiled, and if the seeking of office is branded unless it be supported by proofs of uprightness, how diligently and how carefully ought the dispensing of divine duties and heavenly dignities to be carried out, lest in aught the apostolic and canonical decrees be violated, and the ruling of the Lord's Church be committed to men who being ignorant of the lawful constitutions anti devoid of all humility wish not to rise from the lowest grade, but to begin with the highest: for it is extremely unfair and preposterous that the inexpert should be preferred to the expert, the young to the old, the raw recruits to those who have seen much service. In a great house, indeed, as the Apostle explains , there must needs be divers vessels, some of gold and of silver, and some of wood and of earth: but their purpose varies with the quality of their material, and the use of the precious and of the cheap kinds is not the same. For everything will be in disorder if the earthen ware be preferred to the golden, or the wooden to the silver. And as the wooden or earthen vessels are a figure of those men who are hitherto conspicuous for no virtues; so in the golden or silver vessels they no doubt are represented who, having passed through the fire of long experience, and through the furnace of protracted toil have deserved to be tried gold and pure silver. And if such men get no reward for their devotion, all the discipline of the Church is loosened, all order is disturbed, while men who have undergone no service obtain undeserved preferment by the wrongful choice of the electing body.

V. He Distinguishes Between Laymen Who Have Been Raised to the Bishoprics and Digamous Clerks, Forgiving the Former and Not the Latter.

Since then either the eager wishes of the people or the intrigues of the ambitious have had so much weight among you that we understand not only laymen, but even husbands of second wives or widows have been promoted to the pastoral office, are there not the clearest reasons for requiring that the churches in which such things have been done should be cleansed by a severer judgment than usual, and that not only the rulers themselves, but also those who ordained them should receive condign punishment? But there stand on our one hand the gentleness of mercy, on our other the strictness of justice. And because "all the paths of the Lord are loving-kindness and truth ," we are forced according to our loyalty to the Apostolic See so to moderate our opinion as to weigh men's misdeeds in the balance (for of course they are not all of one measure), and to reckon some as to a certain extent pardonable, but others as altogether to be repressed. For they who have either entered into second marriages or joined themselves in wedlock with widows are not allowed to hold the priesthood, either by the apostolic or legal authority: and much more is this the case with him who, as it was reported to us, is the husband of two wives at once, or him who being divorced by his wife is said to have married another, that is, supposing these charges are in your judgment proved. But the rest, whose preferment only so far incurs blame that they have been chosen to the episcopal function from among the laity, and are not culpable in the matter of their wives, we allow to retain the priesthood upon which they have entered, without prejudice to the statutes of the Apostolic See, and without breaking the rules of the blessed Fathers, whose wholesome ordinance it is that no layman, whatever amount of support he may receive, shall ascend to the first, second, or third rank in the Church until he reach that position by the legitimate steps . For what we now suffer to be to a certain extent venial, cannot hereafter pass unpunished, if any one perpetrates what we altogether forbid: because the forgiveness of a sin does not grant a licence to do wrong, nor will it be right to repeat an offence with impunity which has partly been condoned.

VI. Donatus, a Converted Novatian, and Maximus, an Ex-Donatist, are Retained in Their Episcopal Office.

Donatus of Salacia, who, as we learn, has been converted from the Novatians with his people, we wish to preside over the Lord's flock, on condition that he remembers he must send a certificate of his faith to us, in which he not only condemns the error of the Novatian dogma, but also unreservedly confesses the catholic truth. Maximus, also, although he was culpably ordained when a layman, yet if he is now no longer a Donatist, and has abjured the spirit of schismatic depravity, we do not depose from his episcopal dignity, which he has obtained irregularly, on condition that he declare himself a catholic by drawing Up a certificate for us.

VII. The Case of Aggarus and Tyberianus (Ordained with Tumult) is Referred to the Bishops.

But concerning Aggarus and Tyberianus, whose case is different from the others who were ordained from among the laity, in this that their ordination is reported to have been accompanied by fierce riots and savage disturbances, we have entrusted the whole matter to your judgment, treat relying upon your investigation of the case, we may know what to decide about them.

VIII. Maidens Who Have Suffered Violence are Not to Compare Themselves with Others.

Those handmaids of God who have lost their chastity by the violence of barbarians, will be more praiseworthy in their humility and shame-fastness, if they do not venture to compare themselves to undefiled virgins. For although every sin springs from the desire, and the will may have remained unconquered and unpolluted by the fall of the flesh still this will be less to their detriment, if they grieve over losing even in the body what they did not lose in spirit.

IX. These Injunctions to Be Carried Out Without Contentiousness.

And so now that you see yourselves, beloved, fully instructed through David, our brother and fellow-bishop, who is approved to us both by his personal character and his priestly worth, on[nearly] all the points which our brother Potentius' account contained, it remains, brothers, that you receive our healthful exhortations harmoniously, and that doing nothing in rivalry, but acting unanimously with entire devotion and zeal, you obey the constitution of God and His Apostles, and in nothing suffer the well-considered decrees of the canons to be violated. For what we from the consideration of certain reasons have now relaxed must henceforward be guarded by the ancient rules, lest, what we have on this occasion with merciful lenity conceded, we may hereafter have to visit with condign punishment , acting with special and direct vigour against those who in ordaining bishops have neglected the statutes of the holy fathers, and have consecrated men whom they ought to have rejected. Wherefore if any bishops have consecrated such an one priest as ought not to be, even though in some measure they have escaped any loss of their personal dignity, yet they shall have no further right of ordination, nor shall ever be present at that sacrament which, neglecting the judgment of God, they have improperly conferred.

X. The Appointment of Bishops Over Too Small Places is Inexpedient and Must Be Discontinued.

That of course which pertains to the priestly dignity we wish to be observed in common with all the statutes of the canons, viz., that bishops be not consecrated in any place nor in any hamlet , nor where they have not been consecrated before; for where the flocks are small and the congregations small, the care of the presbyters may suffice, whereas the episcopal authority ought to preside onlyover larger flocks and more crowded cities, lest contrary to the divinely-inspired decrees of the holy Fathers the priestly office be assigned over villages and rural estates or obscure and thinly-populated townships, and the position of honour, to which only the more important charges should be given, be held cheap from the very number of these that hold it. And this bishop Restitutus has reported to have been done in his own diocese, and he has with good reason requested that when the bishops of those places where they ought not to have been ordained die in the natural course, the places themselves should revert to the jurisdiction of the same prelate to whom they formerly belonged and were attached. It is indeed useless for the priestly dignity to be diminished by the superfluous multiplications of the office through the inconsiderate complaisance of the ordainer.

XI. Virgins Violated Against Their Will are to Be Treated as Somewhat Different to the Others, But Not to Be Denied Communion.

Now concerning those who, having made a holy vow of virginity[as we said above, chap. viii.], have suffered the violence of barbarians, and have lost their spotless purity not in spirit but in body, we consider such mode- ration ought to be observed that they should be neither degraded to the rank of widows nor yet reckoned in the number of holy and undefiled virgins: yet, if they persevere in the virgin life, and in heart and mind guard the reality of chastity, participation in the sacraments is not to be denied them, because it is unfair that they should be accused or branded for what their wishes did not surrender, but was stolen by the violence of foes.

XII. The Care of Lupicinus is in Part Dealt with and in Part Referred to Them.

The case also of bishop Lupicinus we order to be heard there, but at his urgent and frequent entreaties we have restored him to communion for this reason, that, as he bad appealed to our judgment, we saw that while the matter was pending he had been undeservedly suspended from communion. Moreover there is this also in addition, that it was clearly rash to ordain one over his head who ought not to have been ordained until Lupicinus, having been placed before you or convicted, or having at least confessed, had opportunity to submit to a just sentence, so that, according to the requirements of ecclesiastical discipline, he who was consecrated might receive his vacant place.

XIII. All Disputes to Be Dealt with on the Spot First and Then Referred to the Apostolic See.

But whenever other eases arise which concern the state of the Church and the harmony of priests, we wish them to be first sifted by yourselves in the fear of the Lord, and a full account of all matters settled or needing settlement sent to us, that those things which have been properly and reasonably decided, according to the usage of the Church, may receive our corroborative sanction also. Dated 10th August.

LETTER XIII. TO THE METROPOLITAN BISHOPS IN THE PROVINCES OF ILLYRICUM.

(Leo congratulates them on accepting the authority of Anastasius over them (given in Lett. IV.).

LETTER XIV. TO ANASTASIUS, BISHOP OF THESSALONICA.

Leo, bishop of the City of Rome, to Anastasius, bishop of Thessalonica.
I. Prefatory.
If with true reasoning you perceived all that has been committed to you, brother, by the blessed apostle Peter's authority, and what has also been entrusted to you by our favour, and would weigh it fairly, we should be able greatly to rejoice at your zealous discharge of the responsibility imposed on you .

II. Anastasius is Taxed with Exceeding the Limits of His Vicariate, Especially in His Violent and Unworthy Treatment of Atticus.

Seeing that, as my predecessors acted towards yours, so too I, following their example, have delegated my authority to you , beloved: so that you, imitating our gentleness, might assist us in the care which we owe primarily to all the churches by Divine institution, and might to a certain extent make up for our personal presence in visiting those I provinces which are far off from us: for it would be easy for you by regular and well-timed inspection to tell what and in what cases you could either, by your own influence, settle or reserve for our judgment. For as it was free for you to suspend the more important matters and the harder issues while you awaited our opinion, there was no reason nor necessity for you to go out of your way to decide what was beyond your powers. For you have numerous written warnings of ours in which we have often instructed you to be temperate in all your actions: that with loving exhortations you might provoke the churches of Christ committed to you to healthy obedience. Because, although as a rule there exist among careless or slothful brethren things which demand a strong hand in rectifying them; yet the correction ought to be so applied as ever to keep love inviolate. Wherefore also it is that the blessed Apostle Paul, in instructing Timothy upon the ruling of the Church, says: "an eider rebuke not, but intreat him as a father: the young men as brethren: old women as mothers: young women as sisters in all purity ." And if this moderation is due by the Apostle's precept to all and any of the lower members, how much more is it to be paid without offence to our brethren and fellow-bishops? in order that although things sometimes happen which have to be reprimanded in the persons of priests, yet kindness may have more effect on those who are to be corrected than severity: exhortation than perturbation: love than power. But they who "seek their own, not the things which are Jesus Christ's ," easily depart from this law, and finding pleasure rather in domineering over their subjects than in consulting their interests, are swoln with the pride of their position, and thus what was provided to secure harmony ministers to mischief. That we are obliged to speak thus causes us no small grief. For I feel myself in a certain measure drawn into blame, on discovering you to have so immoderately departed from the rules handed down to you. If you were careless of your own reputation, you ought at least to have spared my good name: lest what only your own mind prompted should seem done with our approval. Do but read, brother, our pages with care, and peruse all the letters sent by holders of the Apostolic See to your predecessors, and you will find injunctions either from me or from my predecessors on that in which we learn you have presumed.

For there has come to us our brother Atticus, the metropolitan bishop of Old Epirus, with the bishops of his province, and with tearful pleading has complained of the undeserved contumely he has suffered, in the presence of your own deacons who, by giving no contradiction to these woeful complaints, showed that what was impressed upon us did not want for truth. We read also in your letter, which those same deacons of yours brought, that brother Atticus had come to Thessalonica, and that he had also sealed his agreement in a written profession, so that we could not but understand concerning him that it was of his own will and free devotion that he had come, and that he had composed the statement of his promise of obedience, although in the very mention of this statement a sign of injury was betrayed. For it was not necessary that he should be bound in writing, who was already proving his obedience by the very dutifulness of his voluntary coming. Wherefore these words in your letter bore witness to the bewailings of the aforesaid, and through his outspoken account that which had been passed over in silence is laid bare, namely that the Praefecture of Illyricum had been approached, and the most exalted functionary among the potentates of the world had been set in motion to expose an innocent prelate: so that a company was sent to carry out the aweful deed who were to enlist all the public servants in giving effect to their orders, and from the church's holy sanctuary charged with no crime, or at best a false one, was dragged a priest, to whom no truce was granted in consideration of his grievous ill-health or the cruel winter weather: but he was forced to take a journey full of hardships and dangers through the pathless snows. And this was a task of such toil and peril that some of those who accompanied the bishop are said to have succumbed .

I am quite dumb-founded, beloved brother, yea and I am also sore grieved that you brought yourself to be so savagely and violently moved against one about whom you had laid no further information than that when summoned to appear he put off and excused himself on the grounds of illness; especially when, even if he deserved any such treatment, you should have waited till I had replied to your consulting letter. But, as I perceive, you thought too well of my habits, and most truly foresaw how fair-minded an answer I was likely to make to preserve harmony among priests: and therefore you made haste to carry out your movements without concealment, lest when you had received the letter of our forbearance dictating another course, you should have no licence to do that which is done. Or perhaps some crime had reached your ears, and metropolitan bishop that you are, the weight of some new charge pressed you hard? But that this is not consistent with the fact, you yourself make certain by laying nothing against him. Yet even if he had committed some grave and intolerable misdemeanour, you should have waited for our opinion: so as to arrive at no decision by yourself until you knew our pleasure. For we made you our deputy, beloved, on the understanding that you were engaged to share our responsibility, not to take plenary powers on yourself. Wherefore as what you bestow a pious care on delights us much, so your wrongful acts grieve us sorely. And after experience in many cases we must show greater foresight, and use more diligent precaution: to the end that through the spirit of love and peace all matter of offence may be removed from the Lord's churches, which we have commended to you: the pre-eminence of your bishopric being retained in the provinces, but all your usurping excesses being shorn off.

III. The Rights of the Metropolitans Under the Vicariate of Anastasius are to Be Observed.

Therefore according to the canons of the holy Fathers, which are framed by the spirit of God and hollowed by the whole world's reverence, we decree that the metropolitan bishops Of each province over which your care. brother, extends by our delegacy shall keep untouched the rights of their position which have been handed down to them from olden times: but on condition that they do not depart from the existing regulations by any carelessness or arrogance.

IV. The Negative Qualifications of a Bishop Determined.

In cities whose governors have died let this form be observed in filling up their place: he, who is to be ordained, even though his good life be not attested, shall be not a layman, not a neophyte, nor yet the husband of a second wife, or one who, though he has or has had but one, married a widow. For the choosing of priests is of such surpassing importance that things which in other members of the Church are not blame-worthy, are yet held unlawful in them.

V. Continence is Required Even in Sub Deacons.

For although they who are not within the ranks of the clergy are free to take pleasure in the companionship of wedlock and the procreation of children, yet for the exhibiting of the purity of complete continence, even sub-deacons are not allowed carnal marriage: that "both those that have, may be as though they had not ," and those who have not, may remain single. But if in this order, which is the fourth from the Head , this is worthy to be observed, how much more is it to be kept in the first, or second, or third, lest any one be reckoned fit for either the deacon's duties or the presbyter's honourable position, or the bishop's pre-eminence, who is discovered not yet to have bridled his uxorious desires.

VI. The Election of a Bishop Must Proceed by the Wishes of the Clergy and People.

When therefore the choice of the chief priest is taken in hand, let him be preferred before all whom the unanimous consent of clergy and people demands, but if the votes chance to be divided between two persons, the judgment of the metropolitan should prefer him who is supported by the preponderance of votes and merits: only let no one be ordained against the express wishes of the place: lest a city should either despise or hate a bishop whom they did not choose, and lamentably fall away from religion because they have not been allowed to have when they wished.

VII. Metropolitans are to Refer to Their Vicar: the Made of Electing Metropolitans is Laid Down.

However the metropolitan bishop should refer to you, brother, about the person to be consecrated bishop, and about the consent of the clergy and people: and he should acquaint you with the wishes of the province: that the due celebration of the ordination may be strengthened by your authority also. But to right selections it will be your duty to cause no delay or hindrance, lest the Lord's flocks should remain too long with their shepherd's care.

Moreover when a metropolitan is defunct and another has to be elected in to his place, the bishops of the province must meet together in the metropolitical city: that after the wishes of all the clerics and all the citizens have been sifted, the best man may be chosen from the presbyters of that same church or from the deacons, and you are to be informed of his name by the priests of the province, who will carry out the wishes of his supporters on ascertaining that you agree with their choice . For whilst we desire proper elections to be hampered by no delays, we yet allow nothing to be done presumptuously without your knowledge.

VIII. Bishops are to Hold Provincial Councils Twice a Year.

Concerning councils of bishops we give no other instructions than those laid down for the Church's health by the holy Fathers : to wit that two meetings should be held a year, in which judgment should be passed upon all the complaints which are wont to arise between the various ranks of the Church. But if perchance among the rulers themselves a cause arise (which God forbid) concerning one of the greater sins, such as cannot be decided by a provincial trial, the metropolitan shall take care to inform you, brother, concerning the nature of the whole matter, and if, after both parties have come before you, the thing be not set at rest even by your judgment, whatever it be, let it be transferred to our jurisdiction.

IX. Translation from One See to Another is to Be Prohibited.

If any bishop, despising the insignificance of his city, shall intrigue for the government of a more populous place, and transfer himself by whatever means to a larger flock, he shall first be driven from the chair he has usurped, and also shall be deprived of his own: so shall he preside neither over those whom in his greed he coveted, nor over those whom in his arrogance he spurned. Therefore let each be content with his own bounds, and not seek to be raised above the limits of his present post.

X. Bishops are Not to Entice or Receive the Clergy of Another Diocese.

A cleric from another diocese let no (bishop) accept or invite against the wishes of his own bishop: but only when giver and receiver agree together thereupon by friendly compact. For a man is guilty of a serious injury who ventures either to entice or withhold from a brother's church that which is of great use or high value. And so, if such a thing happen within the province, the metropolitan shall force the deserting cleric to return to his church: but if he has withdrawn himself still further off, he shall be recalled by your authoritative command: so that no occasion be left for either desire of gain or intrigue.

XI. When the Vicar Shall Require a Meeting of Bishops, Two from Each Province Will Be Sufficient.

In summoning bishops to your presence, we wish you to show great forbearance: lest under a show of much diligence you seem to exult in your brethren's injuries. Wherefore if any greater case arise for which it is reasonable and necessary to convene a meeting of brethren, it may suffice, brother, that two bishops should attend from each province, whom the metropolitans shall think proper to be sent, on the understanding that those who answer the summons be not detained longer than fifteen days from the time fixed.

XII. In Case of Difference of Opinion Between the Vicar and the Bishops, the Bishop of Rome Must Be Consulted. The Subordination of Authorities in the Church Expounded.

But if in that which you believed necessary to be discussed and settled with the brethren, their opinion differs from your own wishes, let all be referred to us, with the minutes of your proceedings attested, that all ambiguities may be removed, and what is pleasing to God decided. For to this end we direct all our desires and pains, that what conduces to our harmonious unity and to the protection of discipline may be marred by no dissension and neglected by no slothfulness. Therefore, dearly beloved brother, you and those our brethren who are offended at your extravagant conduct (though the matter of complaint is not the same with all), we exhort and warn not to disturb by any wrangling what has been rightfully ordained and wisely settled. Let none "seek what is his own, but what is another's," as the Apostle says: "Let each one of you please his neighbour for his good unto edifying ." For the cementing of our unity cannot be firm unless we be bound by the bond of love into an inseparable solidity: because "as in one body we have many members, but all the members have not the same office; so we being many are one body in Christ, and all of us members one of another ." The connexion of the whole body makes all alike healthy, all alike beautiful: and this connexion requires the unanimity indeed of the whole body, but it especially demands harmony among the priests. And though they have a common dignity, yet they have not uniform rank; inasmuch as even among the blessed Apostles, notwithstanding the similarity of their honourable estate, there was st certain distinction of power, and while the election of them all was equal, yet it was given to one to take the lead of the rest. From which model has arisen a distinction between bishops also, and by an important ordinance it has been provided that every one should not claim everything for himself: but that there should be in each province one whose opinion should have the priority among the brethren: and again that certain whose appointment is in the greater cities should undertake a fuller responsibility, through whom the care of the universal Church should converge towards Peter's one seat, and nothing anywhere should be separated from its Head. Let not him then who knows he has been set over certain others take it ill that some one has been set over him, but let him himself render the obedience which he demands of them: and as he does not wish to bear a heavy load of baggage, so let him not dare to place on another's shoulders a weight that is insupportable. For we are disciples of the humble and gentle Master who says: "Learn of Me, for I am gentle and humble of heart, and ye shall find rest for your souls. For My yoke is easy and My burden light ." And how shall we experience this, unless this too comes to our remembrance which the same Lord says: "He that is greater among you, shall be your servant. But he that exalteth himself, shall be humbled: and he that humbleth himself, shall be exalted ."

LETTER XV. TO TURRIBIUS, BISHOP OF ASTURIA , UPON THE ERRORS OF THE PRISCILLIANISTS.

Leo, bishop, to Turribius, bishop, greeting.
I. Introductory.
Your laudable zeal for the truth of the catholic Faith, and the painstaking devotion you expend in the exercise of your pastoral office upon the Lord's flock is proved by your letter, brother, which your deacon has handed to us, in which you have taken care to bring to our knowledge the nature of the disease which has burst forth in your district from the remnants of an ancient plague. For the language of your letter, and your detailed statement, and the text of your pamphlet , explains clearly that the filthy puddle of the Priscillianists again teems with life amongst you . For there is no dirt which has not flowed into this dogma from the notions of all sorts of heretics: since they have scraped together the motley dregs from the mire of

earthly opinions and made for themselves a mixture which they alone may swallow whole, though others have tasted little portions of it.

In fact, if all the heresies which have arisen before the time of Priscillian were to be studied carefully, hardly any mistake will be discovered with which this impiety has not been infected: for not satisfied with accepting the falsehoods of those who have departed from the Gospel under the name of Christ, it has plunged itself also in the shades of heathendom, so as to rest their religious faith and their moral conduct upon the power of demons and the influences of the stars through the blasphemous secrets of the magic arts and the empty lies of astrologers. But if this may be believed and taught, no reward will be due for virtues, no punishment for faults, and all the injunctions not only of human laws but also of the Divine constitutions will be broken down: because there will be no criterion of good or bad actions possible, if a fatal necessity drives the impulses of the mind to either side, and all that men do is through the agency not of men but of stars. To this madness belongs that monstrous division of the whole human body among the twelve signs of the zodiac, so that each part is ruled by a different power: and the creature, whom God made in His own image, is as much under the domination of the stars as his limbs are connected one with the other. Rightly then our fathers, in whose times this abominable heresy sprung up, promptly pursued it throughout the world, that the blasphemous error might everywhere be driven from the Church: for even the leaders of the world so abhorred this profane folly that they laid low its originator, with most of his disciples, by the sword of the public laws. For they saw that all desire for honourable conduct was removed, all marriage-ties undone, and the Divine and the human law simultaneously undermined, if it were allowed for men of this kind to live anywhere under such a creed. And this rigourous treatment was for long a help to the Church's law of gentleness which, although it relies upon the priestly judgment, and shuns blood-stained vengeance, yet is assisted by the stern decrees of Christian princes at times when men, who dread bodily punishment, have recourse to merely spiritual correction. But since many provinces have been taken up with the invasions of the enemy , the carrying out of the laws also has been suspended by these stormy wars. And since intercourse came to be difficult among God's priests and meetings rare, secret treachery was free to act through the general disorder, and was roused to the upsetting of many minds by those very ills which ought to have counteracted it. But which of the peoples and how many of them are free from the contagion of this plague in a district where, as you point out, dear brother, the minds even of certain priests have sickened of this deadly disease: and they who were believed the necessary quellers of falsehood and champions of the Truth are the very ones through whom the Gospel of God is enthralled to the teaching of Priscillian: so that the fidelity of the holy volumes being distorted to profane meanings, under the names of prophets and apostles, is proclaimed not that which the Holy Spirit has taught, but what the devil's servant has inserted. Therefore as you, beloved, with all the faithful diligence in your power, have dealt under 16 heads with these already condemned opinions , we also subject them once more to a strict examination; lest any of these blasphemies should be thought either bearable or doubtful.

II. (1) ThePriscillianists' Denial of the Trinity Refuted.

And so under the first head is shown what unholy views they hold about the Divine Trinity: they affirm that the person of the Father, the Son, and the Holy Ghost is one and the same, as if the same God were named now Father, now Son, and now Holy Ghost: and as if He who begot were not one, He who was begotten, another, and He who proceeded from both, yet another; but an undivided unity must be understood, spoken of under three names, indeed, but not consisting of three persons. This species of blasphemy they borrowed from Sabellius, whose followers were rightly called Patripassians also: because if the Son is identical with the Father, the Son's cross is the Father's passion (patris-passio): and the Father took on Himself all that the Son took in the form of a slave, and in obedience to the Father. Which without doubt is contrary to the catholic faith, which acknowledges the Trinity of the Godhead to be of one essence (oJmoouvsion) in such a way that it believes the Father, the Son, and the Holy Ghost indivisible without confusion, eternal without time, equal without difference: because it is not the same person but the same essence which fills the Unity in Trinity

III. (2) Their Fancy About Virtues Proceeding from God Refuted.

Under the second head is displayed their foolish and empty fancy about the issue of certain virtues from God which he began to possess, and which were posterior to God Himself in His own essence. In this again they support the Arians' mistake, who say that the Father is prior to the Son, because there was a time when He was without the Son: and became the Father then when He begot the Son. But as the catholic Church abhors them, so also does it abhor these who think that what is of the same essence was ever wanting to God. For it is as wicked to speak of Him as progressing as it is to call Him changeable. For increase implies change as much as does decrease.

IV. (3) Their Account of the Epithet "Only Begotten" Refuted.

Again the third head is concerned with these same folk's impious assertion that the Son of God is called "only-begotten" for this reason that He alone was born of a virgin. To be sure they would not have dared to say this, had they not drunk the poison of Paul of Samosata and Photinus: who said that our Lord Jesus Christ did not exist till He was born of the virgin Mary. But if they wish something else to be understood by their tenet, and do not date Christ's beginning from His mother's womb, they must necessarily assert that there is not one Son of God, but others also were begotten of the most High Father, of whom this one is born of a woman, and therefore called only-begotten, because no other of God's sons underwent this condition of being born. Therefore, whithersoever they betake themselves, they fall into an abyss of great impiety, if they either maintain that Christ the Lord took His beginning from His mother, or do not believe Him to be the only-begotten of God the Father: since He who was God was born of a mother, and no one was born of the Father except the Word.

V. (4) Their Fasting on the Nativity and Sunday Disapproved of.

The fourth head deals with the fact that the Birth-day of Christ, which the catholic Church thinks highly of as the occasion of His taking on Him true man, because "the Word became flesh and dwelt in us ," is not truly honoured by these men, though they make a show of honouring it, for they fast on that day, as they do also on the Lord's day, which is the day of Christ's resurrection. No doubt they do this, because they do not believe that Christ the Lord was born in true man's nature, but maintain that by a sort of illusion there was an appearance of what was not a reality, following the views of Cerdo and Marcion, and being in complete agreement with their kinsfolk, the Manichaeans. For as our examination has disclosed and brought home to them, they drag out in mournful fasting the Lord's day which for us is hollowed by the resurrection of our Saviour: devoting this abstinence, as the explanation goes, to the worship of the sun: so that they are throughout out of harmony with the unity of our faith, and the day which by us is spent in gladness is past in self-affliction by them. Whence it is fitting that these enemies of Christ's cross and resurrection should accept an opinion (like this) which tallies with the doctrine they have selected.

VI. (5) Their View that the Soul is Part of the Divine Being Refuted.

The fifth head refers to their assertion that man's soul is part of the Divine beings , and that the nature of our human state does not differ from its Creator's nature. This impious view has its source in the opinions of certain philosophers, and the Manichaeans and the catholic Faith condemns it: knowing that nothing that is made is so sublime and so supreme as that its nature should be itself God. For that which is part of Himself is Himself, and none other than the Son and Holy Spirit. And besides this one consubstantial, eternal, and unchangeable Godhead of the most high Trinity there is nothing in all creation which, in its origin, is not created out of nothing. Besides anything that surpasses its fellow-creatures is not *ipso facto* God, nor, if a thing is great and wonderful, is it identical with Him "who alone doeth great wonders ." No *man* is truth, wisdom, justice; but many are partakers of truth, wisdom, and justice. But God alone is exempt from any participating: and anything which is in any degree worthily predicated of Him is not an attribute, but His very essence. For in the Unchangeable there is nothing added, there is nothing lost: because "to be " is ever His peculiar property, and that is eternity. Whence abiding in Himself He renews all things , and receives nothing which He did not Himself give. Accordingly they are over-proud and stone-blind who, when they say the soul is part of the Divine Being, do not understand that they merely assert that God is changeable, and Himself suffers anything that may be inflicted upon His nature.

VII. (6) Their View that the Devil Was Never Goad, and is Therefore Not God's Creation, Refuted.

The sixth notice points out that they say the devil never was good, and that his nature is not God's handiwork, but he came forth out of chaos and darkness: because I suppose he has no instigator, but is himself the source and substance of all evil: whereas the true Faith, which is the catholic, acknowledges that the substance of all creatures spiritual or corporeal is good, and that evil has no positive existence ; because God, who is the Maker of the Universe, made nothing that was not good. Whence the devil also would be good, if he had remained as he was made. But because he made a bad use of his natural excellence, and "stood not in the truth ," he did not pass into the opposite substance, but revolted from the highest good to which he owed adherence: just as they themselves who make such assertions run headlong from truth into falsehood, and accuse nature of their own spontaneous delinquencies, and are condemned for their voluntary perversity: though of course this evil is in them, but is itself not a substance but a penalty inflicted on substance.

VIII. (7) Their Rejection of Marriage Condemned.

In the seventh place follows their condemnation of marriages and their horror of begetting children: in which, as in almost all points, they agree with the Manichaeans' impiety. But it is for this reason, as their own practices prove, that they detest the marriage tie, because there is no liberty for lewdness where the chastity of wedlock and of offspring is preserved.

IX. (8) Their Disbelief in the Resurrection of the Body Has Been Already Condemned by the Church.

Their eighth point is that the formation of men's bodies is the device of the devil, and that the seed of conception is shaped by the aid of demons in the wombs of women: and that for this reason the resurrection of the flesh is not to be believed because the stuff of which the body is made is not consistent with the dignity of the soul. This falsehood is without doubt the devil's work, and such monstrous opinions are the devices of demons who do not mould men in women's bellies, but concoct such errors in heretics' hearts. This unclean poison which flows especially from the fount of the Manichaean wickedness has been already arraigned and condemned by the catholic Faith.

X. (9) Their Nation that "The Children of Promise" Are Conceived by the Holy Ghost is Utterly Unscriptural and Uncatholic.

The ninth notice declares that they say the sons of promise are born indeed of women but conceived by the Holy Spirit: lest that offspring which is born of carnal seed should seem to share in God's estate. This is repugnant and contrary to the catholic Faith which acknowledges every man to be formed by the Maker of the Universe in the substance of his body and soul, and to receive the breath of life within his mother's womb: though thattaint of sin and liability to die remains which passed from the first parent into his descendants; until the sacrament of Regeneration comes to succour him, whereby through the Holy Spirit we are re-born the sons of promise, not in the fleshly womb, but in the power of baptism. Whence David also, who certainly was a son of promise, says to God: "Thy hands have made me and fashioned me ." And to Jeremiah says the Lord, "Before I formed thee in the womb I knew thee, and in thy mother's belly I sanctified thee ."

XI. (10) Their Theory that Souls Have a Previous Existence Before Entering Man Refuted.

Under the tenth head they are reported as asserting that the souls which are placed in men's bodies have previously been without body and have sinned in their heavenly habitation, and for this reason having fallen from their high estate to a lower one alight upon ruling spirits of divers qualities, and after passing through a succession of powers of the air and stars, some fiercer, some milder, are enclosed in bodies of different sorts and conditions, so that whatever variety and inequality is meted out to us in this life, seems the result of previous causes. This blasphemous fable they have woven for themselves out of many persons' errors : but all of them the catholic Faith cuts off from union with its body, persistently and truthfully proclaiming that men's souls did not exist until they were breathed into their bodies, and that they were not there implanted by any other than God, who is thecreator both of the souls and of the bodies. And because through the transgression of the first man the whole stock of the human race was tainted, no one can be set free from the state of the old Adam save through Christ's sacrament of baptism, in which there are no distinctions between the re-born, as says the Apostle: "For as many of you as were baptized in Christ did put on Christ: there is neither Jew nor Greek: there is neither bond nor free: there is neither male nor female: for ye are all one in Christ Jesus ." What then have the course of the stars to do with it, or the devices of destiny?

what the changing state of mundane things and their restless diversity? Behold how the grace of God makes all these unequals equal, who, whatever their labours in this life, if they abide faithful, cannot be wretched, for they can say with the Apostle in every trial: "who shall separate us from the love of Christ? shall tribulation, or distress, or persecution, or famine, or nakedness, or peril, or sword? As it is written, 'For thy sake we are killed all the day long, we are accounted as sheep for the slaughter.' (Ps. xliv. 22.) But in all these things we overcome through Him that loved us ." And therefore the Church, which is the body of Christ, has no fear about the inequalities of the world, because she has no desire for temporal goods: nor does she dread being overwhelmed by the empty threats of destiny, for she knows she is strengthened by patience in tribulations.

XII. (11) Their Astrological Notions Condemned.

Their eleventh blasphemy is that in which they suppose that both the souls and bodies of men are under the influence of fatal stars: this folly compels them to become entangled in all the errors of the heathen, and to strive to attract stars that are as they think favourable to them, and to soften those that are against them. But for those who follow such pursuits there is no place in the catholic Church; a man who gives himself up to such convictions separates himself from the body of Christ altogether.

XIII. (12) Their Belief that Certain Powers Rule the Soul and the Stars the Body, is Unscriptural and Preposterous.

The twelfth of these points is this, that they map out the parts of the soul under certain powers, and the limbs of the body under others: and they suggest the characters of the inner powers that rule the soul by giving them the names of the patriarchs, and on the contrary they attribute the signs of the stars to those under which they put the body. And in all these things they entangle themselves in an inextricable maze, not listening to the Apostle when he says. "See that no one deceive you through philosophy and vain deceit after the tradition of men, after the rudiments of the world, and not after Christ; for in Him dwells all the fulness of the Godhead bodily, and in Him ye are made full, who is the head of every principality and power ." And again: "let no man beguile you by a voluntary humility and worshipping of angels, treading on things which he hath not seen, vainly puffed up by the senses of his flesh, not holding fast the Head from whom all the body, being supplied and knit together through the joints and bands, increaseth withthe increase of God ." What then is the use of admitting into the heart what the law has not taught, prophecy has not sung, the truth of the Gospel has not proclaimed, the Apostles' teaching has not handed down? But these things are suited to the minds of those of whom the Apostle speaks, "For the time will come when they will not endure sound doctrine, but having itching ears, will heap to themselves teachers after their own lusts: and will turn away indeed their hearing from the truth, and turn aside unto fables ." And so we can have nothing in common with men who dare to teach or believe such things, and strive by any means in their power to persuade men that the substance of flesh is foreign to the hope of resurrection, and so break down the whole mystery of Christ's incarnation: because it was wrong for Christ to take upon Him complete manhood if it was wrong for Him to emancipate complete manhood.

XIV. (13) Their Fanciful Division of the Scriptures Rejected.

In the thirteenth place comes their assertion that the whole body of the canonical Scriptures is to be accepted, under the names of the patriarchs : because those twelve virtues which work the reformation of the inner man are pointed out in their names, and without this knowledge no soul can effect its reformation, and return to that substance from which it came forth. But this wicked delusion the Christian wisdom holds in disdain, for it knows that the nature of the true Godhead is inviolable and immutable: but the soul, whether living in the body or separated from the body, is subject to many passions: whereas, of course, if it were part of the divine essence, no adversity could happen to it. And therefore there is no comparison between them: One is the Creator, the other is the creature. For He is always the same, and suffers no change: but the soul is changeable, even if not changed, because its power of not changing is a gift, and not a property.

XV. (14) Their Idea that the Scriptures Countenance Their Subjecting of the Body to the Starry Influences Denied.

Under the fourteenth heading their sentiments upon the state of the body are stated, viz., that it is, on account of its earthly properties, held under the power of stars and constellations, and that many things are found in the holy books which have reference to the outer man with this object, that in the Scriptures themselves a certain opposition may be seen at work between the divine and the earthly nature: and that which the powers that rule the soul claim for themselves may be distinguished from that which the fashioners of the body claim. These stories are invented that the soul may be maintained to be part of the divine substance, and the flesh believed to belong to the bad nature: since the world itself, with its elements, they hold to be not the work of the good God, but the outcome of an evil author: and that they might disguise these sacrilegious lies under a fair cloak, they have polluted almost all the divine utterances with the colouring of their unholy notions.

XVI. (15) Their Falsified Copies of the Scriptures, and Their Apocryphal Books Prohibited.

And on this subject your remarks under the fifteenth head make a complaint, and express a well-deserved abhorrence of their devilish presumption, for we too have ascertained this from the accounts of trustworthy witnesses, and have found many of their copies most corrupt, though they are entitled canonical. For how could they deceive the simple- minded unless they sweetened their poisoned cups with a little honey, lest what was meant to be deadly should be detected by its over-nastiness? Therefore care must be taken, and the priestly diligence exercised to the uttermost, to prevent falsified copies that are out of harmony with the pure Truth being used in reading. And the apocryphal scriptures, which, under the names of Apostles , form a nursery-ground for many falsehoods, are not only to be proscribed, but also taken away altogether and burnt to ashes in the fire. For although there are certain things in them which seem to have a show of piety, yet they are never free from poison, and through the allurements of their stories they have the secret effect of first beguiling men with miraculous narratives, and then catching them in the noose of some error. Wherefore if any bishop has either not forbidden the possession of apocryphal writings in men's houses, or under the name of being canonical has suffered those copies to be read in church which are vitiated with the spurious alterations of Priscillian, let him know that he is to be accounted heretic, since he who does not reclaim others from error shows that he himself has gone astray.

XVII. (16) About the Writings of Dictinius.

Under the last head a just complaint was made that the treatises of Dictinius which he wrote in agreement with Priscillian's tenets were read by many with veneration: for if they think any respect is due to Dictinius' memory, they ought to admire his restoration rather than his fall. Accordingly it is not Dictinius but Priscillian that they read: and they approve of what he wrote in error, not what he preferred after recantation. But let no one venture to do this with impunity, nor let any one be reckoned among catholics who makes use of writings that have been condemned not by the catholic Church alone but by the author himself as well. Let not those who have gone astray be allowed to make a fictitious show, and under the veil of the Christian name shirk the provisions of the imperial decrees. For they attach themselves to the catholic Church with all this difference of opinion in their heart, with the object of both making such converts as they can, and escaping the rigour of the law by passing themselves off as ours. This is done by Priscillianists and Manichaeans alike; for there is such a close bond of union between the two that they are distinct only in name, but in their blasphemies are found at one: because although the Manichaeans reject the Old Testament which the others pretend to accept, yet the purpose of both tends to the same end, seeing that the one side corrupts while receiving what the other assails and rejects.

But in their abominable mysteries, which the more unclean they are, are so much the more carefully concealed, their crime is but one, their filthy-mindedness one, and their foul conduct similar. And although we blush to speak so plainly, yet we have tracked it out with the most painful searches, and exposed it by the confession of Manichaeans who have been arrested, and thus brought it to the public knowledge: lest by any means it might seem matter of doubt, although it has been disclosed by the mouth of the men themselves, who had performed the crime, in our court, which was attended not only by a large gathering of priests, but also by men of repute and dignity, and a certain number of the senate and the people, even as the missive which we have addressed to you, beloved, shows to have been done. And there has been found out and widely published about the immoral practices of the Priscillianists just what was also found out about the foul wickedness of the Manichaeans. For they who are throughout on a level of depravity in their ideas, cannot be unlike in their religious matters.

So having run through all that the detailed refutation contains, with which the contents of the memorial of their views does not disagree, we have, I think, satisfactorily shown what our opinion on the matters which you, brother, have referred to us, and how unbearable it is if such blasphemous errors find acceptance in the hearts even of some priests, or to put it more mildly, are not actively opposed by them. With what conscience can they maintain the honourable position which has been given them, who do not labour for the souls entrusted to them? Beasts rush in, and they do not close the fold. Robbers lay wait, and they set no watch. Diseases multiply, and they seek out no remedies. But when in addition they refuse assent to those who act more warily, and shrink from anathematizing by their written confession blasphemies which the whole world has already condemned, what do they wish men to understand except that they are not of the number of the brethren, but on the enemy's side?

XVIII. The Body of Christ Really Rested in the Tomb, and Really Rose Again.

Furthermore in the matter which you placed last in your confidential letter, I am surprised that any intelligent Christian should be in difficulty as to whether when Christ descended to the realms below, his flesh rested in the tomb: for as it truly died and was buried, so it was truly raised the third day. For this the Lord Himself also had announced, saying to the Jews, "destroy this temple, and in three days I will raise it up ." Where the evangelist adds this comment: "but this He spake of the temple of His body." The truth of which the prophet David also had predicted, speaking in the person of the Lord and Saviour, and saying: "Moreover my flesh also shall rest in hope; because Thou will not leave my soul in Hades, nor give Thy Holy One to see corruption " From these words surely it is clear that the Lord's flesh being buried, both truly rested and did not undergo corruption: because it was quickly revived by the return of the soul, and rose again. Not to believe this is blasphemous enough, and is undoubtedly of a piece with the doctrine of Manichaeus and Priscillian, who with their blasphemous conceptions pretend to confess Christ, but only in such a way as to destroy the reality of His incarnation, and death, and resurrection.

Therefore let a council of bishops be held among you, and let the priests of neighbouring provinces meet at a place suitable to all: that, on the lines of our reply to your request for advice, a full inquiry may be made as to whether here are any of the bishops who are tainted with the contagion of this heresy: for they must without doubt be cut off from communion, if they refuse to condemn this most unrighteous sect with all its wrongful conceptions. For it can nohow be permitted that one who has undertaken the duty of preaching the Faith should dare to maintain opinions contrary to Christ's gospel and the creed of the universal Church. What kind of disciples will there be in a place where such masters teach? What will the people's religion, or the salvation of the laity be, where against the interests of human society the holiness of chastity is uprooted, the marriage-bond overthrown, the propagation of children forbidden, the nature of the flesh condemned, and, in opposition to the true worship of the true God, the Trinity of the Godhead is denied, the individuality of the persons confounded, man's soul declared to be the Divine essence, and enclosed in flesh at the Devil's will, the Son of God proclaimed only-begotten in right of being born of a Virgin, not begotten of the Father, and at the same time maintained to be neither true offspring of God, nor true child of the virgin: so that after a false passion and an unreal death, even the resurrection of the flesh reassumed out of the tomb should be considered fictitious? But it is vain for them to adopt the name of catholic, as they do not oppose these blasphemies: they must believe them, if they can listen so patiently to such words. And so we have sent a letter to our brethren and fellow-bishops of the provinces of Tarraco, Carthago, Lusitania and Gallicia, enjoining a meeting of the general synod. It will be yours, beloved, to take order that our authoritative instructions be conveyed to the bishops of the aforesaid provinces. But should anything, which God forbid, hinder the coming together of a general council of Gallicia , at least let the priests come together, the assembling of whom our brothers Idacius and Ceponius shall look to, assisted by your own strenuous efforts to hasten the applying of remedies to these serious wounds by a provincial synod also. Dated July 21, in the consulship of the illustrious Calipius and Ardaburis (447).

LETTER XVI. TO THE BISHOPS OF SICILY.

Leo the bishop to all the bishops throughout Sicily greeting in the Lord.
I. Introductory.

By God's precepts and the Apostle's admonitions we are incited to keep a careful watch over the state of all the churches: and, if anywhere ought is found that needs rebuke, to recall men with speedy care either from the stupidity of ignorance or from forwardness and presumption. For inasmuch as we are warned by the Lord's own command whereby the blessed Apostle Peter had the thrice repeated mystical injunction pressed upon him, that he who loves Christ should feed Christ's sheep, we are compelled by reverence for that see which, by the abundance of the Divine Grace, we hold, to shun the danger of sloth as much as possible: lest the confession of the chief Apostle whereby he testified that he loved God be not found in us: because if he (through us) carelessly feed the flock so often commended to him he is proved not to love the chief Shepherd.

II. Baptism is to Be Administered at Easter-Tide and Not on the Epiphany.

Accordingly when it reached my ears on reliable testimony (and I already felt a brother's affectionate anxiety about your acts, beloved)that in what is one of the chief sacraments of the Church you depart from the practice of the Apostles' constitution by administering the sacrament of baptism to greater numbers on the feast of the Epiphany than at Easter-tide, I was surprised that you or your predecessors could have introduced so unreasonable an innovation as to confound the mysteries of the two festivals and believe there was no difference between the day on which Christ was worshipped by the wise men and that on which He rose again from the dead. You could never have fallen into this fault, if you had taken the whole of your observances from the source whence you derive your consecration to the episcopate; and if the see of the blessed Apostle Peter, which is the mother of your priestly dignity, were the recognized teacher of church-method. We could indeed have endured your departure from its rules with less equanimity, if you had received any previous rebuke by way of warning from us. But now as we do not despair of correcting you, we must show gentleness. And although an excuse which affects ignorance is scarce tolerable in priests, yet we prefer to moderate our needful rebuke and to instruct you plainly in the true method of the Church.

III. One Must Distinguish One Festival from Another in Respect of Dignity and Occasion.

The restoration of mankind has indeed ever remained immutably fore-ordained in God's eternal counsel: but the series of events which had to be accomplished in time through Jesus Christ our Lord was begun at the Incarnation of the Word. Hence there is one time when at the angel's announcement the blessed Virgin Mary believed she was to be with child through the Holy Ghost and conceived: another, when without loss of her virgin purity the Boy was born and shown to the shepherds by the exulting joy of the heavenly attendants: another, when the Babe was circumcised: another, when the victim required by the Law is offered for him: another, when the three wise men attracted by the brightness of the new star arrive at Bethlehem from the East and worship the Infant with the mystic offering of Gifts.

And again the days are not the same on which by the divinely appointed passage into Egypt He was withdrawn from wicked Herod, and on which He was recalled from Egypt into Galilee on His pursuer's death. Among these varieties of circumstance must be included His growth of body: the Lord increases, as the evangelist bears witness, with the progress of age and grace: at the time of the Passover He comes to the temple at Jerusalem with His parents, and when He was absent from the returning company, He is found sitting with the ciders and disputing among the wondering masters and rendering an account of His remaining behind: "why is it," He says, "that ye sought Me? did ye not know that I must be in that which is My Father's ," signifying that He was the Son of Him whose temple He was in. Once more when in later years He was to be declared more openly and sought out the baptism of His forerunner John, was there any doubt of His being God remaining when after the baptism of the Lord Jesus the Holy Spirit in form of a dove descended and rested upon Him, and the Father's voice was heard from the skies, "Thou art My beloved Son: in Thee I am well pleased ?" All these things we have alluded to with as much brevity as possible for this reason, that you may know, beloved, that though all the days of Christ's life were hallowed by many mighty works of His , and though in all His actions mysterious sacraments shone forth, yet at one time intimations of events were given by signs, and at one time fulfilment realized: and that all the Saviour's works that are recorded are not suitable to the time of baptism. For if we were to commemorate with indiscriminate honour these things also which we know to have been done by the Lord after His baptism by the blessed John, His whole life- time would have to be observed in a continuous succession of festivals, because all His acts were full of miracles. But because the Spirit of wisdom and knowledge so instructed the Apostles and teachers of the whole Church as to allow nothing disordered or confused to exist in our Christian observances, we must discern the relative importance of the various solemnities and observe a reasonable distinction in all the institutions of our fathers and rulers: for we cannot otherwise "be one flock and one shepherd ," except as the Apostle teaches us, "that we all speak the same thing: and that we be perfected in the same mind and in the same judgment ."

IV. The Reason Explained Why Easier and Whitsuntide are the Proper Seasons for Baptism.

Although, therefore, both these things which are connected with Christ's humiliation and those which are connected with His exaltation meet in one and the same Person, and all that is in Him of Divine power and human weakness conduces to the accomplishment of our restoration: yet it is appropriate that the power of baptism should change the old into the new creature on the death-day of the Crucified and the Resurrection-day of the Dead: that Christ's death and His resurrection may operate in the re-born , as the blessed Apostle says: "Are ye ignorant that all we who were baptized in Christ Jesus, were baptized in His death? We were buried with Him through baptism into death; that as Christ rose from the dead through the glory of the Father, so we also should walk in newness of life. For if we have become united with the likeness of His death, we shall be also (with the likeness) of His resurrections ," and the rest which the Teacher of the Gentiles discusses further in recommending the sacrament of baptism: that it might be seen from the spirit of this doctrine that that is the day, and that the time chosen for regenerating the sons of men and adopting them among the sons of God, on which by a mystical symbolism and form , what is done in the limbs coincides with what was done in the

Head Himself, for in the baptismal office death ensues through the slaying of sin, and threefold immersion imitates the lying in the tomb three days, and the raising out of the water is like Him that rose again from the tomb. The very nature, therefore of the act teaches us that that is the recognized day for the general reception of the grace, on which the power of the gift and the character of the action originated. And this is strongly corroborated by the consideration that the Lord Jesus Christ Himself, after He rose from the dead, handed on both the form and power of baptizing to His disciples, in whose person all the chiefs of the churches received their instructions with these words, "Go ye and teach all nations, baptizing them in the name of the Father and of the Son and of the Holy Ghosts." On which of course He might have instructed them even before His passion, had He not especially wished it to be understood that the grace of regeneration began with His resurrection. It must be added, indeed, that the solemn season of Pentecost, hallowed by the coming of the Holy Ghost is also allowed, being as it were, the sequel and completion of the Paschal feast. And while other festivals are held on other days of the week, this festival (of Pentecost) always occurs on that day, which is marked by the Lord's resurrection: holding out, so to say, the hand of assisting grace and inviting those, who have been cut off from the Easter feast by disabling sickness or length of journey or difficulties of sailing, to gain the purpose that they long for through the gift of the Holy Spirit. For the Only-begotten of God Himself wished no difference to be felt between Himself and the Holy Spirit in the Faith of believers and in the efficacy of His works: because there is no diversity in their nature, as He says, "I will ask the Father and He shall give you another Comforter that He may be with you for ever, even the Spirit of Truth ;" and again: "But the Comforter which is the Holy Ghost, whom the Father will send in My name, He shall teach you all things and bring to your remembrance all that I said unto you ;" and again: "When He, the Spirit of Truth, is come, He shall guide you into all the Truth." And thus, since Christ is the Truth, and the Holy Spirit the Spirit of Truth, and the name of "Comforter" appropriate to both, the two festivals are not dissimilar, where the sacrament is the same.

V. S. Peter's Example as an Authority for Whitsuntide Baptisms.

And that we do not contend for this on ours own conviction but retain it on Apostolic authority, we prove by a sufficiently apt example, following the blessed Apostle Peter, who, on the very day on which the promised coming of the Holy Ghost filled up the number of those that believed, dedicated to God in the baptismal font three thousand of the people who had been converted by his preaching. The Holy Scripture, which contains the Acts of Apostles, teaches this in its faithful narrative, saying, "Now when they heard this they were pricked in the heart, and said unto Peter and to the rest of the Apostles, what shall we do, brethren? But Peter said unto them, Repent ye and be baptized every one of you in the name of Jesus Christ, unto the remission of your sins, and ye shall receive the gift of the Holy Ghost. For to you is the promise, and to your children and to all that are afar off, even as many as the Lord our God shall call unto Him. With many other words also he testified and exhorted them saying, Save yourselves from this crooked generation. They then that received his word were baptized, and there were added in that day about three thousand."

VI. In Cases of Urgency Other Times Art Allowable for Baptism.

Wherefore, as it is quite clear that these two seasons of which we have been speaking are the rightful ones for baptizing the chosen in Church, we admonish you, beloved, not to add other days to this observance. Because, although there are other festivals also to which much reverence is due in God's honour, yet we must rationally guard this principal and greatest sacrament as a deep mystery and not part of the ordinary routine : not, however, prohibiting the licence to succour those who are in danger by administering baptism to them at any time. For whilst we put off the vows of those who are not pressed by ill health and live in peaceful security to those two closely connected and cognate festivals, we do not at any time refuse this which is the only safeguard of true salvation to any one in peril of death, in the crisis of a siege, in the distress of persecution, in the terror of shipwreck.

VII. Our Lord's Baptism by John Very Different to the Baptism of Believers.

But if any one thinks the feast of the Epiphany, which in proper degree is certainly to be held in due honour, claims the privilege baptism because, according to some the Lord came to St. John's baptism on the same day, let him know that the grace of that baptism and the reason of it were quite different, and is not on an equal footing with the power by which they are re-born of the Holy Ghost, of whom it is said, "which were born not of blood, nor of the will of the flesh, nor of the will of man, but of God ." For the Lord who needed no remission of sin and sought not the remedy of being born again, desired to be baptized just as He desired to be circumcised, and to have a victim offered for His purification: that He, who had been "made of a woman)," as the Apostle says, might become also "under the law" which He had come, "not to destroy but to fulfil ," and by fulfilling to end, as the blessed Apostle proclaims, saying: "but Christ is the end of the law unto righteousness to every one that believeth ." But the sacrament of baptism He founded in His own person , because "in all things having the pre-eminence ," He taught that He Himself was the Beginning. And He ratified the power of re-birth on that occasion, when from His side flowed out the blood of ransom and the water of baptism . As, therefore, the Old Testament was the witness to the new, and "the law was given by Moses: but grace and truth came through Jesus Christ ;" as the divers sacrifices prefigured the one Victim, and the slaughter of many lambs was ended by the offering up of Him, of whom it is said, "Behold the Lamb of God; behold Him that taketh away the sin of the world ;" so too John, not Christ, but Christ's forerunner, not the bridegroom, but the friend of the bridegroom, was so faithful in seeking, "not His own, but the things which are Jesus Christ's ," as to profess himself unworthy to undo the shoes of His feet: seeing that He Himself indeed baptized "in water unto repentance," but He who with twofold power should both restore life and destroy sins, was about to "baptize in the Holy Ghost and fire ." then, beloved brethren, all these distinct proofs come before you, whereby to the removal of all doubt you recognize that in baptizing the elect who, according to the Apostolic rule have to be purged by exorcisms, sanctified by fastings and instructed by frequent sermons, two seasons only are to be observed, viz. Easter and Whitsuntide: we charge you, brother, to make no further departure from the Apostolic institutions. Because hereafter no one who thinks the Apostolic rules can be set at defiance will go unpunished.

VIII. The Sicilian Bishops are to Send Three Theirnumber to Each of the Half-Yearly Meetings of Bishops at Rome.

Wherefore we require this first and foremost for the keeping of perfect harmony, that, according to the wholesome rule of the holy Fathers that there should be two meetings of bishops every year, three of you should appear without fail each time, on the 29th of September, to join in the council of the brethren: for thus, by the aid of Gov's grace, we shall the easier guard against the rise of offences and errors in Christ's Church: and this council must always meet and deliberate in the presence of the blessed Apostle Peter, that all his constitutions and canonical decrees may remain inviolate with all the Lord's priests.

These matters, upon which we thought it necessary to instruct you by the inspiration of the Lord, we wish brought to your knowledge by our brothers and fellow-bishops, Bacillus and Paschasinus. May we learn by their report that the institutions of the Apostolic See are reverently observed by you. Dated 21 Oct., in the consulship of the illustrious Alipius and Ardaburis (447).

LETTER XVII.

To all the bishops of Sicily (forbidding the sale of church property except for the advantage of the church).

Leo, the pope( ), to all the bishops of Sicily.

The occasion of specific complaints claims our attention as having "the care of all the churches," that we should make a perpetual decree precluding all bishops from adopting as a practice what in two churches of your province has been unscrupulously suggested and wrongfully carried out. Upon the clergy of the church in Tauromenium deploring the destitution they were in from the bishop having squandered all its estates by selling giving away, and otherwise disposing of them, the clergy of Panormus, who have lately had a new bishop, raised a similar complaint about the misgovernment of the former bishop in the holy synod, at which we were presiding. Although, therefore, we have already given instructions as to what is for the advantage of both Churches, yet test this vicious example of abominable plundering should hereafter be taken as a precedent, we wish to make this our formal command binding on you, beloved, for ever. We decree, therefore, that no bishopwithout exception shall dare to give away, or to exchange, or to sell any of the property of his church: unless he foresees an advantage likely to accrue from so doing, and after consultation with the whole of the clergy, and with their consent he decides upon what will undoubtedly profit that church. For presbyters, or deacons, or clerics of any rank who have connived at the churches losses, must know that they will be deprived of both rank and communion: because it is absolutely fair, beloved brethren, that not only the bishop, but also the whole of the clergy should advance the interests of their church and keep the gifts unimpaired of those who have contributed their own substance to tile churches for the salvation of their souls. Dated 20 Oct., in the consulship of the illustrious Calepius (447).

LETTER XVIII. TO JANUARIUS, BISHOP OF AQUILEIA

Leo, bishop of the city of Rome, to Januarius, bishop of Aquileia.

Those who renounce heresy and schism and return to the Church must make their recantation very clear: those who are clerics may retain their rank but not be promoted.

On reading your letter, brother, we recognized the vigour of your faith, which we already were aware of, and congratulate you on the watchful care you bestow as pastor. on the keeping of Christ's flock: lest the wolves, that enter in under guise of sheep, should tear the simple ones to pieces in their bestial fierce- ness, and not only themselves run riot without restraint, but also spoil those which are sound. And lest the vipery deceit should effect this, we have thought it meet to warn you, beloved, reminding you that it is at the peril of his soul, for any one of them who has fallen away from us into a sect of heretics and schismatics , and stained himself to whatever extent with the pollution of heretical communion, to be received into catholic communion on coming to his senses without making legitimate and express satisfaction. For it is most wholesome and full of all the benefits of spiritual healing that presbyters or deacons, or sub-deacons or clerics of any rank, who wish to appear reformed, and entreat to return once more to the catholic Faith which they had long ago lost, should first confess without ambiguity that their errors and the authors of the errors themselves are condemned by them, that their base opinions may be utterly destroyed, and no hope survive of their recurrence, and that no member may be harmed by contact with them, every point having been met with its proper recantation. With regard to them we also order the observance of this regulation of the canons , that they consider it a great indulgence, if they be allowed to remain undisturbed in their present rank without any hope of further advancement: but only on consideration of their not being defiled with second baptism . No slight penalty does he incur from the Lord, who judges any such person fit to be advanced to Holy Orders. If advancement is granted to those who are without blame, only after full examination, how much more ought it to be refused to those who are under suspicion. Accordingly, beloved brother, in whose devotion we rejoice, bestow your care on our directions, and take order for the circumspect and speedy carrying out of these laudable suggestions and wholesome injunctions, which affect the welfare of the whole Church. But do not doubt, beloved, that, if what we decree for the observance of the canons, and the integrity of the Faith be neglected (which we do not anticipate), we shall be strongly moved: because the faults of the lower orders are to be referred to none more than to slothful and careless governors, who often foster much disease by refusing to apply the needful remedy. Dated 30 Dec., in the consulship of the illustrious Calepius and Ardaburis (447).

LETTER XIX. TO DORUS, BISHOP OF BENEVENTUM.

Leo, bishop, to Dorus his well-beloved brother.
I. He Rebukes Dorus Far Allowing a Junior Presbyter to Be Promoted Over the Heads of the Seniors, and the First and Second in Seniority for Acquiescing.

We grieve that the judgment, which we hoped to entertain of you, has been frustrated by our ascertaining that you have done things which by their blame-worthy novelty infringe the whole system of Church discipline: although you know full well with what care we wish the provisions of the canons to be kept through all the churches of the Lord, and the priests of all the peoples to consider it their especial duty to prevent the violation of the rules of the holy constitutions by any extravagances. We are surprised, therefore, that you who ought to have been a strict observer of the injunctions of the Apostolic See have acted so carelessly, or rather so contumaciously, as to show yourself not a guardian, but a breaker of the laws handed on to you. For from the report of your presbyter, Paul, which is subjoined, we have learnt that the order of the presbyterate has been thrown into confusion with you by strange intrigues and vile collusion; in such a way that one man has been hastily and prematurely promoted, and others passed over whose advancement was recommended by their age, and who were charged with no fault. But if the eagerness of an intriguer or the ignorant zeal of his supporters demanded that which custom never allowed, viz., that a beginner should be preferred to veterans, and a mere boy to men of years, it was your duty by diligence and teaching to check the improper desires of the petitioners with all reasonable authority: lest he whom you advanced hastily to the priestly rank should enter on his office to the detriment of those with whom he associated and become demoralized by the growth within him, not of the virtue of humility, but of the vice of conceit . For you were not unaware that the Lord had said that "he that humbleth himself shall be exalted: but he that exalteth himself shall be humbled ," and also had said, "but ye seek from little to increase, and from the greater to be less ." For both actions are out of order and out of place : and all the fruit of men's labours is lost, all the measure of their deserts is rendered void, if the gaining of dignity is proportioned to the amount of flattery used: so that the eagerness to be eminent belittles not only the aspirer himself, but also him that connives at him. But if, as is asserted, the first and second presbyter were so agreeable to Epicarpius being put over their heads as to demand his being honoured to their own disgrace, that which they wished ought not to have been granted them when they were voluntarily degrading themselves: because it would have been worthier of you to oppose than to yield to such a pitiable wish. But their base and cowardly submission could not be to the prejudice of others whose consciences were good, and who had not done despite to God's grace; so that, whatever the transaction was whereby they gave up their precedence to another, they could not lower the dignity of those that came next to them, nor because they had placed the last above themselves, could he take precedence of the rest.

II. The Presbyters, Who Gave Way, to Be Degraded with the Usurper to the Bottom: the Rest to Keep Their Places.

The aforesaid presbyters, therefore, who have declared themselves unworthy of their proper rank, though they even deserved to be deprived of their priesthood; yet, that we may show the gentleness of the Apostolic See in sparing them, are to be put last of all the presbyters of the Church: and that they may bear their own sentence, they shall be below him also whom they preferred to themselves by their own judgment: all the other presbyters remaining in the order which the time of his ordination assigns to each. And let none except the two aforesaid suffer any loss of dignity, but let this disgrace attach to those only who chose to put themselves below a junior who had only lately been ordained: that they may feel that that sentence of the gospels applies to themselves when it is said: "with what judgment ye judge, ye shall be judged: and with what measure ye mete, the same shall be measured unto you ." But let Paul the presbyter retain his place from which with praiseworthy firmness he did not budge: and let no further encroachments be made to any one's harm: so that you, beloved, who not undeservedly get the discredit of the whole matter, may with all speed take measures to cure it at least by putting these our injunctions into effect; lest, if a second time a just complaint be lodged with us, we be forced into stronger displeasure: for we would rather restore discipline by correcting what is done wrong, than increase the punishment. Know that we have entrusted the carrying out of our commands to our brother and fellow-bishop Julius, that all things may straightway be established, as we have ordained. Dated 8th March, in the consulship of the illustrious Postumianus (448).

LETTER XX. TO EUTYCHES, AN ABBOT OF CONSTANTINOPLE.

Leo, the bishop, to his dearly-beloved son, Eutyches, presbyter.

He thanks him for his information about the revival of Nestorianism and commends his zeal.

You have brought to our knowledge, beloved, by your letter that through the activity of some the heresy of Nestorius has been again reviving. We reply that your solicitude in this matter has pleased us, since the remarks we have received are an indication of your mind. Wherefore do not doubt that the Lord, the Founder of the catholic Faith, will befriend you in all things. And when we have been able to ascertain more fully by whose wickedness this happens, we must make provision with the help of God for the complete uprooting of this poisonous growth which has long ago been condemned. God keep thee safe, my beloved son. Dated 1st June, in the consulship of the illustrious Postumianus and Zeno (448).

LETTER XXI. FROM EUTYCHES TO LEO.

I. He States His Account of the Proceedings at the Synod.

God the Word is before all else my witness, being confident of my hope and faith in Christ the Lord and God of all, and discerning the proof of my holding the truth in these matters: but I call on your holiness, too, to bear witness to my heart and to the reasonableness of my opinions and words. But the wicked devil has exercised his evil influence upon my zeal and determination, whereby his power ought to have been destroyed. Whereupon he has exerted all his proper power and aroused Eusebius, bishop of the town of Dorylaeum, against me, who presented an allegation to the holy bishop of the church in Constantinople, Flavian, and to certain others whom he found in the same city assembled on various matters of their own: in this he called me heretic, not raising any true accusation but contriving destruction for me and disturbance for the churches of God.

Their holinesses summoned me to reply to his accusation: but though I was delayed by a serious illness besides my advanced age, I came to clear myself, knowing well that a faction had been formed against my safety. And, indeed, together with a writ of appeal to which my signature was appended, I offered them a statement showing my confession upon the holy Faith. But when the holy Flavian did not receive the document, nor order it to be read, yet heard me in reply utter word for word that Faith which was put forth at Nicaea by the holy Synod, and confirmed at Ephesus, I was required to acknowledge two natures, and to anathematize those who denied this. But I, fearing the decision of the synod, and not wishing either to take away or to add one word contrary to the Faith put forth by the holy Synod of Nicaea, knowing, too, that our holy and blessed fathers and bishops Julius, Felix, Athanasius, and Gregorius rejected the phrase "two natures," and not daring to discuss the nature of God the Word, who came into flesh in the last days entering the womb of the holy virgin Mary unchangeably as he willed and knew, becoming man in reality, not in fancy, nor yet venturing to anathematize our aforesaid Fathers, I asked them to let your holiness know these things, that you might judge what seemed right to you, undertaking by all means co follow your ruling.

II. His Explanations Were Allowed No Hearing.

But without listening to any thing which I said, they broke up the Synod and published the sentence of my degradation, which they were getting ready against me before the inquiry. So much slander were they factiously making up against me that even my safety would have been endangered had not the help of God at the intercession of your holiness quickly snatched me from the assault of military force. Then they began to force the heads of other monasteries to subscribe to my degradation (a thing which was never done either towards those who have professed themselves heretics, nor even against Nestorius himself), insomuch that when to reassure the people I tried to set forth statements of my faith, not only did they, who were plotting the aforesaid faction against me, prevent them being heard, but also seized them that straightway I might be held a heretic before all.

III. He Appeals to Leo for Protection.

I take refuge, therefore, with you the defender of religion and abhorrer of such factions, bringing in even still nothing strange against the faith as it was originally handed down to us, but anathematizing Apollinaris, Valentinus, Manes, and Nestorius, and those who say that the flesh of our Lord Jesus Christ, the Saviour, descended from heaven and not from the Holy Ghost and from the holy Virgin, along with all heresies down to Simon Magus. Yet nevertheless I stand in jeopardy of my life as a heretic. I beseech you not to be prejudiced against me by their insidious designs about me, but to pronounce the sentence which shall seem to you right upon the Faith, and in future not to allow any slander to be uttered against me by this faction, nor let one be expelled and banished from the number of the orthodox who has spent his seventy years of lite in continence and all chastity, so that at the very end of life he should suffer shipwreck. I have subjoined to this my letter both documents, that which was presented by my accuser at the Synod, and that which was brought by me but not received, as well as the statement of my faith and those things which have been decreed upon the two natures by our holy Fathers .

Eutyches' Confession of Faith.

I call upon you before God, who gives life to all things, and Christ Jesus, who witnessed that good confession under Pontius Pilate, that you do nothing by favour. For I have held the same as my forefathers and from my boyhood have been illuminated by the same Faith as that which was laid down by the holy Synod of 318 most blessed bishops who were gathered at Nicaea from the whole world, and which was confirmed and ratified afresh for sole acceptance by the holy Synod assembled at Ephesus: and I have never thought otherwise than as the right and only true orthodox Faith has enjoined. And I agree to everything that was laid down about the same Faith by the same holy Synod: of which Synod the leader and chief was Cyril of blessed memory bishop of the Alexandrians, the partner and sharer in the preaching and in the Faith of those saints and elect ot God, Gregory the greater, and the other Gregory , Basil, Athanasius, Atticus and Proclus. Him and all of them I have held orthodox and faithful, and have honoured as saints, and have esteemed my masters. But I utter an anathema on Nestorius, Apollinaris, and all heretics down to Simon, and those who say that the flesh of our Lord Jesus Christ came down from heaven. For He who is the Word of God came down from heaven without flesh and was made flesh in the holy Virgin's womb unchangeably and unalterably as He Himself knew and willed. And He who was always perfect God before the ages, was also made perfect man in the end of the days for us and for our salvation. This my full profession may your holiness consider.

I, Eutyches, presbyter and archimandrite, have subscribed to this statement with my own hand.

LETTER XXII . THE FIRST FROM FLAVIAN, BP. OF CONSTANTINOPLE TO POPE LEO.

To the most holy and God-loving father and fellow-bishop, Leo, Flavian greeting in the Lord.
I. The Designs of the Devil Have Led Eutyches Astray.

There is nothing which can stay the devil's wickedness, that "restless evil, full of deadly poison ." Above and below it "goes about," seeking "whom it may" strike, dismay, and "devour ." Whence to watch, to be sober unto prayer, to draw near to God, to eschew foolish questionings, to follow the fathers and not to go beyond the eternal bounds, this we have learnt from Holy Writ. And so I give up the excess of grief and abundant tears over the capture of one of the clergy who are under me, and whom I could not save nor snatch from the wolf, although I was ready to lay down my life for him. How was he caught, how did he leap away, hating the voice of the caller and turning aside also from the memory of the Fathers and thoroughly detesting their paths. And thus I proceed with my account.

II. The Seductions of Heretics Capture the Unwary.

There are some "in sheep's clothing, but inwardly they are ravening wolves :" whom we know by their fruit. These men seem indeed at first to be of us, but they are not of us: "for if they had been of us, they would no doubt have continued with us ." But when they have spewed out their impiety, throwing out the guile that is in them, and seizing the weaker ones, and those who have their senses unpractised in the divine utterances, they carry them along with themselves to destruction, wresting and doing despite to the Fathers' doctrines, just as they do the Holy Scriptures also to their own destruction: whom we must be forewarned of and take heed lest some should be misled by their wickedness and shaken in their firmness. "For they have sharpened their tongues like serpents: adder's poison is under their lips ," as the prophet has cried out about them.

III. Eutyches' Heresy Stated.

Such a one, therefore, has now shown himself amongst us, Eutyches, for many years a presbyter and archimandrite , pretending to hold the same belief as ours, and to have the right Faith in him: indeed he resists the blasphemy of Nestorius, and feigns a controversy with him, but the exposition of the Faith composed by the 318 holy fathers, and the letter that Cyril of holy memory wrote to Nestorius, and one by the same author on the same subject to the Easterns, these writings, to which all have given their assent, he has tried to upset, and revive the old evil dogmas of the blasphemous Valentinus and Apollinaris. He has not feared the warning of the True

King: "Whoso shall cause one of the least of these little ones to stumble, it was better that a millstone should be hanged about his neck, and that he should be sunk in the depth of the sea " But casting away all shame, and shaking off the cloak which covered his error , he openly in our holy synod persisted in saying that our Lord Jesus Christ ought not to be understood by us as having two natures after His incarnation in one substance and in one person: nor yet that the Lord's flesh was of the same substance with us, as if assumed from us and united to God the Word hypostatically: but he said that the Virgin who bare him was indeed of the same substance with us according to the flesh, but the Lord Himself did not assume from her flesh of the same substance with us: but the Lord's body was not a man's body, although that which issued from the Virgin was a human body. resisting all the expositions of the holy Fathers.

IV. He Has Sent Leo the Minutes of Their Proceedings that He May See All the Details.

But not to make my letter too long by detailing everything, we have sent your holiness the proceedings which some time since we took in the matter: therein we deprived him as convicted on these charges, of his priesthood, of the management of his monastery and of our communion: in order that your holiness also knowing the facts of his case may make his wickedness manifest to all the God-loving bishops who are under your reverence; lest perchance if they do not know the views which he holds, and of which he has been openly convicted, they may be found to be in correspondence with him as a fellow-believer by letter or by other means. I and those who are with me give much greeting to you and to all the brotherhood in Christ. The Lord keep you in safety and prayer for us, O most God-Loving Father

LETTER XXIII. TO FLAVIAN, BISHOP OF CONSTANTINOPLE.

To his well-beloved brother Flavian the bishop, Leo the bishop.

I. He Complains that Flavian Has Not Sent Him a Full Account of Eutyches' Case.

Seeing that our most Christian and merciful Emperor, in his holy and praiseworthy faith and anxiety for the peace of the Catholic Church, has sent us a letter upon the matters which have roused the din of disturbance among you, we wonder, brother, that you have been able to keep silence to us upon the scandal that has been caused, and that you did not rather take measures for our being at once informed by your own report, that we might not have any doubt about the truth of the case. For we have received a document from the presbyter Eutyches , who complains that on the accusation of bishop Eusebius he has been wrongfully deprived of communion, notwithstanding that he says he attended your summons and did not refuse his presence: and moreover asserts that he presented a deed of appeal in the very court, which was however not accepted: whereupon he was forced to put forth letters of defence in the city of Constantinople. Pending which matter we do not yet know with what justice he has been separated from the communion of the Church. But having regard to the importance of the matter, we wish to know the reason of your action and to have the whole thing brought to our knowledge: for we, who desire the judgments of the Lord's priests to be deliberate, cannot without information decide one way or another, until we have all the proceedings accurately before us.

II. And Now Demands It.

And therefore, brother, signify to us in a full account by the hand of the most fit and competent person, what innovation has arisen against the ancient faith, which needed to be corrected by so severe a sentence. For both the moderation of the Church and the devout faith of our most godly prince insist upon our showing much anxiety for the peace of Christendom: that dissensions may be cleared away and the Catholic Faith kept unimpaired, and that those whose faith has been proved may be fortified by our authority, when those who maintain what is wrong have been recalled from their error. And no difficulty can arise on this side, since the said presbyter has professed himself by his own statement, ready to be corrected if anything be found in him worthy of rebuke. For it beseems us in such matters to take every precaution that charity be kept and the Truth defended without the din of strife. And therefore because you see, beloved, that we are anxious about so great a matter, hasten to inform us of everything in as full and clear a manner as possible (for this ought to have been done before), lest in the cross-statements of both sides we be misled by some uncertainty, and the dissension, which ought to be stifled in its infancy, be fostered for our heart is impressed by God's inspiration with the need of saving from violation by anyone's misinterpretation those constitutions of the venerable fathers which have received Divine ratification and belong to the groundwork of the Faith. God keep thee safe, dear brother. Dated 18 February (449), in the consulship of the illustrious Asturius and Protogenes.

LETTER XXIV. TO THEODOSIUS AUGUSTUS II.

Leo the bishop, to Theodosius Augustus.

I. He Praises the Emperor's Piety and Mentions Eutyches' Appeal.

How much protection the Lord has vouchsafed His Church through your clemency and faith, is shown again by this letter which you have sent me: so that we rejoice at there being not only a kingly, but also a priestly mind within you. Seeing that, besides your imperial and public cares, you have a most devout anxiety for the Christian religion, lest schisms or heresies or other offences should grow up among God's people. For your realm is then in its best state when men serve the eternal and unchangeable Trinity by the confession of one Godhead . What the disturbance was which occurred in the Church of Constantinople, and which could have so moved my brother and fellow-bishop Flavian, that he deprived Eutyches, the presbyter, of communion, I have not yet been able to understand clearly. For although the aforesaid presbyter sent in writing a complaint concerning his trouble to the Apostolic See, yet he only briefly touched on some points, asserting that he kept the constitutions of the Nicene synod and had been vainly blamed for difference of faith.

II. He Finds Fault with Flavian's Silence.

But the statement of bishop Eusebius, his accuser, copies of which the said presbyter has sent us, contained nothing clear about his objections, and though he charged a presbyter with heresy, he did not say expressly what opinion he disapproved of in him: although the bishop himself also professed that he adhered to the decrees of the Nicene synod: for which reason we had no means of learning anything more fully. And because the method of our Faith and the laudable anxiety shown by your piety requires the merits of the case to be known, there must now be no place allowed for deception, but we must be informed of the points on which he considers him unsound, that the right judgment may be passed after full information. I have sent a letter to the aforesaid bishop, from which he may gather that I am displeased at his still keeping silence upon what has been done in so grave a matter, when he ought to have been forward in disclosing all to us at the outset: and we believe that even after the reminder he will acquaint us with the whole, in order that, when what now seems obscure, has been brought into the light, judgment may be passed agreeably to the teaching of the Gospels and the Apostles. Dated the 18th of February , in the consulship of the illustrious Asturius and Protogenes (449).

LETTER XXV. FROM PETER CHRYSOLOGUS, BISHOP OF RAVENNA, TO EUTYCHES, THE PRESBYTER.

[In answer to a letter from Eutyches, he urges him to accept the decisions of the Church on the Faith in fear and without too close inquiry, and to abide by the ruling of the bishop of Rome.]

LETTER XXVI . A SECOND ONE FROM FLAVIAN TO LEO.

To the most holy and blessed father and fellow-minister Leo, Flavian greeting in the Lord.
I. Eutyches' Heresy Restated.
Nothing, as you know, most beloved of God, is more precious to priests than piety and he right dividing of the word of truth. For all our hope and safety, and the recompense of promised good depend thereon. For this reason we must take all pains about the true Faith, and those things which have been set forth and decreed by the holy Fathers, that always, and in all circumstances, they may be kept and guarded whole and uninjured. And so it was necessary on the present occasion for us, who see the orthodox Faith suffering harm, and the heresy of Apollinaris and Valentinus being revived by the wicked monk Eutyches, not to overlook it, but publicly to disclose it for the people's safety. For this man: this Eutyches, keeping his diseased and sickly opinion hid within him, has dared to attack our gentleness, and unblushingly and shamelessly to instil his own blasphemy into many minds: saying that before the Incarnation indeed, our Saviour Jesus Christ had two natures, Godhead and manhood: but that after the union they became one nature not knowing what he says, or on what he is speaking so decidedly. For even the union of the two natures that came together in Christ did not, as your piety knows, confuse their properties in the process: but the properties of the two natures remain entire even in the union. And he added another blasphemy also, saying that the Lord's body which sprang from Mary was not of our substance, nor of human matter: but, though he calls it human, he refuses to say it was con-substantial with us or with her who bare him, according to the flesh .
II. The Means Eutyches Has Taken to Circumvent the Synod.
And this notwithstanding that the acts of Ephesus , in the letter written by the holy and ecumenical synod to the wicked and deposed Nestorius, contain these express words "the natures which came together to form true unity are indeed different: and yet from then both there is but one Christ and Son. Not as if the

difference between the two natures was done away with through the union, but rather that these same natures, His Godhead and His Manhood perfected for us one Lord Jesus Christ, through an ineffable and incomprehensible meeting which resulted in unity." And this does not escape your holiness, who have no doubt read the record of what was done at Ephesus. Yet this same Eutyches attaching no weight to these words, thinks he is not liable to the penalties fixed by that holy and ecumenical synod. For this reason, finding that many of the simpler-minded folk were injured in their faith by his contention, upon his being accused by the devout Bishop Eusebius, and upon his attending at the holy council, and with his own mouth declaring what he thought to the members of the synod, we have deposed him for his estrangement from the true Faith, as your holiness will learn from the resolutions passed about him: which we have sent with this our letter. Moreover, it is fair in my opinion that you should be told this also that this same Eutyches, after suffering just and canonical deposition, instead of making amends for his earlier by his later conduct , and appeasing God by careful penitence and many tears, and by a true repentance, comforting our heart which was greatly saddened at his fall: not only did not do so, but even made every effort to throw the most holy church of this place into confusion: setting up in public placards full of insults and maledictions, and beyond this addressing his entreaties to our most religious and Christ-loving Emperor, and these too over-flowing with arrogance and sauciness, whereby he tried to override the divine canons in everything.

III. He Acknowledges the Receipt of Leo's Letter.

But after all this had occurred, your holiness' letter was conveyed to us by the most honourable count Pansophius: and from it we learnt that the same Eutyches had sent you a letter full of falsehood and cunning, saying that at the time of trial he had presented letters of appeal to us, and to the holy synod of bishops who were then present, and had appealed to your holiness: this he certainly never did, but in this matter, too, he has been guilty of deceit, like the father of lies, thinking to gain your ear. Therefore, most holy father, being stirred by all that he has ventured, and by what has been done, and is being done against us and the most holy Church, use your accustomed promptitude as becomes the priesthood, and in defending the commonweal and peace of the holy churches, consent by your own letter to endorse the resolution that has been canonically passed against him, and to confirm the faith of our most religious and Christ-loving Emperor. For the matter only requires your weight and support, which through your wisdom will at once bring about general peace and quietness. For thus both the heresy which has arisen, and the disorder it has excited, will easily be appeased by God's assistance through a letter from you: and the rumoured synod will also be prevented, and so the most holy churches throughout the world need not be disturbed. I and all that are with me salute all the brethren that are with you. May you be granted to us safe in the Lord, and still praying for us, O most God-Loving and Holy Father.

LETTER XXVII. TO FLAVIAN, BISHOP OF CONSTANTINOPLE.

Leo to Flavian, bishop of Constantinople. An acknowledgment of Flavian's first letter and a promise of a fuller reply.

On the first opportunity we could find, which was the coming of our honourable son Rodanus, we acknowledge, beloved, the arrival of your packet, which was to give us information about the case which has been stirred up to our grief among you by misguided error. Since this man, who has long seemed to be religiously disposed, has expressed himself in the Faith otherwise than is right, though he never ought to have departed from the catholic tradition, but to have persevered in the same belief as is held by all. But on this matter we are replying more fully by him who brought your letter to us, beloved: that we may give you all necessary instructions, beloved, on the whole matter. For we do not allow either him to persist in his perverse conviction; or you, beloved, who with such faithful zeal are resisting his wrong and foolish error to be long disturbed by the adversary's opposition. Our aforesaid son, by whom we are sending this letter, we desire you to receive with the affection he deserves, and to reply when he returns to us. Dated 21st May in the consulship of Asturius and Protogenes (449).

LETTER XXVIII. TO FLAVIAN COMMONLY CALLED "THE TOME"

I. Eutyches Has Been Driven into His Error by Presumption and Ignorance.

Having read your letter, beloved, at the late arrival of which we are surprised, and having perused the detailed account of the bishops' acts, we have at last found out what the scandal was which had arisen among you against the purity of the Faith: and what before seemed concealed has now been unlocked and laid open to our view: from which it is shown that Eutyches, who used to seem worthy of all respect in virtue of his priestly office, is very unwary and exceedingly ignorant, so that it is even of him that the prophet has said: "he refused to understand so as to do well: he thought upon iniquity in his bed." But what more iniquitous than to hold blasphemous opinions, and not to give way to those who are wiser and more learned than ourself. Now into this unwisdom fall they who, finding themselves hindered from knowing the truth by some obscurity, have recourse not to the prophets' utterances, not to the Apostles' letters, nor to the injunctions of the Gospel but to their own selves: and thus they stand out as masters of error because they were never disciples of truth. For what learning has he acquired about the pages of the New and Old Testament, who has not even grasped the rudiments of the Creed? And that which, throughout the world, is professed by the mouth of every one who is to be born again, is not yet taken in by the heart of this old man.

II. Concerning the Twofold Nativity and Nature of Christ.

Not knowing, therefore, what he was bound to think concerning the incarnation of the Word of God, and not wishing to gain the light of knowledge by researches through the length and breadth of the Holy Scriptures, he might at least have listened attentively to that general and uniform confession, whereby the whole body of the faithful confess that they *believe in God the Father Almighty, and in Jesus Christ, His only*

Son , our Lord, who was born of the Holy Spirit and the Virgin Mary. By which three statements the devices of almost all heretics are overthrown. For not only is God believed to be both Almighty and the Father, but the Son is shown to be co-eternal with Him, differing in nothing from the Father because He is *God from. God* , Almighty from Almighty, and being born from the Eternal one is co-eternal with Him; not later in point of time, not lower in power, not unlike in glory, not divided in essence: but at the same time the only begotten of the eternal Father was born eternal of the Holy Spirit and the Virgin Mary. And this nativity which took place in time took nothing from, and added nothing to that divine and eternal birth, but expended itself wholly on the restoration of man who had been deceived : in order that he might both vanquish death and overthrow by his strength , the Devil who possessed the power of death. For we should not now be able to overcome the author of sin and death unless He took our nature on Him and made it His own, whom neither sin couldpollute nor death retain. Doubtless then, He was conceived of the Holy Spirit within the womb of His Virgin Mother, who brought Him forth without the loss of her virginity, even as she conceived Him without its loss.

But if He could not draw a rightful understanding (of the matter) from this pure source of the Christian belief, because He had darkened the brightness of the clear truth by a veil of blindness peculiar to Himself, He might have submitted Himself to the teaching of the Gospels. And when Matthew speaks of "the Book of the Generation of Jesus Christ, the Son of David, the Son of Abraham ," He might have also sought out the instruction afforded by the statements of the Apostles. And reading in the Epistle to the Romans, "Paul, a servant of Jesus Christ, called an Apostle, separated unto the Gospel of God, which He had promised before by His prophets in the Holy Scripture concerning His son, who was made unto Him of the seed of David after the flesh ," he might have bestowed a loyal carefulness upon the pages of the prophets. And finding the promise of God who says to Abraham, "In thy seed shall all nations be blest ," to avoid all doubt as to the reference of this seed, he might have followed the Apostle when He says, "To Abraham were the promises made and to his seed. He saith not and to seeds, as if in many, but as it in one, and to thy seed which is Christ ." Isaiah's prophecy also he might have grasped by a closer attention to what he says, "Behold, a virgin shall conceive and bear a Son and they shall call His name Immanuel," which is interpreted "God with us ." And the same prophet's words he might have read faithfully. "A child is born to us, a Son is given to us, whose power is upon His shoulder, and they shall call His name the Angel of the Great Counsel, Wonderful, Counsellor, the Mighty God, the Prince of Peace, the Father of the age to come ." And then he would not speak so erroneously as to say that the Word became flesh in such a way that Christ, born of the Virgin's womb, had the form of man, but had not the reality of His mother's body . Or is it possible that he thought our Lord Jesus Christ was not of our nature for this reason, that the angel, who was sent to the blessed Mary ever Virgin, says, "The Holy Ghost shall come upon thee and the power of the Most High shall overshadow thee: and therefore that Holy Thing also that shall be born of thee shall be called the Son of God ," on the supposition that as the conception of the Virgin was a Divine act, the flesh of the conceived did not partake of the conceiver's nature? But that birth so uniquely wondrous and so wondrously unique, is not to be understood in such wise that the properties of His kind were removed through the novelty of His creation.

For though the Holy Spirit imparted fertility to the Virgin, yet a real body was received from her body; and, "Wisdom building her a house ," "the Word became flesh and dwelt in us ," that is, in that flesh which he took from man and which he quickened with the breath of a higher life .

III. The Faith and Counsel of God In Regard to the Incarnation of the Word are Set Forth.

Without detriment therefore to the properties of either nature and substance which then came together in one person , majesty took on humility, strength weakness, eternity mortality: and for the paying off of the debt belonging to our condition inviolable nature was united with possible nature, so that, as suited the needs of our case , one and the same Mediator between God and men, the Man Christ Jesus, could both die with the one and not die with the other. Thus in the whole and perfect nature of true man was true God born, complete in what was His own, complete in what was ours. And by "ours" we mean what the Creator formed in us from the beginning and what He undertook to repair. For what the Deceiver brought in and man deceived committed, had no trace in the Saviour. Nor, because He partook of man's weaknesses, did He therefore share our faults. He took the form of a slave without stain of sin, increasing the human and not diminishing the divine: because that emptying of Himself whereby the Invisible made Himself visible and, Creator and Lord of all things though He be, wished to be a mortal, was the bending down of pity, not the failing of power. Accordingly He who while remaining in the form of God made man, was also made man in the form of a slave. For both natures retain their own proper character without loss: and as the form of God did not do away with the form of a slave, so the form of a slave did not impair the form of God. For inasmuch as the Devil used to boast that man had been cheated by his guile into losing the divine gifts, and bereft of the boon of immortality had undergone sentence of death, and that he had found some solace in his troubles from having a partner in delinquency , and that God also at the demand of the principle of justice had changed His own purpose towards man whom He had created in such honour: there was need for the issue of a secret counsel, that the unchangeable God whose will cannot be robbed of its own kindness, might carry out the first design of His Fatherly care towards us by a more hidden mystery ; and that man who had been driven into his fault by the treacherous cunning of the devil might not perish contrary to the purpose of God .

IV. The Properties of the Twofold Nativity and Nature of Christ are Weighed One Against Another.

There enters then these lower parts of the world the Son of God, descending from His heavenly home and yet not quitting His Father's glory, begotten in a new order by a new nativity. In a new order, because being invisible in His own nature, He became visible in ours, and He whom nothing could contain was content to be contained : abiding before all time He began to be in time: the Lord of all things, He obscured His immeasurable majesty and took on Him the form of a servant: being God that cannot suffer, He did not disdain to be man that can, and, immortal as He is, to subject Himself to the laws of death. The Lord assumed His mother's nature without her faultiness: nor in the Lord Jesus Christ, born of the Virgin's womb, does the wonderfulness of His birth make His nature unlike ours. For He who is true God is also true man: and in this union there is no lie , since the humility of manhood and the loftiness of the Godhead both meet there. For as God is not changed by the showing of pity, so man is not swallowed up by the dignity. For each form does what is proper to it with the co-operation of the other ; that is the Word performing what appertains to the Word, and the flesh carrying out what appertains to the flesh. One of them sparkles with miracles, the other succumbs to injuries. And as the Word does not cease to be on an equality with His Father's glory, so the flesh does not forego the nature of our race. For it must again and again be repeated that one and the same is truly Son of God and truly son of man. God in that "in the beginning was the Word, and the Word was with God, and the Word was God ;" man in that "the Word became flesh and dwelt in us ." God in that "all things were made by Him , and without Him was nothing made:" man in that "He was made of a woman, made under law ." The nativity of the flesh was the manifestation of human nature: the childbearing of a virgin is the proof of Divine power. The infancy of a babe is shown in the humbleness of its cradle : the greatness of the Most High is proclaimed by the angels' voices . He whom Herod treacherously endeavours to destroy is like ourselves in our earliest stage : but He whom the Magi delight to worship on their knees is the Lord of all. So too when He came to the baptism of John, His forerunner, lest He should not be known through the veil of flesh which covered His Divinity, the Father's voice thundering from the sky, said, "This is My beloved Son, in whom I am well pleased ." And thus Him whom the devil's craftiness attacks as man, the ministries of angels serve as God. To be hungry and thirsty, to be weary, and to sleep, is clearly human: but to satisfy 5,000 men with five loaves, and to bestow on the woman of Samaria living water, droughts of which can secure the drinker from thirsting any more, to walk upon the surface of the sea with feet that do not sink, and to quell the risings of the waves by rebuking the winds, is, without any doubt, Divine. Just as therefore, to pass over many other instances, it is not part of the same nature to be moved to tears of pity for a dead friend, and when the stone that closed the four-days' grave was removed, to raise that same friend to life with a voice of command: or, to hang on the cross, and turning day to night, to make all the elements tremble: or, to be pierced with nails, and yet open the gates of paradise to the robber's faith: so it is not part of the same nature to say, "I and the Father are one," and to say, "the Father is greater than I ." For although in the Lord Jesus Christ God and man is one person, yet the source of the degradation, which is shared by both, is one, and the source of the glory, which is shared by both, is another. For His manhood, which is less than the Father, comes from our side: His Godhead, which is equal to the Father, comes from the Father.

V. Christ's Flesh is Proved Real from Scripture.

Therefore in consequence of this unity of person which is to be understood in both natures , we read of the Son of Man also descending from heaven, when the Son of God took flesh from the Virgin who bore Him. And again the Son of God is said to have been crucified and buried, although it was not actually in His Divinity whereby the Only-begotten is co-eternal and con-substantial with the Father, but in His weak human nature that He suffered these things. And so it is that in the Creed also we all confess that the Only-begotten Son of God was crucified and buried, according to that saying of the Apostle: "for if they had known, they would never have crucified the Lord of glory ." But when our Lord and Saviour Himself would instruct His disciples' faith by His questionings, He said, "Whom do men say that I, the Son of Man, am?" And when they had put on record the various opinions of other people, He said, "But ye, whom do ye say that I am?" Me, that is, who am the Son of Man, and whom ye see in the form of a slave, and in true flesh, whom do ye say that I am? Whereupon blessed Peter, whose divinely inspired confession was destined to profit all nations, said, "Thou art Christ, the Son of the living God ." And not undeservedly was he pronounced blessed by the Lord, drawing from the chief corner-stone the solidity of power which his name also expresses, he, who, through the revelation of the Father, confessed Him to be at once Christ and Son of God: because the receiving of the one of these without the other was of no avail to salvation, and it was equally perilous to have believed the Lord Jesus Christ to be either only God without man, or only man without God. But after the Lord's resurrection (which, of course, was of His true body, because He was raised the same as He had died and been buried), what else was effected by the forty days' delay than the cleansing of our faith's purity from all darkness? For to that end He talked with His disciples, and dwelt and ate with them, He allowed Himself to be handled with diligent and curious touch by those who were affected by doubt, He entered when the doors were shut upon the Apostles, and by His breathing upon them gave them the Holy Spirit , and bestowing on them the light of understanding, opened the secrets of the Holy Scriptures . So again He showed the wound in His side, the marks of the nails, and all the signs of His quite recent suffering, saying, "See My hands and feet, that it is I. Handle Me and see that a spirit hath not flesh and bones, as ye see Me have ;" in order that the properties of His Divine and human nature might be acknowledged to remain still inseparable: and that we might know the Word not to be different from the flesh, in such a sense as also to confess that the one Son of God iS both the Word and flesh . Of this mystery of the faith your opponent Eutyches must be reckoned to have but little sense if he bus recognized our nature in the Only-begotten of God neither through the humiliation of His having to die, nor through the glory of His rising again. Nor has he any fear of the blessed apostle and evangelist John's declaration when he says, "every spirit which confesses Jesus Christ to have come in the flesh, is of God: and every spirit which destroys Jesus is not of God, and this is Antichrist ." But what is "to destroy Jesus," except to take away the human nature from Him, and to render void the mystery, by which alone we were saved, by the most barefaced fictions. The truth is that being in darkness about the nature of Christ's body, he must also be befooled by the same blindness in the matter of His sufferings. For if he does not think the cross of the Lord fictitious, and does not doubt that the punishment He underwent to save the world is likewise true, let him acknowledge the flesh of Him whose death he already believes: and let him not disbelieve Him man with a body like ours, since he acknowledges Him to have been able to suffer: seeing that the denial of His true flesh is also the denial of His bodily suffering. If therefore he receives the Christian faith, and does not turn away his ears from the preaching of the Gospel: let him see what was the nature that hung pierced with nails on the wooden cross, and, when the side of the Crucified was opened by the soldier's spear, let him understand whence it was that blood and water flowed, that the Church of God might be watered from the font and from the cup . Let him hear also the blessed Apostle Peter, proclaiming that the sanctification of the Spirit takes place through the sprinkling of Christ's blood . And let him not read cursorily the same Apostle's words when he says, "Knowing that not with corruptible things, such as silver and gold, have ye been redeemed from your vain manner of life which is part of your fathers' tradition, but with the precious blood of Jesus Christ as of a lamb without spot and blemish ." Let him not resist too the witness of the blessed Apostle John, who says: "and the blood of Jesus the Son of God cleanseth us from all sin ." And again: "this is the victory which overcometh the world, our faith." And "who is He that overcometh the world save He that believeth that Jesus is the Son of God. This is He that came by water and blood, Jesus Christ: not by water only, but by water and blood. And it is the Spirit that testifieth, because the Spirit is the truth , because there are three that bear witness, the Spirit, the water and the blood, and the three are one ." The Spirit, that is, of sanctification, and the blood of redemption, and the water of baptism: because the three are one, and remain undivided, and none of them is separated from this connection; because the catholic Church lives and progresses by this faith, so that in Christ Jesus neither the manhood without the true Godhead nor the Godhead without the true manhood is believed in.

VI. The Wrong and Mischievous Concession of Eutyches. The Terms on Which He May Be Restored to Communion. The Sending of Deputies to the East.

But when during your cross-examination Eutyches replied and said, "I confess that our Lord had two natures before the union but after the union I confess but one ," I am surprised that so absurd and mistaken a statement of his should not have been criticised and rebuked by his judges, and that an utterance which reaches the height of stupidity and blasphemy should be allowed to pass as if nothing offensive had been heard: for the impiety of saying that the Son of God was of two natures before His incarnation is only equalled by the iniquity of asserting that there was but one nature in Him after "the Word became flesh." And to the end that Eutyches may not think this a right or defensible opinion because it was not contradicted by any expression of yourselves, we warn you beloved brother, to take anxious care that if ever through the inspiration of God's mercy the case is brought to a satisfactory conclusion, his ignorant mind be purged from this pernicious idea as well as others. He was, indeed, just beginning to beat a retreat from his erroneous conviction, as the order of proceedings shows , in so far as when hemmed in by your remonstrances he agreed to say what he had not said before and to acquiesce in that belief to which before he had been opposed. However, when he refused to give his consent to the anathematizing of his blasphemous dogma, you understood, brother , that he abode by his treachery and deserved to receive a verdict of condemnation. And yet, if he grieves over it faithfully and to good purpose, and, late though it be, acknowledges how rightly the bishops' authority has been set in motion; or if with his own mouth and hand in your presence he recants his wrong opinions,no mercy that is shown to him when penitent can be found fault with : because our Lord,that true and "good shepherd" who laid downHis life for His sheep and who came to save not lose men's souls , wishes us to imitate His kindness ; in order that while justice constrains us when we sin, mercy may prevent our rejection when we have returned. For then at last is the true Faith most profitably defended when a false belief is condemned even by the supporters of it.

Now for the loyal and faithful execution of the whole matter, we have appointed to represent us our brothers Julius Bishop and Renatus priest [of the Title of S. Clement], as well as my son Hilary , deacon. And with them we have associated

Dulcitius our notary, whose faith is well approved: being sure that the Divine help will be given us, so that he who had erred may be saved when the wrongness of his view has been condemned. God keep you safe, beloved brother.

The 13 June, 449, in the consulship of the most illustrious Asturius and Protogenes.

LETTER XXIX. TO THEODOSIUS AUGUSTUS.

To Caesar Theodosius, the most religious and devout Augustus Leo pope of the Catholic Church of the city of Rome. He notifies the appointment of his representatives at the Council of Ephesus.

How much God's providence vouchsafes to consult for the interests of men is shown by your merciful care which, incited by God's Spirit, is unwilling that thereshould be any disturbance or difference: since the Faith, which is absolutely one, cannot be different from itself in any thing. Hence although Eutyches, as the minutes of the bishops' proceeds reveals, has been detected in an ignorant and unwise error, and ought to have withdrawn from his conviction which is rightly condemned, yet since your piety which loves the Catholic Truth with great jealousy for God's honour, has determined on a synodal judgment at Ephesus, that that Truth on which he is blind may be brought home to the ignorant old man; I have sent my brothers Julius the Bishop, Renatus the presbyter, and my son Hilary the deacon to act as my representatives as the matter requires, and they shall bring with them such a spirit of justice and kindness that while the whole misguided error is condemned (for there can be no doubt as to what is the integrity of the Christian Faith), yet if he who has gone astray repents and entreats for pardon, he may receive the succour of priestly indulgence: seeing that in his appeal which he sent us, he reserved to himself the right of earning our forgiveness by promising to correct whatever our opinion disapproved of in his opinion. But what the catholic Church universally believes and teaches on the mystery of the Lord's Incarnation is contained more fully in the letter which I have sent to my brother and fellow-bishop Flavian. Dated 13th June in the consulship of the illustrious Asturius and Protogenes (449).

LETTER XXX. TO PULCHERIA AUGUSTA.

Much shorter than, but to nearly the same effect as, xxxi., which was written on the same day as this. As xxx. has a Greek translation accompanying it and is duly dated, whereas xxxi. has neither, the Ballerinii would seem to be correct in thinking that xxx. was despatched but did not reach Pulcheria (cf. Lett. xlv. i.) and that xxxi. was for some reason never used. Of the two we have printed xxxi. by preference, as being the fuller discussion of the subject.

LETTER XXXI. TO PULCHERIA AUGUSTA.

Leo to Pulcheria Augusta.

I. He Reminds Pulcheria of Her Former Services to the Church, and Suggests Her Interference in the Eutychian Controversy.

How much protection the Lord has extended to His Church through your clemency, we have often tested by many signs. And whatever stand the strenuousness of the priesthood has made in our times against the assailers of the catholic Truth, has redounded chiefly to your glory: seeing that, as you have learnt from the teaching of the Holy Spirit, you submit your authority in all things to Him, by whose favour and under whose protection you reign. Wherefore, because I have ascertained from my brother and fellow-bishop Flavian's report, that a certain dispute has been raised through the agency of Eutyches in the church of Constantinople against the integrity of the Christian faith (and the text of the synod's minutes has shown me the exact nature of the whole matter), it is worthy of your great name that the error which in my opinion proceeds rather from ignorance than ingenuity, should be dispelled before, with the pertinacity of wrong-headedness, it gains any strength from the support of the unwise. Because even ignorance sometimes falls into serious mistakes, and very frequently the simple-minded rush through unwariness into the devil's pit: and it is thus, I believe, that the spirit of falsehood has crept over Eutyches: so that, whilst he imagines himself to appreciate the majesty of the Son of God more devoutly, by denying in Him the real presence of our nature, he came to the conclusion that the whole of that Word which "became flesh" was of one and the same essence. And greatly as Nestorius fell away from the Truth, in asserting that Christ was only born man of His mother, this man also departs no less far from the catholic path, who does not believe that our substance was brought forth from the same Virgin: wishing it of course to be understood as belonging to His Godhead only; so that that which took the form of a slave, and was like us and of the same form, was a kind of image, not the reality of our nature.

II. Man's Salvation Required the Union of the Two Natures in Christ.

But it is of no avail to say that our Lord, the Son of the blessed Virgin Mary, was true and perfect man, if He is not believed to be Man of that stock which is attributed to Him in the Gospel. For Matthew says, "The book of the generation of Jesus Christ, the son of David, the son of Abraham :" and follows the order of His human origin, so as to bring the lines of His ancestry down to Joseph to whom the Lord's mother was espoused. Whereas Luke going backwards step by step traces His succession to the first of the human race himself, to show that the first Adam and the last Adam were of the same nature. No doubt the Almighty Son of God could have appeared for the purpose of teaching, and justifying men in exactly the same way that He appeared both to patriarchs and prophets in the semblance of flesh ; for instance, when He engaged in a struggle, and entered into conversation (with Jacob), or when He refused not hospitable entertainment, and even partook of the food set before Him. But these appearances were indications of that Man whose reality it was announced by mystic predictions would be assumed from the stock of preceding patriarchs. And the fulfilment of the mystery of our atonement, which was ordained from all eternity, was not assisted by any figures because the Holy Spirit had not yet come upon the Virgin, and the power of the Most High had not over-shadowed her: so that "Wisdom building herself a house " within her undefiled body, "the Word became flesh;" and the form of God and the form of a slave coming together into one person, the Creator of times was born in time; and He Himself through whom all things were made, was brought forth in the midst of all things. For if the New Man had not been made in the likeness of sinful flesh, and taken on Him our old nature, and being consubstantial with the Father, had deigned to be consubstantial with His mother also, and being alone free from sin, had united our nature to Him the whole human race would be held in bondage beneath the Devil's yoke , and we should not be able to make use of the Conqueror's victory, if it had been won outside our nature.

III. From the Union of the Two Natures Flows the Grace of Baptism. He Makes a Direct Appeal to Pulcheria for Her Help.

But from Christ's marvellous sharing of the two natures, the mystery of regeneration shone upon us that through the self-same spirit, through whom Christ was conceived and born, we too, who were born through the desire of the flesh, might be born again from a spiritual source: and consequently, the Evangelist speaks of believers as those "who were born not of bloods, nor of the will of the flesh, nor of the will of man, but of God ." And of this unutterable grace no one is a partaker, nor can be reckoned among the adopted sons of God, who excludes from his faiththat which is the chief means of our salvation. Wherefore, I am much vexed and saddened that this man, who seemed before so laudably disposed towards humility, dares to make these empty and stupid attacks on the one Faith of ourselves and of our fathers. When he saw that his ignorant notion offended the ears of catholics, he ought to have withdrawn from his opinion, and not to have so disturbed the Church's rulers, as to deserve a sentence of condemnation: which, of course, no one will be able to remit, if he is determined to abide by his notion. For the moderation of the Apostolic See uses its leniency in such a way as to deal severely with the contumacious, while desiring to offer pardon to those who accept correction. Seeing then that I possess great confidence in your lofty faith and piety, I entreat your illustrious clemency, that, as the preaching of the catholic Faith has always been aided by your holy zeal, so now, also, you will maintain its free action. Perchance the Lord allowed it to be thus assailed for this reason that we might discover what sort of persons lurked within the Church. And clearly, we must not neglect to look after such, lest we be afflicted with their actual loss.

IV. His Personal Presence at the Council Must Be Excused.the Question at Issue is a Verygrave One.

But the most august and Christian Emperor, being anxious that the disturbances may be set at rest with all speed, has appointed too short and early a date for the council of bishops, which he wishes held at Ephesus, in fixing the first of August for the meeting: for from the fifth of May, on which we received His Majesty's letter, most of the time remaining has to be spent in making complete arrangements for the journey of such priests as are competent to represent me. For as to the necessity of my attending the council also, which his piety suggested, even if there were any precedent for the request, it could by no means be managed now: for the very uncertain state of things at present would not permit my absence from the people of this great city: and the minds of the riotously-disposed might be driven to desperate deeds, if they were to think that I took occasion of ecclesiastical business to desert my country and the Apostolic See. As then you recognize that it concerns the public weal that with your merciful indulgence I should not deny myself to the affectionate prayers of my people, consider that in these my brethren, whom I have sent in my stead, I also am present with the rest who appear: to them I have clearly and fully explained what is to be maintained in view of the satisfactory exposition of the case which has been given, me by the detailed report, and by the defendant's own statement to me. For the question is not about some small portion of our Faith on which no very distinct declaration has been made: but the foolish opposition that is raised ventures to impugn that which our Lord desired no one of either sex in the Church to be ignorant of. For the short but complete confession of the catholic creed which contains the twelve sentences of the twelve apostles is so well furnished with the heavenly panoply, that all the opinions of heretics can receive their death-blow from that one weapon. And if Eutyches had been content to receive that creed in its entirety with a pure and simple heart, he would at no point go astray from the decrees of the most sacred council of Nicaea, and he would understand that the holy Fathers laid this down, to the end that no mental or rhetorical ingenuity should lift itself up against the Apostolic Faith which is absolutely one. Deign then, with your accustomed piety to do your best endeavour, that this blasphemous and foolish attack upon the one and only sacrament of man's salvation may be driven from all men's minds. And if the man himself, who has fallen into this temptation, recover his senses, so as to condemn his own error by a written recantation, let him not be denied communion with his order . Your clemency is to know that I have written in the same strain to the holy bishop Flavian also: that loving-kindness be not lost sight of, if the error be dispelled. Dated 13 June in the consulship of the illustrious Asturius and Protogenes (449).

LETTER XXXII. TO THE ARCHIMANDRITES OF CONSTANTINOPLE .

To his well-beloved sons Faustus, Martinus, and the rest of the archimandrites, Leo the bishop. He acknowledges their zeal and refers them to the Tome.As on behalf of the faith which Eutyches has tried to disturb, I was sending legates de latere to assist the defence of the Truth, I thought it fitting that I should address a letter to you also, beloved: whom I know for certain to be so zealous in the cause of religion that you can by no means listen calmly to such blasphemous and profane utterances: for the Apostle's command lingers in your hearts, in which it is said, "If any man hath preached unto you any gospel other than that which he received, let him be anathema ." And we also decide that the opinion of the said Eutyches is to be rejected, which, as we have learnt from perusing the proceedings, has been deservedly condemned: so that, if its foolish maintainer will abide by his perverseness, he may have fellowship with those whose error he has followed. For one who says that Christ had not a human, that is our, nature, is deservedly put out of Christ's Church. But, if he be corrected through the pity of God's Spirit and acknowledge his wicked error, so as to condemn unreservedly what catholics reject, we wish him not to be denied mercy, that the Lord's Church may suffer no loss: for the repentant can always be readmitted, it is only error that must be shut out. Upon the mystery of great godliness , whereby through the Incarnation of the Word of God comes our justification and redemption, what is our opinion, drawn from the tradition of the fathers, is now sufficiently explained according to my judgment in the letter which I have sent to our brother Flavian the bishop : so that through the declaration of your chief you may know what, according to the gospel of our Lord Jesus Christ, we desire to be fixed in the hearts of all the faithful. Dated 13th June, in the consulship of the illustrious Asturius and Protogenes (449).

LETTER XXXIII. TO THE SYNOD OF EPHESUS.

Leo, bishop, to the holy Synod which is assembled at Ephesus.

I. He commends the Emperor's appeal to the chair of Peter. The devout faith of our most clement prince, knowing that it especially concerns his glory to prevent any seed of error from springing up within the catholic Church, has paid such deference to the Divine institutions as to apply to the authority of the Apostolic See for a proper settlement: as if he wished it to be declared by the most blessed Peter himself what was praised in his confession, when the Lord said, "whom do men say that I, the Son of man, am 5?" and the disciples mentioned various people's opinion: but, when He asked what they themselves believed, the chief of the apostles, embracing the fulness of the Faith in one short sentence, said, "Thou art the Christ, the son of the living God :" that is, Thou who truly art Son of man art also truly Son of the living God: Thou, I say, true in Godhead, true in flesh and one altogether , the properties of the two natures being kept intact. And if Eutyches had believed this intelligently and thoroughly, he would never have retreated from the path of this Faith. For Peter received this answer from the Lord for his confession. "Blessed art thou, Simon Barjona; for flesh and blood hath not revealed it unto thee, but My Father which is in heaven. And I say unto thee, that thou art Peter, and upon this rock I will build My Church: and the gates of Hades shall not prevail against it ." But he who both rejects the blessed Peter's confession, and gainsays Christ's Gospel, is far removed from union with this building; for he shows himself. never to have had any zeal for understanding the Truth, and to have only the empty appearance of high esteem, who did not adorn the hoary hairs of old age with any ripe judgment of the heart.

II. The Heresy of Eutyches is to Be Condemned Though His Full Repentance May Lead to His Restitution.

But because the healing even of such men must not be neglected, and the most Christian Emperor has piously and devoutly desired a council of bishops to be held, that all error may be destroyed by a fuller judgment, I have sent our brothers Julius the bishop, Renatus the presbyter, and my son Hilary the deacon, and with them Dulcitius the notary, whose faith we have proved, to be present in my stead at your holy assembly, brethren, and settle in common with you what is in accordance with the Lord's will. To wit, that the pestilential error may be first condemned, and then the restitution of him, who has so unwisely erred, discussed, but only if embracing the true doctrine he fully and openly with his own voice and signature condemns those heretical opinions in which his ignorance has been ensnared: for this he has promised in the appeal which he sent to us, pledging himself to follow our judgment in all things . On receiving our brother and fellow-bishop Flavian's letter, we have replied to him at some length on the points which he seems to have referred to us : that when this error which seems to have arisen, has been destroyed, there may be one Faith and one and the same confession throughout the whole world to the praise and glory of God, and that "in the name of Jesus every knee should bow, of things in heaven, and things on earth, and things under the earth, and that every tongue should confess that the Lord Jesus Christ is in the glory of God the Father ." Dated 13th June in the consulship of the illustrious Asturius and Protogenes (449).

LETTER XXXIV. TO JULIAN, BISHOP OF COS.

Leo, the bishop, to Julian, the bishop, his well-beloved brother.
I. Eutyches is Now Clearly, Seen to Have Deviated from the Faith.

Your letter, beloved, which has just reached me, shows with what spiritual love of the Catholic Faith you are inspired: and it makes me very glad that devout hearts all agree in the same opinion, so that according to the teaching of the Holy Ghost there may be fulfilled in us what the Apostle says: "Now I beseech you, brethren, through the name of our Lord Jesus Christ, that ye all speak the same things, and there be no divisions among you: but that ye be perfect in the same mind and in the same judgment ." But Eutyches has put himself quite outside this unity, if he perseveres in his perversity, and still does not understand the bonds with which the devil has bound him, and thinks any one is to be reckoned among the Lord's priests, who is a party to his ignorance and madness. For some time we were uncertain in what he was displeasing to catholics: and when we received no letter from our brother Flavian, and Eutyches himself complained in his letter that the Nestorian heresy was being revived, we could not fully learn the source or the motive of so crafty an accusation. But as soon as the minutes of the bishops' proceedings reached us, all those things which were hidden beneath the veil of his deceitful complaints were revealed in their abomination.

II. He Announces the Appointment of Legates a Latere.

And because our most clement Emperor in the loving-kindness and godliness of his mind wished a more careful judgment to be passed about the position of one who hitherto has seemed to be in high esteem, and for this purpose has thought fit to convene a council of bishops, by the hands of our brothers Julius the bishop, and Renatus the presbyter, and also my son Hilary, the deacon whom I have sent *ex latere* in my stead, I have addressed a letter suited to the needs of the case to our brother Flavian. from which you also, beloved, and the whole Church may know about the ancient and unique Faith, which this unlearned opponent has assailed, what we hold as handed down from God and what we preach without alteration. Yet, because we must not forget the duty of mercy, we have considered it consonant with our moderation as priests, that, if the condemned presbyter corrects himself unreservedly, the sentence by which he is bound should be remitted: if, however, he chooses to lie in the mire of his foolishness, let the decree remain, and let him have his lot with those whose error he has followed. Dated 13th June in the consulship of the illustrious Asturius and Protogenes (449) .

LETTER XXXV.TO JULIAN, BISHOP OF COS .

Leo, bishop of the city of Rome to his well-beloved brother, Julian the bishop.
I. Eutyches' Heresy Involves Many Other Heresies.

Although by the hands of our brothers, whom we have despatched from the city on behalf of the Faith, we hare sent a most full refutation of Eutyches' excessive heresy to our brother Flavian, yet because we have received, through our son Basil, your letter, beloved, which has given us much pleasure from the fervour of its catholic spirit, we have added this page also which agrees with the other document, that you may offer a united and strenuous resistance to those who seek to corrupt the gospel of Christ, since the wisdom and the teaching of the Holy Spirit is one and the same in you as in us: and whosoever does not receive it, is not a member of Christ's body and cannot glory in that Head in which he denies the presence of his own nature. What advantage is it to that most unwise old man under the name of the Nestorian heresy to mangle the belief of those, whose most devout faith he cannot tear to pieces: when in declaring the only-begotten Son of God to have been so born of the blessed Virgin's womb that He wore the appearance of a human body without the reality of human flesh being united to the Word, he departs as far from the right path as did Nestorius in separating the Godhead of the Word from the substance of His assumed Manhood ? From which prodigious falsehood who does not see what monstrous opinions spring? for he who denies the true Manhood of Jesus Christ, must needs be filled with many blasphemies, being claimed by Apollinaris as his own, seized upon by Valentinus, or held fast by Manichaeus: none of whom believed that there was true human flesh in Christ. But, surely, if that is not accepted, not only is it denied that He. who was in the form of God, but yet abode in the form of a slave, was born Man according to the flesh and reasonable soul: but also that He was crucified, dead, and buried, and that on the third day He rose again, and that, sitting at the right hand of the Father, he will come to judge the quick and the dead in that body in which He Himself was judged,: because these pledges of our redemption are rendered void if Christ is not believed to have the true and whole nature of true Manhood.

II. The Two Natures are to Be Found in Christ.

Or because the signs of His Godhead were undoubted, shall the proof of his having a human body be assumed false, and thus theindications of both natures be accepted to prove Him Creator, but not be accepted for the salvation of the creature ? No, for the flesh did not lessen what belongs to His Godhead, nor the Godhead destroy what belongs to His flesh. For He is at once both eternal from His Father and temporal from His mother, inviolable in His strength, possible in our weakness: in the Triune Godhead, of one and the same substance with the Father and the Holy Spirit, but in taking Manhood on Himself, not of one substance but of one and the same person [so that He was at once rich in poverty, almighty in submission, impossible in punishment, immortal in death]. For the Word was not in any part of It turned either into flesh or into soul, seeing that the absolute and unchangeable nature of the Godhead is ever entire in its Essence, receiving no loss nor increase, and so beatifying the nature that It had assumed that that nature remained for ever glorified in the person of the Glorifier. [But why should it seem unsuitable or impossible that the Word and flesh and soul should be one Jesus Christ, and that the Son of God and the Son of Man should be one, if flesh and soul which are of different natures make one person even without the Incarnation of the Word: since it is much easier for the power of the Godhead to produce this union of Himself and man than for the weakness of manhood by itself to effect it in its own substance.] Therefore neither was the Word changed into flesh nor flesh into the Word: but both remains in one and one is in both, not divided by the diversity and not confounded by intermixture: He is not one by His Father and another by His mother, but the same, in one way by His Father before every beginning, and in another by His mother at the end of the ages: so that He was "mediator between God and men, the man Christ Jesus ," in whom dwelt "the fulness of the Godhead bodily :" because it was the assumed (nature) not the Assuming (nature) which was raised, because God "exalted Him and gave Him the Name which is above every name: that in the name of Jesus every knee should bow, of things in heaven and things on earth and things under the earth, and that every tongue should confess that Jesus Christ the Lord is in the glory of God the Father ."

III. The Soul of Christ and the Body of Christ Were Real in the Full Human Sense, Though the Circumstances of His Birth Were Unique.

[But as to that which Eutyches dared to say in the court of bishops "that before the Incarnation there were two natures in Christ, but after the Incarnation one ,"he ought to have been pressed by the frequent and anxious questions of the judges to render an account of his acknowledgment, lest it should be passed over as something trivial, though it was seen to have issued from the same fount as his other poisonous opinions. For I think that in saying this he was convinced that the soul, which the Saviour assumed, had had its abode in the heavens before He was born of the Virgin Mary, and that the Word joined it to Himself in the womb. But this is intolerable to catholic minds and ears: because the Lord who came down from heaven brought with Him nothing that belonged to our state: for He did not receive either a soul which had existed before nor a flesh which was not of his mother's body. Undoubtedly our nature was not assumed in such a way that it was created first and then assumed, but it was created by the very assumption. And hence that which was deservedly condemned in Origen must be punished in Eutyches also, unless he prefers to give up his opinion, viz. the assertion that souls have had not only a life but also different actions before they were inserted in men's bodies]. For although the Lord's nativity according to the flesh has certain characteristics wherein it transcends the ordinary beginnings of man's being, both because He alone was conceived and born without concupiscence of a pure Virgin, and because He was so brought forth of His mother's womb that her fecundity bare Him without loss of virginity: yet His flesh was not of another nature to ours: nor was the soul breathed into Him from another source to that of all other men, and it excelled others not in difference of kind but in superiority of power. For He had no opposition in His flesh [nor did the strife of desires give rise to a conflict of wishes]. His bodily senses were active without the law of sin, and the reality of His emotions being under the control of His Godhead and His mind, was neither assaulted by temptations nor yielded to injurious influences. But true Man was united to God and was not brought down from heaven as regards a pro-existing soul, nor created out of nothing as regards the flesh: it wore the same person in the Godhead of the Word and possessed a nature in common with us in its body and soul. For He would not be "the mediator between God and man," unless God and man had co-existed in both natures forming one true Person. The magnitude of the subject urges us to a lengthy discussion: but with one of your learning there is no need for such copious dissertations, especially as we have already sent a sufficient letter to our brother Flavian by our delegates for the confirmation of the minds, not only of priests but also of the laity. The mercy of God will, we believe, provide that without the loss of one soul the sound may be defended against the devil's wiles, and the wounded healed. Dated 13th June in the consulship of the illustrious Asturius and Protogenes (449).

LETTER XXXVI. TO FLAVLAN, BISHOP OF CONSTANTINOPLE.

(He acknowledges the receipt of Flavian's second letter (xxvi) and protests against the necessity for a general council, though at the same time he acquiesces in it. Dated 21 June, a week after the Tome).

LETTER XXXVII. TO THEODOSLUS AUGUSTUS.

Leo to Theodosius Augustus. Unity of Faith is essential but the point at issue hardly required a general council, it is so clear.

On receiving your clemency's letter, I perceived that the universal Church has much cause for joy, that you will have the Christian Faith, whereby the Divine Trinity is honoured and worshipped, to be different or out of harmony with itself in nothing. For what more effectual support can be given to human affairs in calling upon God's mercy than when one thanksgiving, and the sacrifice of one confession is offered to His majesty by all. Wherein the devotions of the priests and all the faithful will reach at last their completeness, if in what was done for our redemption by God the Word, the only Son of God nothing else be believed than what He Himself ordered to be preached and believed. Wherefore although every consideration prevents my attendance on the day which your piety has fixed for the councils of bishops : for there are no precedents for such a thing, and the needs of the times do not allow me to leave the city, especially as the point of Faith at issue is so clear, that it would have been more reasonable to abstain from proclaiming a synod: yet as far as the Lord vouchsafes to help me, I have bestowed my zeal upon obeying your clemency's commands, by appointing my brethren who are competent to act as the case requires in removing offences, and who can represent me: because no question has arisen on which there can or ought to be any doubt. Dated 21st of June, in the consulship of the illustrious Asturius and Protogenes, (449).

LETTER XXXVIII. TO FLAVIAN, BISHOP OF CONSTANTINOPLE.

Leo to Flavian, bishop of Constantinople. He acknowledges the receipt of a letter and advises mercy if Eutyches will recant.

When our brethren had already started whom we despatched to you in the cause of the Faith, we received your letter, beloved, by our son Basil the deacon, in which you rightly said very little on the subject of our common anxiety, both because the accounts which had already arrived had given us full information on every thing, and because for purposes of private inquiry it was easy to converse with the aforesaid Basil, by whom now through the grace of God, in whom we trust, we exhort you, beloved, in reply, using the Apostle's words, and saying: "Be ye in nothing affrighted by the adversaries; which is for them a cause of perdition, but to you of salvation ." For what is so calamitous as to wish to destroy all hope of man's salvation by denying the reality of Christ's Incarnation, and to contradict the Apostle who says distinctly: "great is the mystery of Godliness which was manifest in the flesh ?" What so glorious as to fight for the Faith of the gospel against the enemies of Christ's nativity and cross? About whose most pure light and unconquered power we have already disclosed what was in our heart, in the letter which has been sent to you beloved : lest anything might seem doubtful between us on those things which we have learnt, and teach in accordance with the catholic doctrine. But seeing that the testimonies to the Truth are so clear and strong that a man must be reckoned thoroughly blind and stubborn, who does not at once shake himself free from the mists of falsehood in the bright light of reason; we desire you to use the remedy of long-suffering in curing the madness of ignorance that through your fatherly admonitions they who though old in years are infants in mind, may learn to obey their elders. And if they give up the vain conceits of their ignorance and come to their senses, and if they condemn, all their errors and receive the one true Faith, do not deny them the mercifulness of a bishop's kind heart: although your judgment must remain, if their impiety which you have deservedly condemned persists in its depravity. Dated 23 July in the consulship of the illustrious Asturius and Protogenes (449).

LETTER XXXIX. TO FLAVIAN, BISHOP OF CONSTANTINOPLE.

Leo, the bishop, to Flavian, the bishop. He rebukes Flavian for not answering his repeated letters.

Our anxiety is increased by your silence, for it is long now since we received a letter from you, beloved: while we who bear a chief share in your cares , through our anxiety for the defence of the Faith, have several times , as occasion served, sent letters to you: that we might aid you with the comfort of our exhortations not to yield to the assaults of your adversaries in defence of the Faith, but to feel that we were the sharers in your labour. Some time since we believe our messengers have reached you, brother, through whom you find yourself fully instructed by our writings and injunctions, and we have ourselves sent back Basil to you as you desired . Now, lest you should think we had omitted any opportunity of communicating with you, we have sent this note by our son Eupsychius, a man whom we hold in great honour and affection, asking you to reply to our letter with all speed, and inform us at once about your own actions and those of our representatives, and about the completion of the whole matter: so that we may allay the anxiety which we now feel in defence of the Faith, by happier tidings. Dated 11th August in the consulship of the illustrious Asturius and Protogenes (449).

LETTER XL. TO THE BISHOPS OF THE PROVINCE OF ARLES IN GAUL.

To his well-beloved brethren Constantinus Audentius, Rusticus, Auspicius, Nicetas, Nectarius, Florus, Asclepius, Justus, Augustalis, Ynantius, and Chrysaphius , Leo the pope. He approves of their having unanimously elected Ravennius, Bishop of Arles.

We have just and reasonable reason for rejoicing, when we learn that the Lord's priests have done what is agreeable both to the rules of the Father's canons and to the Apostles' institutions. For the whole body of the Church must needs increase with a healthy growth, if the governing members excel in the strength of their authority, and in peaceful management. Accordingly, we ratify with our sanction your good deed, brethren, in unanimously, on the death of Hilary of holy memory, consecrating our brother Ravennius, a man well approved by us, in the city of Arles, in accordance with the wishes of the clergy, the leading citizens, and the laity. Because a peace-making and harmonious election, where neither personal merits nor the good will of the congregation are wanting, is we believe the expression not only of man's choice, but of God's inspiration. So dearly beloved brethren, let the said priest use God's gift, and understand what self-devotion is expected of him, that by diligently and prudently carrying out the office entrusted to him, he may prove himself equal to your testimony, and fully worthy of our favour. God keep you safe, beloved brethren. Dated 22 August in the consulship of Asturius and Protogenes (449).

LETTER XLI. TO RAVENNIUS, BISHOP OF ARLES.

(He congratulates him on his appointment, exhorts him to firm but gentle government, and advises him frequently to consult the Apostolic See. Undated, but no doubt sent about the same time as XL.)

LETTER XLII. TO RAVENNIUS, BISHOP OF ARLES.

Leo the Pope to his well-beloved brother Ravennius. He asks him to deal with the imposture of a certain Petronianus.

We wish you to be circumspect and careful lest any blameworthy presumption should put forth undue claims: for, when it once finds an entrance by crafty stealth, it spreads itself into greater rashness in the name of the dignity it has assumed. We have learnt, on the trustworthy evidence of your clergy, that a certain wandering and vagabond Petronianus has boasted himself throughout the provinces of Gaul as our deacon, and under cover of this office is going about the various churches of that country. We desire you, beloved brother, so to check his abominable effrontery, as to disclose his imposture, by warning the bishops of the whole district. and to expel him from communion with all the Churches, lest he continue his claim. The Lord keep you safe, dearly beloved brother. Dated 26th, August, in the consulship of the illustrious Asturius and Protogenes (449).

LETTER XLIII . TO THEODOSIUS AUGUSTUS.

To the most glorious and serene Emperor Theodosius. Leo the bishop.

I. He complains of the conduct of Dioscorus at the Council of Ephesus. Already and from the beginning, in the synods which have been held, we have received such freedom of speech from the most holy Peter, chief of the Apostles, as to have the power both to maintain the Truth in the cause of peace, and to allow no one to disturb it in its firm position, but at once to repel the mischief, Since then the council of bishops which you ordered to be held in the city of Ephesus on account of Flavian, does mischief to the Faith itself and inflicts wounds on all the churches— ; and this has been brought to our knowledge not by some untrustworthy messenger, but by the most reverend bishops themselves who were sent by us and by the most trusty Hilarus our deacon, who have narrated to us what took place. And the occurrences are to be put down to the fault of those who met, not having, as is customary, with a pure conscience and right judgment made a definite statement about the faith and those who erred therefrom. For we have learnt that all did not come together in the conference who ought, some being ejected and others received: who were ensnared into an ungodly act of subscription by the designs of the aforesaid priest . For the declaration effected by him is of such a nature as to injure all the churches. For when those who were sent by us saw how exceedingly impious and hostile to the Faith it was, they notified it to us.

II. He Asks Him to Restore the Ancient Catholic Doctrine.

Wherefore, most peace-loving prince, vouchsafe for the Faith's sake to avert this danger from your Godly conscience, and let not man's presumption use violence upon Christ's Gospel In my sincere desire, which is shared by the bishops that are with me, that you, most Christian and revered prince, should before all things please God, tO whom the prayers of the whole Church are poured with one accord for your empire, I give you counsel, for fear lest, if we keep silence on so great a matter, we incur punishment before the tribunal of Christ. I entreat you therefore before the undivided Trinity of the one Godhead, which is injured by these evil doings, and which is the guardian of your kingdom, and before Christ's holy angels that all things remain intact as they were before the judgment, and that they await the weightier decision of the Synod at which the whole number of the bishops in the whole world is gathered together: and do not allow yourselves to bear the weight of others' misdoing. We are constrained to say this plainly by the fear of a constraining necessity . But keep before your eyes the blessed Peter's glory, and the crowns which all the Apostles have in common with him, and the joys of the martyrs who had no other incentive to suffering but the confession of the true Godhead and the perfect continuance in Christ .

III. And Asks Far Another Synod to Be Summoned.

And now that this confession is being God lessly impugned by some few men, all the churches of our parts and all the priests implore your clemency with tears in accordance with the request which Flavian makes in his appeal, to command the assembling together of a special Synod in Italy, in order that all opposition may be expelled or pacified, and that there may be no deviation from or ambiguity in the Faith: and to it should also come the bishops of all the Eastern provinces, that, if any have wandered out of the way of Truth, they may be recalled to their allegiance by wholesome remedies, and they who are under a more grievous charge may either be reduced to submission by counsel or cut off from the one Church. So that we are bound to preserve both what the Nicene canon enjoins and what the definitions of the bishops of the whole world enjoin according to the custom of the catholic Church, and also (to maintain) the freedom of our fathers' Faith, on which your tranquillity rests. For we pray that when those who harm the Church are driven out, and your provinces enjoy the possession of justice, anti vengeance has been executed on these heretics your royal power also may be defended by Christ's right hand.

LETTER XLIV. TO THEODOSIUS AUGUSTUS.

Leo, the bishop, and the holy Synod which is assembled at Rome to Theodosius Augustus.

I. He Exposes the Unscrupulous Nature of the Proceedings at Ephesus.

From your clemency's letter,' which in your love of the catholic Faith you sent sometime ago to the see of the blessed Apostle Peter, we drew such confidence in your defence of truth and peace that we thought nothing harmful could happen in so plain and well-ordered a matter; especially when those who were sent to the episcopal council, which you ordered to be held at Ephesus, were so fully instructed that, if the bishop of Alexandria had allowed the letters, which they brought either to the holy synod or to Flavian the bishop, to be read in the ears of the bishops, by the declaration of the most pure Faith, which being Divinely inspired we both have received and hold, all noise of disputings would have been so completely hushed that neither ignorance could any longer disport itself, nor jealousy find occasion to do mischief. But because private interests are consulted under cover of religion, the disloyalty of a few has wrought that which must wound the whole Church. For not from some untrustworthy messenger, but from a most faithful narrator of the things which have been done, Hilary, our deacon, who, lest he should be compelled by force to subscribe to their proceedings, with great difficulty made his escape, we have learnt that a great many priests came together at the synod, whose numbers would doubtless have assisted the debate and decision, if he who claimed for himself the chief place had consented to maintain priestly moderation, in order that, according to custom, when all had freely expressed their opinion, after quiet and fair deliberation, that might be ordained which was both agreeable to the Faith and helpful to those in error. But we have been told that all who had come were not present at the actual decision: for we have learnt that some were rejected while others were admitted, who at the aforesaid priest's requisition surrendered themselves to an unrighteous subscription, knowing they would suffer harm unless they obeyed his commands, and that such a resolution was brought forward by him that in attacking one man he might wreak his fury of the whole Church. Which our delegates from the Apostolic See saw to be so blasphemous and opposed to the catholic Faith that no pressure could force them to assent; for in the same synod they stoutly protested, as they ought, that the Apostolic See would never receive what was being passed: since the whole mystery of the Christian Faith is absolutely destroyed (which Heaven forfend in your Grace's reign), unless this abominable wickedness, which exceeds all former blasphemies, be abolished.

II. And Entreats the Emperor to Help in Reversing Their Decision.

But because the devil with wicked subtlety deceives the unwary, and so mocks the imprudence of some by a show of piety as to persuade them to things harmful instead of profitable, we pray your Grace, renounce all complicity in this endangering of religion and Faith, and afford in the treatment of Divine things that which is granted in worldly matters by the equity of your laws, that human presumption may not do violence to Christ's Gospel. Behold, I, O most Christian and honoured Emperor, with my fellow-priests fulfilling towards your revered clemency the offices of sincere love, and desiring you in all things to please God, to whom prayers are offered for you by the Church, lest before the Lord Christ's tribunal we be judged guilty for our silence,—we beseech you in the presence of the Undivided Trinity of the One Godhead, Whom such an act wrongs (for He is Himself the Guardian and the Author of your empire), and in the presence of Christ's holy angels, order everything to be in the position in which they were before the decision until a larger number of priests be assembled from the whole world. Suffer not yourself to be weighted with another's sin because (and we must say it) we are afraid lest He, Whose religion is being destroyed, be provoked to wrath. Keep before your eyes, and with all your mental vision gaze reverently upon the blessed Peter's glory, and the crowns which all the Apostles have in common with him and the palms of all the martyrs, who had no other reason for suffering than the confession of the true Godhead and the true Manhood in Christ.

III. He Asks for a Council in Italy.

And because this mystery is now being impiously opposed by a few ignorant persons, all the churches of our parts, and all the priests entreat your clemency, with groans and tears seeing that our delegates faithfully protested, and bishop Flavian gave them an appeal in writing, to order a general synod to be held in Italy, which shall either dismiss or appease all disputes in such a way that there be nothing any longer either doubtful in the Faith or divided in love, and to it, of course, the bishops of the Eastern provinces must come, and if any of them were overcome by threats and injury, and deviated from the path of truth, they may be fully restored by health-giving measures, and they themselves, whose case is harder, if they acquiesce in wiser counsels, may not fall from the unity of the Church. And how necessary this request is after the lodging of an appeal is witnessed by the canonical decrees passed at Nicaea by the bishops of the whole world, which are added below . Show favour to the catholics after your own and your parents' custom. Give us such liberty to defend the catholic Faith as no violence, no fear of the world, while your revered clemency is safe, shall be able to take away. For it is the cause not only of the Church but of your Kingdom and prosperity that we plead, that you may enjoy the peaceful sway of your provinces. Defend the Church in unshaken peace against the heretics, that your empire also may be defended by Christ's right hand. Dated the 13th of October, in the consulship of the illustrious Asturius and Protogenes (449).

LETTER XLV. TO PULCHERIA AUGUSTA.

Leo, the bishop, and the holy Synod which is assembled in the City of Rome to Pulcheria Augusta.

I. He Sends a Copy of the Former Letter Which Failed to Reach Her.

If the letters respecting the Faith which were despatched to your Grace by the hands of our clergy had reached you, it is certain you would have been able, the Lord helping you, to provide a remedy for these things which have been done against the Faith. For when have you failed either the priests or the religion or the Faith of Christ? But when those who were sent were so completely hindered from reaching your clemency that only one of them, namely Hilary our deacon, with difficulty fled and returned, we thought it necessary to rewrite our letter: and that our prayers may deserve to receive more weight, we have subjoined a copy of the very document which did not reach your clemency, entreating you even more earnestly than before to take under protection that religion in which you excel which will win you the greater glory in proportion to the heinousness of the crimes against which your royal faith requires you to proceed, lest the integrity of the Christian Faith be violated by any plot of man's devising. For the things which were believed to require setting at rest and healing by the meeting of a Synod at Ephesus, have not only resulted in still greater disturbances of peace but, which is the more to be regretted, even in the overthrow of the very Faith whereby we are Christians.II. He also sends a copy of his letter to the Emperor and explains its contents.

And they indeed, who were sent, and one of whom, escaping the violence of the bishop of Alexandria who claims everything for himself, faithfully reported to us what took place in the Synod, opposed, as it became them, what I will call the frenzy not the judgment of one man, protesting that those things which were being carried through by violence and fear could not reverse the mysteries of the Church and the Creed itself composed by the Apostles, and that no injuries could sever them from that Faith which they had brought fully set forth and expounded from the See of the blessed Apostle Peter to the holy synod. And since this statement was not allowed to be read out at the bishop's request, in order forsooth that by the rejection of that Faith which has crowned patriarchs, prophets, apostles and martyrs, the birth according to the flesh of Jesus Christ our Lord and the confession of His true Death and Resurrection (we shudder to say it) might be overthrown, we have written on this matter according to our ability, to our most glorious and (what is far greater) our Christian Prince, and at the same time have subjoined a copy of the letter to you to the end that he may not allow the Faith, in which he was re-born and reigns through God's grace, to be corrupted by any innovation, since Bishop Flavian continues in communion with us all, and that which has been done without regard to justice and contrary to all the teaching of the canons can, under no consideration, be held valid. And because the Synod of Ephesus has not removed but increased the scandal of disagreement (I have asked him) to appoint a place and time for holding a council within Italy, all quarrels and prejudices on both sides being suspended, that everything which has engendered offence may be the more diligently reconsidered and without wounding the Faith, without injuring religion those priests may return into the peace of Christ, who through irresolution were forced to subscribe, and only their errors be re moved.

III. He Asks Her to Assist His Petition with the Emperor.

And that we may be worthy to obtain this, let your well-tried faith and protection, which has always helped the Church in her labours, deign to advance our petition with our most clement Prince, under a special commission so to act from the blessed Apostle Peter; so that before this civil and destructive war gains strength within the Church, he may grant opportunity of restoring unity by God's aid, knowing that the strength of his empire will be increased by every extension of catholic freedom that his kindly will affects.

Dated 13th of October in the consulship of the illustrious Asturius and Protogenes (449).

LETTER XLVI. FROM HILARY, THEN DEACON (AFTERWARDS BISHOP OF ROME) TO PULCHERIA AUGUSTA.

(Describing his ill-treatment, as Leo's delegate, by Dioscorus.)

LETTER XLVII. TO ANASTASIUS, BISHOP OF THESSALONICA.

(Congratulating him on being present at the synod of Ephesus)

LETTER XLVIII. TO JULIAN, BISHOP OF COS.

(Consoling him after the riots at Ephesus and exhorting him to stand firm.)

LETTER XLIX. TO FLAVIAN, BISHOP OF CONSTANTINOPLE

(Whose death he is unaware of, promising him all the support in his power.)

LETTER L. TO THE PEOPLE OF CONSTANTINOPLE, BY THE HAND OF EPIPHANIUS AND DIONYSIUS, NOTARY OF THE CHURCH OF ROME.

(Exhorting them to stand firm and consoling them for Flavian's deposition.)

LETTER LI. TO FAUSTUS AND OTHER PRESBYTERS AND ARCHIMANDRITES IN CONSTANTINOPLE.

(With the same purport as the last.)

LETTER LII. FROM THEODORET, BISHOP OF CYRUS, TO LEO. (SEE VOL. III. OF THIS SERIES, P. 293.)

To Leo, bishop of Rome.

I. If Paul Appealed to Peter How Much More Must Ordinary Folk Have Recourse to His Successor.

If Paul, the herald of the Truth, the trumpet of the Holy Ghost, had recourse to the great Peter, in order to obtain a decision from him for those at Antioch who were disputing about living by the Law, much more do we small and humble folk run to the Apostolic See to get healing from you for the sores of the churches. For it is fitting that you should in all things have the pre-eminence, seeing that your See possesses many peculiar privileges. For other cities get a name for size or beauty or population, and some that are devoid of these advantages are compensated by certain spiritual gifts: but your city has the fullest abundance of good things from the Giver of all good. For she is of all cities the greatest and most famous, the mistress of the world and teeming with population. And besides this she has created an empire which is still predominant and has imposed her own name upon her subjects. But her chief decoration is her Faith, to which the Divine Apostle is a sure witness when he exclaims "your faith is proclaimed in all the world ;" and if immediately after receiving the seeds of the saving Gospel she bore such a weight of wondrous fruit, what words are sufficient to express the piety which is now found in her? She has, too, the tombs of our common fathers and teachers of the Truth, Peter and Paul , to illumine the souls of the faithful. And this blessed and divine pair arose indeed in the East, and shed its rays in all directions, but voluntarily underwent the sunset of life in the West, from whence now it illumines the whole world. These have rendered your See so glorious: this is the chief of all your goods. And their See is still blest by the light of their God's presence, seeing that therein He has placed your Holiness to shed abroad the rays of the one true Faith.

II. He Commends Leo's Zeal Against the Manichees, and Latterly Against Entychianism, as Evidenced Especially in the Tome.

Of which thing indeed, though there are many other proofs to be found, your zeal against the ill-famed Manichaeans is proof enough, that zeal which your holiness has of late years displayed , thereby revealing the intensity of your devotion to God in things Divine. Proof enough, too, of your Apostolic character is what you have now written. For we have met with what your holiness has written about the Incarnation of our God and Saviour, and have admired the careful diligence of the work . For it has proved both points equally well, viz., the Eternal Godhead of the Only-begotten of the Eternal Father, and at the same time His manhood of the seed of Abraham and David, and His assumption of a nature in all things like ours, except in this one thing, that He remained free from all sin: for sin is engendered not of nature, but of free will . This also was contained in your letter, that the only-begotten Son of God is One and His Godhead impassible, irreversible, unchangeable even as the Father who begat Him and the All-holy Spirit. And since the Divine nature could not suffer, He took the nature that could suffer to this end, that by the suffering of His own Flesh He might give exemption from suffering to those that believed on Him. These points, and all that is akin thereto, the letter contained. And we, admiring your spiritual wisdom, extolled the grace of the Holy Ghost which spoke through and ask and pray, and beg and beseech your holiness to come to the rescue of the churches of God that are now tempest tossed.

III. He Complains of Dioscorus' ILL-Treatment of Himself

For when we expected a stilling of the waves through those who were sent to Ephesus from your holiness, we have fallen into yet worse storm. For the most righteous prelate of Alexandria was not satisfied with the illegal and most unrighteous deposition of the Lord's most holy and God-loving bishop of Constantinople, Flavian, nor was his wrath appeased by the slaughter of the other bishops likewise. But me, too, he murdered with his pen in my absence, without calling me to judgment, without passing judgment on me in person, without questioning me on what I hold about the Incarnation of our God and Saviour. But even murderers, tomb-breakers, and ravishers of other men's beds, those who sit in judgment do not condemn until they either themselves corroborate the accusations by their confessions, or are clearly convicted by others. But us, when five and thirty days' journey distant, he, though brought up on Divine laws, has condemned at his will. And not now only has he done this, but also last year, after that two persons infected with the Apollinarian disorder had come hither and laid false information against us, he rose up in church and anathematized us, and that when I had written to him and expressed what I hold in a letter.

IV. This ILL-Treatment Has Come After 20 Years' Good Work in His Diocese of Cyrus.

I bemoan the distress of the Church and yearn after its peace. For having ruled through your prayers the church committed to me by the God of the universe for 20 years, neither in the time of the blessed Theodotus, president of the East, nor in the time of those who have succeeded him in the See of Antioch, have I received the slightest blame, but, the Divine Grace working with me, have freed more than 1,000 souls from the disease of Marcion, and have won over many others from the company of Arius and Eunomius to the Master, Christ. And 800 churches have I had to shepherd: for that is the number of parishes in Cyrus, in which not a single tare through your prayers has lingered. But our flock has been freed from every heretical error. He that sees all things knows how I have been stoned by the ill-famed heretics that have been sent against me, and what struggles I have had in many cities of the East against Greeks, Jews, and every heretical error. And after all these toils and troubles, I have been condemned without a hearing.

V. He Appeals to the Apostolic See with Confidence.

I however await the verdict of your Apostolic See, and beg and pray your Holiness to succour me when I appeal to your upright and just tribunal, and bid me come to you and show that my teaching follows in the track of the Apostles. For there are writings of mine some 20 years ago, some 18, some 15, and some 12, some again against the Arians and Eunomians, some against the Jews and Greeks some against the Magi in Persia, some also about the universal Providence, Others about the nature of God and about the Divine Incarnation. I have interpreted, through the Divine grace, both the Apostolic writings and the prophetic utterances, and it is easy therefrom to gather whether I have kept unswervingly the standard of the Faith, or have turned aside from its straight path. And I beg you not to spurn my petition, nor to overlook the insults heaped on my poor white hairs.

VI. Ought He to Acquiesce in His Deposition?

First of all, I beg you to tell me, whether I ought to acquiesce in this unrighteous deposition or not. For I await your verdict and, if you bid me abide by my condemnation, I will abide by it, and will trouble no one hereafter, but await the unerring verdict of our God and Saviour. I indeed, the Master God is my witness, care nought for honour and glory, but only for the stumbling-block that is put in men's way: because many of the simpler folk, and especially those who have been rescued by us from divers heresies, will give credence to those who have condemned us, and perchance reckon us heretics, not being able to discern the exact truth of the dogma, and because, after my long episcopate, I have acquired neither house, nor land, nor obol, nor tomb, only a voluntary poverty, having straightway distributed even what came to me from my fathers after their death, as all know who live in the East.

VII. Being Prevented Himself, He Has Sent Delegates to Plead His Cause.

And before all things I entreat you, holy and God-loved brother, render assistance to my prayers. These things I have brought to your Holiness' knowledge, by the most religious and God-beloved presbyters, Hypatius and Abramius the chorepiscopi , and Alypius, superintendent of the monks in our district: seeing that I was hindered from coming to you myself by the Emperor's restraining letter, and likewise the others. And I entreat your holiness both to look on them with fatherly regard, and to lend them your ears in sincere kindness, and also to deem my slandered and falsely attacked position worthy of your protection, and above all to defend with all your might the Faith that is now plotted against, and to keep the heritage of the fathers intact for the churches, so shall your holiness receive from the Bountiful Master a full reward. (Date about the end of 449.)

LETTER LIII. A FRAGMENT OF A LETTER FROM ANATOLIUS, BISHOP OF CONSTANTINOPLE, TO LEO

(about his consecration).

LETTER LIV. TO THEODOSIUS AUGUSTUS

(asking for a synod in Italy).

LETTERS LV TO LVIII.

A series of Letters.
(1) From Valentinian the Emperor to Theodosius Augustus.
(2) From Galla Placidia Augusta to Theodosius Augustus.
(3) From Licinia Eudoxia Augusta to Theodosius Augustus.
(4) From Galla Placidia Augusta to Pulcheria Augusta, all graphically describing how Leo had appealed to them in public to press his suit with Theodosius. Of these, LVI. is subjoined as perhaps the most interesting specimen.

LETTER LVI. (FROM GALLA PLACIDIA AUGUSTA TO THEODOSIUS).

To the Lord Theodosius, Conqueror and Emperor, her ever august son, Galla Placidia, most pious and prosperous, perpetual Augusta and mother.

When on our very arrival in the ancient city, we were engaged in paying our devotion to the most blessed Apostle Peter, at the martyr's very altar, the most reverend Bishop Leo waiting behind awhile after the service uttered laments over the catholic Faith to us, and taking to witness the chief of the Apostles himself likewise, whom we had just approached, and surrounded by a number of bishops whom he had brought together from numerous cities in Italy by the authority and dignity of his position, adding also tears to his words, called upon us to join our moans to his own. For no slight harm has arisen from those occurrences, whereby the standard of the catholic Faith so long guarded since the days of our most Divine father Constantine, who was the first in the palace to stand out as a Christian, has been recently disturbed by the assumption of one man, who in the synod held at Ephesus is alleged to have rather stirred up hatred and contention, intimidating by the presence of soldiers, Flavianus, the bishop of Constantinople, because he had sent an appeal to the Apostolic See, and to all the bishops of these parts by the hands of those who had been deputed to attend the Synod by the most reverend Bishop of Rome, who have been always wont so to attend, most sacred Lord and Son and adored King, in accordance with the provisions of the Nicene Synod . For this cause we pray your clemency to oppose such disturbances with the Truth, and to order the Faith of the catholic religion to be preserved without spot, in order that according to the standard and decision of the Apostolic See, which we likewise revere as preeminent, Flavianus may remain altogether uninjured in his priestly office, and the matter be referred to the Synod of the Apostolic See, wherein assuredly he first adorned the primacy, who was deemed worthy to receive the keys of heaven: for it becomes us in all things to maintain the respect due to this great city, which is the mistress of all the earth; and this too we must most carefully provide that what in former times our house guarded seem not in our day to be infringed, and that by the present example schisms be not advanced either between the bishops or the most holy churches.

LETTER LIX. TO THE CLERGY AND PEOPLE OF THE CITY OF CONSTANTINOPLE.

Leo the bishop to the clergy, dignitaries, and people, residing at Constantinople.
I. He Congratulates Them on Their Outspoken Resistance to Error.

Though we are greatly grieved at the things reported to have been done recently in the council of priests at Ephesus, because, as is consistently rumoured, and also demonstrated by results, neither due moderation nor the strictness of the Faith was there observed, yet we rejoice in your devoted piety and in the acclamations of the holy people , instances of which have been brought to our notice, we have approved of the right feeling of you all; because there lives and abides in good sons due affection for their excellent Father, and because you suffer the fulness of catholic teaching to be in no part corrupted. For undoubtedly, as the Holy Spirit has unfolded to you, they are leagued with the Manichaeans' error, who deny that the only-begotten Son of God took our nature's true Manhood, and maintain that all His bodily actions were the actions of a false apparition. And lest you should in aught give your assent to this blasphemy, we have now sent you, beloved, by my son Epiphanius and Dionysius, notary of the Roman Church, letters of exhortation wherein we have of our own accord rendered you the assistance which you sought, that you may not doubt of our bestowing all a father's care on you, and labouring in every way, by the help of God's mercy, to destroy all the stumbling-blocks which ignorant and foolish men have raised. And let no one venture to parade his priestly dignity who can be convicted of holding such detestably blasphemous opinions. For if ignorance seems hardly tolerable in laymen, how much less excusable or pardonable is it in those who govern; especially when they dare even to defend their mendacious and perverse views, and persuade the unsteadfast to agree with them either by intimidation or by cajoling.

II. They are to Be Rejected Who Deny the Truth of Christ's Flesh, a Truth Repeated by Every Recipient at the Holy Eucharist.

Let such men be rejected by the holy members of Christ's Body, and let not catholic liberty suffer the yoke of the unfaithful to be laid upon it. For they are to be reckoned outside the Divine grace, and outside the mystery of man's salvation, who, denying the nature of our flesh in Christ, gainsay the Gospel and oppose the Creed. Nor do they perceive that their blindness leads them into such an abyss that they have no sure footing in the reality either of the Lord's Passion or His Resurrection: because both are discredited in the Saviour, if our fleshly nature is not believed in Him. In what density of ignorance, in what utter sloth must they hitherto have lain, not to have learnt from hearing, nor understood from reading, that which in God's Church is so constantly in men's mouths, that even the tongues of infants do not keep silence upon the truth of Christ's Body and Blood at the rite of Holy Communion ? For in that mystic distribution of spiritual nourishment, that which is given and taken is of such a kind that receiving the virtue of the celestial food we pass into the flesh of Him, Who became our flesh . Hence to confirm you, beloved, in your laudably faithful resistance to the foes of Truth, I shall filly and opportunely use the language and sentiments of the Apostle, and say: "Therefore I also hearing of your faith, which is in the Lord Jesus, and love towards all saints, do not cease to give thanks for you, making mention of you in my prayers that the God of our Lord Jesus Christ, the Father l of glory, may give you the spirit of wisdom and revelation in the knowledge of Him, the eyes of your hearts being enlightened that you may know what is the hope of His calling, and what the riches of the glory of His inheritance among the saints, and what is the exceeding greatness of His power in us, who believed according to the working of His mighty power which he has wrought in Christ, raising Him from the dead, and setting Him at His right hand in heavenly places above every principality, and power, and strength, and dominion, and every name which is named not only in this age, but also in that which is to come: and hath put all things under His feet, and given Him to be the head over all the Church which is His body, and the fulness of Him Who filleth all in all ."

III. Perfect God And Perfect Man Were United in Christ.

In this passage let the adversaries of the Truth say when or according to what nature did the Almighty Father exalt His Son above all things, or to what substance did He subject all things. For the Godhead of the Word is equal in all things, and consubstantial with the Father, and the power of the Begetter and the Begotten is one and the same always and eternally. Certainly, the Creator of all natures, since "through Him all things were made, and without Him was nothing made ," is above all things which He created, nor were the things which He made ever not subject to their Creator, Whose eternal property it is, to be from none other than the Father, and in no way different to the Father. If greater power, grander dignity, more exalted loftiness was granted Him, then was He that was so increased less than He that promoted Him, and possessed not the full riches of His nature from Whose fulness He received. But one who thinks thus is hurried off into the society of Arius, whose heresy is much assisted by this blasphemy which denies the existence of human nature in the Word of God, so that, in rejecting the combination of humility with majesty in God, it either asserts a false phantom-body in Christ, or says that all His bodily actions and passions belonged to the Godhead rather than to the flesh. But everything he ventures to uphold is absolutely foolish: because neither our religious belief nor the scope of the mystery admits either of the Godhead suffering anything or of the Truth belying Itself in anything. The impassible Son of God, therefore, whose perpetually it is with the Father and with the Holy Spirit to be what He is in the one essence of the Unchangeable Trinity, when the fullness of time had come which had been fore-ordained by an eternal purpose, and promised by the prophetic significance of words and deeds, became man not by conversion of His substance but by assumption of our nature, and "came to seek and to save that which was lost ." But He came not by local approach nor by bodily motion, as if to be present where He had been absent, or to depart where He had come: but He came to be manifested to onlookers by that which was visible and common to others, receiving, that is to say, human flesh and soul in the Virgin mother's womb, so that, abiding in the form of God, He united to Himself the form of a slave, and the likeness of sinful flesh, whereby He did not lessen the Divine by the human, but increased the human by the Divine.

IV. The Sacrament of Baptism Typifies and Realizes This Union to Each Individual Believer.

For such was the state of all mortals resulting from our first ancestors that, after the transmission of original sin to their descendants, no one would have escaped the punishment of condemnation, had not the Word become flesh and dwelt in us, that is to say, in that nature which belonged to our blood and race. And accordingly, the Apostle says: "As by one man's sin (judgment passed) upon all to condemnation, so also by one man's righteousness (it) passed upon all to justification of life. For as by one man's disobedience many were made sinners, so also by one man's obedience shall many be made righteous ;" and again, "For because by man (came) death, by man also (came) the resurrection of the dead. And as in Adam all die, so also in Christ shall all be made alive ." All they to wit who though they be born in Adam, yet are found reborn in Christ, having a sure testimony both to their justification by grace, and to Christ's sharing in their nature ; for he who does not believe that God's only-begotten Son did assume our nature in the womb of the Virgin-daughter of David, is without share in the Mystery of the Christian religion, and, as he neither recognizes the Bridegroom nor knows the Bride, can have no place at the wedding-banquet. For the flesh of Christ is the veil of the Word, wherewith every one is clothed who confesses Him unreservedly. But he that is ashamed of it and rejects it as unworthy, shall have no adornment from Him, and though he present i himself at the Royal feast, and unseasonably join in the sacred banquet, yet the intruder will not be able to escape the King's discernment, but, as the Lord Himself asserted, will be taken, and with hands and feet bound, be cast into outer darkness; where will be weeping and gnashing of teeth . Hence whosoever confesses not the human body in Christ, must know that he is unworthy of the mystery of the Incarnation, and has no share in that sacred union of which the Apostle speaks, saying, "For we are His members, of His flesh and of His bones. For this cause a man shall leave father and mother and shall cleave to his wife, and there shall be two in one flesh ." And explaining what was meant by this, he added, "This mystery is great, but I speak in respect of Christ and the Church." Therefore, from the very commencement of the human race, Christ is announced to all men as coming in the flesh. In which, as was said, "there shall be two in one flesh," there are undoubtedly two, God and man, Christ and the Church, which issued from the Bridegroom's flesh, when it received the mystery of redemption and regeneration, water and blood flowing from the side of the Crucified. For the very condition of a new creature which at baptism puts off not the covering of true flesh but the taint of the old condemnation, is this, that a man is made the body of Christ, because Christ also is the body of a man .

V. The True Doctrine of the Incarnation Restated and Commended to Their Keeping.

Wherefore we call Christ not God only, as the Manichaean heretics, nor Man only, as the Photinian heretics, nor man in such a way that anything should be wanting in Him which certainly belongs to human nature, whether soul or reasonable mind or flesh which was not derived from woman, but made from the Word turned and changed into flesh; which three false and empty propositions have been variously advanced by the three sections of the Apollinarian heretics . Nor do we say that the blessed Virgin Mary conceived a Man without Godhead, Who was created by the Holy Ghost and afterwards assumed by the Word, which we deservedly and properly condemned Nestorius for preaching: but we call Christ the Son of God, true God, born of God the Father without any beginning in time, and likewise true Man, born of a human Mother, at the ordained fulness of time, and we say that His Manhood, whereby the Father is the greater, does not in anything lessen that nature whereby He is equal with the Father. But these two natures form one Christ, Who has said most truly both according to His Godhead: "I and the Father are one ," and according to His manhood "the Father is greater than I ." This true and indestructible Faith, dearly-beloved, which alone makes us true Christians, and which, as we hear with approval, you are defending with loyal zeal and praiseworthy affection, hold fast and maintain boldly. And since, besides God's aid, you must win the favour of catholic Princes also, humbly and wisely make request that the most clement Emperor be pleased to grant our petition, wherein we have asked for a plenary synod to be convened; that by the aid of God's mercy the sound may be increased in courage, and the sick, if they consent to be treated, have the remedy applied. (Dated October 15, in the consulship of the illustrious Asturius and Protogenes, 449.)

LETTER LX. TO PULCHERIA AUGUSTA.

(He hopes for her intercession to procure the condemnation of Eutyches.)

LETTER LXI. TO MARTINUS AND FAUSTUS, PRESBYTERS.

(Reminding them of a former letter he has written to them, viz. Lett. LI.)

(Letters LXII., LXIII., LXIV., are the Emperor Theodosius' answers (a) to Valentinian, (b) to Galla Placidia, and (c) to Licinia Eudoxia (assuring them of his orthodoxy and care for the Faith.)

LETTER LXV. FROM THE BISHOPS OF THE PROVINCE OF ARLES.

(Asking Leo to confirm the privileges of that city, which they allege date from the mission of Trophimus, by S. Peter, and more recently ratified by the Emperor Constantine.)

LETTER LXVI. LEO'S REPLY TO LETTER LXV.

Leo, the pope, to the dearly-beloved brethren Constantinus, Armentarius, Audientius Severianus, Valerianus, Ursus, Stephanus, Nectarius, Constantius, Maximus, Asclepius, Theodorus, Justus Ingenuus, Augustalis, Superventor, Ynantius, Fonteius, and Palladius.

I. The Bishop of Vienne Has Anticipated Their Appeal. He Proposes to Arbitrate with Impartiality.

When we read your letter, beloved, which was brought to us by our sons Petronius the presbyter and Regulus the deacon, we recognized how affectionate is the regard in which you hold our brother and fellow-bishop, Ravennius: for your request is that what his predecessor deservedly lost for his excessive presumption may be restored to him. But your petition, brothers, was forestalled by the bishop of Vienne, who sent a letter and legates with the complaint that the bishop of Aries had unlawfully claimed the ordination of the bishop of Vasa. Accordingly, as we had to show such respect both for the canons of the fathers and for your good opinion of us, that in the matter of the churches' privileges we should allow no infringement or deprivation, it were incumbent on us to preserve the peace within the province of Vienne by employing such righteous moderation as should disregard neither ancient usage nor your desires.

II. The Bishop of Vienne is to Retain Jurisdiction Over Four Neighbouring Cities: the Rest to Belong to Arles.

For after considering the arguments advanced by the clergy present on either side, we find that the cities of Vienne and Arles within your province have always been so famous, that in certain matters of ecclesiastical privilege, now one, now the other, has alternately taken precedence, though the national tradition is that formerly they had community of rights. And hence we suffer not the city of Vienne to be altogether without honour, so far as concerns ecclesiastical jurisdiction, especially as it already possesses the authority of our decree for the enjoyment of its privilege: to wit the power which, when taken away from Hilary, we thought proper to confer on the bishop of Vienne. And that he seem not suddenly and unduly lowered, he shall hold rule over the four neighbouring towns, that is, Valentia, Tarantasia, Genava and Gratianopolis, with Vienne herself for the fifth, to the bishop of which shall belong the care of all the said churches. But the other churches of the same province shall be placed under the authority and management of the bishop of Arles, who from his temperate moderation we believe will be so anxious for love and peace as by no means to consider himself deprived of that which he sees conceded to his brother. Dated 5th of May, in the consulship of Valentinianus Augustus (7th time), and the most famous Avienus (450.)

LETTER LXVII. TO RAVENNIUS, BISHOP OF ARLES.

To his dearly-beloved brother Ravennius, Leo the pope.

We have kept our sons Petronius the presbyter, and Regulus the deacon, long in the City, both because they deserved this from their favour in our eyes, and because the needs of the Faith, which is now being assailed by the error of some, demanded it. For we wished them to be present when we discussed the matter, and to ascertain everything which we desire through you, beloved, should reach the knowledge of all our brethren and fellow-bishops, specially deputing this to you, dear brother, that through your watchful diligence our letter, which we have issued to the East in defence of the Faith, or else that of Cyril of blessed memory, which agrees throughout with our views, may become known to all the brethren; in order that being furnished with arguments they may fortify themselves with spiritual strength against those who think fit to insult the Lord's Incarnation with their misbeliefs. You have a favourable opportunity, beloved brother, of recommending the commencement of your episcopacy to all the churches and to our God, if you will carry out these things in the way we have charged and enjoined you. But the matters which were not to be committed to paper, in reliance on God's aid, you shall carry out effectually, as we have said, and laudably, when you have learnt about them from the mouths of our aforesaid sons. God keep you safe, dearest brother. Dated 5th of May, in the consulship of the most glorious Valentinianus (for the 7th time) and of the famous Avienus (450).

LETTER LXVIII. FROM THREE GALLIC BISHOPS TO ST. LEO.

Ceretius, Salonius and Veranus to the holy Lord, most blessed father, and pope most worthy of the Apostolic See, Leo.

I. They Congratulate and Thank Leo for the Tome.

Having perused your Excellency's letter, which you composed for instruction in the Faith, and sent to the bishop of Constantinople, we thought it our duty, being enriched with so great a wealth of doctrine, to pay our debt of thanks by at least inditing you a letter. For we appreciate your fatherly solicitude on our behalf, and confess that we are the more indebted to your preventing care because we now have the benefit of the remedy before experiencing the evils. For knowing that those remedies are well-nigh too late which are applied after the infliction of the wounds, you admonish us with the voice of loving forethought to arm ourselves with those Apostolic means of defence. We acknowledge frankly, most blessed pope , with what singular loving-kindness you have imparted to us the innermost thoughts of your breast, by the efficacy of which you secure the safety of others: and while you extract the old Serpent's infused poison from the hearts of others, standing as it were on the watch-tower of Love, with Apostolic care and watchfulness you cry aloud, lest the enemy come on us unawares and off our guard, lest careless security expose us to attack, O holy Lord, most blessed father and pope, most worthy of the Apostolic See. Moreover we; who specially belong to you , are filled with a great and unspeakable delight, because this special statement of your teaching is so highly regarded wherever the Churches meet together, that the unanimous opinion is expressed that the primacy of the Apostolic See is rightfully there assigned, from whence the oracles of the Apostolic Spirit still receive their interpretations.

II. They Ask Him to Correct or Add to Their Copy of the Tome.

Therefore, if you deem it worth while, we entreat your holiness to run through and correct any mistake of the copyist in this work, so valuable both now and in the future, which we have had committed to parchment , in our desire to preserve it, or if you have devised anything further in your zeal, which will profit all who read, give orders in your loving care that it be added to this copy, so that not only many holy bishops our brethren throughout the provinces of Gaul, but also many of your sons among the laity, who greatly desire to see this letter for the revelation of the Truth, may be permitted, when it is sent back to us, corrected by your holy hand, to transcribe, read and keep it. If you think fit, we are anxious that our messengers should return soon, in order that we may the speedier have an account of your good health over which to rejoice: for your well-being is our joy and health.

May Christ the Lord long keep your eminence mindful of our humility, O holy Lord, most blessed father and pope most worthy of the Apostolic See.

I, Ceretius, your adopted (son?), salute your apostleship, commending me to your prayers.

I, Salonius, your adorer, salute your apostleship, entreating the aid of your prayers.

I, Veranus, the worshipper of your apostleship, salute your blessedness, and beseech you to pray for me.

LETTER LXIX. (TO THEODOSIUS AUGUSTUS.)

Leo, the bishop, to Theodosius ever Augustus.

I. He Suspends His Opinion on the Appointment of Anatolius Till He Has Made Open Confession of the Catholic Faith.

In all your piously expressed letters amid the anxieties, which we suffer for the Faith, you have afforded us hope of security by supporting the Council of Nicaea so loyally as not to allow the priests of the Lord to budge from it, as you have often written us already. But lest I should seem to have done anything prejudicial to the catholic defence, I thought nothing rash on either side ought meanwhile to be written back on the ordination of him who has begun to preside over the church of Constantinople, and this not through want of loving interest, but waiting for the catholic Truth to be made clear. And I beg your clemency to bear this with equanimity that when he has proved himself such as we desire towards the catholic Faith, we may the more fully and safely rejoice over his sincerity. But that no evil suspicion may assail him about our disposition towards him, I remove all occasion of difficulty, and demand nothing which may seem either hard or controvertible but make an invitation which no catholic would decline. For they are well known and renowned throughout the world, who before our time have shone in preaching the catholic Truth whether in the Greek or the Latin tongue, to whose learning and teaching some even of our own day have recourse, and from whose writings a uniform and manifold statement of doctrine is produced: which, as it has pulled down the heresy of Nestorius, so has it cut off this error too which is now sprouting out again. Let him then read again what is the belief on the Lord's Incarnation which the holy fathers guarded and has always been similarly preached,and when he has perceived that the letter of Cyril of holy memory, bishop of Alexandria, agrees with the view of those who preceded him [wherein he wished to correct and cure Nestorius, refuting his wrong statements and setting out more clearly the Faith as defined at Nicaea, and which was sent by him and placed in the library of the Apostolic See], let him further reconsider the proceedings of the Ephesian Synod wherein the testimonies of catholic priests on the Lord's Incarnation are inserted and maintained by Cyril of holy memory. Let him not scorn also to read my letter over, which he will find to agree throughout with the pious belief of the fathers. And when he has realized that that is required and desired from him which shall serve the same good end, let him give his hearty assent to the judgment of the catholics, so that in the presence of all the clergy and the whole people he may without any reservation declare his sincere acknowledgment of the common Faith, to be communicated to the Apostolic See and all the Lord's priests and churches, and thus the world being at peace through the one Faith, we may all be able to say what the angels sang at the Saviour's birth of the Virgin Mary, "Glory in the highest to God and on earth peace to men of good will ."

II. He Promises to Accept Anatolius on Making This Confession, and Asks for a Council in Italy to Finally Define the Faith.

But because both we and our blessed fathers, whose teaching we revere and follow, are in concord on the one Faith, as the bishops of all the provinces attest, let your clemency's most devout faith see to it that such a document as is due may reach us as soon as may be from the bishop of Constantinople, as from an approved and catholic priest, that is, openly and distinctly affirming that he will separate from his communion any one who believes or maintains any other view about the Incarnation of the Word of God than my statement and that of all catholics lays down, that we may fairly be able to bestow on him brotherly love in Christ. And that swifter and fuller effect, God aiding us, may be given through your clemency's faith to our wholesome desires, I have sent to your piety my brethren and fellow-bishops Abundius and Asterius, together with Basilius and Senator presbyters, whose devotion is well proved to me, through whom, when they have displayed the instructions which we have sent, you may be able properly to apprehend what is the standard of our faith, so that, if the bishop of Constantinople gives his hearty assent to the same confession, we may securely, as is due, rejoice over the peace of the Church and no ambiguity may seem to lurk behind which may trouble us with perhaps ungrounded suspicions. But if any dissent from the purity of our Faith and from the authority of the Fathers, the Synod which has met at Rome for that purpose joins with me in asking your clemency to permit a universal council within the limits of Italy; so that, if all those come together in one place who have fallen either through ignorance or through fear, measures may be taken to correct and cure them, and no one any longer may be allowed to quote the Synod of Niches in a way which shall prove him opposed to its Faith; since it will be of advantage both to the whole Church and to your rule, if one God, one Faith and one mystery of man's Salvation, be held by the one confession of the whole world.

Dated 17th July in the consulship of the illustrious Valentinianus for the seventh time) and Avienus (450).

LETTER LXX. TO PULCHERIA AUGUSTA.

(In which he again says he is waiting for Anatolius' acceptance of Cyril's and his own statement of the Faith, and looks forward to a Synod in Italy.)

LETTER LXXI. TO THE ARCHIMANDRITES OF CONSTANTINOPLE.

(Complaining of Anatolius' silence.)

LETTER LXXII. TO FAUSTUS, ONE OF THE ARCHIMANDRITES AT CONSTANTINOPLE.

(Commending his faith and exhorting him to steadfastness.)

LETTER LXXIII. FROM VALENTINIAN AND MARCIAN.

(Announcing their election as Emperors (a.d. 450), and asking his prayers that (per celebrandam synodum, te auctore), peace may be restored to the Church.)

LETTER LXXIV. TO MARTINUS, ANOTHER OF THE ARCHIMANDRITES AT CONSTANTINOPLE.

(Commending his steadfastness in the Faith.)

LETTER LXXV. TO FAUSTUS AND MARTINUS TOGETHER.

(Condemning the Latrocinium and maintaining that Eutyches equally with Nestorius promotes the cause of Antichrist.)

LETTER LXXVI. FROM MARCIANUS AUGUSTUS TO LEO.

(Proposing that he should either attend a Synod at Constantinople or help in arranging some other more convenient place of meeting.)

LETTER LXXVII. FROM PULCHERIA AUGUSTA TO LEO.

(In which she expresses her assurance that Anatolius is orthodox, and begs him to assist her husband in arranging for the Synod, and announces that Flavian's body has been buried in the Basilica of the Apostles at Constantinople and the exiled bishops restored.)

LETTER LXXVIII. LEO'S ANSWER TO MARCIANUS.

(Briefly thanking him.)

LETTER LXXIX. TO PULCHERIA AUGUSTA.

Leo, bishop of the city of Rome to Pulcheria Augusta.

I. He Rejoices at Pulcheria's Zeal Both Against Nestorius and Eutyches.

That which we have always anticipated concerning your Grace's holy purposes, we have now proved fully true, viz. that, however varied may be the attacks of wicked men upon the Christian Faith, yet when you are present and prepared by the Lord for its defence, it cannot be disturbed. For God will not forsake either the mystery of His mercy or the deserts of your labours, whereby you long ago repelled the crafty foe of our holy religion from the very vitals of the Church: when the impiety of Nestorius failed to maintain his heresy because it did not escape you the handmaid and pupil of the Truth, how much poison was instilled into simple folk by the coloured falsehoods of that glib fellow. And the sequel to that mighty struggle was that through your vigilance the things which the devil contrived by means of Eutyches, did not escape detection, and they who had chosen to themselves one side in the twofold heresy, were overthrown by the one and undivided power of the catholic Faith. This then is your second victory over the destruction of Eutyches' error: and, if he had had any soundness of mind, that error having been once and long ago routed and put to confusion in the person of his instigators, he would easily have been able to avoid the attempt to rekindle into life the smouldering ashes, and thus only share the lot of those, whose example he had followed, most glorious Augusta. We desire, therefore, to leap for joy and to pay due vows for your clemency's prosperity to God, who has already bestowed on you a double palm and crown through all the parts of the world, in which the Lord's Gospel is proclaimed.

II. He Thanks Her for Her Aid to the Catholic Cause, and Explains His Wishes About the Restoration of the Lapsed Bishops.

Your clemency must know, therefore, that the whole church of Rome is highly grateful for all your faithful deeds, whether that you have with pious zeal helped our representatives throughout and brought back the catholic priests, who had been expelled from their churches by an unjust sentence, or that you have procured the restoration with due honour of the remains of that innocent and holy priest, Flavian, of holy memory, to the church, which he ruled so well. In all which things assuredly your glory is increased manifold, so long as you venerate the saints according to their deserts, and are anxious that the thorns and weeds should be removed from the Lord's field. But we learn as well from the account of our deputies as from that of my brother and fellow-bishop, Anatolius, whom you graciously recommend to me, that certain bishops crave reconciliation for those who seem to have given their consent to matters of heresy, and desire catholic communion for them: to whose request we grant effect on condition that the boon of peace should not be vouchsafed them till, our deputies acting in concert with the aforesaid bishop, they are corrected, and with their own hand condemn their evil doings; because our Christian religion requires boil that true justice should constrain the obstinate, and love not reject the penitent.

III. He Commends Certain Bishops and Churches to Her Care.

And because we know how much pious care your Grace deigns to bestow on catholic priests, we have ordered that you should be informed that my brother and fellow-bishop, Eusebius, is living with us, and sharing our communion, whose church we commend to you; for he that is improperly asserted to have been elected in his place, is said to be ravaging it. And this too we ask of you, Grace, which we doubt not you will do of your own free will, to extend the favour which is due as well to my brother and fellow-bishop, Julian, as to the clergy of Constantinople, who clung to the holy Flavian with faithful loyalty. On all things we have instructed your Grace by our deputies as to what ought to be done or arranged. Dated April 13, in the consulship of the illustrious Adelfius (451).

LETTER LXXX. (TO ANATOLIUS, BISHOP OF CONSTANTINOPLE.)

Leo, the bishop, to Anatolius, the bishop.

I. He Rejoices at Anatolius Having Proved Himself Orthodox.

We rejoice in the Lord and glory in the gift of His Grace, Who has shown you a follower of Gospel-teaching as we have found from your letter, beloved, and our brothers' account whom we sent to Constantinople: for now through the approved faith of the priest, we are justifying in presuming that the whole church committed to him will have no wrinkle nor spot of error, as says the Apostle, "for I have espoused you to one husband to present you a pure virgin to Christ ." For that virgin is the Church, the spouse of one husband Christ, who suffers herself to be corrupted by no error, so that through the whole world we have one entire and pure communion in which we now welcome you as a fellow, beloved, and give our approval to the order of proceedings which we have received, ratified, as was proper, with the necessary signatures. In order, therefore, that your spirit in turn, beloved, might be strengthened by words of ours, we sent back after the Easter festival with our letters, our sons, Casterius, the Presbyter, and Patricius and Asclepias, the Deacons, who brought your writings to us, informing you, as we said above, that we rejoice at the peace of the church of Constantinople, on which we have ever spent such care that we wish it to be polluted by no heretical deceit.

II. The Penitents Among the Backsliding Bishops are to Be Received Back into Full Communion Upon Some Plan to Be Settled by Anatolius and Leo's Delegates.

But concerning the brethren whom we learn from your letters, and from our delegates' ac count, to be desirous of communion with us, on the ground of their sorrow that they did not remain constant against violence and intimidation, but gave their assent to another's crime when terror had so bewildered them, that with hasty acquiescence they ministered to the condemnation of the catholic and guiltless bishop (Flavian), and to the acceptance of the detestable heresy (of Eutyches), we approve of that which was determined upon in the presence and with the co operation of our delegates, viz., that they should be content meanwhile with the communion of their own churches, but we wish our delegates whom we have sent to consult with you, and come to some arrangement whereby those who condemn their ill-doings with full assurances of penitence, and choose rather to accuse than to defend themselves, may be gladdened by being at peace and in communion with us; on condition that what has been received against the catholic Faith is first condemned with complete anathema. For otherwise in the Church of God, which is Christ's Body, there are neither valid priesthoods nor true sacrifices, unless in the reality of our nature the true High Priest makes atonement for us, and the true Blood of the spotless Lamb makes us clean. For although He be set on the Father's right hand, yet in the same flesh which He took from the Virgin, he carries on the mystery of propitiation, as says the Apostle, "Christ Jesus Who died, yea, Who also rose, Who is on the right hand of God, Who also maketh intercession for us ." For our kindness cannot be blamed in any case where we receive those who give assurance of penitence, and at whose deception we were grieved. The boon of communion with us, therefore, must neither harshly be withheld nor rashly granted, because as it is fully consistent with our religion to treat the oppressed with a Christlike charity, so it is fair to lay the full blame upon the authors of the disturbance.

III. The Names of Dioscorus, Juvenal, and Eustathius are Not to Be Read Aloud at the Holy Altar.

Concerning the reading out of the names of Dioscorus, Juvenal, and Eustathius at the holy altar, it beseems you, beloved, to observe that which our friends who were there present said ought to be done, and which is consistent with the honourable memory of S. Flavian, and will not turn the minds of the laity away from you. For it is very wrong and unbecoming that those who have harassed innocent catholics with their attacks, should be mingled indiscriminately with the names of the saints, seeing that by not forsaking their condemned heresy, they condemn themselves by their perversity: such men should either be chastised for their unfaithfulness; or strive hard after forgiveness.

IV. One or Two Instructions About Individuals.

But our brother and fellow-bishop, Julian, and the clergy who adhered to Flavian of holy memory, rendering him faithful service, we wish to adhere to you also beloved, that they may know him who we are sure lives by the merits of his faith with our God to be present with them in you. We wish you to know this too, beloved, that our brother and fellow-bishop Eusebius , who for the Faith's sake endured many dangers and toils, is at present staying with us and continuing in our communion; whose church we would that your care should protect, that nothing may be destroyed in his absence, and no one may venture to injure him in anything until he come to you bearing a letter from us. And that our or rather all Christian people's affection for you may be stirred up in greater measure, we wish this that we have written to you, beloved, to come to all men's knowledge, that they who serve our God may give thanks for the consummation of the peace of the Apostolic See with you. But on other matters and persons you will be more fully instructed, beloved, by the letter you will have received through our delegates. Dated 13 April, in the consulship of the illustrious Adelfius (451).

LETTER LXXXI. TO BISHOP JULIAN.

(Warning him to be circumspect in receiving the lapsed.)

LETTER LXXXII. TO MARCLAN AUGUSTUS.

I. After Congratulating the Emperor on His Noble Conduct, He Deprecates Random Inquiries into the Tenets of the Faith.

Although I have replied already to your Grace by the hand of the Constantinopolitan clergy, yet on receiving your clemency's mercy through the illustrious prefect of the city, my son Tatian, I found still greater cause for congratulation, because I have learnt your strong eagerness for the Church's peace. And this holy desire as in fairness it deserves, secures for your empire the same happy condition as you seek for religion. For when the Spirit of God establishes harmony among Christian princes, a twofold confidence is produced throughout the world, because the progress of love and faith makes the power of their arms in both directions unconquerable, so that God being propitiated by one confession, the falseness of heretics and the enmity of barbarians are simultaneously overthrown, most glorious Emperor. The hope, therefore, of heavenly aid being increased through the Emperor's friendship, I venture with the greater confidence to appeal to your Grace on behalf of the mystery of man's salvation, not to allow any one in vain and presumptuous craftiness to inquire what must be held, as if it were uncertain. And although we may not in a single word dissent from the teaching of the Gospels and Apostles, nor entertain any opinion on the Divine Scriptures different to what the blessed Apostles and our Fathers learnt and taught, now in these latter days unlearned and blasphemous inquiries are set on foot, which of old the Holy Spirit crushed by the disciples of the Truth, so soon as the devil aroused them in hearts which were suited to his purpose.

II. The Points to Be Settled are Only Which of the Lapsed Shall Be Restored, and on What Terms.

But it is most inopportune that through the foolishness of a few we should be brought once more into hazardous opinions, and to the warfare of carnal disputes, as if the wrangle was to be revived, and we had to settle whether Eutyches held blasphemous views, and whether Dioscorus gave wrong judgment, who in condemning Flavian of holy memory struck his own death-blow, and involved the simpler folk in the same destruction. And now that many, as we have ascertained, have betoken themselves to the means of amendment, and entreat forgiveness for their weak hastiness, we have to determine not the character of the Faith, but whose prayers we shall receive, and on what terms. And hence that most religious anxiety which you deign to feel for the proclamation of a Synod, shall have fully and timely put before it all that I judge pertinent to the needs of the case, by means of the deputies who will with all speed, if God permit, reach your Grace. Dated the 23rd of April in the consulship of the illustrious Adelfius (451).

LETTER LXXXIII. TO THE SAME MARCIAN.

(Congratulating him on his benefits to the Church, and deprecating a Synod as inopportune.)

LETTER LXXXIV. TO PULCHERIA AUGUSTA.

(Announcing the despatch of his legates to deal with the lapsed, and asking that Eutyches should be superseded in his monastery by a catholic, and dismissed from Constantinople.)

LETTER LXXXV. TO ANATOLIUS, BISHOP OF CONSTANTINOPLE.

Leo, the bishop, to the bishop Anatolius.

I. Anatolius with Leo's Delegates is to Settle the Question of the Receiving Back of Those Who Had Temporarily Gone Astray After Eutyches.

Although I hope, beloved, you are devoted to every good work, yet that your activity may be rendered the more effective, it was needful and fitting to despatch my brothers Lucentius the bishop and Basil the presbyter, as we promised, to ally themselves with you, beloved, that nothing may be done either indecisively or lazily in matters, which concern the welfare of the universal Church; for as long as you are on the spot, to whom we have entrusted the carrying out of our will, all things can be conducted with such moderation that the claims of neither kindness nor justice may be neglected, but without the accepting of persons, the Divine judgment may be considered in everything. But that this may be properly observed and guarded, the integrity of the catholic Faith must first of all be preserved, and, because in all cases "narrow" and steep "is the way that leadeth unto life ," there must be no deviation from its track, either to the right hand or to the left. And because the evangelical and Apostolic Faith has to combat all errors, on the one side casting down Nestorius, on the other crushing Eutyches and his accomplices, remember the need of observing this rule, that all those who in that synod , which cannot, and does not deserve to have the name of Synod, and in which Dioscorus displayed his bad feeling, and

Juvenal his ignorance, grieve as we learn from your account, beloved, that they were conquered by fear, and being overcome with terror, were able to be forced to assent to that iniquitous judgment, and who now desire to obtain catholic communion, are to receive the peace of the brethren after due assurance of repentance, on condition that in no doubtful terms they anathematize, execrate and condemn Eutyches and his dogma and his adherents.

II. The Case of the More Serious Offenders Must Be Reserved for the Present.

But concerning those who have sinned more gravely in this matter, and claimed for themselves a higher place in the same unhappy synod, in order to irritate the simple minds of their lowlier brethren by their pernicious arrogance, if they return to their right mind, and ceasing to defend their action, turn themselves to the condemnation of their particular error, if these men give such assurance of penitence as shall seem indisputable, let their case be reserved for the maturer deliberations of the Apostolic See, that when all things have been sifted and weighed, the right conclusion may be arrived at about their real actions. And in the Church over which the Lord has willed you to rule, let none such as we have already written have their names read at the altar until the course of events shows what ought to be determined concerning them.

III. Anatolius is Requested to Co-Operate Loyally with Leo's Delegates.

But concerning the address presented to us by your clergy, beloved, there is no need to put my sentiments into a letter: it is sufficient to entrust all to my delegates, whose words shall carefully instruct you on every point. And so, dearest brother, do your endeavour with these brethren whom we have chosen as suitable agents in so great a matter faithfully and effectually to carry out what is agreeable to the Church of God: especially as the very nature of the case, and the promise of Divine aid incite you, and our most gracious princes show such holy faith, such religious devotion, that we find in them not only the general sympathy of Christians, but even that of the priesthood. Who assuredly in accordance with that piety, whereby they boast themselves to be servants of God, will receive all your suggestions for the benefit of the catholic Faith in a worthy spirit, so that by their aid also the peace of Christendom can be restored and wicked error destroyed. And if on any points more advice is needed, let word be quickly sent to us, that after investigating the nature of the case, we may carefully prescribe the rightful measures. Dated 9th of June in the consulship of the illustrious Adelfius (451).

LETTER LXXXVI. TO JULIAN, BISHOP OF COS.

(Begging him for friendship's and the Church's sake to assist his legates in quelling the remnants of heresy.)

LETTER LXXXVII. TO ANATOLIUS, BISHOP OF CONSTANTINOPLE.

(Commending to him two presbyters, Basil and John, who being accused of heresy had come to Rome, and quite convinced Leo of their orthodoxy.)

LETTER LXXXVIII. TO PASCHASINUS, BISHOP OF LILYBAEUM.

Leo, the bishop, to Paschasinus, bishop of Lilybaeum.

I. He Sends a Copy of the Tome and Still Further Explains the Heterodoxy of Eutyches.

Although I doubt not all the sources of scandal are fully known to you, brother, which have arisen in the churches of the East about the Incarnation of our Lord Jesus Christ, yet, test anything might have chanced to escape your care, I have despatched for your attentive perusal and study our letter , which deals with this matter in the fullest way, which we sent to Flavian of holy memory, and which the universal Church has accepted; in order that, understanding how completely this whole blasphemous error has with God's aid been destroyed, you yourself also in your love towards God may show the same spirit, and know that they are utterly to be abhorred, who, following the blasphemy and madness of Eutyches, have dared to say there are not two natures, i.e. perfect Godhead and perfect manhood, in our Lord, the only-begotten Son of God, who took upon Himself to restore mankind; and think they can deceive our wariness by saying they believe the one nature of the Word to be Incarnate, whereas the Word of God in the Godhead of the Father, and of Himself, and of the Holy Spirit has indeed one nature; but when He took on Him the reality of our flesh, our nature also was united to His unchangeable substance: for even Incarnation could not be spoken of, unless the Word took on Him the flesh. And this taking on of flesh forms so complete a union, that not only in the blessed Virgin's child-bearing, but also in her conception, no division must be imagined between the Godhead and the life-endowed flesh , since in the unity of person the Godhead and the manhood came together both in the conception and in the childbearing of the Virgin.

II. Eutyches Might Have Been Warned by Tire Fate of Former Heretics.

A like blasphemy, therefore, is to be abhorred in Eutyches, as was once condemned and overthrown by the Fathers in former heretics: and their example ought to have benefited this foolish fellow, in putting him on his guard against that which he could not grasp by his own sense, lest he should render void the peerless mystery of our salvation by denying the reality of human flesh in our Lord Jesus Christ. For, if there is not in Him true and perfect human nature, there is no taking of us upon Him, and the whole of our belief and teaching according to his heresy is emptiness and lying. But because the Truth does not lie and the Godhead is not possible, there abides in God the Word both substances in one Person, and the Church confesses her Saviour in such a way as to acknowledge Him both impossible in Godhead and possible in flesh, as says the Apostle, "although He was crucified through (our) weakness, yet He lives by the power of God ."

III. He Sends Quotations from the Fathers, and Announces that the Churches of the East Have Accepted the Tome.

And in order that you may be the fuller instructed in all things, beloved, I have sent you certain quotations from our holy Fathers, that you may clearly gather what they felt and what they preached to the churches about the mystery of the Lord's Incarnation, which quotations our deputies produced at Constantinople also together with our epistle. And you must understand that the whole church of Constantinople, with all the monasteries and many bishops, have given their assent to it, and by their subscription have anathematized Nestorius and Eutyches with their dogmas. You must also understand that I have recently received the bishop of Constantinople's letter, which states that the bishop of Antioch has sent instructions to all the bishops throughout his provinces, and gained their assent to my epistle, and their condemnation of Nestorius and Eutyches in like manner.

IV. He Asks Him to Settle the Discrepancy Between the Alexandrine and the Roman Calculation of Easter for 455, by Consulting the Proper Authority.

This also we think necessary to enjoin upon your care that you should diligently inquire in those quarters where you are sure of information concerning that point in the reckoning of Easter, which we have found in the table of Theophilus, and which greatly exercises us, and that you should discuss with those who are learned in such calculations, as to the date, when the day of the Lord's resurrection should be held four years hence. For, whereas the next Easter is to be held by God's goodness on March 23rd, the year after on April 12th, the year after that on April 4th, Theophilus of holy memory has fixed April 24th to be observed in 455, which we find to be quite contrary to the rule of the Church; but in our Easter cycles as you know very well, Easter that year is set down to be kept on April 17th. And therefore, that all our doubts may be removed, we beg you carefully to discuss this point with the best authorities, that for the future we may avoid this kind of mistake. Dated June 24th in the consulship of the illustrious Adelfius (451).

LETTER LXXXIX. TO MARCIAN AUGUSTUS.

(Appointing Paschasinus the bishop and Boniface a presbyter, and Julian the bishop, his representatives at the Synod, as the Emperor is determined it should be held at once.)

LETTER XC. TO MARCIAN AUGUSTUS.

(Assenting perforce to the meeting of the Synod, but begging him to see that the Faith be not discussed as doubtful.)

LETTER XCI. TO ANATOLIUS, BISHOP OF CONSTANTINOPLE.

(Telling him that he has appointed Paschasinus, Boniface, and Julian, bishop of Cos, to represent him at the Synod.)

LETTER XCII. TO JULIAN, BISHOP OF COS.

(Asking him to act as one of his representatives at the Synod.)

LETTER XCIII. TO THE SYNOD OF CHALCEDON.

Leo, the bishop of the city of Rome, to the holy Synod, assembled at Nicaea .

I. He Excuses His Absence from the Synod, and Introduces His Representatives.

I had indeed prayed, dearly beloved, on behalf of my dear colleagues that all the Lord's priests would persist in united devotion to the catholic Faith, and that no one would be misled by favour or fear of secular powers into departure from the way of Truth; but because many things often occur to produce penitence and God's mercy transcends the faults of delinquents, and vengeance is postponed in order that reformation may have place, we must make much of our most merciful prince's piously intentioned Council, in which he has desired your holy brotherhood to assemble for the purpose of destroying the snares of the devil and restoring the peace of the Church, so far respecting the rights and dignity of the most blessed Apostle Peter as to invite us too by letter to vouchsafe our presence at your venerable Synod. That indeed is not permitted either by the needs of the times or by any precedent. Yet in these brethren, that is Paschasinus and Lucentius, bishops, Boniface and Basil, presbyters, who have been deputed by the Apostolic See, let your brotherhood reckon that I am presiding at the Synod; for my presence is not withdrawn from you, who am now represented by my vicars, and have this long time been really with you in the proclaiming of the catholic Faith: so that you who cannot help knowing what we believe in accordance with ancient tradition, cannot doubt what we desire.

II. He Entreats Them to Re-State the Faith as Laid Down in the Tome.

Wherefore, brethren most dear, let all attempts at impugning the Divinely-inspired Faith be entirely put down, and the vain unbelief of heretics be laid to rest: and let not that be defended which may not be believed: since in accordance with the authoritative statements of the Gospel, in accordance with the utterances of the prophets, and the teaching of the Apostles, with the greatest fulness and clearness in the letter which we sent to bishop Flavian of happy memory, it has been laid down what is the loyal and pure confession upon the mystery of our Lord Jesus Christ's Incarnation.

III. The Ejected Bishops Must Be Restored, and the Nestorian Canons Retain Their Force.

But because we know full well that through evil jealousies the state of many churches has been disturbed, and a large number of bishops have been driven from their Sees for not receiving the heresy and conveyed into exile, while others have been put into their places though yet alive, to these wounds first of all must the healing of justice be applied, nor must any one be deprived of his own possession that some one else may enjoy it: for if, as we desire, all forsake their error, no one need lose his present rank, and those who have laboured for the Faith ought to have their rights restored with every privilege. Let the decrees specially directed against Nestorius of the former Synod of Ephesus, at which bishop Cyril of holy memory presided; still retain their force, lest the heresy then condemned flatter itself in aught because Eutyches is visited with condign execration. For the purity of the Faith and doctrine which we proclaim in the same spirit as our holy Fathers, equally condemns and impugns the Nestorian and the Eutychian misbelief with its supporters. Farewell in the Lord, brethren most dear. Dated 26th , of June, in the consulship of the illustrious Adelfius (451).

LETTER XCIV. TO MARCIAN AUGUSTUS.

(Commending his legates to him and praying for the full success of the Synod, if it adhere to the Faith once delivered to the saints.)

LETTER XCV. TO PULCHERIA AUGUSTA BY THE HAND OF THEOCTISTUS THE MAGISTRIAN.

Leo, the bishop to Pulcheria Augusta.

I. He Informs the Empress that He Has Loyally Recognized the Council Ordered by Her, and Sent Representatives with Letters to It.

Your clemency's religious care which you unceasingly bestow on the catholic Faith, I recognize in everything, and give God thanks at seeing you take such interest in the universal Church, that I can confidently suggest what I think agreeable to justice and kindness, and so what thus far your pious zeal through the mercy of Christ has irreproachably accomplished, may the more speedily be brought to an issue which we shall be thankful for, O most noble Augusta. Your clemency's command, therefore, that a Synod should be held at Nicaea , and your gently expressed refusal of my request that it should be held in Italy, so that all the bishops in our parts might be summoned and assemble, if the state of affairs had permitted them, I have received in a spirit so far removed from scorn as to nominate two of my fellow-bishops and fellow-presbyters respectively to represent me, sending also to the venerable synod an appropriate missive from which the brotherhood therein assembled might learn the standard necessary to be maintained in their decision, lest any rashness should do detriment either to the rules of the Faith, or to the provisions of the canons, or to the remedies required by the spirit of loving kindness.

II. In the Settlement of This Matter that Moderation Must Be Observed Which Was Entirely Absent at Ephesus.

For, as I have very often stated in letters from the beginning of this matter, I have desired that such moderation should be observed in the midst of discordant views and carnal jealousies that, whilst nothing should be allowed to be wrested from or added to the purity of the Faith, yet the remedy of pardon should be granted to those who return to unity and peace. Because the works of the devil are then more effectually destroyed when men's hearts are recalled to the love of God and their neighbours. But how contrary to my warnings and entreaties were their actions then, it is a long story to explain, nor is the need to put down in the pages of a letter all that was allowed to be perpetrated in that meeting, not of judges but of robbers, at Ephesus; where the chief men of the synod spared neither those brethren who opposed them nor those who assented to them, seeing that for the breaking down of the catholic Faith and the strengthening of execrable heresy, they stripped some of their rightful rank and tainted others with complicity in guilt; and surely their cruelty was worse to those whom by persuasion they divorced from innocence, than to those whom by persecution they made blessed confessors.

III. Those Who Recant Their Error Must Be Treated with Forbearance.

And yet because such men have harmed themselves most by their wrong-doing, and because the greater the wounds, the more careful must be the application of the remedy, I have never in any letter maintained that pardon must be withheld even from them if they came to their right mind. And although we unchangeably abhor their heresy, which is the greatest enemy of Christian religion, yet the men themselves, if they without any doubt amend their ways and clear themselves by full assurances of repentance, we do not judge to be outcasts from the unspeakable mercy of God: but rather we lament with those that lament, "we weep with those that weep ," and obey the requirements of justice in deposing without neglecting the remedies of loving-kindness: and this, as your piety knows, is not a mere word-promise, but is also borne out by our actions, inasmuch as nearly all who had been either misled or forced into assenting to the presiding bishops, by rescinding what they had decreed and by condemning what they had written, have obtained complete acquittal from guilt and the boon of Apostolic peace.

IV. Even the Authors of the Mischief May Find Room Far Forgiveness by Repentance.

If, therefore, your clemency deigns to reflect upon my motives, it will be satisfied that I have acted throughout with the design of bringing about the abolition of the heresy without the loss of one soul; and that in the case of the authors of these cruel disturbances I have modified my practice somewhat in order that their slow minds might be aroused by some feelings of compunction to ask for lenient treatment. For although since their decision, which is no less blasphemous than unjust, they cannot be held in such honour by the catholic brotherhood as they once were, yet they still retain their sees and their rank as bishops, with the prospect either of receiving the peace of the whole Church, after true and necessary signs of repentance or, if (which God forbid) they persist in their heresy, of reaping the reward of their misbelief. Dated 20th of July, in the consulship of the illustrious Adelfius (451).

LETTER XCVI. TO RAVENNIUS, BISHOP OF ARLES.

(Requesting him to keep Easter on March 23 in 452.)

LETTER XCVII. FROM EUSEBIUS, BISHOP OF MILAN, TO LEO.

(Informing him that the Tome has been approved by the Synod of Milan, and containing the subscriptions of the bishops there assembled.)

LETTER XCVIII. FROM THE SYNOD OF CHALCEDON TO LEO.

The great and holy and universal Synod, which by the grace of God and the sanction of our most pious and Christ-loving Emperors has been gathered together in the metropolis of Chalcedon in the province of Bithynia, to the most holy and blessed archbishop of Rome, Leo.

I. They Congratulate Leo on Taking the Foremost Part in Maintaining the Faith.

"Our mouth was filled with joy and our tongue with exultation ." This prophecy grace has fitly appropriated to us for whom the security of religion is ensured. For what is a greater incentive to cheerfulness than the Faith? what better inducement to exultation than the Divine knowledge which the Saviour Himself gave us from above for salvation, saying, "go ye and make disciples of all the nations, baptizing them into the name of the Father, and of the Son, and of the Holy Ghost, teaching them to observe all things that I have enjoined you ." And this golden chain leading down from the Author of the command to us, you yourself have stedfastly preserved, being set as the mouthpiece unto all of the blessed Peter, and imparting the blessedness of his Faith unto all. Whence we too, wisely taking you as our guide in all that is good, have shown to the sons of the Church their inheritance of Truth, not giving our instruction each singly and in secret, but making known our confession of the Faith in conceit, with one consent and agreement And we were all delighted, revelling, as at an imperial banquet, in the spiritual food, which Christ supplied to us through your letter: and we seemed to see the Heavenly Bridegroom actually present with us. For if "where two or three are gathered together in His name," He has said that "there He is in the midst of them ," must He not have been much more particularly present with 520 priests, who preferred the spread of knowledge concerning Him to their country and their ease? Of whom you were, chief, as the head to the members, showing your goodwill in the person of those who represented you; whilst our religious Emperors presided to the furtherance of due order, inviting us to restore the doctrinal fabric of the Church, even as Zerubbabel invited Joshua to rebuild Jerusalem .

II. They Detail Dioscorus' Wicked Acts.

And the adversary would have been like a wild beast outside the fold, roaring to himself and unable to seize any one, had not the late bishop of Alexandria thrown himself for a prey to him, who, though he had done many terrible things before, eclipsed the former by the latter deeds; for contrary to all the injunctions of the canons, he deposed that blessed shepherd of the saints at Constantinople, Flavian, who displayed such Apostolic faith, and the most pious bishop Eusebius, and acquitted by his terror-won votes Eutyches, who had been condemned for heresy, and restored to him the dignity which your holiness had taken away from him as unworthy of it, and like the strangest of wild beasts, falling upon the vine which he found in the finest condition, He uprooted it and brought in that which had been cast away as unfruitful, and those who acted like true shepherds he cut off, and set over the flocks those who had shown themselves wolves: and besides all this he stretched forth his fury even against him who had been charged with the custody of the vine by the Saviour, we mean of course your holiness, and purposed excommunication against one who had at heart the unifying of the Church. And instead of showing penitence for this, instead of begging mercy with tears, he exulted as if over virtuous actions, rejecting your holiness' letter and resisting all the dogmas of the Truth.

III. We Have Deposed Eutyches, Treating Him as Mercifully as We Could.

And we ought to have left him in the position where he had placed himself: but, since we profess the teaching of the Saviour "who wishes all men to be saved and to come to a knowledge of the Truth ," as a fact we took pains to carry out this merciful policy towards him, and called him in brotherly fashion to judgment, not as if trying to cut him off but affording him room for defence and healing; and we prayed that he might be victorious over the many charges they had brought against him, in order that we might conclude our meeting in peace and happiness and Satan might gain no advantage over us. But he, being absolutely convicted by his own conscience , by shirking the trial gave countenance to the accusations and rejected the three lawful summonses he received. In consequence of which, we ratified with such moderation as we could the vote which he had passed against himself by his blunders, stripping the wolf of his shepherd's skin, which he had long been convicted of wearing for a pretence. Thereupon our troubles ceased and straightway a time of welcome happiness set in: and having pulled up one tare, we filled the whole world to our delight with pure grain: and having received, as it were, full power to rootup and to plant, we limited the up-rooting to one and carefully plant a crop of good fruit. For it was God who worked, and the triumphant Euphemia who crowned the meeting as for a bridal , and who, taking our definition of the Faith as her own confession, presented it to her Bridegroom by our most religious Emperor and Christ-loving Empress, appeasing all the tumult of opponents and establishing our confession of the Truth asacceptable to Him, and with hand and tonguesetting her seal to the votes of us all in proclamation thereof These are the things we have done, with you present in the spirit and known to approve of us as brethren, and all but visible to us through the wisdom of your representatives.

IV. They Announce Their Decision that Constantinople Should Take Precedence Next to Rome, and Ask Leo's Consent to It.

And we further inform you that we have decided on other things also for the good management and stability of church matters, being persuaded that your holiness will accept and ratify them, when you are told. The long prevailing custom, which the holy Church of God at Constantinople had of ordaining metropolitans for the provinces of Asia, Pontus and Thrace, we have now ratified by the votes of the Synod, not so much by way of conferring a privilege on the See of Constantinople as to provide for the good government of those cities, because of the frequent disorders that arise on the death of their bishops, both clergy and laity being then without a leader and disturbing church order. And this has not escaped your holiness, particularly in the case of Ephesus, which has often caused you annoyance . We have ratified also the canon of the 150 holy Fathers who met at Constantinople in the time of the great Theodosius of holy memory, which ordains that after your most holy and Apostolic See, the See of Constantinople shall take precedence, being placed second: for we are persuaded that with your usual care for others you have often extended that Apostolic prestige which belongs to you, to the church in Constantinople also, by virtue of your great disinterestedness in sharing all your own good things with your spiritual kinsfolk. Accordingly vouchsafe most holy and blessed father to accept as your own wish, and as conducing to good government the things which we have resolved on for the removal of al confusion and the confirmation of church order. For your holiness' delegates, the most pious bishops Paschasinus and Lucentius, and with them the right Godly presbyter Boniface, attempted vehemently to resist these decisions, from a strong desire that this good work also should start from your foresight, in order that the establishment of good order as well as of the Faith should be put to your account. For we duly regarding our most devout and Christ loving Emperors, who delight therein, and the illustrious senate and, so to say, the whole imperial city, considered it opportune to use the meeting of this ecumenical Synod for the ratification of your honour, and confidently corroborated this decision as if it were initiated by you with your customary fostering zeal, knowing that every success of the children rebounds to the parent's glory. Accordingly, we entreat you, honour our decision by your assent, and as we have yielded to the head our agreement on things honourable, so may the head also fulfil for the children what is fitting. For thus will our pious Emperors be treated with due regard, who have ratified your holiness' judgment as law, and the See of Constantinople will receive its recompense for having always displayed such loyalty on matters of religion towards you, and for having so zealously linked itself to you in full agreement. But that you may know that we have done nothing for favour or in hatred, but as being guided by the Divine Will, we have made known to you the whole scope of our proceedings to strengthen our position and to ratify and establish what we have done .

LETTER XCIX. FROM RAVENNUS AND OTHER GALLIC BISHOPS.

(Announcing that the Tome has been accepted in Gaul also as a definitive statement of the Faith, with the bishops' subscriptions.)

LETTER C. FROM THE EMPEROR MARCIAN.

(Dealing much more briefly with the same subjects as Letter XCVIII. above.)

LETTER CI. FROM ANATOLIUS, BISHOP OF CONSTANTINOPLE, TO LEO.

(Dealing with much the same subjects as Letter XCVIII. from Anatolius' own standpoint: Chap. iii. is translated in extenso as illustrating XCVIII., chap. iii.)

III. He Describes the Circumstances Under Which the Doctrine of the Incarnation Had Been Formulated by the Synod.

But since after passing judgment upon him we had to come to an agreement with prayers and tears upon a definition of the right Faith; for that was the chief reason for the Emperor's summoning the holy Synod, at which your holiness was present in the spirit with us, and wrought with us by the God-fearing men who were sent from you; we, having the protection of the most holy and beautiful martyr Euphemia, have all given ourselves to this important matter with all deliberateness. And as the occasion demanded that all the assembled holy bishops should publish a unanimous de cision for clearness and for an explicit statement of the Faith in our Lord-Jesus Christ the Lord God who is found and revealed even to those who seek Him not, yes, even to those who ask not for Him , in spite of some attempts to resist at first, nevertheless showed us His Truth, and ordained that it should be written down and proclaimed by all unanimously and without gainsaying, which thus confirmed the souls of the strong, and invited into the way of Truth all who were swerving therefrom. And, indeed, after unanimously setting our names to this document, we who have assembled in this ecumenical Synod in the name of the Faith of the same most holy and triumphant martyr, Euphemia, and of our most religious and Christ-loving Emperor Marcian, and our most religious and in all things most faithful daughter the Empress Pulcheria Augusta, with prayer and joy and happiness, having laid on the holy altar the definition written in accordance with your holy epistle for the confirmation of our Fathers' Faith, presented it to their pious care; for thus they had asked to receive it, and, having received it, they glorified with us their Master Christ, who had driven away all the mist of heresy and had graciously made clear the word of Truth. And in this way was simultaneously established the peace of the Church and the agreement of the priests concerning the pure Faith by the Saviour's mercy.

LETTER CII. TO THE GALLIC BISHOPS.

(Thanking them for their letter (viz. XCIX.) to him, and announcing the result of the Synod of Chalcedon.)

LETTER CIII. TO THE GALLIC BISHOPS.

(Written later: enclosing a copy of the sentence against Eutyches and Dioscorus.)

LETTER CIV. LEO, THE BISHOP, TO MARCIAN AUGUSTUS.

(To Marcian Augustus, about the presumption of Anatolius, by the hand of Lucian the bishop and Basil the deacon.)

I. He Congratulates the Emperor on His Share in the Triumph of the Catholic Faith.

By the great bounty of God's mercy the joys of the whole catholic Church were multiplied when through your clemency's holy and glorious zeal the most pestilential error was abolished among us; so that our labours the more speedily reached their desired end, because your God-serving Majesty had so faithfully and powerfully assisted them. For although the liberty of the Gospel had to be defended against certain dissentients in the power of the Holy Ghost, and through the instrumentality of the Apostolic See, yet God's grace has shown itself more manifestly (than we could have hoped) by vouchsafing to the world that in the victory of the Truth only the authors of the violation of the Faith should perish and the Church restored to her soundness. Accordingly the war which the enemy of our peace had stirred up, was so happily ended, the Lord's right hand fighting for us, that when Christ triumphed all His priests shared in the one victory, and when the light of Truth shone forth, only the shades of error, with its champions, were dispelled. For as in believing the Lord's own resurrection, with a view to strengthen the beginnings of Faith, confidence was much increased by the fact that certain Apostles doubted of the bodily reality of our Lord Jesus Christ, and by examining the prints of the nails and the wound of the spear with sight and touch removed the doubts of all by doubting; so now, too, while the misbelief of some is refuted, the hearts of all hesitaters are strengthened, and that which caused blindness to some few avails for the enlightenment of the whole body. In which work your clemency duly and rightly rejoices, having faithfully and properly provided that the devil's snares should do no hurt to the Eastern churches, but that to propitiate God everywhere more acceptable holocausts should be offered; seeing that through the mediator between God and man, the Man Christ Jesus, one and the self-same creed is held by people, priests, and princes, O most glorious son and most clement Augustus.

II. Considering All the Circumstances Anatolius Might Have Been Expected to Shaw More Modesty.

But now that these things, about which so great a concourse of priests assembled, have been brought to a good and desirable conclusion, I am surprised and grieved that the peace of the universal Church which had been divinely restored is again being disturbed by a spirit of self-seeking. For although my brother Anatolius seems necessarily to have consulted his own interest in forsaking the error of those who ordained him, and with salutary change of mind accepting the catholic Faith, yet he ought to have taken care not to mar by any depravity of desire that which he is known to have obtained through your means . For we, having regard to your faith and intervention, though his antecedents were suspicious on account of those who consecrated him , wished to be kind rather than just towards him, that by the use of healing measures we might assuage all disturbances which through the operations of the devil had been excited; and this ought to have made him modest rather than the opposite. For even if he had been lawfully and regularly ordained for conspicuous merit, and by the wisest selection yet without respect to the canons of the Fathers, the ordinances of the Holy Ghost, and the precedents of antiquity, no votes could have availed in his favour. I speak before a Christian and a truly religious, truly orthodox prince (when I say that) Anatolius the bishop detracts greatly from his proper merits in desiring undue aggrandizement.

III. The City of Constantinople, Royal Though It Be, Can Never Be Raised to Apostolic Rank.

Let the city of Constantinople have, as we desire, its high rank, and under the protection of God's right hand, long enjoy your clemency's rule. Yet things secular stand on a differentbasis from things divine: and there can be no sure building save on that rock which the Lord has laid for a foundation. He that covets what is not his due, loses what is his own. Let it be enough for Anatolius that by the aid of your piety and by my favour and approval he has obtained the bishopric of so great a city. Let him not disdain a city which is royal, though he cannot make it an Apostolic See ; and let him on no account hope that he can rise by doing injury to others. For the privileges of the churches determined by the canons of the holy Fathers, and fixed by the decrees of the Nicene Synod, cannot be overthrown by any unscrupulous act, nor disturbed by any innovation. And in the faithful execution of this task by the aid of Christ I am bound to display an unflinching devotion; for it is a charge entrusted to me, and it tends to my condemnation if the rules sanctioned by the Fathers and drawn up under the guidance of God's Spirit at the Synod of Nicaea for the government of the whole Church are violated with my connivance (which God forbid), and if the wishes of a single brother have more weight with me than the common good of the Lord's whole house.

IV. He Asks the Emperor to Express His Disapproval of Anatolius' Self-Seeking Spirit.

And therefore knowing that your glorious clemency is anxious for the peace of the Church and extends its protection and approval to those measures which conduce to pacific unity, I pray and beseech you with earnest entreaty to refuse all sanction and protection to these unscrupulous attempts against Christian unity and peace, and put a salutary check upon my brother Anatolius' desires, which will only injure himself, if he persists: that he may not desire things which are opposed to your glory and the needs of the times, and wish to be greater than his predecessors, and that it may be free for him to be as pre-eminent as he can in virtues, in which he will be partaker only if he prefer to be adorned with love rather than puffed up with ambition. The conception of this unwarrantable wish he ought indeed never to have received within the secret of his heart, but when my brothers and fellow-bishops who were there to represent me withstood him, he might at least have desisted from his unlawful self-seeking at their wholesome opposition. For both your gracious Majesty and his own letter affirm that the legates of the Apostolic See opposed him as they ought with the most justifiable resistance, so that his presumption was the less excusable in that not even when rebuked did it restrain itself.

V. And to Try to Bring Him to a Right Mind.

And hence, because it becomes your glorious faith that, as heresy was overthrown, God acting through you, so now all self-seeking should be defeated, do that which beseems both your Christian and your kingly goodness, so that the said bishop may obey the Fathers, further the cause of peace, and not think he had any right to ordain a bishop for the Church of Antioch, as he presumed to do without any precedent and contrary to the provisions of the canons: an act which from a longing to re-establish the Faith and in the interests of peace we have determined not to cancel. Let him abstain therefore from doing despite to the rules of the Church and shun unlawful excesses, lest in attempting things un-favourable to peace he cut himself off from the universal Church. I had much liefer love him for acting blamelessly than find him persist in this presumptuous frame of mind which may separate him from us all. My brother and fellow-bishop, Lucian, who with my son, Basil the deacon, brought your clemency's letter to me, has fulfilled the duties he undertook as legate with all devotion: for he must not be reckoned to have failed in his mission, the course of events having rather failed him. Dated the 22nd of May in the consulship of the illustrious Herculanus (452).

LETTER CV. (TO PULCHERIA AUGUSTA ABOUT THE SELF-SEEKING OF ANATOLIUS.)

Leo the bishop to Pulcheria Augusta.

I. He Congratutates the Empress on the Triumph of the Faith, But Regrets the Introduction of a New Controversy into the Church.

We rejoice ineffably with your Grace that the catholic Faith has been defended against heretics and peace restored to the whole Church through your clemency's holy and God-pleasing zeal: giving thanks to the Merciful and Almighty God that He has suffered none save those who loved darkness rather than light to be defrauded of the gospel-truth: so that by the removal of the mists of error the purest light might arise in the hearts of all, and that darkness-loving foe might not triumph over certain weak souls, whom not only those who stood unhurt but also those whom he had made to totter have overcome, and that by the abolition of error the true Faith might reign throughout the world, and "every tongue might confess that the Lord Jesus Christ is in the glory of God the Father ." But when the whole world had been confirmed in the unity of the Gospel, and the hearts of all priests had been guided into the same belief, it had been better that besides those matters for which the holy Synod was assembled, and which were brought to a satisfactory agreement through your Grace's zeal, nothing should be introduced to counteract so great an advantage, and that a council of bishops should not be made an occasion for the inopportune advancing of an illegitimate desire.

II. The Nicene Canons are Unalterable and Binding Universally.

For my brother and fellow-bishop Anatolius not sufficiently considering your Grace's kindness and the favour of my assent, whereby he gained the priesthood of the church of Constantinople, instead of rejoicing at what he has gained, has been inflamed with undue desires beyond the measure of his rank, believing that his intemperate self-seeking could be advanced by the assertion that certain persons had signified their assent thereto by an extorted signature: notwithstanding that my brethren and fellow-bishops, who represented me, faithfully and laudably expressed their dissent from these attempts which are doomed to speedy failure. For no one may venture upon anything in opposition to the enactments of the Fathers' canons which many long years ago in the city of Nicaea were founded upon the decrees of the Spirit, so that any one who wishes to pass any different decree injures himself rather than impairs them. And if all pontiffs will but keep them inviolate as they should, there will be perfect peace and complete harmony through all the churches: there will be no disagreements about rank, no disputes about ordinations, no controversies about privileges, no strifes about taking that which is another's; but by the fair law of love a reasonable order will be kept both in conduct and in office, and he will be truly great who is found free from all self-seeking, as the Lord says, "Whosoever will become greater among you, let him be your minister, and whosoever will be first among you shall be your slave; even as the Son of Man came not to be ministered unto but to minister ." And yet these precepts were at the time given to men who wished to rise from a mean estate and to pass from the lowest to the highest things; but what more does the ruler of the church of Constantinople covet than he has gained? or what will satisfy him, if the magnificence and renown of so great a city is not enough? It is too arrogant and intemperate thus to step beyond all proper bounds and trampling on ancient custom to wish to seize another's right: to increase one man's dignity at the expense of so many metropolitans' primacy, and to carry a new war of confusion into peaceful provinces which were long ago set at rest by the enactments of the holy Nicene Synod: to break through the venerable Fathers' decrees by alleging the consent of certain bishops, which even the course of so many years has not rendered effective. For it is boasted that this has been winked at for almost 60 years now, and the said bishop thinks that he is assisted thereby; but it is vain for him to look for assistance from that which, even if a man dared to wish for it, yet he could never obtain.

III. Only by Imitating His Predecessor Will He Regain Leo's Confidence: the Assent of the Bishops is Declared Null and Void.

Let him realize what a man he has succeeded, and expelling all the spirit of pride let him imitate Flavian's faith, Flavian's modesty, Flavian's humility, which has raised him right to a confessor's glory. If he will shine with his virtues, he will merit all praise, and in all quarters he will win an abundance of love not by seeking human advancement but by deserving Divine favour. And by this careful course I promise he will bind my heart also to him, and the love of the Apostolic See, which we have ever bestowed on the church of Constantinople, shall never be violated by any change. Because if sometimes rulers fall into errors through want of moderation, yet the churches of Christ do not lose their purity. But the bishops' assents, which are opposed to the regulations of the holy canons composed at Nicaea in conjunction with your faithful Grace, we do not recognize, and by the blessed Apostle Peter's authority we absolutely dis-annul in comprehensive terms, in all ecclesiastical cases obeying those laws which the Holy Ghost set forth by the 318 bishops for the pacific observance of all priests in such sort that even if a much greater number were to pass a different decree to theirs, whatever was opposed to their constitution would have to be held in no respect.

IV. He Requests the Empress to Give His Letter Her Favourable Consideration.

And so I request your Grace to receive in a worthy spirit this lengthy letter, in which I had to explain my views, at the hands of my brother and fellow-bishop Lucianus, who, as far as in him lies, has faithfully executed the anxious duties of his undertaking as my delegate, and of my son Basil, the deacon. And because it is your habit to labour for the peace and unity of the Church, for his soul's health keep my brother Anatolius the bishop, to whom I have extended my love by your advice, within those limits which shall be profitable to him, that as your clemency's glory is magnified already for the restoration of the Faith, so it may be published abroad for the restraint of self-seeking. Dated the 22nd of May, in the consulship of the illustrious Herculanus (452).

LETTER CVI. TO ANATOLIUS, BISHOP OF CONSTANTINOPLE, IN REBUKE OF HIS SELF-SEEKING.

Leo, the bishop, to Anatolius, the bishop.

I. He Commends Anatolius Far His Orthodoxy, But Condemns Him Far His Presumption.

Now that the light of Gospel Truth has been manifested, as we wished, through God's grace, and the night of most pestilential error has been dispelled from the universal Church, we are unspeakably glad in the Lord, because the difficult charge entrusted to us has been brought to the desired conclusion, even as the text of your letter announces, so that, according to the Apostle's teaching, "we all speak the same thing, and that there be no schisms among us: but that we be perfect in the same mind and in the same knowledge ." In devotion to which work we commend you, beloved, for taking part: for thus you benefited those who needed correction by your activity, and purged yourself from all complicity with the transgressors. For when your predecessor Flavian, of happy memory, was deposed for his defence of catholic Truth, not unjustly it was believed that your ordainers seemed to have consecrated one like themselves, contrary to the provision of the holy canons. But God's mercy was present in this, directing and confirming you, that you might make good use of bad beginnings, and show that you were promoted not by men's judgment, but by God's loving-kindness: and this may be accepted as true, on condition that you lose not the grace of this Divine gift by another cause of offence. For the catholic, and especially the Lord's priest, must not only be entangled in no error, but also be corrupted by no covetousness; for, as says the Holy Scripture, "Go not after thy lusts, and decline from thy desire " Many enticements of this world, many vanities must be resisted, that the perfection Of true self-discipline may be attained the first blemish of which is pride, the beginning of transgression and the origin of sin. For the mind greedy of power knows not either how to abstain from things forbidden nor to enjoy things permitted, so long as transgressions go unpunished and run into undisciplined and wicked excesses, and wrong doings are multiplied, which were only endured in our zeal for the restoration of the Faith and love of harmony .

II. Nothing Can Cancel or Modify the Nicene Canons.

And so after the not irreproachable beginning of your ordination, after the consecration of the bishop of Antioch, which you claimed for yourself contrary to the regulations of the canons. I grieve, beloved, that you have fallen into this too, that you should try to break down the most sacred constitutions of the Nicene canons : as if this opportunity had expressly offered itself to you for the See of Alexandria to lose its privilege of second place, and the church of Antioch to forego its right to being third in dignity, in order that when these places had been subjected to your jurisdiction, all metropolitan bishops might be deprived of their proper honour. By which unheard of and never before attempted excesses you went so far beyond yourself as to drag into an occasion of self-seeking, and force connivance from that holy Synod which the zeal of our most Christian prince had convened, solely to extinguish heresy and to confirm the catholic Faith: as if the unlawful wishes of a multitude could not be rejected, and that state of things which was truly ordained by the Holy Spirit in the canon of Nicaea could in any part be overruled by any one. Let no synodal councils flatter themselves upon the size of their assemblies, and let not any number of priests, however much larger, dare either to compare or to prefer themselves to those 318 bishops, seeing that the Synod of Nicaea is hollowed by God with such privilege, that whether by fewer or by more ecclesiastical judgments are supported, whatever is opposed to their authority is utterly destitute of all authority.

III. The Synod of Chalcedon, Which Met for One Purpose, Ought Never to Have Been Used for Another.

Accordingly these things which are found to be contrary to those most holy canons are exceedingly unprincipled and misguided. This haughty arrogance tends to the disturbance of the whole Church, which has purposed so to misuse a synodal council, as by wicked arguments to over-persuade, or by intimidation to compel, the brethren to agree with it, when they had been summoned simply on a matter of Faith, and had come to a decision on the subject which was to engage their care. For it was on this ground that our brothers sent by the Apostolic see, who presided in our stead at the synod with commendable firmness, withstood their illegal attempts, openly protesting against the introduction of any reprehensible innovation contrary to the enactments of the Council of Nicaea. And there can be no doubt about their opposition, seeing that you yourself in your epistle complain of their wish to contravene your attempts. And therein indeed you greatly commend them to me by thus writing, whereas you accuse yourself in refusing to obey them concerning your unlawful designs, vainly seeking what cannot be granted, and craving what is bad for your soul's health, and can never win our consent. For may I never be guilty of assisting so wrong a desire, which ought rather to be subverted by my aid, and that of all who think not high things, but agree with the lowly.

IV. The Nicene Canons are for Universal Application and Not to Be Wrested to Private Interpretations.

These holy and venerable fathers who in he city of Nicaea, after condemning the blasphemous Arius with his impiety, laid down a code of canons for the Church to last till the end of the world, survive not only with us but with the whole of mankind in their constitutions; and, if anywhere men venture upon what is contrary to their decrees, it is *ipso facto* null and void; so that what is universally laid down for our perpetual advantage can never be modified by any change, nor can the things which were destined for the common good be perverted to private interests; and thus so long as the limits remain, which the Fathers fixed, no one may invade another's right but each must exercise himself within the proper and lawful bounds, to the extent of his power, in the breadth of love; of which the bishop of Constantinople may reap the fruits richly enough, if he rather relies on the virtue of humility than is puffed up with the spirit of self-seeking.

V. The Sanction Alleged to Have Been Accorded 60 Years Ago to the Supremacy of Constantinople Over Alexandria and Antioch is Worthless.

"Be not highminded," brother, "but fear ," and cease to disquiet with unwarrantable demands the pious ears of Christian princes, who I am sure will be better pleased by your modesty than by your pride. For your purpose is in no way whatever supported by the written assent of certain bishops given, as you allege, 60 years ago , and never brought to the knowledge of the Apostolic See by your predecessors; and this transaction, which from its outset was doomed to fall through and has now long done so, you now wish to bolster up by means that are too late and useless, viz., by extracting from the brethren an appearance of consent which their modesty from very weariness yielded to their own injury. Remember what the Lord threatens him with, who shall have caused one of the little ones to stumble, and get wisdom to understand what a judgment of God he will have to endure who has not feared to give occasion of stumbling to so many churches and so many priests. For I confess I am so fist bound by love of the whole brotherhood that I will not agree with any one in demands which are against his own interests, and thus you may clearly perceive that my opposition to you, beloved, proceeds from the kindly intention to restrain you from disturbing the universal Church by sounder counsel. The rights of provincial primates may not be overthrown nor metropolitan bishops be defrauded of privileges based on antiquity. The See of Alexandria may not lose any of that dignity which it merited through S. Mark, the evangelist and disciple of the blessed Peter, nor may the splendour of so great a church be obscured by another's clouds, Dioscorus having fallen through his persistence in impiety. The church of Antioch too, in which first at the preaching of the blessed Apostle Peter the Christian name arose , must continue in the position assigned it by the Fathers, and being set in the third place must never be lowered therefrom. For the See is on a different footing to the holders of it; and each individual's chief honour is his own integrity. And since that does not lose its proper worth in any place, how much more glorious must it be when placed in the magnificence of the city of Constantinople, where many priests may find both a defence of the Fathers' canons and an example of uprightness in observing you?

VI. Christian Love Demands Self-Denial Not Self-Seeking.

In thus writing to you, brother, I exhort and admonish you in the Lord, laying aside all ambitious desires to cherish rather a spirit of love and to adorn yourself to your profit with the virtues of love, according to the Apostle's teaching. For love "is patient and kind, and envies not, acts not iniquitously, is not puffed up, is not ambitious, seeks not its own ." Hence if love seeks not its own, how greatly does he sin who covets another's? From which I desire you to keep yourself altogether, and to remember that sentence which says, "Hold what thou hast, that no other take thy crown ." For if you seek what is not permitted, you will deprive yourself by your own action and judgment of the peace of the universal Church. Our brother and fellow-bishop Lucian and our son Basil the deacon, attended to your injunctions with all the zeal they possessed, but justice refused to give effect to their pleadings. Dated the 22nd of May in the consulship of the illustrious Herculanus (452).

LETTER CVII. TO JULIAN, BISHOP OF COS.

(Expostulating with him for putting personal considerations before the good of the Church in the matter of the precedence of the See of Constantinople.)

LETTER CVIII. TO THEODORE, BISHOP OF FORUM JULII.

Leo, the bishop, to Theodore, bishop of Forum Julii.

I. Theodosus Should Not Have Approached Him Except Through His Metropolitan.

Your first proceeding, when anxious, should have been to have consulted your metropolitan on the point which seemed to need inquiry, and if he too was unable to help you, beloved, you should both have asked to be instructed (by us); for in matters, which concern all the Lord's priests as a whole, no inquiry ought to be made without the primates. But in order that the consulter's doubts may in any case be set at rest, I will not keep back the Church's rules about the state of penitents.

II. The Grace of Penitence is for Those Who Fall After Baptism.

The manifold mercy of God so assists men when they fall, that not only by the grace of baptism but also by the remedy of penitence is the hope of eternal life revived, in order that they who have violated the gifts of the second birth, condemning themselves by their own judgment, may attain to remission of their crimes, the provisions of the Divine Goodness having so ordained that God's indulgence cannot be obtained without the supplications of priests. For the Mediator between God and men, the Man Christ Jesus, has transmitted this power to those that are set over the Church that they should both grant a course of penitence to those who confess, and, when they are cleansed by wholesome correction admit them through the door of reconciliation to communion in the sacraments. In which work assuredly the Saviour Himself unceasingly takes part and is never absent from those things, the carrying out of which He has committed to His ministers. saying: "Lo, I am with you all the days even to the completion of the age :" so that whatever is accomplished through our service in due order and with satisfactory results we doubt not to have been vouchsafed through the Holy Spirit.

III. Penitence is Sure Only in This Life.

But if any one of those for whom we entreat God be hindered by some obstacle and lose the benefit of immediate absolution, and before he attain to the remedies appointed, end his days in the course of nature, he will not be able when stripped of the flesh to gain that which when yet in the body he did not receive. And there will be no need for us to weigh tile merits and acts of those who have thus died, seeing that the Lord our God, whose judgments cannot be found out, has reserved for His own decision that which our priestly ministry could not complete: for He wishes His power to be so feared that this fear may benefit all, and every one may dread that which happens to the lukewarm or careless. For it is most expedient and essential that the guilt of sins should be loosed by priestly supplication before the last day of life.

IV. And Yet Penitence and Reconciliation Must Not Be Refused to Men in Extremis.

But to those who in time of need and in urgent danger implore the aid first of penitence, then of reconciliation, must neither means of amendment nor reconciliation be forbidden: because we cannot place limits to God's mercy nor fix times for Him with whom true conversion suffers no delay of forgiveness, as says God's Spirit by the prophet, "when thou hast turned and lamented, then shalt thou be saved;" and elsewhere, "Declare thou thy iniquities beforehand, that thou may'st be justified;" and again, "For with the Lord there is mercy, and with Him is plenteous redemption." And so in dispensing God's gifts we must not be hard, nor neglect the tears and groans of self-accusers, seeing that we believe the very feeling of penitence springs from the inspiration of God, as says the Apostle, "lest perchance God will give them repentance that they may recover themselves from the snares of the devil, by whom they are held captive at his will."

V. Hazardous as Deathbed Repentance Is, the Grace of Absolution Must Not Be Refused Even When It Can Be Asked for Only by Signs.

Hence it behoves each individual Christian to listen to the judgment of his own conscience, lest he put off the turning to God from day to day and fix the time of his amendment at the end of his life; for it is most perilous for human frailty and ignorance to confine itself to such conditions as to be reduced to the uncertainty of a few hours, and instead of winning indulgence by fuller amendment, to choose the narrow limits of that time when space is scarcely found even for the penitent's confession or the priest's absolution. But, as I have said, even such men's needs must be so assisted that the free action of penitence and the grace of communion be not denied them, if they demand it even when their voice is gone, by the signs of a still clear intellect. And if they be so overcome by the stress of their malady that they cannot signify in the priest's presence what just before they were asking for, the testimony of believers standing by must prevail for them, that they may obtain the benefit of penitence and reconciliation simultaneously, so long as the regulations of the Fathers' canons be observed in reference to those persons who have sinned against God by forsaking the Faith.

VI. He is to Bring This Letter to the Notice of the Metropolitan.

These answers, brother, which I have given to your questions in order that nothing different be done under the excuse of ignorance, you shall bring to the notice of your metropolitan; that if there chance to be any of the brethren who before now have thought there was any doubt about these points, they may be instructed by him concerning what I have written to you. Dated June 11th in the consulship of the illustrious Herculanus (452).

LETTER CIX. TO JULIAN, BISHOP OF COS.

Leo, the pope, to Julian, the bishop.
I. He Laments Over the Recent Rioting in Palestine.

The information which you give, brother, about the riotous doings of the false monks is serious and to no slight degree lamentable; for they are due to the war which the wicked Eutyches by the madness of deceivers is waging against the preaching of the Gospel and the Apostles, though it will end in his own destruction and that of his followers but this is delayed by the long-suffering of God, in order that it may appear how greatly the enemies of the cross of Christ are enslaved to the devil; because heretical depravity, breaking through its ancient veil of pretence can no longer restrain itself within the limits of its hypocrisy, and has poured forth all its long-concealed poison, raging against the disciples of the Truth not only with pen but also with deeds of violence , in order to wrest consent from unlearned simplicity or from panic-stricken faith. But the sons of light ought not to be so afraid of the sons of darkness, as being sane to acquiesce in the ideas of madmen or to think that any respect should be shown to men of this kind; for, if they would rather perish than recover their senses, provision must be made lest their escape from punishment should do wider harm, and long toleration of them should lead to the destruction of many.

II. The Ringleaders Must Be Removed to a Distance.

I am not unaware what love and favour is due to our sons, those holy and true monks, who forsake not the moderation of their profession, and carry into practice what they promised by their vows. But these insolent disturbers, who boast of their insults and injuries to priests , are to be held not the slaves of Christ, but the soldiers of Antichrist, and must be chiefly humiliated in the person of their leaders, who incite the ignorant mob to uphold their insubordination. And hence, seeing that our most merciful Prince loves the catholic Faith with all the devotion of a religious heart, and is greatly offended at the effrontery of these rebel heretics, as is everywhere reported, we must appeal to his clemency that the instigators of these seditions be removed from their mad congregations; and not only Eutyches and Dioscorus but also any who have been forward in aiding their wrongheaded madness, be placed where they can hold no intercourse with their partners in blasphemy: for the simpleness of some may chance to be healed by this method, and men will be more easily recalled to soundness of mind, if they be set free from the incitements of pestilential teachers.

III. He Sends a Letter of S. Athanasius to Show that the Present Heresy is Only a Revival of Former Exploded Heresies.

But lest the instruction necessary for the confirmation of faithful spirits or the refutation of heretics should be wanting or not expressed, I have sent the letter of bishop Athanasius of holy memory addressed to bishop Epictetus , whose testimony Cyril of holy memory made use of at the Synod of Ephesus against Nestorius, because it has so clearly and carefully set forth the Incarnation of the Word', as to overthrow both Nestorius and Eutyches by anticipation in the heresies of those times. Let the followers of Eutyches and Dioscorus dare to accuse such an authority as this of ignorance or of heresy, who assert that our preaching goes astray from the teaching and the knowledge of the Fathers. But it ought to avail for the confirmation of the minds of all the Lord's priests, who, having been already detected and condemned of heresy in respect of the authorities they followed, now begin more openly to set forth their blasphemous dogma, lest, if their meaning were hid beneath the cloke of silence it might still be doubtful whether the triple error of Apollinaris , and the mad notion of the Manichees was really revived in them. And as they no longer seek to hide themselves but rise boldly against the churches of Christ, must we not take care to destroy all the strength of their attempts, observing. as I have said, such discrimination as to separate the incorrigible from the more docile spirits: for "evil conversations corrupt good manners ," and "the wise man will be sharper than the pestilent person who is chastised ;" in order that in whatever way the society of the wicked is broken up, some vessels may be snatched from the devil's hand? For we ought not to be so offended at scurrilous and empty words as to have no care for their correction.

IV. He Expresses a Hope that Juvenal's Timely Acknowledgment of Error Will Be Imitated by the Rest.

But bishop Juvenal, whose injuries are to be lamented, joined himself too rashly to those blasphemous heretics, and by embracing Eutyches and Dioscorus, drove many ignorant folk headlong by his example, albeit he afterwards corrected himself by wiser counsels. These men, however, who drank in more greedily the wicked poison, have become the enemies of him, whose disciples they had been before, so that the very food he had supplied them was turned to his own ruin: and yet it is to be hoped they will imitate him in amending his ways, if only the holy associations of the neighbourhood in which they dwell will help them to recover their senses. But the character of him who has usurped the place of a bishop still living cannot be doubted from the character of his actions, nor is it to be disputed that he who is loved by the assailants of the Faith must be a misbeliever. Meanwhile, brother, do not hesitate to continue with anxious care to keep me acquainted with the course of events by more frequent letters. Dated November 25th in the consulship of Herculanus (452).

LETTER CX. FROM MARCIAN AUGUSTUS.

(Expressing surprise that Leo has not by now confirmed the acts of the Synod, and asking for a speedy confirmation.)

LETTER CXI. TO MARCIAN AUGUSTUS.

(About Anatolius' mistake in deposing Actions from the office of archdeacon and putting in Andrew instead.)

LETTER CXII. TO PULCHERIA AUGUSTA.

(On the same subject more briefly.)

LETTER CXIII. TO JULIAN, BISHOP OF COS.

Leo, bishop of Rome, to Julian, bishop of Cos.

I. After Thanks for Julian's Sympathy He Complains of the Deposition of Aetius from the Archdeaconry.

I acknowledge in your letter, beloved, the feelings of brotherly love, in that you sympathize with us in true grief at the many grievous evils we have borne: But we pray that these things which the Lord has either allowed or wished us to suffer, may avail to the correction of those who live through them , and that adversities may cease through the cessation of offences. Both which results will follow through the mercy of God, if only He remove the scourge and turn the hearts of His people to Himself. But as you, brother, are saddened by the hostilities which have raged around us, so I am made anxious because, as your letter indicates, the treacherous attacks of heretics are not set at rest in the church of Constantinople, and men seek occasion to persecute those who have been the defenders of the catholic Fairly. For so long as Aetius is removed from his office of archdeacon under pretence of promotion and Andrew is taken into his place, who had been cast off for associating with heretics; so long as respect is shown to the accusers of Flavian of holy memory, and the partners or disciples of that most pious confessor are put down, it is only too clearly shown what pleases the bishop of the church itself. Towards whom I put off taking action till I hear the merits of the case and await his own dealing with me in the letter our son Aetius tells me he will send, giving opportunity for voluntary correction, whereby I desire my vexation to be appeased. Nevertheless, I have written to our most clement Prince and the most pious Augusta about these things which concern the peace of the Church; and I do not doubt they will in the devoutness of their faith take heed lest a heresy already condemned should succeed in springing up again to the detriment of their own glorious work.

II. He Asks Julian to Act for Him as Anatolius is Deficient in Vigour.

See then, beloved brother, that you bestow the necessary thought on the cares of the Apostolic See, which by her rights as your mother commends to you, who were nourished at her breast, the defence of the catholic Truth against Nestorians and Eutychians, in order that, supported by the Divine help, you may not cease to watch the interests of the city of Constantinople, lest at any time the storms of error arise within her. And because the faith of our glorious Princes is so great that you may confidently suggest what is necessary to them, use their piety for the benefit of the universal Church. But if ever you consult me, beloved, on things which you think doubtful, my reply shall not fail to supply instruction, so that, apart from cases which ought to be decided by the inquiries of the bishops of each particular church, you may act as my legate and undertake the special charge of preventing the Nestorian or Eutychian heresy reviving in any quarter; because the bishop of Constantinople does not possess catholic vigour, and is not very jealous either for the mystery of man's salvation or for his own reputation: whereas if he had any spiritual activity, he ought to have considered by whom he was ordained, and whom he succeeded in such a way as to follows the blessed Flavian rather than the instruments of his promotion. And, therefore, when our most religious Princes deign in accordance with my entreaties to reprimand our brother Anatolius on those matters, which deservedly come under blame, join your diligence to theirs, beloved, that all causes of offences may be removed by the application of the fullest correction and he cease from injuring our son Aetius. For with a catholic-minded bishop even though there was something which seemed calculated to annoy in his archdeacon, it ought to have been passed over from regard for the Faith, rather than that the most worthless heretic should take the place of a catholic. And so when I have learnt the rest of the story, I shall then more clearly gather what ought to be done. For, meanwhile, I have thought better to restrain my vexation and to exercise patience that there might be room for forgiveness.

III. He Asks for Further Information About the Rioting in Palestine and in Egypt.

But with regard to the monks of Palestine, who are said this long time to be in a state of mutiny, I know not by what spirit they are at present moved. Nor has any one yet explained to me what reasons they seem to bring forward for their discontent: whether for instance, they wish to serve the Eutychian heresy by such madness, or whether they are irreconcilably vexed that their bishop could have been misled into that blasphemy, whereby, in spite of the very associations of the holy spots, from which issued instruction for the whole world, he has alienated himself from the Truth of the Lord's Incarnation, and in their opinion that cannot be venial in him which in others had to be wiped out by absolution. And therefore I desire lobe more fully informed about these things that proper means may he taken for their correction; because it is one thing to arm oneself wickedly against the Faith, and another thing to be immoderately disturbed on behalf of it. You must know, too, that the documents which Aetius the presbyter told me before had been dispatched, and the epitome of the Faith which you say you have sent, have not yet arrived. Hence, if an opportunity offers itself of a more expeditious messenger, I shall be glad for any information that may seem expedient to be sent me as soon as possible. I am anxious to know about the monks of Egypt , whether they have regained their peacefulness and their faith, and about the church of Alexandria, what trustworthy tidings reaches you: I wish you to know what I wrote to its bishop or his ordainers, or the clergy, and have therefore sent you a copy of the letter. You will learn also what I have said to our most clement Prince and our most religious Empress from the copies sent.

IV. He Asks for a Latin Translation of the Acts of Chalcedon.

I wish to know whether my letter has been delivered to you, brother, which I sent you by Basil the deacon, upon the Faith of the Lord's Incarnation, while Flavian of holy memory was still alive; for I fancy you have never made any comment on its contents. We have no very clear information about the acts of the Synod, which were drawn up at the time of the council at Chalcedon, on account of the difference of language . And therefore i specially enjoin upon you, brother, that you have the whole collected into one volume, accurately translated of course into Latin, that we may not be in doubt on any portion of the proceedings, and that there may be no manner of uncertainty after you have taken pains to bring it fully within my understanding. Dated March 11th, in the consulship of the illustrious Opilio (453).

LETTER CXIV. TO THE BISHOPS ASSEMBLED IN SYNOD AT CHALCEDON.

(In answer to their Letter (XCVIII.), approving of their acts in the general so long as nothing is contrary to the canons of Nicaea.)

LETTER CXV. TO MARCIAN AUGUSTUS.

(Congratulating him upon the restoration of peace to the Church, and the suppression of the riotous monks; giving his consent also, as a liege subject of the Emperor's, to the acts of Chalcedon, and asking him to make this known to the Synod.)

LETTER CXV. TO PULCHERIA AUGUSTA.

(Commending her pious zeal and informing her of Iris assent to the acts of Chalcedon.)

LETTER CXVII. TO JULIAN, BISHOP OF COS.

Leo to Julian the bishop.

I. He Wishes His Assent to the Acts of Chalcedon to Be Widely Known.

How watchfully and how devotedly you guard the catholic Faith, brother, the tenor of your letter shows, and my anxiety is greatly relieved by the information it contains; supplemented as it is by the most religious piety of our religious Emperor, which is clearly shown to be prepared by the Lord for the confirmation of the whole Church; so that, whilst Christian princes act for the Faith with holy zeal, the priests of the Lord may confidently pray for their realm.

What therefore our most clement Emperor deemed needful I have willingly complied with, by sending letters to all the brethren who were present at the Synod of Chalcedon, in which to show that I approved of what was resolved upon by our holy brethren about the Rule of Faith; on their account to wit, who in order to cloke their own treachery, pretend to consider invalid or doubtful such conciliar ordinances as are not ratified by my assent albeit, after the return of the brethren whom I had sent in my stead, I dispatched a letter to the bishop of Constantinople; so that, if he had been minded to publish it, abundant proof might have been furnished thereby how gladly I approved of what the synod had passed concerning the Faith. But, because it contained such an answer as would have run counter to his self-seeking, he preferred my acceptance of the brethren's resolutions to remain unknown, lest at the same time my reply should become known on the absolute authority of the Nicene canons. Wherefore take heed, beloved, that you warn our most gracious prince by frequent reminders that he add his words to ours and order the letter of the Apostolic See to be sent round to the priests of each single province, that hereafter no enemy of the Truth may venture to excuse himself under cover of my silence.

II. He Expresses His Thanks for the Zeal Shown by the Emperor and the Empress.

And as to the edict of the most Christian Emperor, in which he has shown what the ignorant folly of certain monks deserved and as to the reply of the most gracious

Augusta, in which she rebuked the heads of the monasteries, I wish my great rejoicing to be known, being assured that this fervour of faith is bestowed upon them by Divine inspiration, in order that all men may acknowledge their superiority to rest not only on their royal state but also on their priestly holiness: whom both now and formerly I have asked to treat you with full confidence, being assured of their good will, and that they will not refuse to give ear to necessary suggestions.

III. He Wishes to Know the Effect of His Letter to the Empress Eudocia.

And, because the most clement Emperor has been pleased to charge me secretly by our son Paulus with the task of admonishing our daughter the most clement Augusta Eudocia , I have done what he wished, in order that from my letter she may learn how profitable it will be to her if she espouses the cause of the catholic Faith, and have managed that she should further be admonished by a letter from that most clement prince her son; nothing doubting that she herself, too, will set to work with pious zeal to bring the leaders of sedition to a knowledge of the consequences of their action, and, if they understand not the utterances of those who teach them, to make them at least afraid of the powers of those who will punish them. And so what effect this care of ours produces, I with to know at once by a letter from you, beloved, and whether their ignorant contumacy has at length subsided: as to which if they think there is any doubt about our teaching, let them at least not reject the writings of such holy priests as Athanasius, Theophilus and Cyril of Alexandria, with whom our statement of the Faith so completely harmonizes that any one who professes consent to them disagrees in nothing with us.

IV. Aetius Must Be Content at Present with the Emperor's Favour.

With our son Aetius the presbyter we sympathize in his sorrow; and, as one has been put into his place who had previously been judged worthy of censure, there is no doubt that this change tends to the injury of catholics. But these things must be borne patiently meanwhile, lest we should be thought to exceed the measure of our usual moderation, and for the present Aetius must be content with the encouragement of our most clement prince's favour, to whom I have but lately so commended him by letter that I doubt not his good repute has been increased in their most religious minds.

V. Anatalius Shows No Contrition in His Subsequent Acts.

This too we would have you know, that bishop Anatolius after our prohibition so persisted in his rash presumption as to call upon the bishops of Illyricum to subscribe their names: this news was brought us by the bishop who was sent by the bishop of Thessalonica to announce his consecration. We have declined to write to Anatolius about this, although you might have expected us to do so, because we perceived he did not wish to be reformed. I have made two versions of my letter to the Synod, one with a copy of my letter to Anatolius subjoined, one without it; leaving it to your judgment to deliver the one which you think ought to be given to our most clement prince and to keep the other. Dated 21st March, in the consulship of the illustrious Opilio (453).

LETTER CXVIII. TO THE SAME JULIAN, BISHOP OF COS.

(In which, after speaking of his own efforts for the Faith, he objects to monks being permitted to preach, especially if heretically inclined, and asks Julian to stir up the Emperor's zeal for the Faith.)

LETTER CXIX. TO MAXIMUS, BISHOP OF ANTIOCH, BY THE HAND OF MARIAN THE PRESBYTER, AND OLYMPIUS THE DEACON.

Leo to Maximus of Antioch.
I. The Faith is the Mean Between the Two Extremes of Eutyches and Nestorius.

How much, beloved, you have at heart the most sacred unity of our common Faith and the tranquil harmony of the Church's peace, the substance of your letter shows, which was brought me by our sons, Marian the presbyter and Olympius the deacon, and which was the more welcome to us because thereby we can join as it were in conversation, and thus the grace of God becomes more and more known and greater joy is felt through the whole world over the revelation of catholic Truth. And yet we are sore grieved at some who still (so your messengers indicate) love their darkness; and though the brightness of day has arisen everywhere, even still delight in the obscurity of their blindness, and abandoning the Faith, remain Christians in only the empty name, without knowledge to discern one error from another, and to distinguish the blasphemy of Nestorius from the impiety of Eutyches. For no delusion of theirs can appear excusable, because they contradict themselves in their perverseness. For, though Eutyches' disciples abhor Nestorius, and the followers of Nestorius anathematize Eutyches, yet in the judgment of catholics both sides are condemned and both heresies alike are cut away from the body of the Church: because neither falsehood can be in unison with us. Nor does it matter in which direction of blasphemy they disagree with the truth of the Lord's Incarnation, since their erroneous opinions hold neither with the authority of the Gospel nor with the significance of the mystery .

II. Maximus is to Keep the Churches of the East Free from These Two Opposite Heresies.

And therefore, beloved brother, you must with all your heart consider over which church the Lord has set you to preside, and remember that system of doctrine of which the chief of all the Apostles, the blessed Peter, laid the foundation, not only by his uniform preaching throughout the world, but especially by his teaching in the cities of Antioch and Rome: so that you may understand that he demands of him who is set over the home of his own renown those institutions which he handed down, as he received them from the Truth Itself, which he confessed. And in the churches of the East, and especially in those which the canons of the most holy Fathers at Nicaea assigned to the See of Antioch, you must not by any means allow unscrupulous heretics to make assaults on the Gospel, and the dogmas of either Nestorius or Eutyches to be maintained by any one. Since, as I have said, the rock (petra) of the catholic Faith, from which the blessed Apostle Peter took his name at the Lord's hands, rejects every trace of either heresy; for it openly and clearly anathematizes Nestorius for separating the nature of the Word and of the flesh in the blessed Virgin's conception, for dividing the one Christ into two, and for wishing to distinguish between the person of the Godhead and the person of the Manhood: because He is altogether one and the same who in His eternal Deity was born of the Father without time, and in His true flesh was born of His mother in time; and similarly it eschews Eutyches for ignoring the reality of the human flesh in the Lord Jesus Christ, and asserting the transformation of the Word Himself into flesh, so that His birth, nurture, growth, suffering, death and burial, and resurrection on the third day, all belonged to His Deity only, which put on not the reality but the semblance of the form of a slave.

III. Antioch as the Third See in Christendom is to Retain Her Privileges.

And so it behoves you to use the utmost vigilance, lest these depraved heretics dare to assert themselves; for you must resist them with all the authority of priests, and frequently inform us by your reports what is being done for the progress of the churches. For it is right that you should share this responsibility with the Apostolic See, and realize that the privileges of the third See in Christendom give you every confidence in action, privileges which no intrigues shall in any way impair: because my respect for the Nicene canons is such that I never have allowed nor ever will the institutions of the holy Fathers to be violated by any innovation. For different sometimes as are the deserts of individual prelates, yet the rights of their Sees are permanent: and although rivalry may perchance cause some disturbance about them, yet it cannot impair their dignity. Wherefore, brother, if ever you consider any action ought to be taken to uphold the privileges of the church of Antioch, be sure to explain it in a letter of your own, that we may be able to reply to your application completely and appropriately.

IV. Anatolius' Attempts to Subvert the Decisions of Nicaea are Futile.

But at the present time let it be enough to make a general proclamation on all points, that if in any synod any one makes any attempt upon or seems to take occasion of wresting an advantage against the provisions of the Nicene canons, he can inflict no discredit upon their inviolable decrees: and it will be easier for the compacts of any conspiracy to be broken through than for the regulations of the aforesaid canons to be in any particular invalidated. For intrigue loses no opportunity of stealing an advantage, and whenever the course of things brings about a general assembly of priests, it is difficult for the greediness of the unscrupulous not to try to gain some unfair point: just as in the Synod of Ephesus which overthrew the blasphemous Nestorius with his dogma, bishop Juvenal believed that he was capable of holding the presidency of the province of Palestine, and ventured to rally the insubordinate by a lying letter . At which Cyril of blessed memory, bishop of Alexandria, being properly dismayed, pointed out in his letter to me to what audacity the other's cupidity had led him: and with anxious entreaty begged me hard that no assent should be given his unlawful attempts. For be it known to you that we found the original document of Cyril's letter which was sought for in our book-case, and of which you sent us copies. On this, however, my judgment lays especial stress that, although a majority of priests through the wiliness of some came to a decision which is found opposed to those constitutions of the 318 fathers, it must be considered void on principles of justice: since the peace of the whole Church cannot otherwise be preserved, except due respect be invariably shown to the canons.

V. If Leo's Legates in Any Way Exceeded Their Instructions, They Did So Ineffectually.

Of course, if anything is alleged to have been done by those brethren whom I sent in my stead to the holy Synod, beyond that which was germane to the Faith, it shall be of no weight at all: because they were sent by the Apostolic See only for the purpose of extirpating heresy and upholding the catholic Faith. For whatever is laid before bishops for inquiry beyond the particular subjects which come before synodal councils may admit of a certain amount of free discussion, if the holy Fathers have laid down nothing thereon at Nicaea. For anything that is not in agreement with their rules and constitutions can never obtain the assent of the Apostolic See. But how great must be the diligence with which this rule is kept, you will gather from the copies of the letter which we sent to the bishop of Constantinople, restraining his cupidity; and you shall take order that it reach the knowledge of all our brethren and fellow-priests.

VI. No One But Priests are Allowed to Preach.

This too it behaves you, beloved, to guard against, that no one except those who are the Lord's priests dare to claim the right of teaching or preaching, be he monk or layman, who boasts himself of some knowledge. Because although it is desirable that all the Church's sons should understand the things which are right and sound, yet it is permitted to none outside the priestly rank to assume the office of preacher, since in the Church of God all things ought to be orderly, that in Christ's one body the more excellent members should fulfil their own duties, and the lower not resist the higher. Dated the 11th of June, in the consulship of the illustrious Opilio (453).

LETTER CXX. TO THEODORET, BISHOP OF CYRUS, ON PERSEVERANCE IN THE FAITH.

Leo, the bishop, to his beloved brother Theodoret, the bishop.

I. He Congratulates Theodoret on Their Joint Victory, and Expresses His Approval of an Hottest Inquiry Which Leads to Good Results.

On the return of our brothers and fellow-priests, whom the See of the blessed Peter sent to the holy council, we ascertained, beloved, the victory you and we together had won by assistance from on high over the blasphemy of Nestorius, as well as over the madness of Eutyches. Wherefore we make our boast in tim Lord, singing with the prophet: "our help is in the name of the Lord, who hath made heaven and earth :" who has suffered us to sustain no harm in the person of our brethren, but has corroborated by the irrevocable assent of the whole brotherhood what He had already laid down through our ministry: to show that, what had been first formulated by the foremost See of Christendom, and then received by the judgment of the whole Christian world, had truly proceeded from Himself: that in this, too, the members may be at one with the Head. And herein our cause for rejoicing grows greater when we see that the more fiercely the foe assailed Christ's servants, the more did he afflict himself. For lest the assent of other Sees to that which the Lord of all has appointed to take precedence of the rest might seem mere complaisance, or lest any other evil suspicion might creep in, some were found to dispute our decisions before they were finally accepted. And while some, instigated by the author of the disagreement, rush forward into a warfare of contradictions, a greater good results through his fall under the guiding hand of the Author of all goodness. For the gifts of God's grace are sweeter to us when they are gained with mighty efforts: and uninterrupted peace is wont to seem a lesser good than one that is restored by labours. Moreover, the Truth itself shines more brightly, and is more bravely maintained when what the Faith had already taught is afterwards confirmed by further inquiry. And still further, the good name of the priestly office gains much in lustre where the authority of the highest is preserved without it being thought that the liberty of the lower ranks has been at all infringed. And the result of a discussion contributes to the greater glory of God when the debaters exert themselves with confidence in overcoming the gainsayers: that what of itself is shown wrong may not seem to be passed over in prejudicial silence.

II. Christ's Victory Has Won Back Many to the Faith.

Exult therefore, beloved brother, yes, exult triumphantly in the only-begotten Son of God. Through us He has conquered for Himself the reality of Whose flesh was denied. Through us and for us He has conquered, in whose cause we have conquered. This happy day ranks next to the Lord's Advent for the world. The robber is laid low, and there is restored to our age the mystery of the Divine Incarnation which the enemy of mankind was obscuring with his chicaneries, because the facts would not let him actually destroy it. Nay, the immortal mystery had perished from the hearts of unbelievers, because so great salvation is of no avail to unbelievers, as the Very Truth said to His disciples: "he that believeth and is baptized shall be saved; but he that believeth not shall be condemned ." The rays of the Sun of Righteousness which were obscured throughout the East by the clouds of Nestorius and Eutyches, have shone out brightly from the West, where it has reached its zenith in the Apostles and teachers of the Church. And yet not even in the East is it to be believed that it was ever eclipsed where noble confessors have been found among your ranks: so that, when the old enemy was trying afresh, through the impenitent heart of a modern Pharaoh , to blot out the seed of faithful Abraham and the sons of promise, he grew weary, through God's mercy, and could harm no one save himself. And in regard to him the Almighty has worked this wonder also, in that He has not overwhelmed with the founder of the tyranny those who were associated with him in the slaughter of the people of Israel, but has gathered them into His own people; and as the Source of all mercy knew to be worthy of Himself and possible for Himself alone, He has made them conquerors with us who were conquered by us. For whilst the spirit of falsehood is the only true enemy of the human race, it is undoubted that all whom the Truth has won over to His side share in His triumph over that enemy. Assuredly it now is clear how divinely authorized are these words of our Redeemer, which are so applicable to the enemies of the Faith that one may not doubt they were said of them: "You," He says, "are of your father the devil, and the lusts of your father it is your will to fulfil. He was a murderer from the beginning and stood not in the truth, because the truth is not in him. When he speaketh a lie, he speaketh of his own: for he is a liar and the father thereof ."

III. Dioscorus, Who in His Madness Has Attacked Even the Bishop of Rome, Has Shown Himself the Instrument of Satan.

It is not to be wondered, then, that they who have accepted a delusion as to our nature in the true God agree with their father on these points also, maintaining that what was seen, heard, and in fact, by the witness of the gospel, touched and handled in the only Son of God, belonged not to that to which it was proved to belong, but to an essence co-eternal and consubstantial with the Father: as if the nature of the Godhead could have been pierced on the Cross, as if the Unchangeable could grow from infancy to manhood, or the eternal Wisdom could progress in wisdom, or God, who is a Spirit, could thereafter be filled with the Spirit. In this, too, their sheer madness betrayed its origin, because, as far as it could, it attempted to injure everybody. For he, who afflicted you with his persecutions, led others wrong by driving them to consent to his wickedness. Yea, even us too, although he had wounded us in each one of the brethren (for they are our members), even us he did not exempt from special vexation in attempting to inflict an injury upon his Head with strange and unheard of and incredible effrontery. But would that he had recovered his senses even after all these enormities, and had not saddened us by his death and eternal damnation. There was no measure of wickedness that he did not reach: it was not enough for him that, sparing neither living nor dead, and forswearing truth and allying himself with falsehood, he imbrued his hands, that had been already long polluted, in the blood of a guiltless, catholic priest. And since it is written: "he that hateth his brother is a murderer :" he has actually carried out what he was said already to have done in hate, as if he had never heard of this nor of that which the Lord says, "learn of Me; for I am meek and lowly in heart, and ye shall find rest unto your souls: for My yoke is easy and My burden is light ." A worthy preacher of the devil's errors has been found in this Egyptian plunderer, who, like the cruellest tyrant the Church has had, forced his villainous blasphemies on the reverend brethren through the violence of riotous mobs and the blood-stained hands of soldiers. And when our Redeemer's voice assures us that the author of murder and of lying is one and the same, He has carried out both equally: as if these things were written not to be avoided but to be perpetrated: and thus does he apply to the completion of his destruction the salutary warnings of the Son of God, and turns a deaf ear to what the same Lord has said, "I speak that which I have seen with My Father; and ye do that which ye have seen with your father ."

IV. Those Who Undertake to Speak Authoritatively an Doctrine, Must Preserve the Balance Between the Extremes.

Accordingly while he strove to cut short Flavian of blessed memory's life in the present world, he has deprived himself of the light of true life. While he tried to drive you out of your churches, he has cut off himself from fellowship with Christians. While he drags and drives many into agreement with error, he has stabbed his own soul with many a wound, a solitary convicted offender beyond all, and through all and for all, for he was the cause of all men's being accused. But, although, brother, you who are nurtured on solid food, have little need of such reminders yet that we may fulfil what belongs to our position according to that utterance of the Apostle who says, "Besides these things that are without, that which presseth on me daily, anxiety for all the churches. Who is weakened and I am not weak? Who is made to stumble and I burn not ?" we believe this admonition ought to be given especially on the present occasion, that whenever by the ministration of the Divine grace we either overwhelm or cleanse those who are without, in the pool of doctrine, we go not away in aught from those rules of Faith which the Godhead of the Holy Ghost brought forward at the Council of Choicedon, and weigh our words with every caution so as to avoid the two extremes of new false doctrine : not any longer (God forbid it) as if debating what is doubtful, but with full authority laying clown conclusions already arrived at; for in the letter which we issued from the Apostolic See, and which has been ratified by the assent of the entire holy Synod, we know that so many divinely authorised witnesses are brought together, that no one can entertain any further doubt, except one who prefers to enwrap himself in the clouds of error, and the proceedings of the Synod whether those in which we read the formulating of the definition of Faith, or those in which the aforesaid letter of the Apostolic See was zealously supported by you, brother, and especially the address of the whole Council to our most religious Princes, are corroborated by the testimonies of so many fathers in the past that they must persuade any one, however unwise and stubborn his heart, so long as he be not already joined with the devil in damnation for his wickedness.

V. Theodoret's Orthodoxy Has Been Happily and Thoroughly Vindicated.

Wherefore this, too, it is our duty to provide against the Church's enemies, that, as far as in us lies, we leave them no occasion for slandering us, nor yet, in acting against the Nestorians or Eutychians, ever seem to have retreated before the other side, but that we shun and condemn both the enemies of Christ in equal measure, so that whenever the interests of the hearers in any way require it, we may with all promptitude and clearness strike down them and their doctrines with the anathema that they deserve, lest if we seem to do this doubtfully or tardily, we be thought to act against our will. And although the facts themselves are sufficient to remind your wisdom of this, yet now actual experience has brought the lesson home. But blessed be our God, whose invincible Truth has shown you free from all taint of heresy in the judgment of the Apostolic See. To whom you will repay due thanks for all these labours, if you keep yourself such a defender of the universal Church as we have proved and do still prove you. For that God has dispelled all calumnious fallacies, we attribute to the blessed Peter's wondrous care of us all, for after sanctioning the judgment of his See in defining the Faith, he allowed no sinister imputation to rest on any of you, who have laboured with us for the catholic Faith: because the Holy Spirit adjudged that no one could fail to come out conqueror of those whose Faith had now conquered.

VI. He Asks Theodoret for His Continued Cooperation, and Refers Him to a Letter Which He Has Written to the Bishop of Antioch.

It remains that we exhort you to continue your co-operation with the Apostolic See, because we have learnt that some remnants of the Eutychian and Nestorian error still linger amongst you. For the victory which Christ our Lord has vouchsafed to His Church, although it increases our confidence, does not yet entirely destroy our anxiety, nor is it granted us to sleep but to work on more calmly. Hence it is we wish to be assisted in this too by your watchful care, that you hasten to inform the Apostolic See by your periodic reports what progress the Lord's teaching makes in those regions; to the end that we may assist the priests of that district in whatever way experience suggests.

On those matters which were mooted in the often-quoted council, in unlawful opposition to the venerable canons of Nicaea, we have written to our brother and fellow-bishop. the occupant of the See of Antioch, adding that too which you had given us verbal information about by your delegates with reference to the unscrupulousness of certain monks, and laying down strict injunctions that no one, be he monk or layman, that boasts himself of some knowledge, should presume to preach except the Lord's priests. That letter, however, we wish to reach all men's knowledge for the benefit of the universal Church through our aforesaid brother and fellow-bishop Maximus; and for that reason we have not thought fit to add a copy of it to this; because we have no doubt of the due carrying out of our injunctions to our aforesaid brother and fellow-bishop. (In another hand.) God keep thee safe, beloved brother. Dated 11 June in the consulship of the illustrious Opilio (453).

LETTERS CXXI. AND CXXII. THE FORMER TO MARCIAN AUGUSTUS, AND THE OTHER TO JULIAN THE BISHOP.

Asking him for further inquiries and information about the proper date for Easter in 455; cf. Letter LXXXVIII. chap. 4, above.

LETTER CXXIII. TO EUDOCIA AUGUSTA, ABOUT THE MONKS OF PALESTINE.

Leo, the bishop, to Eudocia Augusta.

I. A Request that She Should Use Her Influence with the Monks of Palestine in Reducing Them to Order.

I do not doubt that your piety is aware how great is my devotion to the catholic Faith, and with what care I am bound, God helping me, to guard against the Gospel of truth being withstood at any time by ignorant or disloyal men. And, therefore, after expressing to you my dutiful greetings which your clemency is ever bound to receive at my hands, I entreat the Lord to gladden me with the news of your safety, and to bring aid evermore and more by your means to the maintenance of that article of the Faith over which the minds of certain monks within the province of Palestine have been much disturbed; so that to the best of your pious zeal all confidence in such heretical perversity may be destroyed. For what but sheer destruction was to be feared by men who were not moved either by the principles of God's mysteries , or by the authority of the Scriptures, or by the evidence of the sacred places themselves . May it advantage then the Churches, as by God's favour it does advantage them, and may it advantage the human race itself which the Word of God adopted at the Incarnation, that you have conceived the wish to take up your abode in that country where the proofs of His wondrous acts and the signs of His sufferings speak to you of our Loan Jesus Christ as not only true God but also true Man.

II. They are to Be Told that the Catholic Faith Rejects Both the Eutychian and the Nestorian Extremes. He Wishes to Be Informed How Far She Succeeds.

If then the aforesaid revere and love the name of "catholic," and wish to be numbered among the members of the Lord's body, let them reject the crooked errors which in their rashness they have committed, and let them show penitence for their wicked blasphemies and deeds of bloodshed . For the salvation of their souls let them yield to the synodal decrees which have been confirmed in the city of Choicedon. And because nothing but true faith and quiet humility attains to the understanding of the mystery of man's salvation, let them believe what they read in the Gospel, what they confess in the Creed, and not mix themselves up with unsound doctrines. For as the catholic Faith condemns Nestorius, who dared to maintain two persons in our one Lord Jesus Christ, so does it also condemn Eutyches and Dioscorus who deny that the true human flesh was assumed in the Virgin Mother's womb by the only-begotten Word of God.

If your exhortations have any success in convincing these persons, which will win for you eternal glory, I beseech your clemency to inform me of it by letter; that I may have the joy of knowing that you have reaped the fruit of your good work, and that they through the Lord's mercy have not perished. Dated the 15th of June, in the consulship of the illustrious Opilio (453).

LETTER CXXIV. TO THE MONKS OF PALESTINE.

Leo, the bishop, to the whole body of monks settled throughout Palestine.

I. They Have Possibly Been Misled by a Wrong Translation of His Letter on the Incarnation to Flavian.

The anxious care, which I owe to the whole Church and to all its sons, has ascertained from many sources that some offence has been given to your minds, beloved, through my interpreters, who being either ignorant, as it appears, or malicious, have made you take some of my statements in a different sense to what I meant, not being capable of turning the Latin into Greek with proper accuracy, although in the explanation of subtle and difficult matters, one who undertakes to discuss them can scarcely satisfy himself even in his own tongue. And yet this has so far been of advantage to me, that by your disapproving of what the catholic Faith rejects, we know you are greater friends to the true than to the false: and that you quite properly refuse to believe what I myself also abhor, in accordance with ancient doctrine. For although my letter addressed to bishop Flavian, of holy memory, is of itself sufficiently explicit, and stands in no need either of correction or explanation, yet other of my writings harmonize with that letter, and in them my position will be found similarly set forth. For necessity was laid upon me to argue against the heretics who have thrown many of Christ's peoples into confusion, both before our most merciful princes and the holy synodal Council, and the church of Constantinople, and thus I have laid down what we ought to think and feel on the Incarnation of the Word according to the teaching of the Gospel and Apostles, and in nothing have I departed from the creed of the holy Fathers: because the Faith is one, true, unique, catholic, and to it nothing can be added, nothing taken away: though Nestorius first, and now Eutyches, have endeavoured to assail it from an opposite standpoint, but with similar disloyalty, and have tried to impose on the Church of God two contradictory heresies, which has led to their both being deservedly condemned by the disciples of the Truth; because the false view which they both held in different ways was exceedingly mad and sacrilegious.

II. Eutyches, Who Confounds the Persons, is as Much to Be Rejected as Nestorius, Who Separates Them.

Nestorius, therefore, must be anathematized for believing the Blessed Virgin Mary to be mother of His manhood only, whereby he made the person of His flesh one thing, and that of His Godhead another, and did not recognize the one Christ in the Word of God and in the flesh, but spoke of the Son of God as separate and distinct from the son of man: although, without losing that unchangeable essence which belongs to Him together with the Father and the Holy Spirit from all eternity and without respect of time, the "Word became flesh" within the Virgin's womb in such wise that by that one conception and one parturition she was at the same time, in virtue of the union of the two substances, both handmaid and mother of the Lord. This Elizabeth also knew, as Luke the evangelist declares, when she said: "Whence is this to me that the mother of my Lord should come to me ?" But Eutyches also must be stricken with the same anathema, who, becoming entangled in the treacherous errors of the old heretics, has chosen the third dogma of Apollinaris : so that he denies the reality of his human flesh and Soul, and maintains the whole of our Lord Jesus Christ to be of one nature, as if the Godhead of the Word had turned itself into flesh and soul: and as if to be conceived and born, to be nursed and grow, to be crucified and die, to be buried and rise again, and to ascend into heaven and to sit on the Father's right hand, from whence He shall come to judge the living and the dead-as if all those things belonged to that essence only which admits of none of them without the reality of the flesh: seeing that the nature of the Only-begotten is the nature of the Father, the nature of the Holy Spirit, and that the undivided unity and consubstantial equality of the eternal Trinity is at once impassible and unchangeable. But if this heretic withdraws from the perverse views of Apollinaris, lest he be proved to hold that the Godhead is passible and mortal: and yet dares to pronounce the nature of the Incarnate Word that is of the Word made Flesh one, he undoubtedly crosses over into the mad view of Manichaeus and Marcion , and believes that the man Jesus Christ, the mediator between God and men, did all things in an unreal way, and had not a human body, but that a phantom-like apparition presented itself to the beholders' eyes.

III. The Acknowledgment of Our Nature in Christ is Necessary to Orthodoxy.

As these iniquitous lies were once rejected by the catholic Faith, and such men's blasphemies condemned by the unanimous votes of the blessed Fathers throughout the world, whoever these are that are so blinded and strange to the light of truth as to deny the presence of human, that is our, nature in the Word of God from the time of the Incarnation, they must show on what ground they claim the name of Christian, and in what way they harmonize with the true Gospel, if the child-bearing of the blessed Virgin produced either the flesh without the Godhead or the Godhead without the flesh. For as it cannot be denied that "the Word became flesh and dwelt in us ," so it cannot be denied that "God was in Christ, reconciling the world to Himself ." But what reconciliation can there be, whereby God might be propitiated for the human race, unless the mediator between God and man took up the cause of all? And in what way could He properly fulfil His mediation, unless He who in the form of God was equal to the Father, were a sharer of our nature also in the form of a slave: so that the one new Man might effect a renewal of the old: and the bond of death fastened on us by one man's wrong-doing might be loosened by the death of the one Man who alone owed nothing to death. For the pouring out of the blood of the righteous on behalf of the unrighteous was so powerful in its effect , so rich a ransom that, if the whole body of us prisoners only believed in their Redeemer, not one would be held in the tyrant's bonds: since as the Apostle says, "where sin abounded, grace also did much more abound ." And since we, who were born under the imputation of sin, have received the power of a new birth unto righteousness, the gift of liberty has become stronger than the debt of slavery.

IV. They Only Benefit by the Blood of Christ Who Truly Share in His Death and Resurrection.

What hope then do they, who deny the reality of the human person in our Saviour's body, leave for themselves in the efficacy of this mystery? Let them say by what sacrifice they have been reconciled, by what blood-shedding brought back. Who is He "who gave Himself for us an offering and a victim to God for a sweet smell :" or what sacrifice was ever more hallowed than that which the true High priest placed upon the altar of the cross by the immolation of His own flesh? For although in the sight of the Lord the death of many of His saints has been precious , yet no innocent's death was the propitiation of the world. The righteous have received, not given, crowns: and from the endurance of the faithful have arisen examples of patience, not the gift of justification. For their deaths affected themselves alone, and no one has paid off another's debt by his own death : one alone among the sons of men, our Load Jesus Christ, stands out as One in whom all are crucified, all dead, all buried, all raised again. Of them He Himself said "when I am lifted from the earth, I will draw all (things) unto Me ." True faith also, that justifies the transgressors and makes them just, is drawn to Him who shared their human natures and wins salvation in Him, in whom alone man finds himself not guilty; and thus is free to glory in the power of Him who in the humiliation of our flesh engaged in conflict with the haughty foe, and shared His victory with those in whose body He had triumphed.

V. The Actions of Christ's Two Natures Must Be Kept Distinct.

Although therefore in our one Lord Jesus Christ, the true Son of God and man, the person of the Word and of the flesh is one, and both beings have their actions in common : yet we must understand the character of the acts themselves, and by the contemplation of sincere faith distinguish those to which the humility of His weakness is brought from those to which His sublime power is inclined: what it is that the flesh without the Word or the Word without the flesh does not do. For instance, without the power of the Word the Virgin would not have conceived nor brought forth: and without the reality of the flesh His infancy would not have laid wrapt in swaddling clothes. Without the power of the Word the Magi would not have adored the Child that a new star had pointed out to them: and without the reality of the flesh that Child would not have been ordered to be carried away into Egypt and withdrawn from Herod's persecution. Without the power of the Word the Father's voice uttered from the sky would not have said, "This is My beloved Son, in whom I am well pleased :" and without the reality of the flesh John would not have been able to point to Him and say: "Behold the Lamb of God, behold Him that beareth away the sins of the world ." Without the power of the Word there would have been no restoring of the sick to health, no raising of the dead to life: and without the reality of the flesh He would not have hungered and needed food, nor grown weary and needed rest. Lastly, without the power of the Word, the Lord would not have professed Himself equal to the Father, and without the reality of the flesh He would not also have said that the Father was greater than He: for the catholic Faith upholds and defends both positions, believing the only Son of God to be both Man and the Word according to the distinctive properties of His divine and human substance.

VI. There is No Confusion of the Two Natures in Christ .

Although therefore from that beginning whereby in the Virgin's womb "the Word became flesh," no sort of division ever arose between the Divine and the human substance, and through all the growth and changes of His body, the actions were of one Person the whole time, yet we do not by any mixing of them up confound those very acts which were done inseparably: and from the character of the acts we perceive what belonged to either form. For neither do His Divine acts affect His human, nor His human acts His Divine, since both concur in this way and to this very end that in their operation His twofold qualities be not absorbed the one by the other, nor His individuality doubled. Therefore let those Christian phantom-mongers tell us, what nature of the Saviour's it was that was fastened to the wood of the Cross, that lay in the tomb, and that on the third day rose in the flesh when the stone was rolled away from the grave: or what kind of body Jesus presented to His disciples' eyes entering when the doors were shut upon them: seeing that to drive away the beholders' disbelief, He required them to inspect with their eyes and to handle with their hands the still open prints of the nails and the flesh wound of His pierced side. But if in spite of the truth being so clear, their persistence in heresy will not abandon their position in the darkness, let them show whence they promise themselves the hope of eternal life, which no one can attain to, save through the mediator between God and man, the man Jesus Christ. For "there is not another name given to men under heaven, in which they must be saved ." Neither is there any ransoming of men from captivity, save in His blood, "who gave Himself a ransom for all :" who, as the blessed apostle proclaims, "when He was in the form of God, thought it not robbery that He was equal with God; but emptied Himself, receiving the form of a slaves Icing made in the likeness of men, and being found in fashion as a man He humbled Himself, being made obedient even unto death, the death of the cross. For which reason God also exalted Him, and gave Him a name which is above every name: that in the name of Jesus every knee may bow of things in heaven, of things on the earth, and of things under the earth, and that every tongue may confess that the Lord Jesus Christ is in the glory of God the Father ."

VII. It Was as Being "In Form of a Slave," Not as Son of God That He Was Exalted.

Although therefore the Lord Jesus Christ is one, and the true Godhead and true Manhood in Him forms absolutely one and the same person, and the entirety of this union cannot be separated by any division, yet the exaltation wherewith "God exalted Him," and "gave Him a name which excels every name," we understand to belong to that form which needed to be enriched by this increase of glory . Of course "in the form of God" the Son was equal to the Father, and between the Father and the Only-begotten there was no distinction in point of essence, no diversity in point of majesty: nor through the mystery of the Incarnation had the Word been deprived of anything which should be restored Him by the Father's gift. But "the form of a slave" by which the impassible Godhead fulfilled a pledge of mighty loving-kindness , is human weakness which was lifted up into the glory of the divine power, the Godhead and the manhood being right from the Virgin's conception so completely united that without the manhood the divine acts, and without the Godhead the human acts were not performed. For which reason as the Lord of majesty is said to have been crucified, so He who from eternity is equal with God is said to have been exalted. Nor does it matter by which substance Christ is spoken of, since the unity of His person inseparably remaining He is at once both wholly Son of man according to the flesh and wholly Son of God according to His Godhead, which is one with the Father. Whatever therefore Christ received in time, He received in virtue of His manhood, on which are conferred whatsoever it had not. For according to the power of the Word, "all things that the Father hath" the Son also hath indiscriminately, and what "in the form of a slave" He received from the Father, He also Himself gave in the form of the Father. He is in Himself at once both rich and poor; rich, because "in the beginning was the Word, and the Word was with God, and God was the Word. This was in the beginning with God. All things were made through Him, and without Him was made nothing:" and poor because "the Word became flesh and dwelt in us ." But what is that emptying of Himself, or that poverty except the receiving of the form of a slave by which the majesty of the Word was veiled, and the scheme for man's redemption carried out? For as the original chains of our captivity could not be loosed, unless a man of our race and of our nature appeared who was not under the prejudice of the old debt, and who with his untainted blood might blot out the bond of death , as it had from the beginning been divinely fore-ordained, so it came to pass in the fulness of the appointed time that the promise which had been proclaimed in many ways might reach its long expected fulfilment, and that thus, what had been frequently announced by one testimony after another, might have all doubtfulness removed.

VIII. A Protest Against Their Faithlessness and Inconsistency in This Matter.

And so, as all these heresies have been destroyed, which through the holy devotion of the presiding Fathers have been cut off from the body of the catholic unity, and which deserved to be exiles from Christ, because they have made the Incarnation of the Word, which is the one salvation of those who believe aright, a stone of offence and a stumbling-block to themselves, I am surprised that you, beloved, have any difficulty in discerning the light of the Truth. And since it has been made clear by numerous explanations that the Christian Faith was right in condemning both Nestorius and Eutyches with Dioscorus, and that a man cannot be called a Christian who gives his assent to the blasphemous opinion of either the one or the other, I am grieved that you are, as I hear, doing despite to the teaching of the Gospel and the Apostles by stirring up the various bodies of citizens with seditions, by disturbing the churches, and by inflicting not only insults, but even death, upon priests and bishops, so that you lose sight of your resolves and profession through your fury and cruelty. Where is your rule of meekness and quietness? where is the long-suffering of patience? where the tranquillity of peace? where the firm foundation of love and courage of endurance?what evil persuasion has carried you off, what persecution has separated you from the gospel of Christ? or what strange craftiness of the Deceiver has shown itself that, forgetting the prophets and apostles, forgetting the health-giving creed and confession which you pronounced before many witnesses when you received the sacrament of baptism you should give yourselves up to the the Devil's deceits? what effect would "the Claws " and other cruel tortures have had on you if the empty comments of heretics have had so much weight in taking the purity of your faith by storm? you think you are acting for the Faith and yet you go against the Faith. You arm yourselves in the name of the Church and yet fight against the Church. Is this what you have learnt from prophets, evangelists, and apostles? to deny the true flesh of Christ, to subject the

, very essence of the Word to suffering and death, to make our nature different from His who repaired it, and to reckon all that the cross uplifted, that the spear pierced, that the stone on the tomb received and gave back, to be only the work: of Divine power, and not also of human humility? It is in reference to this humility that the Apostle says, "For I do not blush for the Gospel ," inasmuch as he knew what a slur was cast upon Christians by their enemies. And, therefore, the Lord also made proclamation, saying: "he that shall confess Me before men him will I also confess before My Father ." For these will not be worthy of the Son and the Father's acknowledgment in whom the flesh of Christ awakens no respect: and they will prove themselves to have gained no virtue from the sign of the cross who blush to avow with their lips what they have consented to bear upon their brows.

IX. An Exhortation to Accept the Catholic View of the Incarnation.

Give up, my sons, give up these suggestions of the devil. God's Truth nothing can impair, but the Truth does not save us except in our flesh. For, as the prophet says, "truth is sprung out of the earth ," and the Virgin Mary conceived the Word in such wise that she ministered flesh of her substance to be united to Him without the addition of a second person, and without the disappearance of her nature: seeing that He who was in the form of God took the form of a slave in such wise that Christ is one and the same in both forms: God bending Himself to the-weak things of man, and man rising up to the high things of the Godhead, as the Apostle says, "whose are the fathers, and from whom, according to the flesh is Christ, who is above all things God blessed for ever. Amen ."

LETTER CXXV. TO JULIAN, THE BISHOP, BY COUNT RODANUS.

(Asking him to write quickly, and not keep him in suspense.)

LETTER CXXVI. TO MARCIAN AUGUSTUS.

(Congratulating him on the restoration of peace in Palestine.)

LETTER CXXVII. TO JULIAN, BISHOP OF COS.

(About (1) affairs in Palestine, (2) a letter from Proterius, (3) the date of Easter, (4) his reply to the Synod of Chalcedon, (5) the deposition of Aetius.)

LETTER CXXVII. TO MARCIAN AUGUSTUS.

(Professing readiness to be reconciled to Anatolius if he will abide by the canons and not infringe the prerogatives of others.)

LETTER CXXIX. TO PROTERIUS, BISHOP OF ALEXANDRIA.

Leo to Proterius, bishop of Alexandria.
I. He Commends His Persistent Loyalty to the Faith.

Your letter, beloved, which our brother and fellow-bishop Nestorius duly brought us, has caused me great joy. For it was seemly that such an epistle should be sent by the head of the church of Alexandria to the Apostolic See, as showed that the Egyptians had from the first learnt from the teaching of the most blessed Apostle Peter through his blessed disciple Mark , that which it is agreed the Romans have believed, that beside the Lord Jesus Christ "there is no other name given to men under heaven, in which they must be saved ." But because "all men have not faith " and the crafty Tempter never delights so much in wounding the hearts of men as when he can poison their unwary minds with errors that are opposed to Gospel Truth, we must strive by the mighty teaching of the Holy Ghost to prevent Christian know ledge from being perverted by the devil's falsehoods. And against this danger it behoves the rulers of the churches especially to guard and to avert from the minds of simple folk lies which are coloured by a certain show of truth . "For narrow and steep is the way which leads to life ." And they seek to entrap men not so much by watching their actions as by nice distinctions of meaning, corrupting the force of sentences by some very slight addition or alteration, whereby sometimes a statement, which made for salvation, by a subtle change is turned to destruction. But since the Apostle says, "there must be heresies, that they which are approved may be made manifest among you ," it tends to tile progress of the whole Church, that, whenever wickedness reveals itself in setting forth wrong opinions, the things which are harmful be not concealed, and that what will inevitably end in ruin may not injure the innocence of others. Wherefore they must put down. their blind wanderings and downfalls to themselves, who with rash obstinacy prefer to glory: in their shame than to accept the offered remedy. You do right, brother, to be displeased at their stubbornness, and we commend. you for holding fast that teaching which has; come down to us from the blessed Apostles and the holy Fathers.

II. Let Him Fortify the Faithful by the Public Reading Aloud of Quotations from the Fathers Bearing on the Question and of the Tome.

For there is no new preaching in the letter which I wrote in reply to Flavian of holy memory, when be consulted me about the Incarnation of our Lord Jesus Christ; for in nothing did I depart from that rule of Faith which was outspokenly maintained by your ancestors and ours. And if Dioscorus had been willing to follow and imitate them, he would have abided in the Body of Christ, having in the works of Athanasius of blessed memory the materials for instruction, and in the discourses of Theophilus and Cyril of holy remembrance the means rather of praise-worthily opposing the already condemned dogma than of choosing to consort with Eutyches in his blasphemy. This therefore, beloved brother, I advise in my anxiety for our common Faith that, because the enemies of Christ's cross lie in watch for all our words and syllables, we give them not the slightest occasion for falsely asserting that we agree with the Nestorian doctrine. And you must so diligently exhort the laity and clergy and all the brotherhood to advance in the Faith as to show that you teach nothing new but instil into all men's breasts those things, which the Fathers of revered memory have with harmony of statement taught, and with which in all things our epistle agrees. And this must be shown not only by your words but also by the actually reading aloud of previous statements, that God's people may know that what the Fathers received from their predecessors and handed on to their descendants, is still instilled into them in the present day. And to this end, when the statements of the aforesaid priests have first been read, then lastly let my writings also be recited, that the ears of the faithful may attest that we preach nothing else than what we received from our forefathers. And because their understandings are but little practised in discerning these things, let them at least learn from the letters of the Fathers, how ancient this evil is, which is now condemned by us in Nestorius as well as in Eutyches, who have both been ashamed to preach the gospel of Christ according to the Lord's own teaching.

III. The Ancient Precedents are to Be Maintained Throughout.

Accordingly, both in the rule of Faith and in the observance of discipline, let the standard of antiquity be maintained throughout, and do thou, beloved, display the firmness of a prudent ruler, that the church of Alexandria may get the benefit of my earnest resistance to the unprincipled ambition of certain people in maintaining its ancient privileges, and of my determination that all metropolitans should retain their dignity undiminished, as you will ascertain from the tenor of my letters, which I have addressed, whether to the holy Synod or to the most Christian Emperor, or to the Bishop of Constantinople; for you will perceive that I have made it my special care to allow no deviation from the rule of Faith in the Lord-churches, nor any diminution of their privileges through any individual's unscrupulousness. And as this is so, hold fast, brother, to the custom of your predecessors, and keep due authority over your comprovincial bishops, who by ancient constitution are subject to the See of Alexandria; so that they resist not ecclesiastical usage, and refuse not to meet together under your presidency, either at fixed times or when any reasonable cause demands it: and that if anything has to be discussed in a general meeting which will be to the benefit of the Church, when the brethren have thus met together, they may unanimously come to some resolution thereupon. For there is nothing which ought to recall them from this obedience, seeing that both for faith and conduct we have such good knowledge of you, brother, that we will not allow you to lose any of your predecessor's authority, nor to be slighted with impunity. Dated March 10th, in the consulship of the illustrious Aetius and Studius (454).

LETTER CXXX. TO MARCIAN AUGUSTUS.

(Praising the orthodoxy of Proterius, advocating the public recital by him of passages bearing on the present controversy from the writings of Athanasius and others, and also of the Tome itself in a new Greek translation.)

LETTER CXXXI. TO JULIAN, BISHOP OF COS.

(Telling him he has received Proterius' letter, and asking for (1) a new Greek translation of the Tome; (2) a report on the Easter difficulty of the next year (455)).

LETTER CXXXII. FROM ANATOLIUS, BISHOP OF CONSTANTINOPLE, TO LEO.

(In which he complains of the intermission in their correspondence, maintains his allegiance to Rome, announces the restitution of Aetius, deprecates the charge of personal ambition, and remits the proceedings of Chalcedon for his approval.)

LETTER CXXXIII. FROM PROTERIUS, BISHOP OF ALEXANDRIA, TO LEO.

(Upon the Easter Difficulty of 455.)

LETTER CXXXIV. TO MARCIAN AUGUSTUS.

(Suggesting that Eutyches should be banished to a still remoter place, where he cannot do so much harm by his false teaching.)

LETTER CXXXV. TO ANATOLIUS.

(in Answer to CXXXII.)

LETTER CXXXVI. TO MARCIAN AUGUSTUS.

(Simultaneously with CXXXV., on the subject of his reconciliation with Anatolius.)

LETTER CXXXVII. TO THE SAME, AND ON THE SAME DAY.

(On the subject of Easter, acknowledging the trouble Proterius has taken, — to which is joined a request that the accounts of the oeconomi should be audited by priests, not lay persons.)

LETTER CXXXVIII. TO THE BISHOPS OF GAUL AND SPAIN.(ON EASTER.)

Letter CXXXIX. To Juvenal, Bishop of Jerusalem.
Leo, bishop of the city of Rome, to Juvenal, bishop of Jerusalem.

1.he Rejoices Over Juvenal's Return to Orthodoxy, Though Chiding Him Far Having Gone Astray.

When I received your letter, beloved, which our sons Andrew the presbyter and Peter the deacon brought me, I rejoiced indeed that you had been allowed to return to the seat of your bishopric; but when all the reasons came to my remembrance, which brought you into such excessive troubles, I grieved to think you had been yourself the source of your adversities by failing in persistency of opposition to the heretics: for men can but think you were not bold enough to refute those with whom when in error you professed yourself satisfied. For the condemnation of Flavian of blessed memory, and the acceptance of the most unholy Eutyches, what was it but the denial of our Lord Jesus Christ according to the flesh? which He Himself of His great mercy caused to be overthrown, when by the authority of the holy Council of Chalcedon He brought to nought that accursed judgment of the Synod of Ephesus without debarring any of the attainted from being healed by correction. And therefore, because in the tithe of long-suffering, you have chosen return to wisdom rather than persistency in folly, I rejoice that you have so sought the heavenly remedies as at last to have become a defender of the Faith which is assailed by heretics. For, though no priest ought to be ignorant of that which he preaches , yet any Christian living at Jerusalem is more inexcusable than all the ignorant, seeing that he is taught to understand the power of the Gospel, not only by the written word but by the witness of the places themselves, and what elsewhere may not be disbelieved, cannot there remain unseen. Why is the understanding in difficulty, where the eyes are its instructors? And why are things read or heard doubtful, where all the mysteries of man's salvation obtrude themselves upon the sight and touch? As if to each individual doubter the Lord still used His human voice and said, why are "ye disturbed and why do thoughts arise into your hearts? see My hands and My feet that it is I myself. Handle Me and see because (or that) a spirit hath not bones and flesh, as ye see Me have ."

II. Let Him Be Strengthened in His Faith by the Holy Associations of Life Place Where He Lives.

Make use, therefore, beloved brother, of these incontrovertible proofs of the catholic Faith and support the preaching of the Evangelists by the testimony of the holy places in which you live. In your country is Bethlehem, in which the Light of Salvation sprang from the womb of the Virgin of the house of David , whom wrapped in swaddling clothes the manger of the crowded inn received. In your country was the Saviour's infancy announced by angels, adored by magi, sought by Herod through the death of many infants. In your country was it that His boyhood grew, His youth ripened, and His true man's nature reached to perfect manhood by the increase of the body, not without food for hunger, not without sleep for rest, not without tears of pity, not without fear and dread: for He is one and the same Person, who in the form of God wrought great miracles of power, and in the form of a slave underwent the cruelty of the passion. This the very cross unceasingly says to you: this the stone of the sepulchre cries out, under which the Lord in human condition lay, and from which by Divine power He rose. And when you approach the mount of Olivet, to venerate the place of the Ascension, does not the angel's voice ring in your ears, which says to those who were dumb-founded at the Lord's uplifting, "ye men of Galilee, why stand ye gazing into heaven? this Jesus, Who was taken up from you into heaven, shall so come, as ye saw Him going into heaven ."

III. The Facts of the Gospel Attest the Incarnation.

The true birth of Christ, therefore, is confirmed by the true cross; since He is Himself born in our flesh, Who is crucified in our flesh, which, as no sin entered into it., could not have been mortal, unless it had been that of our race. But in order that He might restore life to all, He undertook the cause of all and rendered void the force of the old bond, by paying it for all, because He alone of us all did not owe it: that, as by one man's guilt all had become sinners, so by one man's innocence all might become innocent, righteousness being bestowed upon men by Him Who had undertaken man's nature. For in no way is He outside our true bodily nature, of Whom the Evangelist in beginning his story says, "the book of the generation of Jesus Christ, the son of David, the son of Abraham ," with which the blessed Apostle Paul's teaching agrees, when he says "whose are the fathers and of whom is Christ according to the flesh, Who is above all God blessed for ever ," and so to Timothy "remember," he says, "that Jesus Christ has risen from the dead, of the seed of David ."

IV. Those Who are Still in Error Must Be Thoroughly Instructed in the Historic Faith.

But how many are the authorities, both in the New and Old Testaments, by which this truth is declared, as befits the antiquity of your See, you clearly understand, seeing that the belief of the Fathers and my letter written to Flavian, of holy memory, of which you yourself made mention, confirmed, as they have been, by the universal synod, are sufficient for you. And therefore it behoves you, beloved, to take heed that no one raise a murmur against the unspeakable mystery of our Redemption and Hope. But if there are any who are still in the darkness of ignorance or the discord of perversity, let them be instructed by the authority of those whose doctrine in God's Church was apostolical and clear, that they may recognize that on the Incarnation of God's Word we believe what they did, and may not by their obstinacy place themselves outside the Body of Christ, in which we died and rose with Him: because neither loyalty to the Faith nor the plan of the mystery admits that either the Godhead should be possible in its own essence. or the reality be falsified in His taking on Him of our flesh. Dated 4th September, in the consulship of the illustrious Aetius and Studius (454).

LETTER CXL. TO JULIAN, BISHOP OF COS.

(Now that Dioscorus is dead, the peace of the Church will be more easily restored.)

LETTER CXLI. TO THE SAME.

(on Several Minor Points of Detail)

LETTER CXLII. TO MARCIAN AUGUSTUS.

(Inter alia thanking him for the trouble he has taken about the Easter of 455.)

LETTER CXLIII. TO ANATOLIUS, BISHOP OF CONSTANTINOPLE.

(Briefly asking him to extirpate all remains of heresy.)

LETTER CXLIV. TO JULIAN, BISHOP OF COS.

(Speaking of Run, Ours Which Have Reached Him of Disturbances at Alexandria, and Begging of Him to Be on the Alert.)

LETTER CXLV. TO LEO AUGUSTUS.

(Asking him to help the church of Alexandria in appointing a good bishop in place of the murdered Proterius.)

LETTER CXLVI. TO ANATOLIUS, BISHOP OF CONSTANTINOPLE.

(Begging him to take precautions lest the change of Emperor should be made the occasion for fresh outbreaks of heresy.)

LETTER CXLVII. TO JULIAN, BISHOP OF COS, AND AETIUS, THE PRESBYTER.

(Charging him to uphold the acts of Chalcedon, and to help in choosing a good successor to Proterius.)

LETTER CXLVIII. TO LEO AUGUSTUS.

(Thanking him for assurances made that he would guard the interests of the Church.)

LETTER CXLIX. TO BASIL, BISHOP OF ANTIOCH.

(Asking him to give no countenance to the demand for a new Synod.)

LETTER CL TO EUXITHEUS, BISHOP OF THESSALONICA (AND OTHERS)

.(to the Same Effect.)

LETTER CLI. TO ANATOLIUS, BISHOP OF CONSTANTINOPLE.

(He is to keep the church of Constantinople free from all heresy.)

LETTER CLII. TO JULIAN, BISHOP OF COS.

(Charging him to see that the preceding letters reach their destination.)

LETTER CLIII. TO AETIUS, PRESBYTER ,OF CONSTANTINOPLE.

(Asking him to assist in the distribution of these letters.)

LETTER CLIV. TO THE EGYPTIAN BISHOPS.

(See Letter CLVIII.)

LETTER CLV. TO ANATOLIUS, BISHOP OF CONSTANTINOPLE.

(In which he incites him to watchfulness, and complains that certain of the clergy in Constantinople are in collusion with the adversary.)

LETTER CLVI. TO LEO AUGUSTUS.

Leo, the bishop, to Leo Augustus.

I. There is No Need to Open the Question of Doctrine Again Now.

Your clemency's letter, which was full of vigorous faith and of the light of truth, I have respectfully received, which I wish I could obey, even in the matter of my personal attendance, which your Majesty thinks necessary; for then I should gain the greater advantage from the sight of your splendour. But I believe you will approve of my view when reason has shown it preferable. For since with holy and spiritual zeal you consistently maintain the Church's peace, and nothing is more conducive to the defence of the Faith than to adhere to those things which have been incontrovertibly defined under tile unceasing guidance of the Holy Spirit, we shall seem to be doing our best to upset the decrees, and at the bidding of a heretic's petition to overthrow the authorities which the universal Church has adopted, and thus to remove all limits from the conflicts of Churches, and giving full rein to rebellion, to extend rather than appease contentions. And hence because after the disgraceful scenes at the synod of Ephesus, whereat through the wickedness of Dioscorus the catholic Faith was rejected, and Eutyches' heresy accepted, nothing more useful could be devised for the preservation of the Christian Faith than that the holy Synod of Chalcedon should rescind his wicked acts, and that such care should be bestowed thereat on heavenly doctrine, that nothing should linger in any one's mind in disagreement with the utterances of either the Prophets or the Apostles, such moderation of course being observed that only the persistent rebels should be east off from the unity of the Church, and no one who was penitent should be denied pardon, what more in accordance with men's expectations or with religion will your Majesty be able to decree, than that no one henceforth be permitted to attack what has been determined by decrees which are Divine rather than human, lest they be truly worthy but to lose God's gift, who have dared to doubt concerning His Truth?

II. The Proposal to Reconsider the Question Proceeds from Antichrist or the Devil Himself.

Since, therefore, the universal Church has become a rock (*petra*) through the building up of that original Rock , and the first of the Apostles, the most blessed Peter, heard the voice of the Lord saying, "Thou art Peter, and upon this rock (*petra*) I will build My Church ," who is there who dare assail such impregnable strength, unless he be either antichrist or the devil, who, abiding unconverted in his wickedness, is anxious to sow lies by the vessels of wrath which are suited to his treachery, whilst under the false name of diligence he pretends to be in search of the Truth. And his unrestrained madness and blind wickedness has deservedly brought contempt and disrepute on himself, so that while he rages against the holy church of Alexandria with diabolical purpose, men may learn the character of those who desire to reconsider the Synod of Chalcedon. For it cannot possibly have been that an opinion was there expressed contrary to the holy Synod of Nicaea, as the heretics falsely maintain, who pretend that they hold the faith of the Nicene Council, in which our holy and venerable fathers, being assembled against Arius, affirmed not that the Lord's Flesh, but that the Son's Godhead was homoousion with the Father, whereas in the Council of Chalcedon against the blasphemy of Eutyches, it was defined that the Lord Jesus Christ took the reality of our body from the substance of the Virgin-mother.

III. All the Bishops of Christendom Agree with Him in This.

Therefore in addressing our most Christian Emperor, who is worthy to be classed among the champions of Christ, I use the freedom of the catholic Faith and fearlessly exhort you to throw in your lot with Apostles and Prophets; firmly to despise and reject those who have deprived themselves of their Christian name, and not to let blasphemous parricides, who, it is agreed, wish to annul the Faith, discuss that Faith under treacherous pretexts. For since the Lord has enriched your clemency with such insight into His mystery, you ought unhesitatingly to consider that the kinglypower has been conferred on you not for the governance of the world alone but more especially for the guardianship of the Church: that by quelling wicked attempts you may both defend that which has been rightly decreed, and restore true peace where there has been disturbance, that is to say by deposing usurpers of the rights of others and reinstating the ancient Faith in the See of Alexandria, that by your reforms God's wrath may be appeased, and so He take not vengeance for their doings on a people hitherto religious, but forgive them. Set before the eyes of your heart, venerable Emperor, the fact that all the Lord's priests which are in all the world, are beseeching you on behalf of that Faith, wherein is Redemption for the whole world. In which those maintainers of the Apostolic Faith more particularly appeal to you who have presided over the Church of Alexandria, entreating your Majesty not to allow heretics who have rightfully been condemned for their perversity, to continue intheir usurpation ; for, whether you look at the wickedness of their error or consider the deed which their madness has perpetrated, not only are they unable to be admitted to the dignity of the priesthood, but they even deserve to be cut off from the name of Christian. For — and I entreat your Majesty's forgiveness for saying so — they to some extent dim your own splendour, most glorious Emperor, when such treacherous parricides dare to ask for that which even the guiltless could not lawfully obtain.

IV. The Difference Between the Two Petitions Which Have Been Presented to the Emperor.

Petitions have been presented to your Majesty, copies of which you subjoined to your letter. But in that which comes in deprecation from the catholics, a list of signatures is contained: and because their case had good reason in it, the names of individuals, and even their dignified rank is confidently disclosed. But in that, which heretical intrusion has not feared to offer to our orthodox Emperor under the vague sanction of a motley body, all particular names are withheld for this reason, lest not only the paucity of members but also their worth might be discovered. For they think it expedient to conceal their number, though their quality is indicated, and not improperly they are afraid to proclaim their position, seeing that they deserve to be condemned. In the one document therefore is contained the petition of catholics, in the other the fictions of heretics are set forth. Here the overthrow of the Lord's priests, of the whole Christian people, and of the monasteries is bemoaned: there is displayed the continuance of gigantic wrongs, so that what ought never to have been heard of is allowed to be widely extended.

V. It is a Great Opportunity for the Emperor to Show His Faith.

Is it not clear which side you ought to support and which to oppose, if the Church of Alexandria, which has always been the "house of prayer," is not now to be "a den of robbers ?" For surely it is manifest that through the cruellest and maddest savagery all the light of the heavenly mysteries is extinguished. The offering of the sacrifice is cut off, the hallowing of the chrism has failed, and from the murderous hands of wicked men all the mysteries have withdrawn themselves. Nor can there be any manner of doubt what decree ought to be passed on these then, who after unutterable acts of sacrilege, after shedding the blood of a most highly reputed priest, awlscattering the ashes of his burnt body to be the sport of the winds of heaven, dare to demand for themselves the rights of a usurped dignity and to arraign before councils the inviolable Faith of the Apostolic teaching. Great, therefore, is the opportunity for you to add to your diadem from the Lord's hand the crown of faith also, and to triumph over the Church's foes: for, if it be matter of praise to you to vanquish the armies of opposing nations, how great will be the glory of freeing from its mad tyrant the church of Alexandria, the affliction of which is an injury to all Christians?

VI. He Promises More Detailed Statements an the Faith Subsequently, and Begs Him to Correct Certain Things in Which Anatolius is Remiss.

But in order that my correspondence may have the effect on your Majesty of a mouth to mouth colloquy, I have seen that whatever suggestions I would make about our commonFaith, must be conveyed in subsequent communications. And lest the pages of this epistle reach too great a length, I have comprised in another letter what is agreeable to the maintenance of the catholic Faith, in order that, though the published statements of the Apostolic See were sufficient, yet theseadditional statements might also break down the snares of the heretics. For your Majesty's priestly and Apostolic mind ought to be still further kindled to righteous vengeance by this pestilential evil, which mars the purity of the church of Constantinople, in which are found certain clerics, who agree with the interpretations of the heretics and within the very heart of the Church assist them by their support. In removing whom if my brother Anatolius is found remiss through too good-natured leniency, vouchsafe to show your laith by administering this remedy also to the Church, that such men be driven not only from the ranks of the clergy, but also from dwelling in the city. I commend to you your Majesty's loyal subjects, bishop Julian and presbyter Aetius, with a request that you will deign to listen quietly to their suggestions in defence of the catholic Faith, because they are in good truth men who may be found helpful to your faith in all things. Dated the 1st of Dec. in the consulship of the illustrious Constantine and Rufus (457).

LETTER CLVII. TO ANATOLIUS, BISHOP OF CONSTANTINOPLE.

(Urging him to active measures in certain specified matters.)

LETTER CLVIII. TO THE CATHOLIC BISHOPS OF EGYPT SOJOURNING IN CONSTANTINOPLE.

Leo to the catholic Egyptian bishops sojourning in Constantinople. He encourages them in their sufferings for the Faith, and in their entreaties for redress to the Emperor.

I have before now been so saddened by tidings of the crimes committed in Alexandria, and my spirit has been so wounded by the atrocity of the deed itself, that I know not what tears to show and what lamentation to utter over it, and am fain to use the prophet's language, "who will give waters to my head and a fountain of tears to my eyes?" Yet anticipating your complaint, beloved, I have entreated our most clement and Christian Emperor for a remedy of these great evils, and by our sons and assistants Gerontius and Olympius have at a different time demanded that he should make haste to purge of a heresy already condemned the church of that city, in which so many Catholic teachers have flourished, and not allow murderous spirits whom no reverence for place or time could deter from shedding their ruler's blood, to gain anything from his clemency, more particularly when they desire to reconsider the council of Chalcedon to the overthrow of the Faith. Accordingly the same reason, beloved, which drove you from your own Sees, ought to console you for your sufferings; for it, is certain that afflicted souls, that suffer adversity for His name, are in no wise deprived of the Lord's protection. Bear it therefore bravely, and mindful of that country which is yours, rejoice over your present sojourn in a strange land. Abstain from grieving over your exile and indulge not in sorrow for your present weariness, ye who know that the Apostle glories even in his many perils on behalf of the Lord's Faith. You have One who knows your conflicts and has prepared the rewards of recompense. Let no one shrink from this labour, whose guerdon is to reign and live for ever. Let the feet of all who fight be fixed in the halls of Jerusalem; for in the hope of that retribution they will have no cause to fear the camp nor the onsets of the enemy. Victory is never hard nor triumph difficult over the remnants of an abject foe who has been routed by the whole world alike, especially over those whose ringleaders you see already prostrate. With unceasing prayers, therefore (even as I also have not failed to do), entreat the favour of the most Christian Emperor, who in God's mercy is ready to hear: that in accordance with the letter I have sent, he may strengthen the cause of the common Faith with that devotion of mind, which we are well assured he possesses, and in his piety may remove all the harmful charges which the madness of heretics has invented, and arrange for your return, beloved, and so may cause each several province and all the churches with their priests to rejoice in the unshaken peace of Christ. Dated the 1st of Dec. in the consulship of Constantine and Rufus (457).

LETTER CLIX. TO NICAETAS, BISHOP OF AQUILEIA.

(Leo, the bishop, to Nicaetas, bishop of Aquileia, greeting.)
I. Prefatory

My son Adeodatus, deacon of our See, on returning to us has delivered your request, beloved, to receive from us the authority of the Apostolic See upon matters which seem indeed to be hard to decide, but which we must make provision for with a view to the necessities of the times that the wounds which have been inflicted by the attacks of the enemy may be healed chiefly by the agency of religion.

II. About the Women Who Married Again When Their Husbands Were Taken Prisoners.

As then you say that through the disasters of war and through the grievous inroads of the enemy families have in certain cases been so broken up that the husbands have been carried off into captivity and their wives remain forsaken, and these latter thinking their own husbands either dead or never likely to be freed from their masters, have contracted another marriage under stress of loneliness, and as, now that the state of things has im- proved through the Lord's help, some of those who were thought to have perished have returned, you seem, dear brother, naturally to be in doubt what ought to be settled by us about women thus joined to other husbands. But because we know it is written that "a woman is joined to a man by God ," and again, we are aware of the precept that "what God hath joined, man may not put asunder ," we are bound to hold that the compact of the lawful marriage must be renewed, and after the removal of the evils inflicted by the enemy, what each lawfully had must be restored to him; and we must take every pains that each should recover what is his own.

III. Whether He is Blameable Who Has Taken the Prisoner's Wife?

But notwithstanding let him not be held blameable and treated as the invader of another's right, who took the place of the husband, who was thought no longer alive. For thus many things which belonged to those led into captivity happened to pass into the possession of others, and yet it is altogether fair that on their return their property should be restored. And if this is duly observed in the case of slaves or of lands, or even of houses and personal goods, how much more ought it to be done in the restoration of wives, that what has been disturbed by the necessitities of war may be restored by the remedy of peace?

IV. The Wife Must Be Restored to Her First Husband.

And, therefore, if husbands who have returned after a long captivity still feel such affection for their wives as to desire them to return to partnership , that, which necessity brought about, must be passed over and judged blameless and the demands of fidelity satisfied.

V. Women Must Be Excommunicated Who Refuse to Return.

And if any women are so possessed by love of their later husbands as to prefer to remain with them than to return to their lawful partners, they are deservedly to be branded: so that they be even deprived of the Church's communion; for in a pardonable matter they have chosen to taint themselves with crime, showing that they have sought their own pleasure in their incontinence, when a rightful restitution could have obtained their forgiveness. Let them return then to their former state and make voluntary reparation, nor let that which a condition of necessity extorted from them be by any means turned into disgrace through evil desires; because, as those women who refuse to return to their husbands are to be held unholy, so they who return to an affection entered on with God's sanction are deservedly to be praised.

VI. About Captives, Who Were Compelled to Eat of Sacrificial Food.

Concerning those Christians who are asserted to have been polluted with sacrificial food, while among those by whom they were taken prisoners, we have thought it right to make this reply to your enquiry, dear brother, that they be purged by a satisfactory penitence which is to be measured not so much by the duration of the process as by the intensity of the feeling. And whether their compliance was wrung from them by terror or hunger, there need be no hesitation at acquitting them, since the food was taken from fear or want, not from superstitious reverence.

VII. About Those Who in Fear or by Mistake Were Re-Baptized

But as to those about whom you thought. beloved, we ought likewise to be consulted who were either forced by fear or led by mistake to repeat their baptism, and now understand that they acted contrary to the ordinances of the catholic Faith, such moderation must be observed towards them that they be received into full communion with us, but not without the healing of penitence and the imposition of the bishop's hands, the length of the penance (with due regard to moderation) being left to your judgment, as you shall perceive the minds of the penitents to be disposed: in which you must not forget to consider old age, illness, and other risks. For if a man be in so dangerous a case that his life is despaired of, while he is still under penance, he should receive the gracious aid of communion by the priest's tender care.

VIII. About Baptism by Heretics.

For they who have received baptism from heretics, not having been previously baptized, are to be confirmed by imposition of hands with only the invocation of the Holy Ghost, because they have received the bare form of baptism without the power of sanctification . And this regulation, as you know; we require to be kept in all the churches, that the font once entered may not be defiled by repetition, as the Lord says, "One Lord, one faith, one baptism." And that washing may not be polluted by repetition, but, as we have said, only the sanctification of the Holy Ghost invoked, that what no one can receive from heretics may be obtained from catholic priests. This letter of ours, which we have sent in reply to the inquiries of the brotherhood you shall bring to the knowledge of all your brethren and fellow-bishops of the province, that our authority, now that it is given, may avail for the general observance. Dated 21st March, in the consulship of Majorian Augustus (458).

LETTER CLX.

(See Letter CLVIII.)

LETTER CLXI. TO THE PRESBYTERS, DEACONS AND CLERGY OF THE CHURCH OF CONSTANTINOPLE.

(Exhorting them to remain stedfast in the Faith as fixed at Chalcedon, and to have no dealings with Atticus and Andrew unless they recant.)

LETTER CLXII. TO LEO AUGUSTUS.

By the hand of Philoxenus agens in rebus. Leo the Bishop to Leo Augustus.

I. The Decrees of Chalcedon and Nicaea are Identical and Final.

With much joy my mind exults in the Lord, and great is my cause for thankfulness, now that I perceive your clemency's most excellent faith to be in all things enlarged by the gifts of heavenly grace, and I experience by increased diligence the devotion of a priestly mind in you. For in your Majesty's communications! it is beyond doubt revealed what the Holy Spirit is working through you for the good of the whole Church, and how greatly it is to be desired by the prayers of all the faithful that your empire may be everywhere extended with glory, seeing that besides your care for things temporal you so perseveringly exercise a religious foresight in the service of what is divine and eternal: to wit that the catholic Faith, which alone gives life to and alone in hallows mankind, may abide in the one confession, and the dissensions which spring from the variety of earthly opinions may be driven away, most glorious Emperor, from that solid Rock, on which the city of God is built. And these gifts of God will at last be granted us from Him, if we be not found ungrateful for what has been vouchsafed, and as though what we have gained were naught, we seek not rather the very opposite. For to seek what has been discovered, to reconsider what has been completed, and to demolish what has been defined, what else is it but to return no thanks for things gained and to indulge the unholy longings of deadly lust on the food of the forbidden tree? And hence by deigning to show a more careful regard for the peace of the universal Church, you manifestly recognize what is the design of the heretics' mighty intrigues that a more careful discussion should take place between the disciples of Eutyches and Dioscorus and the emissary of the Apostolic See, as if nothing had already been defined, and that what with the glad approval of the catholic priests of the whole world was determined at the holy Synod of Chalcedon should be rendered invalid to the detriment also of the most sacred Council of Nicaea. For what in our own days at Chalcedon was determined concerning our Lord Jesus Christ's Incarnation, was also so defined at Nicaea by that mystic number of Fathers, lest the confession of catholics should believe that God's Only-begotten Son was in aught unequal to the Father, or that when He was made Son of man He had not the true nature of our flesh and soul.

II. The Wicked Designs of Heretics Must Be Stedfastly Resisted.

Therefore we must abhor and persistently avoid what heretical deceit is striving to obtain, nor must what has been well and fully defined be brought again under discussion, lest we ourselves should seem at the will of condemned men to have doubts concerning things which it is clear agree throughout with the authority of Prophets, Evangelists, and Apostles. And hence, if there are any who disagree with these heaven-inspired decisions, let them be left to their own opinions and depart from the unity of the Church with that perverse sect which they have chosen. For it can in no wise be that men who dare to speak against divine mysteries are associated in any communion with us. Let them pride themselves on the emptiness of their talk and boast of the cleverness of their arguments against the Faith: we are pleased to obey the Apostle's precepts, where he says, "See that no one deceive you with philosophy and vain seductions of men ." For according to the same Apostle, "ifI build up those things which I destroyed, I prove myself a transgressor ," and subject myself to those conditions of punishment which not only the authority of Prince Marcian of blessed memory, but I myself also by my consent have accepted. Because as you have justly and truthfully maintained perfection admits of no increase nor fulness of addition. And hence, since I know you, venerable Prince, imbued as you are with the purest light of truth, waver in no part of the Faith, but with just and perfect judgment distinguish right from wrong, and separate what is to be embraced from what is to be rejected, I beseech you not to think that my humility is to be blamed for want of confidence, since my cautiousness is not only in the interests of the universal Church but also for the furtherance of your own glory, that under your reign the unscrupulousness of heretics may not seem to be advanced and the security of catholics disturbed.

III. He Promises to Send Envoys Not to Discuss with the Eutychians, But to Explain the Faith to the Emperor.

Although, therefore, I am very confident of the piety of your heart in all things, and perceive that through the Spirit of Gov dwelling in you, you are sufficiently instructed, nor can any error delude your faith, yet I will endeavour to follow your bidding so far as to send certain of my brothers to represent my person before you, and to set forth what the Apostolic rule of Faith is, although, as I have said, it is well known to you, in all things making it clear and certain that they are not in any way to be reckoned among catholics, who do not accept the definitions of the venerable Synod of Nicaea or the ordinances of the holy Council of Chalcedon, inasmuch as it is evident the holy decrees of both proceed from the Evangelical and Apostolical source, and whatever is not of Christ's watering is like a snake-poisoned draught . Your Majesty should understand beforehand, most venerable Emperor, that those whom I undertake to send will come from the Apostolic See, not to fight with the enemies of the Faith nor to strive against any, because of matters already settled as it has pleased God both at Nicaea and at Chalcedon we dare not enter upon any discussion, as if what so great an authority has fixed by theHoly Spirit were doubtful or weak.

IV. The Heretics Must Be Formed to Give Up Their Usurpations and Left to the Judgment of God.

But we do not refuse the assistance of our ministry for the instruction of our little ones, who after being fed with milk desire to be satisfied with more solid food: and as we do not scorn the simple folk, so we will have no dealings with rebel heretics, remembering the Lord's command, who says, "Give not that which is holy to the dogs, nor cast your pearls before swine ." Surely it is altogether unworthy and unjust to admit to freedom of discussion men whom the Holy Spirit describes in the words of the prophet, "the sons of the stranger have lied unto me ." For even though they resist not the Gospel, yet they have shown themselves to be of those of whom it is written "they profess that they know God but by their deeds they deny Him ," while the blood of just Abel still cries against wicked Cain , who being rebuked by the Lord did not set quietly about his repentance but burst forth into murder. Whose punishment we wish to be reserved for the Lord's judgment in such a way that, unprincipled plunderer and blood-thirsty murderer as he is, he may be thrown back upon himself and relinquish what is ours. We pray you also not to suffer the lamentable captivity of the holy church of Alexandria to be any further prolonged, which by the help of your faith and Justice ought to be restored to its liberty, that through all the cities of Egypt the dignity of the Fathers and their priestly rights may be restored. Dated 21st of March in the consulship of Leo and Majorian Augusti (458).

LETTER CLXIII. TO ANATOLIUS, BISHOP OF CONSTANTINOPLE. BY PATRITIUS THE DEACON THE DEACON.

(Glorying over the harshness of his former letter, to which Anatolius had objected, but persisting that he is not satisfied with the explanation Atticus had furnished of his orthodoxy.)

LETTER CLXIV TO LEO AUGUSTUS.

Leo, the bishop, to Leo Augustus.

I. He Sends Envoys But de Deprecates Any Fresh Discussion of the Faith.

Rejoicing that it has been proved to me by many clear proofs with what earnestness you consult the interests of the universal Church, I have not delayed to obey your Majesty's commands on the first opportunity, by despatching Domitian and Geminian my brothers and fellow-bishops, who in furtherance of my earnest prayers, shall entreat you for the peaceful acceptance of the gospel-teaching and obtain the liberty of the Faith in which through the instruction of the Holy Spirit you yourself are so conspicuously eminent, now that the enemies of Christ are driven far away, who even if they had wished to conceal their madness, could not lie hid, because the holy simplicity of the Lord's flock is very different from the pretences of beasts who hide themselves in sheeps' clothing, nor can they creep in by hypocrisy now that their exceeding madness has revealed them. Recognize, therefore, august and venerable Emperor, how that you are called by Divine providence to the guardianship of the whole world, and understand what aid you owe to your Mother, the Church, who makes especial boast of you. Disputes that are ended must not be allowed to rise with renewed vigour against the triumphs of the Almighty's right hand, especially when this can in no wise be allowed to heretics, whose attempts have long ago been condemned and the labours of the faithful have a just claim to this result, that all the fulness of the Church shall remain secure in the completeness of her unity, and that nothing whatever of what has been well laid down shall be reconsidered, because, after constitutions have been legitimately framed under Divine guidance, to wish still to wrangle is the sign not of a peace-making but of a rebellious spirit, as says the Apostle, "for to strive with words is profitable for nothing, but for the subverting of them that hear."

II. In Matters of Faith Human Rhetoric is Out of Place.

For if it be always free for human fancies to assert themselves in dispute, there never will be wanting men who will dare to oppose the Truth, and to put their trust in the glib utterances of this world's wisdom, whereas the Christian Faith and wisdom knows from the teaching of our Lord Jesus Christ Himself how strictly it ought to shun this most harmful vanity. For when Christ was about to summon all nations to the illumination of the Faith, He chose those who were to devote themselves to the preaching of the Gospel not from among philosophers or orators, but took humble fishermen as the instruments by which He would reveal Himself, lest the heavenly teaching, which was of itself full of mighty power, should. seem to need the aid of words. And hence the Apostle protests and says, "For Christ sent me not to baptize but to preach the Gospel, not in wisdom of words lest the cross of Christ should be made void; for the word of the cross is to them indeed that perish foolishness, but to those which are being saved it is the power of God. For it is written, I will destroy the wisdom of the wise and the prudence of the prudent will I reject. Where is the wise? where is the scribe? where is the inquirer of this age? has not God made foolish the wisdom of this world?" For rhetorical arguments and clever debates of man's device make their chief boast in this, that in doubtful matters which are obscured by the variety of opinions they can induce their hearers to accept that view which each has chosen for his own genius and eloquence to bring forward; and thus it happens that what is maintained with the greatest eloquence is reckoned the truest. But Christ's Gospel needs not this art; for in it the true teaching stands revealed by its own light: nor is there any seeking for that which shall please the ear, when to know Who is the Teacher is sufficient for true faith.

III. Eutyches' Dogma is Condemned by the Testimony of Scripture and Cannot Further Be Entertained.

But nothing severs those who are deceived by their own inventions, from the light of the Gospel so much as their not thinking that the Lord's Incarnation appertains in a true sense to man's, that is, our, nature: as if it were unworthy of God's glory that the majesty of the impossible Word should have taken the reality of human flesh, whereas men's salvation could not otherwise have been restored had not He Who is in the form of God deigned also to take the form of a slave. And hence since the holy Synod of Chalcedon, which was attended by all the provinces of the Roman world and obtained universal acceptance for its decisions, and is in complete harmony therein with the most sacred council of Nicaea, has cut off all the wicked followers of the Eutychian dogma from the body of the catholic communion, how shall any of the lapsed regain the peace of the church, without purging himself by a full course of penitence? For what licence can be granted them for discussing, when they have deserved to be condemned by a just and holy judgment, so that they might most truly fall under that sentence of the blessed Apostle, wherewith at the very outset of the infant Church he overthrew the enemies of Christ's cross, saying: "every spirit which confesses Jesus Christ to have come in the flesh is of God, and every spirit which dissolves Jesus is not of God, but this is antichrist ." And this pre-existent teaching of the Holy Ghost we must faithfully and stedfastly make use of, lest, by admitting the discussions of such men the authority of the divinely inspired decrees be diminished, when in all parts of your kingdom and in all borders of the earth that Faith which was confirmed at Chalcedon is being established on the surest basis of peace, nor is any one worthy of the name of Christian who cuts himself off from communion with us. Of whom the Apostle says, "a man that is heretical after a first and a second admonition, avoid, knowing that such a one is perverse and condemned by his own judgment ."

IV. If the Divine Mercy is to Be Exercised, the Heretics Must Cease Entirely from the Error of Their Ways.

What therefore the unholy parricide has perpetrated by seizing on the holy Church and cruelly murdering its very ruler, cannot be expiated by man's forgiveness, unless He Who alone can rightly punish such things, and alone can of His unspeakable mercy remit them, be propitiated. But though we are not anxious for vengeance, we cannot in any way be allied with the devil's servants. Yet if we learn they are quitting the ranks of heresy, repenting, them of their error and turning from the weapons of discord to the lamentations of sorrow, we also can intercede for them, lest they perish for ever, thus following the example of the Lord's loving-kindness, who, when nailed to the wood of the cross prayed for His persecutors, "Father, forgive them; for they know not what they do ." And that Christian love may do this profitably for its enemies, wicked heretics must cease to harass God's ever religious and ever devout Church; they must not dare to disturb the souls of the simple by their falsehoods, to the end that, where in all former times the purest faith has flourished, the teaching of the Gospel and of the Apostles may now also have free course; because we also imitating, so far as we can, the Divine mercy desire no one to be punished by justice, but all to be released by mercy.

V. Let Him Restore the Refugee Clergy and Laity and Utterly Reject Those Who Persist in Heresy.

I entreat your clemency, listen to the suggestions of my brethren already mentioned, whom, as I some time ago have said in a former letter , I have sent not to wrangle with the condemned, but merely to intercede with you for the stability of the catholic Faith. And in accordance with your faith in and regard for the Divine Majesty this especially you should grant, that completely setting aside the contentions of heretics you should deign to bestow a merciful attention on those who have fallen upon such evil days, and, after restoring the liberty of the church of Alexandria to its pristine state, should set up there a bishop who, upholding the decrees of the Synod of Chalcedon and agreeing with the ordinances of the Gospel, shall be able to restore peace among that greatly disturbed people. Those bishops and clergy also whom the unholy parricide has driven out of their churches, should be recalled at your Majesty's command, all others also, whom a like maliciousness has banished from their dwellings, being restored to their former estate, to the end that we may have due cause fully and perfectly to rejoice in the grace of God and your faith without any further noise of strife. For it any one is so forgetful of the Christian hope and his own salvation as to venture by any dispute to assail the Evangelical and Apostolical decrease of the holy Synod of Chalcedon, thus overthrowing the most sacred Council of Nicaea also, him with all heretics who have held blasphemous and abominable views on the Incarnation of our Lord Jesus Christ we condemn by a like anathema and equal curse, so that, without refusing the remedy of repentance to those who make full and legitimate atonement, the sentence of the Synod, which is based on truth, may rest upon those who still resist. Dated 17th of August, in the consulship of Leo and Majorian Augusti (458).

LETTER CLXV. TO LEO AUGUSTUS.

[This letter, which is sometimes called the Second Tome, contains the detailed statement of the catholic doctrine of the Incarnation, which Leo had promised the Emperor in Letter CLVI. It consists of 9 chapters, but, as chaps. iii. to viii. and parts of ii. and ix. are almost identical in language with Letter CXXIV. already given in full, I have not thought it necessary to reproduce the letter here. At the end a long series of quotations from Hilary, Ambrose and other Fathers bearing upon the doctrine are also added, but these also are dispensed with in accordance with our general practice, as we are now presenting Leo and no one else to the reader.]

LETTER CLXVI. TO NEO, BISHOP OF RAVENNA.

Leo, the bishop, to Neo, bishop of Ravenna, greeting.

I. Those, Who Being Taken Captives in Infancy Cannot Remember or Bring Witnesses of Theirbaptism, Must Not Be Denied This Sacrament.

We have indeed frequently, God's Spirit instructing us, steadied the brethren's hearts, when they were tottering on the slippery places of doubtful questions, by formulating an answer either out of the teaching of the Holy Scriptures or from the rules of the Fathers: but lately in Synod a new and hitherto unheard-of subject of debate has arisen. For at the instance of certain brethren we have discovered that some of the prisoners of war, on their free return to their own homes, such to wit as went into captivity at an age when they could have no sure knowledge of anything, crave the healing waters of baptism, but in the ignorance of infancy cannot remember whether they have received the mystery and rites of baptism, and that therefore in this uncertainty of defective recollection their souls are brought into jeopardy, so long as under a show of caution they are denied a grace, which is withheld, because it is thought to have been bestowed. And so, since certain brethren in a not unjustifiable fear have hesitated to perform the rites of the Lord's mystery, at a synodal meeting, as we have said, we have received a formal request for advice on this matter, and in carefully discussing it, we have desired to weigh each members opinion, and to handle it in so cautious a manner as to arrive with certainty at the truth by making use of the knowledge of many. Consequently the same things, which have come into our mind by the Divine inspiration, have received the assent and confirmation of a large number of the brethren. And so we are bound before all things to take heed, while we hold fast to a certain show of caution, we incur a loss of souls who are to be regenerated. For who is so given over to suspicions as to decide that to be true which without any evidence he suspects by mere guesswork? And so wherever the man himself who is anxious for the new birth does not recollect his baptism, and no one can Bear witness about him being unaware of his consecration to God, there is no possibility for sin to creep In, seeing that, so far as their knowledge goes, neither the bestower or receiver of the consecration is guilty. We know indeed that an unpardonable offence is committed, whenever in accordance with the institutions of heretics which the holy Fathers have condemned, any one is forced twice to enter the font, which is but once available for those who are to be reborn, in opposition to the Apostle's teaching , which speaks to us of One Godhead in Trinity, one confession in Faith, one sacrament in Baptism. But in this nothing similar is to be apprehended, since, what is not known to have been done at all, cannot come under the charge of repetition. And so, whenever such a case occurs, first sift it by careful investigation, and spend a considerable time, unless his last end is near, in inquiring whether there be absolutely no one who by his testimony can assist the other's ignorance. And when it is established that the man who requires the sacrament of baptism is prevented by a mere baseless suspicion, let him come boldly to obtain the grace, of which he is conscious of no trace in himself. Nor need we fear thus to open the door of salvation which has not been shown to have been entered before.

II. Baptism by Heretics Must Not Be Invalidated by Second Baptism.

But if it is established that a man has been baptized by heretics, on him the mystery of regeneration must in no wise be repeated, but only that conferred which was wanting before, so that he may obtain the power of the Holy Ghost by the laying on of the Bishop's hands . This decision, beloved brother, we wish to be brought to the knowledge of you all generally, to the end that God's mercy may not be refused to those who desire to be saved through undue timidity. Dated the 24th of Oct., in the consulship of Ms Majorian Augustus (458).

LETTER CLXVII . TO RUSTICUS, BISHOP OF GALLIA NARBONENSIS, WITH THE REPLIES TO HIS QUESTIONS ON VARIOUS POINTS.

Leo, the bishop, to Rusticus, bishop of Gallia Narbonensis.

I. He Exhorts Him to Act with Moderation Towards Two Bishops Who Have Offended Him.

Your letter, brother. which Hermes your archdeacon brought, I have gladly received; the number of different matters it contains makes it indeed lengthy, but not so tedious to me on a patient perusal that any point should be passed over, amid the cares that press upon me from all sides. And hence having grasped the gist of your allegation and reviewed what took place at the inquiry of the bishops and leading men , we gather that Sabinian and Leo, presbyters, lacked confidence in your action, and that they have no longer any just cause for complaint, seeing that of their own accord they withdrew from the discussion that had been begun. What form or what measure of justice you ought to mete out to them I leave to your own discretion advising you, however, with the exhortation of love that to the healing of the sick you ought to apply spiritual medicine, and that remembering the Scripture which says "be not over just ," you should act with mildness towards these who in zeal for chastity seem to have exceeded the limits of vengeance, lest the devil, who deceived the adulterers, should triumph over the avengers of the adultery.

II. He Expostulates with Him for Wishing to Give Up His Office, Which Would Imply Distrust of God's Promises.

But I am surprised, beloved, that you are so disturbed by opposition in consequence of offences, from whatever cause arising, as to say you would rather be relieved of the labours of your bishopric, and live in quietness and ease than continue in the office committed to you. But since the Lord says, "blessed is he who shall persevere unto the end ," whence shall come this blessed perseverance, except from the strength of patience? For as the Apostle proclaims, "All who would live godly in Christ shall suffer persecution ." And it is not only to be reckoned persecution, when sword or fire or other active means are used against the Christian religion; for the direst persecution is often inflicted by nonconformity of practice and persistent disobedience and the barbs of ill-natured tongues: and since all the members of the Church are always liable to these attacks, and no portion of the faithful are free from temptation, so that a life neither of ease nor of labour is devoid of danger, who shall guide the ship amidst the waves of the sea. if the helmsman quit his post? Who shall guard the sheep from the treachery of wolves, if the shepherd himself be not on the watch? Who, in fine, shall resist the thieves and robbers. if love of quietude draw away the watchman that is set to keep the outlook from the strictness of his watch? One must abide, therefore, in the office committed to him and in the task undertaken. Justice must be stedfastly upheld and mercy lovingly extended. Not men, but their sins must be hated . The proud must be rebuked, the weak must be borne with; and those sins which require severer chastisement must be dealt with in the spirit not of vindictiveness but of desire to heal. And if a fiercer storm of tribulation fall upon us, let us not be terror-stricken as if we had to overcome the disaster in our own strength, since both our Counsel and our Strength is Christ, and through Him we can do all things, without Him nothing, Who, to confirm the preachers of the Gospel and the ministers of the mysteries, says, "Lo, I am with you all the days even to the consummation of the age ." And again He says, "these things I have spoken unto you that in me ye may have peace. In this world ye shall have tribulation, but be of good cheer, because I have overcome the world ." The promises, which are as plain as they can be, we ought not to let any causes of offence to weaken, lest we should seem ungrateful to God for making us His chosen vessels, since His assistance is powerful as His promises are true.

III. Many of the Questions Raised Could Be More Easily Settled in a Personal Interview Than on Paper.

On those points of inquiry, beloved, which your archdeacon has brought me separately written out, it would be easier to arrive at conclusions on each point face to face, if you could grant us the advantage of your presence. For since some questions seem to exceed the limits of ordinary diligence, I perceive that they are better suited to conversation than to writing: for as there are certain things which can in no wise be controverted, so there are many things which require to be modified either by considerations of age or by the necessities of the case; always provided that we remember in things which are doubtful or obscure, that must be followed which is found to be neither contrary to the commands of the Gospel nor opposed to the decrees of the holy Fathers.

Question I. *Concerning a Presbyter or Deacon Who Falsely Claims to Be a Bishop, and Those Whom They Have Ordained.*

Reply. No consideration permits men to be reckoned among bishops who have not been elected by the clergy, demanded by the laity, and consecrated by the bishops of the province with the assent of the metropolitan . And hence, since the question often arises concerning advancement unduly obtained, who need doubt that that can in no wise be which is not shown to have been conferred on them, And if any clerics have been ordained by such false bishops in those churches which have bishops of their own, and their ordination took place with the consent and approval of the proper bishops, it may be held valid on condition that they continue in the same churches. Otherwise it must be held void, not being connected with any place nor resting on any authority.

Question II. *Concerning a Presbyter or Deacon, Who on His Crime Being Known Asks for Public Penance, Whether It is to Be Granted Him by Laying on of Hands?*

Reply. It is contrary to the custom of the Church that they who have been dedicated to the dignity of the presbyterate or the rank of the diaconate, should receive the remedy of penitence by laying on of hands for any crime; which doubtless descends from the Apostles' tradition, according to what is written, "If a priest shall have sinned, who shall pray for him?" And hence such men when they have lapsed in order to obtain God's mercy must seek private retirement, where their atonement may be profitable as well as adequate.

Question III. *Concerning Those Who Minister at the Altar and Have Wives, Whether They May Lawfully Cohabit with Them?*

Reply. The law of continence is the same for the ministers of the altar as for bishops and priests, who when they were laymen or readers, could lawfully marry and have offspring. But when they reached to the said ranks, what was before lawful ceased to be so. And hence, in order that their wedlock may become spiritual instead of carnal, it behaves them not to put away their wives but to "have them as though they had them not ," whereby both the affection of their wives may be retained and the marriage functions cease.

Question IV. *Concerning a Presbyter or Deacon Who Has Given His Unmarried Daughter in Marriage to a Man Who Already Had a Woman Joined to Him, by Whom He Had Also Had Children.*

Reply. Not every woman that is joined to a man is his wife, even as every son is not his father's heir. But the marriage bond is legitimate between the freeborn and between equals: this was laid down by the Lord long before the Roman law had its beginning. And so a wife is different from a concubine, even as a bondwoman from a freewoman. For which reason also the Apostle in order to show the difference of these persons quotes from Genesis, where it is said to Abraham, "Cast out the bondwoman and her son: for the son of the bondwoman shall not be heir with my son Isaac ." And hence, since the marriage tie was from the beginning so constituted as apart from the joining of the sexes to symbolize the mystic union of Christ and His Church, it is undoubted that that woman has no part in matrimony, in whose case it is shown that the mystery of marriage has not taken place. Accordingly a clergyman of any rank who has given his daughter in marriage to a man that has a concubine, must not be considered to have given her to a married man, unless perchance the other woman should appear to have become free, to have been legitimately dowered and to have been honoured by public nuptials.

Question V. *Concerning Young Women Who Have Married Men that Have Concubines.*

Reply. Those who are joined to husbands by their fathers' will are tree from blame, if the women whom their husbands had were not in wedlock.

Question VI. *Concerning Those Who Leave the Women by Whom They Have Children and Take Wives.*

Reply. Seeing that the wife is different from the concubine, to turn a bondwoman from one's couch and take a wife whose free birth is assured, is not bigamy but an honourable proceeding.

Question VII. *Concerning Those Who in Sickness Accept Terms of Penitence, and When They Have Recovered, Refuse to Keep Them.*

Reply. Such men's neglect is to be blamed but not finally to be abandoned, in order that they may be incited by frequent exhortations to carry out faithfully what under stress of need they asked for. For no one is to be despaired of so long as he remain in this body, because sometimes what the diffidence of age puts off is accomplished by maturer counsels.

Question VIII. *Concerning Those Who Their Deathbed Promise Repentance and Die Before Receiving Communion.*

Reply. Their cause is reserved for the judgment of God, in Whose hand it was that their death was put off until the very time of communion. But we cannot be in communion with those, when dead, with whom when alive we were not in communion.

Question IX. *Concerning Those Who Under Pressure of Great Pain Ask for Penance to Be Granted Them, and When the Presbyter Has Come to Give What They Seek, If the Pain Has Abated Somewhat, Make Excuses and Refuse to Accept What is Offered.*

Reply. This tergiversation cannot proceed from contempt of the remedy but from fear of falling into worse sin. Hence the penance which is put off, when it is more earnestly sought must not be denied in order that the wounded soul may in whatever way attain to the healing of absolution.

Question X. *Concerning Those Who Have Professed Repentance, If They Begin to Go to Law in the Forum.*

Reply. To demand just debts is indeed one thing and to think nothing of one's own property from the perfection of love is another. But one who craves pardon for unlawful doings ought to abstain even from many things that are lawful, as says the Apostle, "all things are lawful for me, but all things are not expedient ." Hence, if the penitent has a matter which perchance he ought not to neglect, it is better for him to have recourse to the judgment of the Church than of the forum.

Question XI. *Concerning Those Who During or After Penance Transact Business.*

Reply. The nature of their gains either excuses or condemns the trafficker, because there is an honourable and a base kind of profit. Notwithstanding it is more expedient for the penitent to suffer loss than to be involved in the risks of trafficking, because it is hard for sin not to come into transactions between buyer and seller.

Question XII. *Concerning Those Who Return to Military Service After Doing Penance.*

Reply. It is altogether contrary to the rules of the Church to return to military service in the world after doing penance, as the Apostle says, "No soldier in God's service entangles himself in the affairs of the world ." Hence he is not free from the snares of the devil who wishes to entangle himself in the military service of the world.

Question XIII. *Concerning Those Who After Penance Take Wives or Join Themselves to Concubines.*

Reply. If a young man under fear of death or the dangers of captivity has done penance, and afterwards fearing to fall into youthfulincontinence has chosen to marry a wife lest he should be guilty of fornication, he seems to have committed a pardonable act, so long as he has known no woman whatever save his wife. Yet herein we lay down no rule, but express an opinion as to what is less objectionable. For according to a true view of the matter nothing better suits him who has done penance than continued chastity both of mind and body.

Question XIV. *Concerning Monks Who Take to Military Service or to Marriage.*

Reply. The monk's vow being undertaken of his own will or wish cannot be given up without sin. For that which a man has vowed to God, he ought also to pay. Hence he who abandons his profession of a single life and betakes himself to military service or to marriage, must make atonement and clear himself publicly, because although such service may be innocent and the married state honourable, it is transgression to have forsaken the higher choice.

Question XV. *Concerning Young Women Who Have Worn the Religious Habit for Some Time But Have Not Been Dedicated, If They Afterwards Marry.*

Reply. Young women, who without being forced by their parents' command but of their own free-will have taken the vow and habit of virginity, if afterwards they choose wedlock, act wrongly, even though they have not re- ceived dedication: of which they would doubtless not have been defrauded, if they had abided by their vow.

Question XVI. *Concerning Those Who Have Been Left as Infants by Christian Parents, If No Proof of Their Baptism Can Be Found Whether They Ought to Be Baptized?*

Reply. If no proof exist among their kinsfolk and relations, nor among the clergy or neighbours whereby those, about whom the question is raised, may be proved to have been baptized, steps must be taken for their regeneration: lest they evidently perish; for in their case reason does not allow that what is not shown to have been done should seem to be repeated.

Question XVII. *Concerning Those Who Have Been Captured by the Enemy and are Not Aware Whether They Have Been Baptized But Know, They Were Several Times Taken to Church by Their Parents, Whether They Can or Ought to Be Baptized When They Come Back to Roman Territory?*

Reply. Those who can remember that they used to go to church with their parents can remember whether they received what used to be given to their parents . But if this also has escaped their memory, it seems that that must be bestowed on them which is not known to have been bestowed because there can be no presumptuous rashness where the most loyal carefulness has been exercised.

Question XVIII. *Concerning Those Who Have Come from Africa or Mauretania and Know Not in What Sect They Were Baptized, What Ought to Be Done in Their Case?*

Reply. These persons are not doubtful of their baptism, but profess ignorance as to the faith of those who baptized them: and hence since they have received the form of baptism in some way or other, they are not to be baptized but are to be united to the catholics by imposition of hands, after the invocation of the Holy Spirit's power, which they could not receive from heretics.

Question XIX. *Concerning Those Who After Being Baptized in Infancy Were Captured by the Gentiles, and Lived with Them After the Manner of the Gentiles, When They Come Back to Roman Territory as Still Young Men, If They Seek Communion, What Shall Be Done?*

Reply. If they have only lived with Gentiles and eaten sacrificial food, they can be purged by fasting and laying on of hands, in order that for the future abstaining from things offered to idols, they may be partakers of Christ's mysteries. But if they have either worshipped idols or been polluted with manslaughter or fornication, they must not be admitted to communion, except by public penance.

LETTER CLXVIII. TO ALL THE BISHOPS OF CAMPANIA, SAMNIUM AND PICENUM.

(Rebuking them first for performing baptisms without due preparation or sufficient cause on ordinary saints'-days (Easter and Whitsuntide being the only recognized times), and secondly for requiring from penitents that a list of their offences should be read out publicly, a practice which is in many ways objectionable.)

LETTER CLXIX. TO LEO AUGUSTUS.

Leo, the bishop, to Leo Augustus.

I. He Heartily Thanks the Emperor Far What He Has Done, and Asks Him to Complete the Work in Any Way He Can.

If we should seek to reward your Majesty's glorious resolution in defence of the Faith with all the praise that the greatness of the issue demands, we should be found unequal to the task of giving thanks and celebrating the joy of the universal Church with our feeble tongue. But His worthier recompense awaits your acts and deserts, in whose cause you have shown so excellent a zeal, and are now triumphing gloriously over the attainment of the wished-for end. Your clemency must know therefore that all the churches of God join in praising you and rejoicing that the unholy parricide has been cast off from the neck of the Alexandrine church, and that God's people, on whom the abominable robber has been so great a burden, restored to the ancient liberty of the Faith, can now be recalled into the way of salvation by the preaching of faithful priests, when it sees the whole hotbed of pestilence done away with in the person of the originator himself. Now therefore, because you have accomplished this by firm resolution and stedfast will, complete your tale of work for the Faith by passing such decrees as shall be well-pleasing to God in favour of this city's catholic ruler , who is tainted by no trace of the heresy now so often condemned: lest, perchance, the wound apparently healed but still lurking beneath. the scar should grow, and the Christian laity; which by your public action has been freed from the perversity of heretics, should again fall a prey to deadly poison.

II. Good Works as Well as Integrity of Faith is Required in a Priest.

But you see, venerable Emperor, and clearly understand, that in the person, whose excommunication is contemplated, it is not only the integrity of his faith that must be considered; for even, if that could be purged by any punishments and confessions, and completely restored by any conditions, yet the wicked and bloody deeds that have been committed can never be done away by the protestations of plausible words: because in God's pontiff, and particularly in the priest of so great a church, the sound of the tongue and the utterance of the lips is not enough, and nothing is of avail, if God makes proclamation with His voice and the mind is convicted of blasphemy. For of such the Holy Ghost speaks by the Apostle, "having an appearance of godliness, but denying the power thereof," and again elsewhere, "they profess that they know God, but in deeds they deny Him ." And hence, since in every member of the Church both the integrity of the true Faith and abundance of good works is looked for, how much more ought both these things to predominate in the chief pontiff, because the one without the other cannot be in union with the Body of Christ.

III. Timothy's Request For Indulgence on the Score of Orthodoxy Must Not Be Allowed.

Nor need we now state all that makes Timothy accursed, since what has been done through him and on his account, has abundantly and conspicuously come to the knowledge of the whole world, and whatever has been perpetrated by an unruly mob against justice, all rests on his head, whose wishes were served by its mad hands. And hence, even if in his profession of faith he neglects nothing, and deceives us in nothing, it best consorts with your glory absolutely to exclude him from this design of his, because in the bishop of so great a city the universal Church ought to rejoice with holy exultation, so that the true peace of the Lord may be glorified not only by the preaching of the Faith, but also by the example of men's conduct. Dated 17th of June, in the consulship of Magnus and Apollonius (460). (By the hand of Philoxenus *agens in rebus*.)

LETTER CLXX. TO GENNADIUS, BISHOP OF CONSTANTINOPLE.

(Complaining of Timothy Aelurus having been allowed to come to Constantinople, and saying that there is no hope of his restitution.)

LETTER CLXXI. TO TIMOTHY, BISHOP OF ALEXANDRIA.

Leo, the bishop, to Timothy, catholic bishop of the church of Alexandria.

I. He Congratulates Him on His Election, and Bids Him Win Back Wanderers to the Fold.

It is dearly apparent from the brightness of the sentiment quoted by the Apostle, that "all things work together for good to them that love God ," and by the dispensation of God's pity, where adversities are received, there also prosperity is given. This the experience of the Alexandrine church shows, in which the moderation and long suffering of the humble has laid up for themselves great store in return for their patience: because "the Lord is nigh them that are of a contrite heart, and shall save those that are humble in spirit ," our noble Prince's faith being glorified in all things, through whom "the right-hand of the Lord hath done great acts ," in preventing the abomination of antichrist any longer occupying the throne of the blessed Fathers; whose blasphemy has hurt no one more than himself, because although he has induced some to be partners of his guilt, yet he has inexpiably stained himself with blood. And hence concerning that which under the direction of Faith your election, brother, by the clergy, and the laity, and all the faithful, has brought about, I assure you that the whole of the Lord's Church rejoices with me, and it is my strong desire that the Divine pity will in its loving-kindness confirm this joy with manifold signs of grace, your own devotion ministering thereto in all things, so that you may sedulously win over, through the Church's prayers, those also who have hitherto resisted the Truth, to reconciliation with God, and, as a zealous ruler, bring them into union with the mystic body of the catholic Faith, whose entirety admits of no division, imitating that true and gentle Shepherd, who laid down His life for His sheep, and, when one sheep wandered, drove it not back with the lash, but carried it back to the fold on His own shoulders.

II. Let Him Be Watchful Against Heresy and Send Frequent Reports to Rome.

Take heed, then, dearly beloved brother, lest any trace of either Nestorius' or Eutyches' error be found in God's people: because "no one can lay any foundation except that which is laid, which is Christ Jesus ;" who would not have reconciled the whole world to God the Father, had He not by the regeneration of Faith adopted us all in the reality of our flesh . Whenever, therefore, opportunities arise which you can use for writing, brother, even as you necessarily and in accordance with custom have done in sending a report of your ordination to us by our sons, Daniel the presbyter and Timothy the deacon, so continue to act at all times and send us, who will be anxious for them, as frequent accounts as possible of the progress of peace, in order that by regular intercourse we may feel that "the love of God is shed abroad in our hearts through the Holy Ghost, which is given unto us ." Dated the 18th of August, in the consulship of Magnus and Apollonius (460).

LETTER CLXXII. TO THE PRESBYTERS AND DEACONS OF THE CHURCH OF ALEXANDRIA.

(Inviting them to aid in confirming the peace of the Church, and in winning those who had given way to heresy.)

LETTER CLXXIII. TO CERTAIN EGYPTIAN BISHOPS.

(Congratulating them on the election of Timothy, and begging them to assist in maintaining unity and bringing back wanderers to the fold.)

SERMONS.

SERMON I. PREACHED ON HIS BIRTHDAY, OR DAY OF ORDINATION.

Having been elected in absence he returns thanks for the kindness and earnestly demands the prayers of his church.

"Let my mouth speak the praise or the Lord ," and my breath and spirit, my flesh and tongue bless His holy Name. For it is a sign, not of a modest, but an ungrateful mind, to keep silence on the kindnesses of God: and it is very meet to begin our duty as consecrated pontiff with the sacrifices of the Lord's praise . Because "in our humility" the Lord "has been mindful of us " and has blessed us: because "He alone has done great wonders for me ," so that your holy affection for me reckoned me present, though my long journey had forced me to be absent. Therefore I give and always shall give thanks to our God for all the things with which He has recompensed me. Your favourable opinion also I acknowledge publicly, paying you the thanks I owe, and thus showing that I understand how much respect, love and fidelity your affectionate zeal could expend on me who long with a shepherd's anxiety for the safety of your souls, who have passed so conscientious a judgment on me, with absolutely no deserts of mine to guide you. I entreat you, therefore, by the mercies of the Lord, aid with your prayers him whom you have sought out by your solicitations that both the Spirit of grace may abide in me and that your judgment may not change. May He who inspired you with such unanimity of purpose, vouchsafe to us all in common the blessing of peace: so that all the days of my life being ready for the service of Almighty Can, and for my duties towards you, I may with confidence entreat the Lord: "Holy Father, keep in Thy name those whom Thou hast given me :" and while you ever go on unto salvation, may "my soul magnify the Lord ," and in the retribution of the judgment to come may the account of my priesthood so be rendered to the just Judge that through your good deeds you may be my joy and my crown, who by your good will have given an earnest testimony to me in this present life.

SERMON II. ON HIS BIRTHDAY, II.: DELIVERED ON THE ANNIVERSARY OF HIS CONSECRATION.)

I. The Lord Raises Up the Weak and Gives Him Grace According to His Need.

The Divine condescension has made this an honourable day for me, for it has shown by raising my humbleness to the highest rank, that He despised not any of His own. And hence, although one must be diffident of merit, yet it is one's bounden duty to rejoice over the gift, since He who is the Imposer of the burden is Himself the Aider in its execution: and lest the weak recipient should fall beneath the greatness of the grace, He who conferred the dignity will also give the power. As the day therefore returns in due course on which the Lord purposed that I should begin my episcopal office, there is true cause for me to rejoice to the glory of God, Who that I might love Him much, has forgiven me much, and that I might make His Grace wonderful, has conferred His gifts upon me in whom He found no recommendations of merit. And by this His work what does the Lord suggest and commend to our hearts but that no one should presume upon his own righteousness nor distrust God's mercy which shines out more pre-eminently then, when the sinner is made holy and the downcast lifted up. For the measure of heavenly gifts does not rest upon the quality of our deeds, nor in this world, in which "all life is temptation ," is each one rewarded according to his deserving, for if the Lord were to take count of a man's iniquities, no one could stand before His judgment.

II. The Mighty Assemblage of Prelates Testifies to Men's Loyal Acceptance of Peter in Peter's Unworthy Successor.

Therefore, dearly-beloved, "magnify the Lord with me and let us exalt His name together ," that the whole reason of to-day's concourse may be referred to the praise of Him Who brought it to pass. For so far as my own feelings are concerned, I confess that I rejoice most over the devotion of you all; and when I look upon this splendid assemblage of my venerable brother-priests I feel that, where so many saints are gathered, the very angels are amongst us. Nor do I doubt that we are to-day visited by a more abundant outpouring of the Divine Presence, when so many fair tabernacles of God, so many excellent members of the Body of Christ are in one place and shine with one light. Nor yet I feel sure, is the fostering condescension and true love of the most blessed Apostle Peter absent from this congregation: he has not deserted your devotion, in whose honour you are met together. And so he too rejoices over your good feeling and welcomes your respect for the Lord's own institution as shown towards the partners of His honour, commending the well ordered love of the whole Church, which ever finds Peter in Peter's See, and from affection for so great a shepherd grows not lukewarm even over so inferior a successor as myself. In order therefore, dearly beloved, that this loyalty which you unanimously display towards my humbleness may obtain the fruit of its zeal, on bended knee entreat the merciful goodness of our God that in our days He will drive out those who assail us, strengthen faith, increase love, increase peace and deign to render me His poor slave, whom to show the riches of His grace He has willed to stand at the helm of the Church, sufficient for so great a work and useful in building you up, and to this end to lengthen our time for service that the years He may grant us may be used to His glory through Christ our Lord. Amen.

SERMON III. ON HIS BIRTHDAY, III: DELIVERED ON THE ANNIVERSARY OF HIS ELEVATION TO THE PONTIFICATE.

I. The Honour of Being Raised to the Episcopate Must Be Referred Solely to the Divine Head of the Church.

As often as God's mercy deigns to bring round the day of His gifts to us, there is, dearly-beloved, just and reasonable cause for rejoicing, if only our appointment to the office be referred to the praise of Him who gave it. For though this recognition of God may well be found in all His priests, yet I take it to be peculiarly binding on me, who, regarding my own utter insignificance and the greatness of the office undertaken, ought myself also to utter that exclamation of the Prophet," Lord, I heard Thy speech and was afraid: I considered Thy works and was dismayed ." For what is so unwonted and so dismaying as labour to the frail, exaltation to the humble, dignity to the undeserving? And yet we do not despair nor lose heart, because we put our trust not in ourselves but in Him who works in us. And hence also we have sung with harmonious voice the psalm of David, dearly beloved, not in our own praise, but to the glory of Christ the Lord. For it is He of whom it is prophetically written, "Thou art a priest for ever after the order of Melchizedeck ," that is, not after the order of Aaron, whose priesthood descending along his own line of offspring was a temporal ministry, and ceased with the law of the Old Testament, but after the order of Melchizedeck, in whom was prefigured the eternal High Priest. And no reference is made to his parentage because in him it is understood that He was portrayed, whose generation cannot be declared. And finally, now that the mystery of this Divine priesthood has descended to human agency, it runs not by the line of birth, nor is that which flesh and blood created, chosen, but without regard to the privilege of paternity and succession by inheritance, those men are received by the Church as its rulers whom the Holy Ghost prepares: so that in the people of God's adoption, the whole body of which is priestly and royal, it is not the prerogative of earthly origin which obtains the unction , but the condescension of Divine grace which creates the bishop.

II. From Christ and Through S. Peter the Priesthood is Handed on in Perpetuity.

Although, therefore, dearly beloved, we be found both weak and slothful in fulfilling the duties of our office, because, whatever devoted and vigorous action we desire to do, we are hindered by the frailty of our very condition; yet having the unceasing propitiation of the Almighty and perpetual Priest, who being like us and yet equal with the Father, brought down His Godhead even to things human, and raised His Manhood even to things Divine, we worthily and piously rejoice over His dispensation, whereby, though He has delegated the care of His sheep to many shepherds, yet He has not Himself abandoned the guardianship of His beloved flock. And from His overruling and eternal protection we have received the support of the Apostles' aid also, which assuredly does not cease from its operation: and the strength of the foundation, on which the whole superstructure of the Church is reared, is not weakened by the weight of the temple that rests upon it. For the solidity of that faith which was praised in the chief of the Apostles is perpetual: and as that remains which Peter believed in Christ, so that remains which Christ instituted in Peter. For when, as has been read in the Gospel lesson , the Lord had asked the disciples whom they believed Him to be amid the various opinions that were held, and the blessed Peter bad replied, saying, "Thou art the Christ, the Son of the living God," the Lord says, "Blessed art thou, Simon Bar-Jona, because flesh and flood hath not revealed it to thee, but My Father, which is in heaven. And I say to thee, that thou art Peter, and upon this rock will I build My church, and the gates of Hades shall not prevail against it. And I will give unto thee the keys of the kingdom of heaven. And whatsoever thou shall bind on earth, shall be bound in heaven; and whatsoever thou shall loose on earth, shall be loosed also in heaven ."

III. S. Peter's Work is Still Carried Out by His Successors.

The dispensation of Truth therefore abides, and the blessed Peter persevering in the strength of the Rock, which he has received, has not abandoned the helm of the Church, which he undertook. For he was ordained before the rest in such a way that from his being called the Rock, from his being pronounced the Foundation, from his being constituted the Doorkeeper of the kingdom of heaven, from his being set as the Umpire to bind and to loose, whose judgments shall retain their validity in heaven, from all these mystical titles we might know the nature of his association with Christ. And still to-day he more fully and effectually performs what is entrusted to him, and carries out every part of his duty and charge in Him and with Him, through Whom he has been glorified. And so if anything is rightly done and rightly decreed by us, if anything is won from the mercy of God by our daily supplications, it is of his work and merits whose power lives and whose authority prevails in his See. For this, dearly-beloved, was gained by that confession, which, inspired in the Apostle's heart by God the Father, transcended all the uncertainty of human opinions, and was endued with the firmness of a rock, which no assaults could shake. For throughout the Church Peter daily says, "Thou art the Christ, the Son of the living God," and every tongue which confesses the Lord, accepts the instruction his voice conveys. This Faith conquers the devil, and breaks the bonds of his prisoners. It uproots us from this earth and plants us in heaven, and the gates of Hades cannot prevail against it. For with such solidity is it endued by God that the depravity of heretics cannot mar it nor the unbelief of the heathen overcome it.

IV. This Festival Then is in S. Peter's Honour, and the Progress of His Flock Redounds to His Glory.

And so, dearly beloved, with reasonable obedience we celebrate to-day's festival by such methods, that in my humble person he may be recognized and honoured, in whom abides the care of all the shepherds, together with the charge of the sheep commended to him, and whose dignity is not abated even in so unworthy an heir. And hence the presence of my venerable brothers and fellow-priests, so much desired and valued by me, will be the more sacred and precious, if they will transfer the chief honour of this service in which they have deigned to take part to him whom they know to be not only the patron of this see, but also the primate of all bishops. When therefore we utter our exhortations in your ears, holy brethren, believe that he is speaking whose representative we are: because it is his warning that we give, nothing else but his teaching that we preach, beseeching you to "gird up the loins of your mind ," and lead a chaste and sober life in the fear of God, and not to let your mind forget his supremacy and consent to the lusts of the flesh. Short and fleeting are the joys of this world's pleasures which endeavour to turn aside from the path of life those who are called to eternity. The faithful and religious spirit, therefore, must desire the things which are heavenly, and being eager for the Divine promises, lift itself to the love of the incorruptible Good and the hope of the true Light. But be sure, dearly-beloved, that your labour, whereby you resist vices and fight against carnal desires, is pleasing and precious in God's sight, and in God's mercy will profit not only yourselves but me also, because the zealous pastor makes his boast of the progress of the Lord's flock. "For ye are my crown and joy ," as the Apostle says; if your faith, which from the beginning of the Gospel has been preached in all the world has continued in love and holiness. For though the whole Church, which is in all the world, ought to abound in all virtues, yet you especially, above all people, it becomes to excel in deeds of piety, because founded as you are on the very citadel of the Apostolic Rock, not only has our Lord Jesus Christ redeemed you in common with all men, but the blessed Apostle Peter has instructed you far beyond all men. Through the same Christ our Lord.

SERMON IX. UPON THE COLLECTIONS, IV.

I. The Devil's Wickedness in Leading Men Astray is Now Counteracted by the Work of Redemption in Restoring Them to the Truth.

God's mercy and justice, dearly-beloved, has in loving-kindness disclosed to us through our Lord Jesus Christ's teaching, the manner of His retributions, as they have been ordained from the foundation of the world, that accepting the significance of facts we might take what we believe will happen, to have, as it were, already come to pass. For our Redeemer and Saviour knew what great errors the devil's deceit had dispersed throughout the world and by how many superstitions he had subjected the chief part of mankind to himself. But that the creature formed in God's image might not any longer through ignorance of the Truth be driven on to the precipice of perpetual death, He inserted in the Gospel-pages the nature of His judgment that it might recover every man from the snares of the crafty foe; for now all would know what rewards the good might hope for and what punishments the evil must fear. For the instigator and author of sin in order first to fall through pride and then to injure us through envy, because "he stood not in the Truth" put all his strength in lying and produced every kind of deceit from this poisoned source of his cunning, that he might cut off man's devout hopes from that happiness which he had lost by his own uplifting, and drag them into partnership with his condemnation, to whose reconciliation he himself could not attain. Whoever therefore among men has wronged God by his wickednesses, has been led astray by his guile, and depraved by his villainy. For he easily drives into all evil doings those whom he has deceived in the matter of religion. But knowing that God is denied not only by words but also by deeds, many whom he could not rob of their faith, he has robbed of their love, and by choking the ground of their heart with the weeds of avarice, has spoiled them of the fruit of good works, when he could not spoil them of the confession of their lips.

II. God's Just Judgment Against Sin is Denounced that We May Avoid It by Deeds of Mercy and Love.

On account therefore, dearly-beloved, of these crafty designs of our ancient foe, the unspeakable goodness of Christ has wished us to know, what was to be decreed about all mankind in the day of retribution, that, while in this life healing remedies are legitimately offered, while restoration is not denied to the contrite, and those who have been long barren can at length be fruitful, the verdict on which justice has determined may be fore-stalled and the picture of God's coming to judge the world never depart from the mind's eye. For the Lord will come in His glorious Majesty, as He Himself has foretold, and there will be with Him an innumerable host of angel-legions radiant in their splendour. Before the throne of His power will all the nations of the world be gathered; and all the men that in all ages and on all the face of the earth have been born, shall stand in the Judge's sight. Then shall be separated the just from the unjust, the guiltless from the guilty; and when the sons of piety, their works of mercy reviewed, have received the Kingdom prepared for them, the unjust shall be upbraided for their utter barrenness, and those on the left having naught in common with those on the right, shall by the condemnation of the Almighty Judge be cast into the fire prepared for the torture of the devil and his angels, with him to share the punishment, whose will they choose to do. Who then would not tremble at this doom of eternal torment? Who would not dread evils which are never to be ended? But since this severity is only denounced in order that we may seek for mercy, we too in this present life must show such open-handed mercy that after perilous neglect returning to works of piety it may be possible for us to be set free from this doom. For this is the purpose of the Judge's might and of the Saviour's graciousness, that the unrighteous may forsake his ways and the sinner give up his wicket habits. Let those who wish Christ to spare them, have mercy on the poor; let them give freely to feed the wretched, who desire to attain to the society of the blessed. Let no man consider his fellow vile, nor despise in any one that nature which the Creator of the world made His own. For who that labours can deny that Christ claims that labour as done unto Himself? Your fellow-slave is helped thereby, but it is the Lord who will repay. The feeding of the needy is the purchase money of the heavenly kingdom and the free dispenser of things temporal is made the heir of things eternal. But how has such small expenditure deserved to be valued so highly except because our works are weighed in the balance of love, and when a man loves what God loves, he is deservedly raised into His kingdom, whose attribute of love has in part become his?

III. We Minister to Christ Himself in the Person of His Poor.

To this pious duty of good works, therefore dearly beloved, the day of Apostolic institution invites us, on which the first collection of our holy offerings has been prudently and profitably ordained by the Fathers; in order that, because at this season formerly the Gentiles used superstitiously to serve demons, we might celebrate the most holy offering of our alms in protest against the unholy victims of the wicked. And because this has been most profitable to the growth of the Church, it has been resolved to make it perpetual. We exhort you, therefore, holy brethren throughout the churches of your several regions on Wednesday next to contribute of your goods, according to your means and willingness, to purposes of charity, that ye may be able to win that blessedness in which he shall rejoice without end, who "considereth the needy and poor ." And if we are to "consider" him, dearly beloved, we must use loving care and watchfulness, in order that we may find him whom modesty conceals and shamefastness keeps back. For there are those who blush openly to ask for what they want and prefer to suffer privation without speaking rather than to be put to shame by a public appeal. These are they whom we ought to "consider" and relieve from their hidden straits in order that they may the more rejoice from the very fact that their modesty as well as poverty has been consulted. And rightly in the needy and poor do we recognize the person of Jesus Christ our Lord Himself, "Who though He was rich," as says the blessed Apostle, "became poor, that He might enrich us by His poverty ." And that His presence might never seem to be wanting to us, He so effected the mystic union of His humility and His glory that while we adore Him as King and Lord in the Majesty of the Father, we might also feed Him in His poor, for which we shall be set free in an evil day from perpetual damnation, and for our considerate care of the poor shall be joined with the whole company of heaven.

IV. To Complete Their Acceptance by God, They Must Not Neglect to Lay All Information Against the Manichees Who are in the City.

But in order that your devotion, dearly beloved, may in all things be pleasing to God, we exhort you also to show due zeal in informing your presbyters of Manichees where-ever they be hidden. For it is naught but piety to disclose the hiding-places of the wicked, and in them to overthrow the devil whom they serve. For against them, dearly beloved, it becomes indeed the whole world and the whole Church everywhere to put on the armour of Faith: but your devotion ought to be foremost in this work, who in your progenitors learnt the Gospel of the Cross of Christ from the very mouth of the most blessed Apostles Peter and Paul. Men must not be allowed to lie hid who do not believe that the law given through Moses, in which God is shown to be the Creator of the Universe, ought to be received: who speak against the Prophets and the Holy Ghost, dare in their damnable profanity to reject the Psalms of David which are sung through the universal Church with all reverence, deny the birth of the Lord Christ, according to the flesh, say that His Passion and Resurrection was fictitious, not true, and deprive the baptism of regeneration of all its power as a means of grace. Nothing with them is holy, nothing entire, nothing true. They are to be shunned, lest they harm any one: they are to be given up, lest they should settle in any part of our city. Yours, dearly. beloved, will be the gain before the Lord's judgment-seat of what we bid, of what we ask. For it is but right that the triumph of this deed also should be joined to the oblation of our alms, the Lord Jesus Christ in all things aiding us, Who lives and reigns for ever and ever. Amen.

SERMON X. ON THE COLLECTIONS, V.

I. Our Goods are Given Us Not as Our Own Possessions But for Use in God's Service.

Observing the institutions of the Apostles' tradition, dearly beloved, we exhort you, as watchful shepherds, to celebrate with the devotion of religious practice that day which they purged from wicked superstitions and consecrated to deeds of mercy, thus showing that the authority of the Fathers still lives among us, and that we obediently abide by their teaching. Inasmuch as the sacred usefulness of such a practice affects not only time past but also our own age, so that what aided them in the destruction of vanities, might contribute with us to the increase of virtues. And what so suitable to faith, what so much in harmony with godliness as to assist the poverty of the needy, to undertake the care of the weak, to succour the needs of the brethren, and to remember one's own condition in the toils of others. In which work He only who knows what He has given to each, discerns aright how much a man can and how much he cannot do. For not only are spiritual riches and heavenly gifts received from God, but earthly and material possessions also proceed from His bounty, that He may be justified in requiring an account of those things which He has not so much put in our possession as committed to our stewardship. God's gifts, therefore, we must use properly and wisely, lest the material for good work should become an occasion of sin. For wealth, after its kind and regarded as a means, is good and is of the greatest advantage to human society, when it is in the bands of the benevolent and open-handed, and when the luxurious man does not squander nor the miser hoard it; for whether ill-stored or unwisely spent it is equally lost.

II. The Liberal Use of Riches is Worse Than Vain, If It Be for Selfish Ends Alone.

And, however praiseworthy it be to flee from intemperance, and to avoid the waste of base pleasures, and though many in their magnificence disdain to conceal their wealth, and in the abundance of their goods think scorn of mean and sordid parsimony, yet such men's liberality is not happy, nor their thriftiness to be commended, if their riches are of benefit to themselves alone; if no poor folks are helped by their goods, no sick persons nourished; if out of the abundance of their great possessions the captive gets not ransom, nor the stranger comfort, nor the exile relief. Rich men of this kind are needier than all the needy. For they lose those returns which they might have for ever, and while they gloat over the brief and not always free enjoyment of what they possess, they are not fed upon the bread of justice nor the sweets of mercy: outwardly splendid, they have no light within: of things temporal they have abundance, but utter lack of things eternal: for they inflict starvation on their own souls, and bring them to shame and nakedness by spending upon heavenly treasures none of these things which they put into their earthly storehouses.

III. The Duty of Mercy Outweighs All Other Virtues.

But, perhaps there are some rich people, who, although they are not wont to help the Church's poor by bounteous gifts, yet keep other commands of God, and among their many meritorious acts of faith and uprightness think they will be pardoned for the lack of this one virtue. But this is so important that, though the rest exist without it, they can be of no avail. For although a man be full of faith, and chaste, and sober, and adorned with other still greater decorations, yet if he is not merciful, he cannot deserve mercy: for the Lord says, "blessed are the merciful, for God shall have mercy upon them ." And when the Son of Man comes in His Majesty and is seated on His glorious throne, and all nations being gathered together, division is made between the good and the bad, for what shall they be praised who stand upon the fight except for works of benevolence and deeds of love which Jesus Christ shall reckon as done to Himself? For He who has made man's nature His own, has separated Himself in nothing from man's humility. And what objection shall be made to those on the left except for their neglect of love, their inhuman harshness, their refusal of mercy to the poor? as if those on the right had no other virtues those on the left no other faults. But at the great and final day of judgment large-hearted liberality and ungodly meanness will be counted of such importance as to outweigh all other virtues and all other shortcomings, so that for the one men shall gain entrance into the Kingdom, for the other they shall be sent into eternal fire.

IV. And Its Efficacy, as Scripture Proves, is Incalculable.

Let no one therefore, dearly beloved, flatter himself on any merits of a good life, if works of charity be wanting in him, and let him not trust in the purity of his body, if he be not cleansed by the purification of almsgiving. For "almsgiving wipes out sin ," kills death, and extinguishes the punishment of perpetual fire. But he who has not been fruitful therein, shall have no indulgence from the great Re-compenser, as Solomon says, "He that closeth his ears lest he should hear the weak, shall himself call upon the Lord, and there shall be none to hear him ." And hence Tobias also, while instructing his son in the precepts of godliness, says, "Give alms of thy substance, and turn not thy face from any poor man: so shall it come to pass that the face of God shall not be turned from thee ." This virtue makes all virtues profitable; for by its presence it gives life to that very faith, by which "the just lives ," and which is said to be "dead without works :" because as the reason for works consists in faith, so the strength of faith consists in works. "While we have time therefore," as the Apostle says, "let us do that which is good to all men, and especially to them that are of the household of faith ." "But let us not be weary in doing good; for in His own time we shall reap ."And so the present life is the time for sowing, and the day of retribution is the time of harvest, when every one shall reap the fruit of his seed according to the amount of his sowing. And no one shall be disappointed in the produce of that harvesting, because it is the heart's intentions rather than the sums expended that will be reckoned up. And little sums from little means shall produce as much as great sums from great means. And therefore, dearly beloved, let us carry out this Apostolic institution. And as the first collection will be next Sunday, let all prepare themselves to give willingly, that every one according to his ability may join in this most sacred offering. Your very alms and those who shall be aided by your gifts shall intercede for you, that you may be always ready for every good work in Christ Jesus our Lord, Who lives and reigns for ages without end. Amen.

SERMON XII. ON THE FAST OF THE, TENTH MONTH, I.

I.restoration to the Divine Image in Which We Were Made is Only Possible by Our Imitation of God's Will.

If, dearly beloved, we comprehend faithfully and wisely the beginning of our creation, we shall find that man was made in God's image, to the end that he might imitate his Creator, and that our race attains its highest natural dignity, by the form of the Divine goodness being reflected in us, as in a mirror. And assuredly to this form the Saviour's grace is daily restoring us, so long as that which, in the first Adam fell, is raised up again in the second. And the cause of our restoration is naught else but the mercy of God, Whom we should not have loved, unless He had first loved us, and dispelled the darkness of our ignorance by the light of His truth. And the Lord foretelling this by the holy Isaiah says, "I will bring the blind into a way that they knew not, and will make them walk in paths which they were ignorant of. I will turn darkness into light for them, and the crooked into the straight. These words will I do for them, and not forsake them ." And again he says, "I was found by them that sought Me not, and openly appeared to them that asked not for Me ." And the Apostle John teaches us how this has been fulfilled, when he says. "We know that the Son of God is come, and has given us an understanding, that we may know Him that is true, and may be in Him that is true, even His Son ," and again, "let us therefore love God, because He first loved us ." Thus it is that God, by loving us, restores us to His image, and, in order that He may find in us the form of His goodness, He gives us that whereby we ourselves too may do the work that He does, kindling that is the lamps of our minds, and inflaming us with the fire of His love, that we may love not only Himself, but also whatever He loves. For if between men that is the lasting friendship which is based upon similarity of character notwithstanding that such identity of wills is often directed to wicked ends, how ought we to yearn and strive to differ in nothing from what is pleasing to God. Of which the prophet speaks, "for wrath is in His indignation, and life in His pleasure ," because we shall not otherwise attain the dignity of the Divine Majesty, unless we imitate His will.

II. We Must Love Both God And Our Neighbour, and "Our Neighbour" Must Be Interpreted in Its Widest Sense.

And so, when the Lord says, "Thou shalt love the Lord thy God, from all thy heart and from all thy mind: and thou shalt love thy neighbour as thyself ," let the faithful soul put on the unfading love of its Author and Ruler, and subject itself also entirely to His will in Whose works and judgments true justice and tender-hearted compassion never fail. For although a man be wearied out with labours and many misfortunes, there is good reason for him to endure all in the knowledge that adversity will either prove him good or make him better. But this godly love cannot be perfect unless a man love his neighbour also. Under which name must be included not only those who are connected with us by friendship or neighbourhood, but absolutely all men, with whom we have a common nature, whether they be foes or allies, slaves or free. For the One Maker fashioned us, the One Creator breathed life into us; we all enjoy the same sky and air, the same days and nights, and, though some be good, others bad, some righteous, others unrighteous, yet God is bountiful to all, kind to all, as Paul and Barnabas said to the Lycaonians concerning God's Providence, "who in generations gone by suffered all the nations to walk in their own ways. And yet He left Himself not without witness, doing them good, giving rain from heaven and fruitful seasons, and filling our hearts with food and gladness ." But the wide extent of Christian grace has given us yet greater reasons for loving our neighbour, which, reaching to all parts of the whole world, looks down on no one, and teaches that no one is to be neglected. And full rightly does He command us to love our enemies, and to pray to Him for our persecutors, who, daily grafting shoots of the wild olive from among all nations upon the holy branches of His own olive, makes men reconciled instead of enemies, adopted sons instead of strangers, just instead of ungodly, "that every knee may bow of things in heaven, of things on earth, and of things under the earth, and every tongue confess that the Lord Jesus Christ is in the glory of God the Father ."

III. We Must Be Thankful, and Show, Our Thankfulness for What We Have Received, Whethermuch or Little.

Accordingly, as God wishes us to be good, because He is good, none of His judgments ought to displease us. For not to give Him thanks in all things, what else is it but to blame Him in some degree. Man's folly too often dares to murmur against his Creator, not only in time of want, but also in time of plenty, so that, when something is not supplied, he complains, and when certain things are in abundance he is ungrateful. The Lord of rich harvests thought scorn of his well-filled garners, and groaned over his abundant grape-gathering: he did not give thanks for the size of the crop, but complained of its poorness . And if the ground has been less prolific than its wont in the seed it has reared, and the vines and the olives have failed in their supply of fruit, the year is accused, the elements blamed, neither the air nor the sky is spared, whereas nothing better befits and reassures the faithful and godly disciples of Truth than the persistent and unwearied lifting of praise to God, as says the Apostle, "Rejoice alway, pray without ceasing: in all things give thanks. For this is the will of God in Christ Jesus in all things for you ." But how shall we be partakers of this devotion, unless vicissitudes of fortune train our minds in constancy, so that the love directed towards God may not be puffed up in prosperity nor faint in adversity. Let that which pleases God, please us too. Let us rejoice in whatever measure of gifts He gives. Let him who has used great possessions well, use small ones also well. Plenty and scarcity may be equally for our good, and even in spiritual progress we shall not be east down at the smallness of the results, if our minds become not dry and barren. Let that spring from the soil of our heart, which the earth gave not. To him that fails not in good will, means to give are ever supplied. Therefore, dearly beloved, in all works of godliness let us use what each year gives us, and let not seasons of difficulty hinder our Christian benevolence. The Lord knows how to replenish the widow's vessels, which her pious deed of hospitality has emptied: He knows how to turn water into wine: He knows how to satisfy 5,000 hungry persons with a few loaves. And He who is fed in His poor, can multiply when He takes what He increased when He gave.

IV. Prayer, Fasting and Almsgiving are the Three Comprehensive Duties of a Christian.

But there are three things which most belong to religious actions, namely prayer, fasting, and almsgiving, in the exercising of which while every time is accepted, yet that ought to be more zealously observed, which we have received as hallowed by tradition from the apostles: even as this tenth month brings round again to us the opportunity when according to the ancient practice we may give more diligent heed to those three things of which I have spoken. For by prayer we seek to propitiate God, by fasting we extinguish the lusts of the flesh, by alms we redeem our sins: and at the same time God's image is throughout renewed in us, if we are always ready to praise Him, unfailingly intent on our purification and unceasingly active in cherishing our neighhour. This threefold round of duty, dearly beloved, brings all other virtues into action: it attains to God's image and likenessand unites us inseparably with the Holy Spirit. Because in prayer faith remains stedfast, in fastings life remains innocent, in almsgiving the mind remains kind. On Wednesday and Friday therefore let us fast: and on Saturday let us keep vigil with the most blessed Apostle Peter, who will deign to aid our supplications and fast and alms with his own prayers through our Lord Jesus Christ, who with the Father and the Holy Ghost lives and reigns for ever and ever. Amen.

SERMON XVI. ON THE FAST OF THE TENTH MONTH.

I. The Prosperous Must Show Forth Their Thankfulness to God, by Liberality to the Floor and Needy.

The transcendant power of God's grace, dearly beloved, is indeed daily effecting in Christian hearts the transference of our every n desire from earthly to heavenly things. But this present life also is passed through the Creator's aid and sustained by His providence, because He who promises things eternal is also the the Supplier of things temporal. As therefore we ought to give God thanks for the hope of future happiness towards which we run by faith, because He raises us up to a perception of the happiness in store for us, so for those things also which we receive in the course of every year, God should be honoured and praised, who having from the beginning given fertility to the earth and laid down laws of bearing fruit for every germ and seed, will never forsake his own decrees but will as Creator ever continue His kind administration of the things that He has made. Whatever therefore the cornfields, the vineyards and the olive groves have bornefor man's purposes, all this God in His bounteous goodness has produced: for under the varying condition of the elements He has mercifully aided the uncertain toils of the husbandmen so that wind, and rain, cold and heat, day and night might serve our needs. For men's methods would not have sufficed to give effect to their works, had not God given the increase to their wonted plantings and waterings. And hence it is but godly and just that we too should help others with that which the Heavenly Father has mercifully bestowed on us. For there are full many, who have no fields, no vineyards, no olive-groves, whose wants we must provide out of the store which God has given, that they too with us may bless God for the richness of the earth and rejoice at its possessors having received things which they have shared also with the poor and the stranger. That garner is blessed and most worthy that all fruits should increase manifold in it, from which the hunger of the needy and the weak is satisfied from which the wants of the stranger are relieved, from which the desire of the sick is gratified. For these men God has in His justice permitted to be afflicted with divers troubles, that He might both crown the wretched for their patience and the merciful for their loving-kindness.

II. Almsgiving and Fasting are the Most Essential Aids to Prayer.

And while all seasons are opportune for this duty, beloved, yet this present season is specially suitable and appropriate, at which our holy fathers, being Divinely inspired, sanctioned the Fast of the tenth month, that when all the ingathering of the crops was complete, we might dedicate to God our reasonable service of abstinence, and each might remember so to use his abundance as to be more abstinent in himself and more open-handed towards the poor. For forgiveness of sins is most efficaciously prayed for with almsgiving and fasting, and supplications that are winged by such aids mount swiftly to God's ears: since as it is written, "the merciful man doeth good to his own soul ," and nothing is so much a man's own as that which he spends on his neighbour. For that part of his material possessions with which he ministers to the needy, is transformed into eternal riches, and such wealth is begotten of this bountifulness as can never be diminished or in any way destroyed, for "blessed are the merciful, for God shall have mercy on them ," and He Himself shall be their chief Reward, who is the Model of His own command.

III. Christians' Pious Activity Has So Enraged Satan that He Has Multiplied Heresies to Wreak Them Harm.

But at all these acts of godliness, dearly-beloved, which commend us more and more to God, there is no doubt that our enemy, who is so eager and so skilled in harming us, is aroused with keener stings of hatred, that under a false profession of the Christian name he may corrupt those whom he is not allowed to attack with open and bloody persecutions, and for this work he has heretics in his service whom he has led astray from the catholic Faith, subjected to himself, and forced under divers errors to serve in his camp. And as for the deception of primitive man he used the services of a serpent, so to mislead the minds of the upright he has armed these men's tongues with the poison of his falsehoods. But these treacherous designs, dearly beloved, with a shepherd's care, and so far as the Lord vouchsafes His aid, we will defeat. And taking heed lest any of the holy flock should perish, we admonish you with fatherly warnings to keep aloof from the "lying lips" and the "deceitful tongue" from which the prophet asks that his soul should be delivered ; because "their words," as says the blessed Apostle, "do creep as doth a gangrene ." They creep in humbly, they arrest softly, they bind gently, they slay secretly. For they "come," as the Saviour foretold, "in sheeps' clothing, but inwardly they are ravening wolves ;"

because they could not deceive the true and simple sheep, unless they covered their bestial rage with the name of Christ. But in them all he is at work who, though he is really the enemy of enlightenment, "transforms himself into an angel of light ." His is the craft which inspires Basilides; his the ingenuity which worked in Marcion; he is the leader under whom Sabellius acted; he the author of Photinus' headlong fall, his the authority and his the spirit which Arius and Eunomius served: in fine under his command and authority the whole herd of such wild beasts has separated from the unity of the Church and severed connexion with the Truth.

IV. Of All Heresies Manicheism is the Worst and Foulest.

But while he retains this ever-varying supremacy over all the heresies, yet he has built his citadel upon the madness of the Manichees, and found in them the most spacious court in which to strut and boast himself: for there he possesses not one form of misbelief only, but a general compound of all errors and ungodlinesses. For all that is idolatrous in the heathen, all that is blind in carnal Jews, all that is unlawful in the secrets of the magic art, all finally that is profane and blasphemous in all the heresies is gathered together with all manner of filth in these men as if in a cesspool . And hence it is too long a matter to describe all their ungodlinesses: for the number of the charges against them exceeds my supply of words. It will be sufficient to indicate a few instances, that you may, from what you hear, conjecture what from modesty we omit. In the matter of their rites, however, which are as indecent morally as they are religiously, we cannot keep silence about that which the Lord has been pleased to reveal to our inquiries, lest any one should think we have trusted in this thing to vague rumours and uncertain opinions. And so with bishops and presbyters sitting beside me, and Christian nobles assembled in the same place, we ordered their elect men and women to be brought before us. And when they had made many disclosures concerning their perverse tenets and their mode of conducting festivals, they revealed this story of utter depravity also, which I blush to describe but which has been so carefully investigated that no grounds for doubt are left for the incredulous or for cavillers. For there were present all the persons by which the unutterable crime had been perpetrated, to wit a girl at most ten years old, and two women who had nursed her and prepared her for this outrage. There was also present the stripling who had outraged her, and the bishop, who had arranged their horrible crime. All these made one and the same confession, and a tale of such foul orgies was disclosed as our ears could scarcely bear. And lest by plainer speaking we offend chaste ears, the account Of the proceedings shall suffice, in which it is most fully shown that in that sect no modesty, no sense of honour, no chastity whatever is found: for their law is falsehood, their religion the devil, their sacrifice immorality.

V. Every One Should Abjure Such Men, and Give All the Information They Possess About Them to the Authorities.

And so, dearly beloved, renounce all friendship with these men who are utterly abominable and pestilential, and whom disturbances in other districts have brought in great numbers to the city : and you women especially refrain from acquaintance and intercourse with such men, lest while your ears are charmed unawares by their fabulous stories, you fall into the devil's noose, who, knowing that he seduced the first man by the woman's mouth, and drove all men from the bliss of paradise through feminine credulity, still lies in watch for your sex with more confident craft that he may rob both of their faith and of their modesty those whom he has been able to ensnare by the servants of his falseness. This, too, dearly beloved, I entreat and admonish you loyally to inform us , if any of you know where they dwell, where they teach, whose houses they frequent, and in whose company they take rest: because it is of little avail to any one that through the Holy Ghost's protection he is not caught by them himself, if he takes no action when he knows that others are being caught. Against common enemies for the common safety all alike should exercise the same vigilance lest from one member's wound other members also be injured, and they that think such men should not be given up, in Christ's judgment be found guilty for their silence even though they are not contaminated by their approval.

VI. Zeal in Rooting Out Heresy Will Make Other Pious Duties More Acceptable.

Display then a holy zeal of religious vigilance, and let all the faithful rise in one body against these savage enemies of their souls. For the merciful God has delivered a certain portion of our noxious foes into our hands in order that by revelation of the danger the utmost caution might be aroused. Let not what has been done suffice, but let us persevere in searching them out: and by God's aid the result will be not only the continuance in safety of those who still stand, but also the recovery from error of many who have been deceived by the devil's seduction. And the prayers, and alms, and fasts that you offer to the merciful God shall be the holier for this very devotion, when this deed of faith also is added to all your other godly duties. OnWednesday and Friday, therefore, let us fast, and on Saturday let us keep vigil in the presence of the most blessed Apostle Peter; who, as we experience and know, watches unceasingly like a shepherd over the sheep entrusted to him by the Lord, and who will prevail in his entreaties that the Church of God, which was rounded by his preaching, may be free from all error, through Christ our Lord. Amen.

SERMON XVII. ON THE FAST OF THE TENTH MONTH, VI.

I. The Duty of Fasting is Based on Both the Old and New Testaments, and is Closely Connected with the Duties of Prayer and Almsgiving.

The teaching of the Law, dearly beloved, imparts great authority to the precepts of the Gospel, seeing that certain things are transferred from the old ordinances to the new, and by the very devotions of the Church it is shown that the Lord Jesus Christ "came not to destroy but to fulfil the Law ." For since the cessation of the signs by which our Saviour's coming was announced, and the abolition of the types in the presence of the Very Truth, those things which our religion instituted, whether for the regulation of customs or for the simple worship of God, continue with us in the same form in which they were at the beginning, and what was in harmony with both Testaments has been modified by no change. Among these is also the solemn fast of the tenth month, which is now to be kept by us according to yearly custom, because it is altogether just and godly to give thanks to the Divine bounty for the crops which the earth has produced for the use of men under the guiding hand of supreme Providence. And to show that we do this with ready mind, we must exercise not only the self-restraint of fasting, but also diligence in almsgiving, that from the ground of our heart also may spring the germ of righteousness and the fruit of love, and that we may deserve God's mercy by showing mercy to His poor. For the supplication, which is supported by works of piety, is most efficacious in prevailing with God, since he who turns not his heart away from the poor soon turns himself to hear the Lord, as the Lord says: "be ye merciful as your Father also is merciful .... release and ye shall be released ." What is kinder than this justice? what more merciful than this retribution, where the judge's sentence rests in the power of him that is to be judged? "Give," he says, "and it shall be given to you ." How soon do the misgivings of distrust and the puttings off of avarice fall to the ground, when humanity may fearlessly spend what the Truth pledges Himself to repay.

II. He that Lends to the Lord Makes a Better Bargain Than He that Lends to Man.

Be stedfast, Christian giver: give what you may receive, sow what you may reap, scatter what you may gather. Fear not to spend, sigh not over the doubtfulness of the gain. Your substance grows when it is wisely dispensed. Set your heart on the profits due to mercy, and traffic in eternal gains. Your Recompenser wishes you to be munificent, and He who gives that you may have, commands you to spend, saying, "Give, and it shall be given to you." You must thankfully embrace the conditions of this promise. For although you have nothing that you did not receive, yet you cannot fail to have what you give. He therefore that loves money, and wishes to multiply his wealth by immoderate profits, should rather practise this holy usury and grow rich by such money-lending, in order not to catch men hampered with difficulties, and by treacherous assistance entangle them in debts which they can never pay, but to be His creditor and His money-lender, who says, "Give, and it shall be given to you," and "with what measure ye measure, it shall be measured again to you ." But he is unfaithful and unfair even to himself, who does not wish to have for ever what he esteems desirable. Let him amass what he may, let him hoard and store what he may, he will leave this world empty and needy, as David the prophet says, "for when he dieth he shall take nothing away, nor shall his glory descend with him ." Whereas if he were considerate of his own soul, he would trust his good to Him, who is both the proper Surety for the poor and the generous Repayer of loans. But unrighteous and shameless avarice, which promises to do some kind act but eludes it, trusts not God, whose promises never fail, and trusts man, who makes such hasty bargains; and while he reckons the present more certain than the future, often deservedly finds that his greed for unjust gain is the cause of by no means unjust loss.

III. Money-Lending at High Interest is in All Respects Iniquitous.

And hence, whatever result follow, the money-lender's trade is always bad, for it is sin either to lessen or increase the sum, in that if he lose what he lent he is wretched, and if he takes more than he lent he is more wretched still. The iniquity of money-lending must absolutely be abjured, and the gain which lacks all humanity must be shunned. A man's possessions are indeed multiplied by these unrighteous and sorry means, but the mind's wealth decays because usury of money is the death of the soul . For what God thinks of such men the most holy Prophet David makes clear, for when he asks, "Lord, who shall dwell in thy tabernacle, or who shall rest upon thy holy hill ?" he receives the Divine utterance in reply, from which he learns that that man attains to eternal rest who among other rules of holy living "hath not given his money upon usury :" and thus he who gets deceitful gain from lending his money on usury is shown to be both an alien from God's tabernacle and an exile from His holy hill, and in seeking to enrich himself by other's losses, he deserves to be punished with eternal neediness.

IV. Let Us Avoid Avarice, and Share God's Benefits with Others.

And so, dearly beloved, do ye who with the whole heart have put your trust in the Lord's promises, flee from this unclean leprosy of avarice, and use God's gift piously and wisely. And since you rejoice in His bounty, take heed that you have those who may share in your joys. For many lack what you have in plenty, and some men's needs afford you opportunity for imitating the Divine goodness, so that through you the Divine benefits may be transferred to others also, and that by being wise stewards of your temporal goods, you may acquire eternal riches. On Wednesday and Friday next, therefore, let us fast, and on Saturday keep vigil with the most blessed Apostle Peter, by whose prayers we may in all things obtain the Divine protection through Christ our Lord. Amen.

SERMON XIX. ON THE FAST OF THE TEN MONTH, VIII.

I. Self-Restraint Leads to Higher Enjoyments.

When the Saviour would instruct His disciples about the Advent of God's Kingdom and the end of the world's times, and teach His whole Church, in the person of the Apostles, He said, "Take heed lest haply your hearts be overcharged with surfeiting and drunkenness, and care of this life ." And assuredly, dearly beloved, we acknowledge that this precept applies more especially to us, to whom undoubtedly the day denounced is near, even though hidden. For the advent of which it behoves every man to prepare himself, lest it find him given over to gluttony, or entangled in cares of this life. For by daily experience, beloved, it is proved that the mind's edge is blunted by over-indulgence of the flesh, and the heart's vigour is dulled by excess of food, so that the delights of eating are even opposed to the health of the body, unless reasonable moderation withstand the temptation and the consideration of future discomfort keep from the pleasure. For although the flesh desires nothing without the soul, and receives its sensations from the same source as it receives its motions also, yet it is the function of the same soul to deny certain things to the body which is subject to it, and by its inner judgment to restrain the outer parts from things unseasonable, in order that it may be the oftener free from bodily lusts, and have leisure for Divine wisdom in the palace of the mind, where, away from all the noise of earthly cares, it may in silence enjoy holy meditations and eternal delights. And, although this is difficult to maintain in this life, yet the attempt can frequently be renewed, in order that we may the oftener and longer be occupied with spiritual rather than fleshly cares; and by our spending ever greater portions of our time on higher cares, even our temporal actions may end in gaining the incorruptible riches.

II. The Teaching of the Four Yearly Fasts is that Spiritual Self-Restraint is as Necessary as Corporeal.

This profitable observance, dearly beloved, is especially laid down for the fasts of the Church, which, in accordance with the Holy Spirit's teaching, are so distributed over the whole year that the law of abstinence may be kept before us at all times. Accordingly we keep the spring fast in Lent, the summer fast at Whitsuntide, the autumn fast in the seventh month, and the winter fast in this which is the tenth month, knowing that there is nothing unconnected with the Divine commands, and that all the elements serve the Word of God to our instruction, so that from the very hinges on which the world turns, as if by four gospels we learn unceasingly what to preach and what to do. For, when the prophet says, "The heavens declare the glory of God, and the firmament showeth His handiwork: day unto day uttereth speech, and night showeth knowledge ," what is there by which the Truth does not speak to us? By day and by night His voices are heard, and the beauty of the things made by the workmanship of the One God ceases not to instil the teachings of Reason into our hearts' ears, so that "the invisible things of God may be perceived and seen through the things which are made," and men may serve the Creator of all, not His creatures . Since therefore all vices are destroyed by self-restraint, and whatever avarice thirsts for, pride strives for, luxury lusts after, is overcome by the solid force of this virtue, who can fail to understand the aid which is given us by fastings? for therein we are bidden to restrain ourselves, not only in food, but also in all carnal desires. Otherwise it is lost labour to endure hunger and yet not put away wrong wishes; to afflict oneself by curtailing food, and yet not to flee from sinful thoughts. That is a carnal, not a spiritual fast, where the body only is stinted, and those things persisted in, which are more harmful than all delights. What profit is it to the soul to act outwardly as mistress and inwardly to be a captive and a slave, to issue orders to the limbs and to lose the right to her own liberty? That soul for the most part (and deservedly) meets with rebellion in her servant, which does not pay to God the service that is due. When the body therefore fasts from food, let the mind fast from vices, and pass judgment upon all earthly cares and desires according to the law of its King

III. Thus Fasting in Mind as Well as Body, and Giving Alms Freely, We Shall Win God's Highest Favour.

Let us remember that we owe love first to God, secondly to our neighbour, and that all our affections must be so regulated as not to draw us away from the worship of God, or the benefiting our fellow slave. But how shall we worship God unless that which is pleasing to Him is also pleasing to us? For, if our will is His will, our weakness will receive strength from Him, from Whom the very will came; "for it is God," as the Apostle says, "who worketh in us both to will and to do for (His) good pleasure ." And so a man will not be puffed up with pride, nor crushed with despair, if he uses the gifts which God gave to His glory, and withholds his inclinations from those things, which he knows will harm him. For in abstaining from malicious envy, from luxurious and dissolute living, from the perturbations of anger, from the lust after vengeance, he will be made pure and holy by true fasting, and will be fed upon the pleasures of incorruptible delights, and so he will know how, by the spiritual use of his earthly riches, to transform them into heavenly treasures, not by hoarding up for himself what he has received, but by gaining a hundred-fold on what he gives. And hence we warn you, beloved, in fatherly affection, to make this winter fast fruitful to yourselves by bounteous alms, rejoicing that by you the Lord feeds and clothes His poor, to whom assuredly He could have given the possessions which He has bestowed on you, had He not in His unspeakable mercy wished to justify them for their patient labour, and you for your works of love. Let us therefore fast on Wednesday and Friday, and on Saturday keep vigil with the most blessed Apostle Peter, and he will deign to assist with his own prayers our supplications and fastings and alms which our Lord Jesus Christ presents, Who with the Father and the Holy Ghost lives and reigns for ever and ever. Amen.

SERMON XXI. ON THE FEAST OF THE NATIVITY, I.

I. All Share in the Joy of Christmas.

Our Saviour, dearly-beloved, was born today: let us be glad. For there is no proper place for sadness, when we keep the birthday of the Life, which destroys the fear of mortality and brings to us the joy of promised eternity. No one is kept from sharing in this happiness. There is for all one common measure of joy, because as our Lord the destroyer of sin and death finds none free from charge, so is He come to free us all. Let the saint exult in that he draws near to victory. Let the sinner be glad in that he is invited to pardon. Let the gentile take courage in that he is called to life. For the Son of God in the fulness of time which the inscrutable depth of the Divine counsel has determined, has taken on him the nature of man, thereby to reconcile it to its Author: in order that the inventor of death, the devil, might be conquered through that (nature) which he had conquered. And in this conflict undertaken for us, the fight was fought on great and wondrous principles of fairness; for the Almighty Lord enters the lists with His savage foe not in His own majesty but in our humility, opposing him with the same form and the same nature, which shares indeed our mortality, though it is free from all sin. Truly foreign to this nativity is that which we read of all others, "no one is clean from stain, not even the infant who has lived but one day upon earth ." Nothing therefore of the lust of the flesh has passed into that peerless nativity, nothing of the law of sin has entered. A royal Virgin of the stem of David is chosen, to be impregnated with the sacred seed and to conceive the Divinely-human offspring in mind first and then in body. And lest in ignorance of the heavenly counsel she should tremble at so strange a result , she learns from converse with the angel that what is to be wrought in her is of the Holy Ghost. Nor does she believe it loss of honour that she is soon to be the Mother of God . For why should she be in despair over the novelty of such conception, to whom the power of the most High has promised to effect it. Her implicit faith is confirmed also by the attestation of a precursory miracle, and Elizabeth receives unexpected fertility: in order that there might be no doubt that He who had given conception to the barren, would give it even to a virgin.

II. The Mystery of the Incarnation is a Fitting Theme for Joy Both to Angels and to Men.

Therefore the Word of God, Himself God,the Son of God who "in the beginning was with God," through whom "all things were made" and "without" whom "was nothing made ," with the purpose of delivering man from eternal death, became man: so bending Himself to take on Him our humility without decrease in His own majesty, that remaining what He was and assuming what He was not, He might unite the true form of a slave to that form in which He is equal to God the Father, and join both natures together by such a compact that the lower should not be swallowed up in its exaltation nor the higher impaired by its new associate. Without detriment therefore to the properties of either substance which then came together in one person, majesty took on humility, strength weakness, eternity mortality: and for the paying off of the debt, belonging to our condition, inviolable naturewas united with possible nature, and true God and true man were combined to form one Lord, SO that, as suited the needs of our case, one and the same Mediator between God and men, the Man Christ Jesus, could both die with the one and rise again with the other.

Rightly therefore did the birth of our Salvation impart no corruption to the Virgin's purity, because the bearing of the Truth was the keeping of honour. Such then beloved was the nativity which became the Power of God and the Wisdom of God even Christ, whereby He might be one with us in manhood and surpass us in Godhead. For unless He were true God, He would not bring us a remedy, unless He were true Man, He would not give us an example. Therefore the exulting angel's song when the Lord was born is this, "Glory to God in the Highest," and their message, "peace on earth to men of good will ." For they see that the heavenly Jerusalem is being built up out of all the nations of the world: and over that indescribable work of the Divine love how ought the humbleness of men to rejoice, when the joy of the lofty angels is so great?

III. Christians Then Must Live Worthily of Christ Their Head.

Let us then, dearly beloved, give thanks to God the Father, through His Son, in the Holy Spirit , Who "for His great mercy, wherewith He has loved us," has had pity on us: and "when we were dead in sins, has quickened us together in Christ ," that we might be inHim a new creation and a new production. Let us put off then the old man with his deeds: and having obtained a share in the birth of Christ let us renounce the works of the flesh. Christian, acknowledge thy dignity, and becoming a partner in the Divine nature, refuse to return to the old baseness by degenerate conduct. Remember the Head and the Body of which thou art a member. Recollect that thou wert rescued from the power of darkness and brought out into God's light and kingdom. By the mystery of Baptism thou weft made the temple of the Holy Ghost: do not put such a denizen to flight from thee by base acts, and subject thyself once more to the devil's thraldom: because thy purchase money is the blood of Christ, because He shall judge thee in truth Who ransomed thee in mercy, who with the Father and the Holy Spirit reigns for ever and ever. Amen.

SERMON XXII. ON THE FEAST OF THE NATIVITY, II.

I. The Mystery of the Incarnation Demands Our Joy.

Let us be glad in the Lord, dearly-beloved, and rejoice with spiritual joy that there has dawned for us the day of ever-new redemption. of ancient preparation , of eternal bliss. For as the year rolls round, there recurs for us the commemoration of our salvation, which promised from the beginning, accomplished in the fulness of time will endure for ever; on which we are bound with hearts up-lifted to adore the divine mystery: so that what is the effect of God's great gift may be celebrated by the Church's great rejoicings. For God the almighty and merciful, Whose nature as goodness, Whose will is power, Whose work is mercy: as soon as the devil's malignity killed us by the poison of his hatred, foretold at the very beginning of the world the remedy His piety had prepared for the restoration of us mortals: proclaiming to the serpent that the seed of the woman should come to crush the lifting of his baneful head by its power, signifying no doubt that Christ would come in the flesh, God and man, Who born of a Virgin should by His uncorrupt birth condemn the despoiler of the human stock. Thus in the whole and perfect nature of true man was true God born, complete in what was His own, complete in what was ours. And "ours" we call what the Creator formed in us from the beginning and what He undertook to repair. For what, the deceiver brought in and the deceived admitted had no trace in the Saviour Nor because He partook of man's weaknesses, did He therefore share our faults. He took the form of a slave without stain of sin, increasing the human and not diminishing the Divine: because that "emptying of Himself" whereby the Invisible made Himself visible and Creator and Lord Of all things as He was, wished to be mortal, was the condescension of Pity not the failing of Power .

II. The New Character of the Birth of Christ Explained.

Therefore, when the time came, dearly beloved, which had been fore-ordained for men's redemption , there enters these lower parts of the world, the Son of God, descending from His heavenly throne and yet not quitting His Father's glory, begotten in a new order, by a new nativity. In a new order, because being invisible in His own nature He became visible in ours, and He whom nothing could contain, was content to be contained: abiding before all time He began to be in time: the Lord of all things, He obscured His immeasurable majesty and took on Him the form of a servant: being God, that cannot suffer, He did not disdain to be man that can, and immortal as He is, to subject Himself to the laws of death . And by a new nativity He was begotten, conceived by a Virgin, born of a Virgin, without paternal desire, without injury to the mother's chastity: because such a birth as knew no taint of human flesh, became One who was to be the Saviour of men, while it possessed in itself the nature of human substance. For when God was born in the flesh, God Himself was the Father, as the archangel witnessed to the Blessed Virgin Mary: "because the Holy Spirit shall come upon thee, and the power of the most High shall overshadow thee: and therefore, that which shall be born of thee shall be called holy, the Son of God ." The origin is different but the nature like: not by intercourse with man but by the power of God was it brought about: for a Virgin conceived, a Virgin bare, and a Virgin she remained. Consider here not the condition of her that bare but the will of Him that was born; for He was born Man as He willed and was able. If you inquire into the truth of His nature, you must acknowledge the matter to be human: if you search for the mode of His birth, you must confess the power to be of God. For the Lord Jesus Christ came to do away with not to endure our pollutions: not to succumb to our faults but to heal them . He came that He might cure every weakness of oar corruptness and all the sores of our defiled souls: for which reason it behoved Him to be born by a new order, who brought to men's bodies the new gift of unsullied purity. For the uncorrupt nature of Him that was born had to guard the primal virginity of the Mother, and the infused power of the Divine Spirit had to preserve in spotlessness and holiness that sanctuary which He had chosen for Himself: that Spirit (I say) who had determined to raise the fallen, to restore the broken, and by overcoming the allurements of the flesh to bestow on us in abundant measure the power of chastity: in order that the virginity which in others cannot be retained in child-bearing, might be attained by them at their second birth.

III. Justice Required that Satan Should Be Vanquished by God Made Man.

And, dearly beloved, this very fact that Christ chose to be born of a Virgin does it not appear to be part of the deepest design? I mean, that the devil should not be aware that Salvation had been born for the human race, and through the obscurity of that spiritual conception, when he saw Him no different to others, should believe Him born in no different way to others. For when he observed that His nature was like that of all others, he thought that He had the same origin as all had: and did not understand that He was free from the bonds of transgression because he did not find Him a stranger to the weakness of mortality. For though the true mercy of God had infinitely many schemes to hand for the restoration of mankind, it chose that particular design which put in force for destroying the devil's work, not the efficacy of might but the dictates of justice. For the pride of the ancient foe not undeservedly made good its despotic rights over all men, and with no unwarrantable supremacy tyrannized over those who had been of their own accord lured away from God's commands to be the slaves of his will. And so there would be no justice in his losing the immemorial slavery of the human race, were he not conquered by that which he had subjugated. And to this end, without male seed Christ was conceived of a Virgin, who was fecundated not by human intercourse but by the Holy Spirit. And whereas in all mothers conception does not take place without stain of sin, this one received purification from the Source of her conception. For no taint of sin penetrated, where no intercourse occurred. Her unsullied virginity knew no lust when it ministered the substance. The Lord took from His mother our nature, not our fault. The slave's form is, created without the slave's estate, because the New Man is so commingled with the old, as both to assume the reality of our race and to remove its ancient flaw.

IV. The Incarnation Deceived the Devil and Caused Him to Break the Bond Under Which He Held Men.

When, therefore, the merciful and almighty Saviour so arranged the commencement of His human course as to hide the power of His Godhead which was inseparable from His manhood under the veil of our weakness, the crafty foe was taken off his guard and he thought that the nativity of the Child, Who was born for the salvation of mankind, was as much subject to himself as all others are at their birth. For he saw Him crying and weeping, he saw Him wrapped in swaddling clothes, subjected to circumcision, offering the sacrifice which the law required. And then he perceived in Him the usual growth of boyhood, and could have had no doubt of His reaching man's estate by natural steps. Meanwhile, he inflicted insults, multiplied injuries, made use of curses, affronts, blasphemies, abuse, in a word, poured upon Him all the force of his fury and exhausted all the varieties of trial: and knowing how he had poisoned man's nature, had no conception that He had no share in the first transgression Whose mortality he had ascertained by so many proofs. The unscrupulous thief and greedy robber persisted in assaulting Him Who had nothing of His own, and in carrying out the general sentence on original sin, went beyond the bond on which he rested, and required the punishment of iniquity from Him in Whom he found no fault. And thus the malevolent terms of the deadly compact are annulled, and through the injustice of an overcharge the whole debt is cancelled. The strong one is bound by his own chains, and every device of the evil one recoils on his own head. When the prince of the world is bound, all that he held in captivity is released. Our nature cleansed from its old contagion regains its honourable estate, death is destroyed by death, nativity is restored by nativity: since at one and the same time redemption does away with slavery, regeneration changes our origin, and faith justifies the sinner.

V. The Christian is Exhorted to Share in the Blessings of the Incarnation.

Whoever then thou art that devoutly and faithfully boastest of the Christian name, estimate this atonement at its right worth. For to thee who wast a castaway, banished from the realms of paradise, dying of thy weary exile, reduced to dust and ashes, without further hope of living, by the Incarnation of the Word was given the power to return from afar to thy Maker, to recognize thy parentage, to become free after slavery, to be promoted from being an outcast to sonship: so that, thou who wast born of corruptible flesh, mayest be reborn by the Spirit of God, and obtain through grace what thou hadst not by nature, and, if thou acknowledge thyself the son of God by the spirit of adoption, dare to call God Father. Freed from the accusings of a bad conscience, aspire to the kingdom of heaven, do God's will supported by the Divine help, imitate the angels upon earth, feed on the strength of immortal sustenance, fight fearlessly on the side of piety against hostile temptations, and if thou keep thy allegiance in the heavenly warfare, doubt not that thou wilt be crowned for thy victory in the triumphant camp of the Eternal King, when the resurrection that is prepared for the faithful has raised thee to participate in the heavenly Kingdom.

VI. The Festival Has Nothing to Do with Sunworship, as Some Maintain.

Having therefore so confident a hope, dearly beloved, abide firm in the Faith in which you are built: lest that same tempter whose tyranny over you Christ has already destroyed, win you back again with any of his wiles, and mar even the joys of the present festival by his deceitful art, misleading simpler souls with the pestilential notion of some to whom this our solemn feast day seems to derive its honour, not so much from the nativity of Christ as, according to them, from the rising of the new sun . Such men's hearts are wrapped in total darkness, and have no growing perception of the true Light: for they are still drawn away by the foolish errors of heathendom, and because they cannot lift the eyes of their mind above that which their carnal sight beholds, they pay divine honourto the luminaries that minister to the world.Let not Christian souls entertain any suchwicked superstition and portentous lie. Beyond all measure are things temporal removed from the Eternal, things corporeal from the Incorporeal, things governed from the Governor. For though they possess a wondrous beauty, yet they have no Godhead to be worshipped. That power then, that wisdom, that majesty is to be adored which created the universe out of nothing, and framed by His almighty methods the substance of the earth and sky into what forms and dimensions He willed. Sun, moon, and stars may be most useful to us, most fair to look upon; but only if we render thanks to their Maker for them and worship God who made them, not the creation which does Him service. Then praise God, dearly beloved, in all His works and judgments. Cherish an undoubting belief in the Virgin's pure conception. Honour the sacred and Divine mystery of man's restoration with holy and sincere service. Embrace Christ born in our flesh, that you may deserve to see Him also as the God of glory reigning in His majesty, who with the Father and the Holy Spirit remains in the unity of the Godhead for ever and ever. Amen.

SERMON XXIII. ON THE FEAST OF THE NATIVITY, III.

I. The Truths of the Incarnation Never Suffer from Being Repeated.

The things which are connected with the mystery of to-day's solemn feast are well known to you, dearly-beloved, and have frequently been heard: but as yonder visible light affords pleasure to eyes that are unimpaired, so to sound hearts does the

Saviour's nativity give eternal joy; and we must not keep silent about it, though we cannot treat of it as we ought. For we believe that what Isaiah says, "who shall declare his generation ?" applies not only to that mystery, whereby the Son of God is co-eternal with the Father, but also to this birth whereby "the Word became flesh." And SO God, the Son of God, equal and of the same nature from the Father and with the Father, Creator and Lord of the Universe, Who is completely present everywhere, and completely exceeds all things, in the due course of time, which runs by His own disposal, chose for Himself this day on which to be born of the blessed virgin Mary for the salvation of the world, without loss of the mother's honour. For her virginity was violated neither at the conception nor at the birth: "that it might be fulfilled," as the Evangelist says, "which was spoken by the Lord through Isaiah the prophet, saying, behold the virgin shall conceive in the womb, and shall bear a son, and they shall call his name Emmanuel, which is interpreted, God with us ." For this wondrous child-bearing of the holy Virgin produced in her offspring one person which was truly human and truly Divine , because neither substance so retained their properties that there could be any division of persons in them; nor was the creature taken into partnership with its Creator in such a way that the One was the in-dweller, and the other the dwelling; but so that the one nature was blended with the other. And although the nature which is taken is one, and that which takes is another, yet these two diverse natures come together into such close union that it is one and the same Son who says both that, as true Man, "He is less than the Father," and that, as true God, "He is equal with the Father."

II.the Arians Could Not Comprehend the Union of God And Man.

This union, dearly beloved, whereby the Creator is joined to the creature, Arian blindness could not see with the eyes of intelligence, but, not believing that the Only-begotten of God was of the same glory and substance with the Father, spoke of the Son's Godhead as inferior, drawing its arguments front those words which are to be referred to the "form of a slave," in respect of which, in order to show that it belongs to no other or different person in Himself, the same Son of God with the same form, says, "The Father is greater than I ," just as He says with the same form, "I and my Father are one ." For in "the form of a slave," which He took at the end of the ages for our restoration, He is inferior to the Father: but in the form of God, in which He was before the ages, He is equal to the Father. In His human humiliation He was "made of a woman, made under the Law :" in His Divine majesty He abides the Word of God, "through whom all things were made ." Accordingly, He Who in the form of God made man, in the form of a slave was made man. For both natures retain their own proper character without loss: and as the form of God did not do away with the form of a slave, so the form of a slave did not impair the form of God . And so the mystery of power united to weakness, in respect of the same human nature, allows the Son to be called inferior to the Father: but the Godhead, which is One in the Trinity of the Father, Son, and Holy Ghost, excludes all notion of inequality. For the eternity of the Trinity has nothing temporal, nothing dissimilar in nature: Its will is one, Its substance identical, Its power equal, and yet there are not three Gods, but one God ; because it is a true and inseparable unity, where there can be no diversity . Thus in the whole and perfect nature of true man was true God born, complete in what was His own, complete in what was ours. And by "ours" we mean what the Creator formed in us from the beginning, and what He undertook to repair. For what the deceiver brought in, and man deceived committed, had no trace in the Saviour; nor because He partook of man's weaknesses, did He therefore share our faults. He took the form of a slave without stain of sin, increasing the human and not diminishing the divine: for that "emptying of Himself," whereby the Invisible made Himself visible, was the bending down of pity, not the failing of power.

III. The Incarnation Was Necessary to the Taking Away of Sin.

In order therefore that we might be called to eternal bliss from our original bond and from earthly errors, He came down Himself to us to Whom we could not ascend, because, although there was in many the love of truth, yet the variety of our shifting opinions was deceived by the craft of misleading demons, and man's ignorance was dragged into diverse and conflicting notions by a falsely-called science. But to remove this mockery, whereby men's minds were taken captive to serve the arrogant devil, the teaching of the Law was not sufficient, nor could our nature be restored merely by the Prophets' exhortations; but the reality of redemption had to be added to moral injunctions, and our fundamentally corrupt origin had to be re-born afresh. A Victim had to be offered for our atonement Who should be both a partner of our race and free from our contamination, so that this design of God whereby it pleased Him to take away the sin of the world in the Nativity and Passion of Jesus Christ, might reach to all generations : and that we should not be disturbed but rather strengthened by these mysteries, which vary with the character of the times, since the Faith, whereby we live, has at no time suffered variation.

IV. the Blessings of the Incarnation Stretch Backwards as Well as Reach Forward.

Accordingly let those men cease their complaints who with disloyal murmurs speak against the dispensations of God, and babble about the lateness of the Lord's Nativity as if that, which was fulfilled in the last age of the world, had no bearing upon the times that are past. For the Incarnation of the Word did but contribute to the doing of that which was done : and the mystery of man's salvation was never in the remotest age at a standstill. What the apostles foretold, that the prophets announced: nor was that fulfilled too late which has always been believed. But the Wisdom and Goodness of God made us more receptive of His call by thus delaying the work which brought salvation: so that what through so many ages had been foretold by many signs, many utterances, and many mysteries, might not be doubtful in these days of the Gospel: and that the Saviour's nativity, which was to exceed all wonders and all the measure of human knowledge, might engender in us a Faith so much the firmer, as the foretelling of it had been ancient and oft-repeated. And so it was no new counsel, no tardy pity whereby God took thought for men: but from the constitution of the world He ordained one and the same Cause of Salvation for all. For the grace of God, by which the whole body of the saints is ever justified, was augmented, not begun, when Christ was born: and this mystery of God's great love, wherewith the whole world is now filled, was so effectively presignified that those who believed that promise obtained no less than they, who were the actual recipients.

V. The Coming of Christ in Our Flesh Corresponds with Our Becoming Members of His Body.

Wherefore since the loving-kindness is manifest, dearly beloved, wherewith all the riches of Divine goodness are showered on us, whose call to eternal life has been assisted not only by the profitable examples of those who went before, but also by the visible and bodily appearing of the Truth Itself, we are bound to keep the day of the Lord's Nativity with no slothful nor carnal joy. And we shall each keep it worthily and thoroughly, if we remember of what Body we are members, and to what a Head we are joined, lest any one as an ill-fitting joint cohere not with the rest of the sacred building. Consider, dearly beloved and by the illumination of the Holy Spirit thoughtfully bear in mind Who it was that received us into Himself, and that we have received in us: since, as the Lord Jesus became our flesh by being born, so we also became His body by being re-born. Therefore are we both members of Christ, and the temple of the Holy Ghost: and for this reason the blessed Apostle says, "Glorify and carry God in your body :" for while suggesting to us the standard of His own gentleness and humility, He fills us with that power whereby He redeemed us, as the Lord Himself promises: "come unto Me all ye who labour and are heavy-laden, and I will refresh you. Take My yoke upon you and learn of Me, for I am meek and lowly of heart, and ye shall find rest to your souls " Let us then take the yoke, that is not heavy nor irksome, of the Truth that rules us, and let us imitate His humility, to Whose glory we wish to be conformed: He Himself helping us and leading us to His promises, Who, according to His great mercy, is powerful to blot out our sins, and to perfect His gifts in us, Jesus Christ our Lord, Who lives and reigns for ever and ever. Amen.

SERMON XXIV. ON THE FEAST OF THE NATIVITY, IV.

I. The Incarnation Fulfils All Its Types and Promises.

The Divine goodness, dearly beloved, has indeed always taken thought for mankind in divers manners, and in many portions, and of His mercy has imparted many gifts of His providence to the ages of old; but in these last times has exceeded all the abundance of His usual kindness, when in Christ the very Mercy has descended to sinners, the very Truth to those that are astray, the very Life to those that are dead: so that Word, which is co-eternal and co-equal with the Father, might take our humble nature into union with His Godhead, and, being born God of God, might also be bern Man of man. Tiffs was indeed promised from the foundation of the world, and had always been prophesied by many intimations of facts and words : but how small a portion of mankind would these types and fore-shadowed mysteries have saved, had not the coming of Christ fulfilled those long and secret promises: and had not that which then benefited but a few believers in the prospect, now benefited myriads of the faithful in its accomplishment. Now no longer then are we led to believe by signs and types, but being confirmed by the gospel story we worship that which we believe to have been done; the prophetic lore assisting our knowledge, so that we have no manner of doubt about that which we know to have been predicted by such sure oracles. For hence it is that the Lord says to Abraham: "In thy seed shall all nations be blessed :" hence David, in the spirit of prophecy, sings, saying: "The Lord swore truth to David, and He shall not frustrate it: of the fruit of thy loins will I set upon thy seat ;" hence the Lord again says through Isaiah: "behold a virgin shall conceive in her womb, and shall bear a Son, and His Name shall be called Emmanuel, which is interpreted, God with us ," and again, "a rod shall come forth from the root of Jesse, and a flower shall arise froth his root ." In which rod, no doubt the blessed Virgin Mary is predicted, who sprung from the stock of Jesse and David and fecundated by the Holy Ghost, brought forth a new flower of human flesh, becoming a virgin-mother.

II. The Incarnation Was the Only Effective Remedy to the Fall.

Let the righteous then rejoice in the Lord, and let the hearts of believers turn to God's praise, and the sons of men confess His wondrous acts; since in this work of God especially our humble estate realizes how highly its Maker values it: in that, after His great gift to mankind in making us after His image, He contributed far more largely to our restoration when the Land Himself took on Him "the form of a slave." For though all that the Creator expends upon His creature is part of one and the same Fatherly love, yet it is less wonderful than man should advance to divine things than that God should descend to humanity. But unless the Almighty God did deign to do this, no kind of righteousness, no form of wisdom could rescue any one from the devil's bondage and from the depths of eternal death. For the condemnation that passes with sin from one upon all would remain, and our nature, corroded by its deadly wound, would discover no remedy, because it could not alter its state in its own strength. For the first man received the substance of flesh from the earth, and was quickened with a rational spirit by the in-breathing of his Creator , so that living after the image and likeness of his Maker, he might preserve the form of God's goodness and righteousness as in a bright mirror. And, if he had perseveringly maintained this high dignity of his nature by observing the Law that was given him, his uncorrupt mind would have raised the character even Of his earthly body to heavenly glory. But because in unhappy rashness he trusted the envious deceiver, and agreeing to his presumptuous counsels, preferred to forestall rather than to win the increase of honour that was in store for him, not only did that one man, but in him all that came after him also hear the verdict: "earth thou art, and unto earth shalt thou go ;" "as in the earthy," therefore, "such are they also that are earthy ," and no one is immortal, because no one is heavenly.

III. We All Became Partakers in the Birth of Christ, by the Re-Birth of Baptism.

And so to undo this chain of sin and death, the Almighty Son of God, that fills all things and contains,all things, altogether equal to the Father and co-eternal in one essence from Him and with Him, took on Him man's nature, and the Creator and Land of all things deigned to be a mortal: choosing for His mother one whom He had made, one who, without loss of her maiden honour, supplied so much of bodily substance, that without the pollution of human seed the New Man might be possessed of purity and truth. In Christ, therefore, born of the Virgin's womb, the nature does not differ from ours, because His nativity is wonderful. For He Who is true God, is also true man: and there is no lie in either nature. "The Word became flesh" by exaltation of the flesh, not by failure of the Godhead: which so tempered its power and goodness as to exalt our nature by taking it, and not to lose His own by imparting it. In this nativity of Christ, according to the prophecy of David, "truth sprang out of the earth, and righteousness looked down from heaven ." In this nativity also, Isaiah's saying is fulfilled, "let the earth produce and bring forth salvation, and let righteousness spring up together ." For the earth of human flesh, which in the first transgressor, was cursed, in this Offspring of the Blessed Virgin only produced a seed that was blessed and free from the fault of its stock. And each one is a partaker of this spiritual origin in regeneration; and to every one when he is re-born, the water of baptism is like the Virgin's womb; for the same Holy Spirit fills the font, Who filled the Virgin, that the sin, which that sacred conception overthrew, may be taken away by this mystical washing.

IV. The Manichaeans, by Rejecting the Incarnation, Have Fallen into Terrible Iniquities.

In this mystery, dear beloved, the mad error of the Manichaeans has no part, nor have they any partnership in the regeneration of Christ, who say that He was corporeally born of the Virgin Mary: so that, as they do not believe in His real nativity, they do not accept His real passion either; and, not acknowledging Him really buried, they reject His genuine resurrection. For, having entered on the perilous path of their abominable dogma, where all is dark and slippery, they rush into the abyss of death over the precipice of falsehood, and find no sure ground on which to rest; because, besides all their other diabolical enormities, on the very chief feast of Christ's worship, as their latest confession has made manifest , they revel in bodily as well as mental pollution, losing their own modesty as well as the purity of their Faith; so that they are found to be as filthy in their rites as they are blasphemers in their doctrines.

V. Other Heresies Contain Some Portion of Truth, But the Manichoeans Contain None Whatever.

Other heresies, dearly beloved, although they are all rightly to be condemned in their variety, yet have each in some part of them that which is true. Arius, in laying down that the Son of God is less than the Father and a creature, and in thinking that the Holy Spirit was like all else made by the same (Father), has lost himself in great blasphemy; but he has not denied the eternal and unchangeable Godhead in the essence of the Father, though he could not see it in the Unity of the Trinity. Macedonius was devoid of the light of the Truth when he did not receive the Godhead of the Holy Spirit, but he did acknowledge one power and the same nature in the Father and the Son. Sabellius was plunged into inextricable error by holding the unity of substance to be inseparable in the Father, Son and Holy Spirit, but granted to a singleness of nature what he should have attributed to an equality of nature , and because he could not understand a true Trinity, he believed in one and the same person under a threefold appellation. Photinus, misled by his mental blindness, acknowledged in Christ true man of our substance, but did not believe Him born God of God before all ages, and so losing the entirety of the Faith, believed the Son of God tO have taken on Him the true nature of human flesh in such a way as to assert that there was no soul in it, because the Godhead Itself took its place . Thus, if all the errors which the catholic Faith has anathematized are recanted, something is found in one after another which can be separated from its damnable setting. But in the detestable dogma of the Manicheans there is absolutely nothing which can be adjudged tolerable in any degree.

VI. Christians Must Cling to the One Faith and Not Be Led Astray.

But you, dearly beloved, whom I address in no less earnest terms than those of the blessed Apostle Peter, "a chosen race, a royal priesthood, a holy nation, a people for God's own possession ," built upon the impregnable rock, Christ, and joined to the Lord our Saviour by His true assumption of our flesh, remain firm in that Faith, which you have professed before many witnesses, and in which you were reborn through water and the Holy Ghost, and received the anointing of salvation, and the seal of eternal life . But "if any one preach to you any thing beside that which you have learnt, let him be anathema :" refuse to put wicked fables before the clearest truth, and what you may happen to read or hear contrary to the rule of the catholic and Apostolic creed, judge it altogether deadly and diabolical. Be not carried away by their deceitful keepings of sham and pretended fasts which tend not to the cleansing, but to the destroying of men's souls. They put on indeed a cloke of piety and chastity, but under this deceit they conceal the filthiness of their acts, and from the recesses of their ungodly heart hurl shafts to wound the simple; that, as the prophet says, "they may shoot in darkness at the upright in heart ." A mighty bulwark is a sound faith, a true faith, to which nothing has to be added or taken away: because unless it is one, it is no faith, as the Apostle says, "one Lord, one faith, one baptism, one God and Father of all, who is above all, and through all, and in us all ." Cling to this unity, dearly beloved, with minds unshaken, and in it "follow after" all "holiness ," in it carry out the Lord's commands, because "without faith it is impossible to please God ," and without it nothing is holy, nothing is pure, nothing alive: "for the just lives by faith ," and he who by the devil's deception loses it, is dead though living, because as righteousness is gained by faith, so too by a true faith is eternal life gained, as says our Lord and Saviour. And this is life eternal, that they may know Thee, the only true God, and Jesus Christ, whom Thou hast sent . May He make you to advance and persevere to the end, Who lives and reigns with the Father and the Holy Spirit, for ever and ever. Amen.

SERMON XXVI. ON THE FEAST OF THE NATIVITY, VI.

I. Christmas Morning is the Most Appropriate Time for Thoughts on the Nativity.

On all days and at all times, dearly beloved, does the birth of our Lord and Saviour from the Virgin-mother occur to the thoughts of the faithful, who meditate on divine things, that the mind may be aroused to the acknowledgment of its Maker, and whether it be occupied in the groans of supplication, or in the shouting of praise, or in the offering of sacrifice, may employ its spiritual insight on nothing more frequently and more trustingly than on the fact that God the Son of God, begotten of the co-eternal Father, was also born by a human birth. But this Nativity which is to be adored in heaven and on earth is suggested to us by no day more than this when, with the early light still shedding its rays on nature , there is borne in upon our senses the brightness of this wondrous mystery. For the angel Gabriel's converse with the astonished Mary and her conception by the Holy Ghost as wondrously promised as believed, seem to recur not only to the memory but to the very eyes. For to day the Maker of the world was born of a Virgin's womb, and He, who made all natures, became Son of her, whom He created. To-day the Word of God appeared clothed in flesh, and That which had never been visible to human eyes began to be tangible to our hands as well. Today the shepherds learnt from angels' voices that the Saviour was born in the substance of our flesh and soul; and to-day the form of the Gospel message was pre-arranged by the leaders of the Lord's flocks , so that we too may say with the arm), of the heavenly host: "Glory in the highest to God, and on earth peace to men of good will."

II. Christians are Essentially Participators in the Nativity of Christ.

Although, therefore, that infancy, which the majesty of God's Son did not disdain, reached mature manhood by the growth of years and, when the triumph of His passion and resurrection was completed, all the actions of humility which were undertaken for us ceased, yet to-day's festival renews for us the holy childhood of Jesus born of the Virgin Mary: and in adoring the birth of our Saviour, we find we are celebrating the commencement of our own life. For the birth of Christ is the source of life for Christian folk, and the birthday of the Head is the birthday of the body. Although every individual that is called has his own order, and all the sons of the Church are separated from one another by intervals of time, yet as the entire body of the faithful being born in the font of baptism is crucified with Christ in His passion, raised again in His resurrection, and placed at the Father's right hand in His ascension, so with Him are they born in this nativity. For any believer in whatever part of the world that is re-born in Christ, quits the old paths of his original nature and passes into a new man by being re-born; and no longer is he reckoned of his earthly father's stock but among the seed of the Saviour, Who became the Son of man in order that we might have the power to be the sons of God. For unless He came down to us in this humiliation, no one would reach His presence by any merits of his own. Let not earthly wisdom shroud in darkness the hearts of the called on this point, and let not the frailty of earthly thoughts raise itself against the loftiness of God's grace, for it will soon return to the lowest dust. At the end of the ages is fulfilled that which was ordained from all eternity: and in the presence of realities, when signs and types have ceased, the Law and prophecy have become Truth: and so Abraham is found the father of all nations, and the promised blessing is given to the world in his seed: nor are they only Israelites whom blood and flesh begot, but the whole body of the adopted eater into possession of the heritage prepared for the sons of Faith. Be not disturbed by the cavils of silly questionings, and let not the effects of the Divine word be dissipated by human calculation; we with Abraham believe in God and "waver not through unbelief" but "know most assuredly that what the Lord promised, He is able to perform."

III. Peace with God Is His Best Gift to Man.

The Saviour then, dearly beloved, is born not of fleshly seed but of the Holy Spirit, in such wise that the condemnation of the first transgression did not touch Him. And hence the very greatness of the boon conferred demands of us reverence worthy of its splendour. For, as the blessed Apostle teaches, "we have received not the spirit of this world but the Spirit which is of God, that we may know the things which are given us by God:" and that Spirit can in no other way be rightly worshipped, except by offering Him that which we received from Him. But in the treasures of the Lord's bounty what can we find so suitable to the honour of the present feast as the peace, which at the Lord's nativity was first proclaimed by the angel-choir? For that it is which brings forth the sons of God, the nurse of love and the mother of unity: the rest of the blessed and our eternal home; whose proper work and special office it is to join to God those whom it removes from the world. Whence the Apostle incites us to this good end, in saying, "being justified therefore by faith let us have peace towards God." In which brief sentence are summed up nearly all the commandments; for where true peace is, there can be no lack of virtue. But what is it, dearly beloved, to have peace towards God, except to wish what He bids, and not to wish what He forbids? For if human friendships seek out equality of soul and similarity of desires, and difference of habits can never attain to full harmony, how will he be partaker of divine peace, who is pleased with what displeases God and desires to get delight from what he knows to be offensive to God? That is not the spirit of the sons of God; such wisdom is not acceptable to the noble family of the adopted. That chosen and royal race must live up to the dignity of its regeneration, must love what the Father loves, and in nought disagree with its Maker, lest the Lord should again say: "I have begotten and raised up sons, but they have scorned Me: the ox knoweth his owner and the ass his master's crib: but Israel hath not known Me and My people hath not acknowledged Me ."

IV. We Must Be Worthy of Our Calling as Sans and Friends of God.

The mystery of this boon is great, dearly beloved, and this gift exceeds all gifts that God should call man son, and man should name God Father: for by these terms we perceive and learn the love which reached so great a height. For if in natural progeny and earthly families those who are born of noble parents are lowered by the faults of evil intercourse, and unworthy offspring are put to shame by the very brilliance of their ancestry; to what end will they come who through love of the world do not fear to be outcast from the family of Christ? But if it gains the praise of men that the father's glory should shine again in their descendants, how much more glorious is it for those who are born of God to regain the brightness of their Maker's likeness and display in themselves Him Who begat them, as saith the Lord: "Let your light so shine before men that they may see your good works and glorify your Father which is in heaven ?" We know indeed, as the Apostle John says that "the whole world lieth in the evil one ," and that by the stratagems of the Devil and his angels numberless attempts are made either to frighten man in his struggle upwards by adversity or to spoil him by prosperity, but "greater is He that is in us, than he that is against us ," and they who have peace with God and are always saying to the Father with their whole hearts "thy will be done " can be overcome in no battles, can be hurt by no assaults. For accusing ourselves in our confessions and refusing the spirit's consent to our fleshly lusts, we stir up against us the enmity of him who is the author of sin, but secure a peace with God that nothing can destroy, by accepting His gracious service, in order that we may not only surrender ourselves in obedience to our King but also be united to Him by our free-will. For if we are like-minded, if we wish what He wishes, and disapprove what He disapproves, He will finish all our wars for us, He Who gave the will, will also give the power: so that we may be fellow-workers in His works, and with the exultation of Faith may utter that prophetic song: "the Lord is my light and my salvation: whom shall I fear? the Lord is the defender of my life: of whom shall I be afraid ?"

V. The Birth of Christ is the Birth of Peace to the Church.

They then who "are born not of blood nor of the will of the flesh nor of the will of man but of God ," must offer to. the Father the unanimity of peace-loving sons, and all the members of adoption must meet in the First-begotten of the new creation, Who came to do not His own Will but His that sent Him; inasmuch as the Father in His gracious favour has adopted as His heirs not those that are discordant nor those that are unlike Him, but those that are in feeling and affection one. They that are re-modelled after one pattern must have a spirit like the model. The birthday of the Lord is the birthday of peace: for thus says the Apostle, "He is our peace, who made both one ;" since whether we be Jew or Gentile, "through Him we have access in one Spirit to the Father ." And it was this in particular that He taught His disciples before the day of His passion which He had of His own free-will fore-ordained, saying, "My peace I give unto you, My peace I leave for you ;" and lest under the general term the character of His peace should escape notice, He added. "not as the world give I unto you ." The world, He Says, has its friendships, and brings many that are apart into loving harmony. There are also minds which are equal in vices. and similarity of desires produces equality of affection. And if any are perchance to be found who are not pleased with what is mean and dishonourable, and who exclude from the terms of their connexion unlawful compacts, yet even such if they be either Jews, heretics or heathens , belong not to God's friendship but to this world's peace. But the peace of the spiritual and of catholics coming down from above and leading upwards refuses to hold communion with the lovers of the world resists all obstacles and flies from pernicious pleasures to true joys, as the Lord says: "Where thy treasure is, there will thy heart be also :" that is, if what you love is below you will descend to the lowest depth: if what you love is above, you will reach the topmost height: thither may the Spirit of peace lead and bring us, whose wishes and feeling are at one, and who are of one mind in faith and hope and in charity: since "as many as are led by the Spirit of God these are sons of God " Who reigneth with the Son and Holy Spirit for ever and ever. Amen.

SERMON XXVII. ON THE FEAST OF THE NATIVITY, VII.

I. It is Equally Dangerous to Deny the Godhead or the Manhood in Christ.

He is a true and devout worshipper, dearly-beloved, of to-day's festival who thinks nothing that is either false about the Lord's Incarnation or unworthy about His Godhead. For it is an equally dangerous evil to deny in Him the reality of our nature and the equality with the Father in glory. When, therefore, we attempt to understand the mystery of Christ's nativity, wherein He was born of the Virgin-mother, let all the clouds of earthly reasonings be driven far away and the smoke of worldly wisdom be purged from the eyes of illuminated faith: for the authority on which we trust is divine, the teaching which we follow is divine. Inasmuch as whether it be the testimony of the Law, or the oracles of the prophets, or the trumpet of the gospel to which we apply our inward ear, that is true which the blessed John full of the Holy Spirit uttered with his voice of thunder : "in the beginning was the Word: and the Word was with God, and the Word was God. The same was in the beginning with God. All things were made through Him, and without Him was nothing made ." And similarly is it true what the same preacher added: "the Word became flesh and dwelt in us: and we beheld His glory, the glory as of the only-begotten of the Father ." Therefore in both natures it is the same Son of God taking what is ours and not losing what is His own; renewing man in His manhood, but enduring unchangeable in Himself. For the Godhead which is His in common with the Father un lerwent no loss of omnipotence, nor did the "form of a slave" do despite to the "form of God," because the supreme and eternal Essence, which lowered Itself for the salvation of mankind, transferred us into Its glory, but did not cease to be what It was. And hence when the Only-begotten of God confesses Himself less than the Father , and yet calls Himself equal with Him , He demonstrates the reality of both forms in Himself: so that the inequality proves the human nature, and the equality the Divine.

II. The Incarnation Has Changed All the Possibilities of Man's Existence.

The bodily Nativity therefore of the Son of God took nothing from and added nothing to His Majesty because His unchangeable substance could be neither diminished nor increased. For that "the Word became flesh" does not signify that the nature of God was changed into flesh, but that the Word took the flesh into the unity of His Person: and therein undoubtedly the whole man was received, with which within the Virgin's womb fecundated by the Holy Spirit, whose virginity was destined never to be lost , the Son of God was so inseparably united that He who was born without time of the Father's essence was Himself in time born of the Virgin's womb. For we could not otherwise be released from the chains of eternal death but by Him becoming humble in our nature, Who remained Almighty in His own. And so our Lord Jesus Christ, being at birth true man though He never ceased to be true God, made in Himself the beginning of a new creation, and in the "form" of His birth started the spiritual life of mankind afresh, that to abolish the taint of our birth according to the flesh there might be a possibility of regeneration without our sinful seed for those of whom it is said, "Who were born not of blood, nor of the will of the flesh, nor of the will of man, but of God ." What mind can grasp this mystery, what tongue can express this gracious act? Sinfulness returns to guiltlessness and the old nature becomes new; strangers receive adoption and outsiders enter upon an inheritance. The ungodly begin to be righteous, the miserly benevolent, the incontinent chaste, the earthly heavenly. And whence comes this change, save by the right hand of the Most High? For the Son of God came to "destroy the works of the devil ,"and has so united Himself with us and us with Him that the descent of God to man's estate became the exaltation of man to God's.

III. The Devil Knows Exactly What Temptations to Offer to Each Several Person.

But in this mercifulness of God, dearly beloved, the greatness of which towards us we cannot explain, Christians must be extremely careful lest they be caught again in the devil's wiles and once more entangled in the errors which they have renounced. For the old enemy does not cease to "transform himself into an angel of light ," and spread everywhere the snares of his deceptions, and make every effort to corrupt the faith of believers. He knows whom to ply with the zest of greed, whom to assail with the allurements of the belly, before whom to set the attractions of self-indulgence, in whom to instil the poison of jealousy: he knows whom to overwhelm with grief, whom to cheat with joy, whom to surprise with fear, whom to bewilder with wonderment: there is no one whose habits he does not sift, whose cares he does not winnow, whose affections he does not pry into: and wherever he sees a man most absorbed in occupation, there he seeks opportunity to injure him. Moreover he has many whom he has bound still more tightly because they are suited for his designs, that he may use their abilities and tongues to deceive others. Through them are guaranteed the healing of sicknesses, the prognosticating of future, events, the appeasing of demons and the driving away of apparitions . They also are to be added who falsely allege that the entire condition of human life depends on the influences of the stars, and that that which is really either the divine will or ours rests with the unchangeable fates. And yet, in order to do still greater harm, they promise that they can be changed if supplication is made to those constellations which are adverse. And thus their ungodly fabrications destroy themselves; for if their predictions are not reliable, the fates are not to be feared: if they are, the stars are not to be venerated.

IV. The Foolish Practice of Some Who Turn to the Sun and Bow to It is Reprehensible.

From such a system of teaching proceeds also the ungodly practice of certain foolish folk who worship the sun as it rises at the beginning of daylight from elevated positions: even some Christians think it is so proper to do this that, before entering the blessed Apostle Peter's basilica, which is dedicated to the One Living and true God, when they have mounted the steps which lead to the raised platform, they turn round and bow themselves towards the rising sun and with bent neck do homage to its brilliant orb. We are full of grief and vexation that this should happen, which is partly due to the fault of ignorance and partly to the spirit of heathenism: because although some of them do perhaps worship the Creator of that fair light rather than the Light itself, which is His creature, yet we must abstain even flora the appearance of this observance: for if one who has abandoned the worship of gods, finds it in our own worship, will he not hark back again to this fragment of his old superstition, as if it were allowable, when he sees it to be common both to Christians and to infidels?

V. The Sun and Moon Were Created for Use, Not for Worship.

This objectionable practice must be given up therefore by the faithful, and the honour due to God alone must not be mixed up with those men's rites who serve their fellow-creatures. For the divine Scripture says: "Thou shalt worship the Lord thy God, and Him only shalt thou serve." Anti the blessed Job, "a man without complaint," as the Lord says, "and one that eschews every evil ," said, "Have I seen the sun when it shone or the moon walking brightly, and my heart hath rejoiced in secret, and I have kissed my hand: what is my great iniquity and denial against the most High God ?" But what is the sun or what is the moon but elements of visible creation and material light: one of which is of greater brightness and the other of lesser light? For as it is now day time and now night time, so the Creator has constituted divers kinds of luminaries, although even before they were made there had been days without the sun and nights without the moon . But these were fashioned to serve in making man, that he who is an animal endowed with reason might be sure of the distinction of the months, the recurrence of the year, and the variety of the seasons, since through the unequal length of the various periods, and the clear indications given by the changes in its risings, the sun doses the year and the moon renews the months. For on the fourth day, as we read, God said: "Let there be lights in the firmament of the heaven, and let them shine upon the earth, and let them divide between day and night, and let them be for signs and for seasons, and for days and years, and let them be in the firmament of heaven that they may shine upon earth."

VI. Let Us Awake to the Proper Use of All Our Parts and Facilities.

Awake, O man, and recognize the dignity of thy nature. Recollect thou wast made in the image of God, which although it was corrupted in Adam, was yet re-fashioned in Christ. Use visible creatures as they should be used, as thou usest earth, sea, sky, air, springs, and rivers: and whatever in them is fair and wondrous, ascribe to the praise and glory of the Maker. Be not subject to that light wherein birds and serpents, beasts and cattle, flies and worms delight. Confine the material light to your bodily senses, and with all your mental powers embrace that "true light which lighteth every man that cometh into this world ," and of which the prophet says, "Come unto Him and be enlightened, and your faces shall not blush ." For if we "are a temple of God, and the Spirit of God dwelleth in " us, what every one of the faithful has in his own heart is more than what he wonders at in heaven. And so, dearly beloved, we do not bid or advise you to despise God's works or to think there is anything opposed to your Faith in what the good God has made good, but to use every kind of creature and the whole furniture of this world reasonably and moderately: for as the Apostle says, "the things which are seen are temporal: but the things which are not seen are eternal ." Hence because we are born for the present and reborn for the future, let us not give ourselves up to temporal goods, but to eternal: and in order that we may behold our hope nearer, let us think on what the Divine Grace has bestowed on our nature on the very occasion when we celebrate the mystery of the Lord's birthday. Let us hear the Apostle, saying: "for ye are dead, and your life is hid with Christ in God. But when Christ, who is your life, shall appear, then shall ye also appear with Him in glory :" who lives and reigns with the Father and the Holy Ghost for ever and ever. Amen.

SERMON XXVIII. ON THE FESTIVAL OF THE NATIVITY, VIII.

I. The Incarnation an Unceasing Source a Joy.

Though all the divine utterances exhort us, dearly beloved, to "rejoice in the Lord always ," yet to-day we are no doubt incited to a full spiritual joy, when the mystery of the Lord's nativity is shining brightly upon us , so that we may have recourse to that unutterable condescension of the Divine Mercy, whereby the Creator of men deigned to become man, and be found ourselves in His nature whom we worship in ours. For God the Son of God, the only-begotten of the eternal and not-begotten Father, remaining eternal "in the form of God," and unchangeably and without time possessing the property of being no way different to the Father He received "the form of a slave" without loss of His own majesty, that He might advance us to His state and not lower Himself to ours. Hence both natures abiding in possession of their own properties such unity is the result of the union that whatever of Godhead is there is inseparable from the manhood: and whatever of manhood, is indivisible from the Godhead.

II. The Virgin's Conception Explained.

In celebrating therefore the birthday of our Lord and Saviour, dearly beloved, let us entertain pure thoughts of the blessed Virgin's child-bearing, so as to believe that at no moment of time was the power of the Word wanting to the flesh and soul which she conceived, and that the temple of Christ's body did not previously receive its form and soul that its Inhabitant might come and take possession but through Himself and in Himself was the beginning given to the New Man, so that in the one Son of God and Man there might be Godhead without a mother, and Manhood without a Father. For her virginity fecundated by the Holy Spirit at one and the same time brought forth without trace of corruption both the offspring and the Maker of her race. Hence also the same Lord, as the Evangelist relates, asked of the Jews whose son they had learnt Christ to be on the authority of the Scriptures, and when they replied that the tradition was He would come of David's seed, "How," saith He, "doth David in the Spirit call Him Lord, saying, the Lord said to my Lord: sit thou on My right hand till I place thy enemies as the footstool of thy feet ?" And the Jews could not solve the question put, because they did not understand that in the one Christ both the stock of David and the Divine nature were there prophesied.

III. In Redeeming Man, Justice as Well as Mercy Ad to Be Considered.

But the majesty of the Son of God in which He is equal with the Father in its garb of a slave's humility feared no diminution, required no augmentation: and the very effect of His mercy which He expended on the restitution of man, He was able to bring about solely by the power of His Godhead; so as to rescue the creature that was made in the image of God from the yoke of his cruel oppressor. But because the devil had not shown himself so violent in his attack on the first man as to bring him over to his side without the consent of His free will, man's voluntary sin and hostile desires had to be destroyed in such wise that the standard of justice should not stand in the way of the gift of Grace. And therefore in the general ruin of the entire human race there was but one remedy in the secret of the Divine plan which could succour the fallen, and that was that one of the sons of Adam should be born free and innocent of original transgression, to prevail for the rest both by His example and His merits. Still further, because this was not permitted by natural generation, and because there could be no offspring from our faulty stock without seed, of which the Scripture saith, "Who can make a clean thing conceived of an unclean seed? is it not Thou who art alone ?" David's Lord was made David's Son, and from the fruit of the promised branch sprang. One without fault, the twofold nature coining together into one Person, that by one and the same conception and birth might spring our Lord Jesus Christ, in Whom was present both true Godhead for the performance of mighty works and true Manhood for the endurance of sufferings.

IV. All Heresies Proceed from Failure to Believe the Twofold Nature of Christ.

The catholic Faith then, dearly beloved, may scorn the errors of the heretics that bark against it, who, deceived by the vanity of worldly wisdom, have forsaken the Gospel of Truth, and being unable to understand the Incarnation of the Word, have constructed for themselves out of the source of enlighten-merit occasion of blindness. For after investigating almost all false believers' opinions, even those which presume to deny the Holy Spirit, we come to the conclusion that hardly any one has gone astray, unless he has refused to believe the reality of the two natures in Christ under the confession of one Person. For some have ascribed to the Lord only manhood , others only Deity . Some have said that, though there was in the true Godhead, His flesh was unreal . Others have acknowledged that He took true flesh but say that He had not the nature of God the Father; and by assigning to His Godhead what belonged to His human substance, have made for themselves a greater and a lesser God, although there can be in true Godhead no grades: seeing that whatever is less than God, is not God . Others recognizing that there is no difference between Father and Son, because they could not understand unity of Godhead except in unity of Person, have maintained that the Father is the same as the Son : so that to be born and nursed, to suffer and die, to be buried and rise again, belonged to the same Father who sustained throughout the Person of both Man and the Word. Certain have thought that our Lord Jesus Christ had a body not of our substance but assumed from higher and subtler elements : whereas certain others have considered that in the flesh of Christ there was no human soul, but that the Godhead of the Word Itself fulfilled the part of soul. But their unwise assertion passes into this form that, though they acknowledge the existence of a soul in the Lord, yet they say it was devoid of mind, because the Godhead of Itself was sufficient for all purposes of reason to the Man as well as to the God in Christ. Lastly the same people have dared to assert that a certain portion of the Word was turned into Flesh, so that in the manifold varieties of this one dogma, not only the nature of the flesh and of the soul but also the essence of the Word Itself is dissolved.

V. nestorianism and Eutychianism are Particularly to Be Avoided at the Present Time.

There are many other astounding falsehoods also which we must not weary your ears, beloved, with enumerating. But after all these various impieties, which are closely connected by the relationship that exists between one form of blasphemy and another, we call your devout attention to the avoiding of these two errors in particular: one of which, with Nestorius for its author, some time ago attempted to gainground, but ineffectually; the other, which is equally damnable, has more recently sprung up with Eutyches as its propounder. The former dared to maintain that the blessed Virgin Mary was the mother of Christ's manhood only, so that in her conception and childbearing no union might be believed to have taken place of the Word and the Flesh: because the Son of God did not Himself become Son of Man, but of His mere condescension linked Himself with created man. This can in no wise be tolerated by catholic ears, which are so imbued with the gospel of Truth that they know of a surety there is no hope of salvation for mankind unless He were Himself the Son of the Virgin who was His mother's Creator. On the other hand this blasphemous propounder of more recent profanity has confessed the union of the two Natures in Christ, but has maintained that the effect of this very union is that of the two one remained while the substance of the other no longer existed, which of course could not have been brought to an end except by either destruction or separation. But this is so opposed to sound faith that it cannot be entertained without loss of one's Christian name. For if the Incarnation of the Word is the uniting of the Divine and human natures, but by the very fact of their coming together that which was twofold became single, it was only the Godhead that was born of the Virgin's womb, and went through the deceptive appearance of receiving nourishment and bodily growth: and to pass over all the changes of the human state, it was only the Godhead that was crucified, dead, and buried: so that according to those who thus think, there is no reason to hope for the resurrection, and Christ is not "the first-begotten from the dead;" because He was not One who ought to have been raised again, if He had not been One who could be slain.

VI. The Deity and the Manhood Were Present in Christ from the Very First.

Keep far from your hearts, dearly beloved, the poisonous lies of the devil's inspirations, and knowing that the eternal Godhead of the Son underwent no growth while with the Father, be wise and consider that to the same nature to which it was said in Adam, "Thou art earth, and unto earth shall thou go," it is said in Christ, "sit Thou on My right hand." According to that Nature, whereby Christ is equal to the Father, the Only-begotten was never inferior to the sublimity of the Father; nor was the glory which He had with the Father a temporal possession; for He is on the very right hand of the Father, of which it is said in Exodus, "Thy right hand, O Lord, is glorified in power ;" and in Isaiah, "Lord, who hath believed our report? and the arm of the Lord, to whom is it revealed ?" The man, therefore, assumed into the Son of God, was in such wise received into the unity of Christ's Person from His very commencement in the body, that without the Godhead He was not conceived, without the Godhead He was not brought forth, without the Godhead He was not nursed. It was the same Person in the wondrous acts, and in the endurance of insults; through His human weakness crucified, dead and buried: through His Divine power, being raised the third day, He ascended to the heavens, sat down at the right hand of the Father, and in His nature as man received from the Father that which in His nature as God He Himself also gave .

VII. The Fulness of the Godhead is Imparted to the Body (the Church) Through the Head, (Christ).

Meditate, dearly beloved on these things with devout hearts, and be always mindful of the apostle's injunction, who admonishes all men, saying, "See lest any one deceive you through philosophy and vain deceit according to the tradition of men, and not according to Christ; for in Him dwelleth all the fulness of the Godhead bodily, and ye have been filled in Him ." He said not "spiritually" but "bodily," that we may understand the substance of flesh to be real, where there is the dwelling in the body of the fulness of the Godhead: wherewith, of course, the whole Church is also filled, which, clinging to the Head, is the body of Christ; who liveth and reigneth with the Father and the Holy Ghost, God for ever and ever. Amen.

SERMON XXXI. ON THE FEAST OF THE EPIPHANY, I.

I. The Epiphany a Necessary Sequel to the Nativity.

After celebrating but lately the day on which immaculate virginity brought forth the Saviour of mankind, the venerable feast of the Epiphany, dearly beloved, gives us continuance of joy, that the force of our exultation and the fervour of our faith may not grow cool, in the midst of neighbouring and kindred mysteries . For it concerns all men's salvation, that the infancy of the Mediator between God and men was already manifested to the whole world, while He was still detained in the tiny town. For although He had chosen the Israelitish nation, and one family out of that nation, from whom to assume the nature of all mankind, yet He was unwilling that the early days of His birth should be concealed within the narrow limits of His mother's home: but desired to be soon recognized by all, seeing that He deigned to be born for all. To three wise men, therefore, appeared a star of new splendour in the region of the East, which, being brighter and fairer than the other stars, might easily attract the eyes and minds of those that looked on it, so that at once that might be observed not to be meaningless, which had so unusual an appearance. He therefore who gave the sign, gave to the beholders understanding of it, and caused inquiry to be made about that, of which He had thus caused understanding, and after inquiry made, offered Himself to be found.

II. Herod's Evil Designs Were Fruitless. The Wise Men's Gifts Were Consciously Symbolical.

These three men follow the leading of the light above, and with stedfast gaze obeying the indications of the guiding splendour, are led to the recognition of the Truth by the brilliance of Grace, for they supposed that a king's birth was notified in a human sense , and that it must be sought in a royal city. Yet He who had taken a slave's form, and had come not to judge, but to be judged, chose Bethlehem for His nativity, Jerusalem for His passion. But Herod, hearing that a prince of the Jews was born, suspected a successor, and was in great terror: and to compass the death of the Author of Salvation, pledged himself to a false homage. How happy had he been, if he had imitated the wise men's faith, and turned to a pious use what he designed for deceit. What blind wickedness of foolish jealousy, to think thou canst overthrow the Divine plan by thy frenzy. The Lord of the works, who offers an eternal Kingdom, seeks not a temporal. Why dost thou attempt to change the unchangeable order of things ordained, and to forestall others in their crime? The death of Christ belongs not to thy time. The Gospel must be first set on foot, the Kingdom of God first preached, healings first given to the sick, wondrous acts first performed. Why dost thou wish thyself to have the blame of what will belong to another's work, and why without being able to effect thy wicked design, dost thou bring on thyself alone the charge of wishing the evil? Thou gainest nothing and cattiest out nothing by this intriguing. He that was born voluntarily shall die of His own free will. The Wise men, therefore, fulfil their desire, and come to the child, the Lord Jesus Christ, the same star going before them. They adore the Word in flesh, the Wisdom in infancy, the Power in weakness, the Lord of majesty in the reality of man: and by their gifts make open acknowledgment of what they believe in their hearts, that they may show forth the mystery of their faith and understanding . The incense they offer to God, the myrrh to Man, the gold to the King, consciously paying honour to the Divine and human Nature in union: because while each substance had its own properties, there was no difference in the power of either.

III. The Massacre of the Innocents is in Harmony with the Virgin's Conception, Which Again Teaches Us Purity of Life.

And when the wise men had returned to their own land, and Jesus had been carried into Egypt at the Divine suggestion, Herod's madness blazes out into fruitless schemes. He orders all the little ones in Bethlehem to be slain, and since he knows not which infant to fear, extends a general sentence against the age he suspects. But that which the wicked king removes from the world, Christ admits to heaven: and on those for whom He had not yet spent His redeeming blood, He already bestows the dignity of martyrdom. Lift your faithful hearts then, dearly-beloved, to the gracious blaze of eternal light, and in adoration of the mysteries dispensed for man's salvation give your diligent heed to the things which have been wrought on your behalf. Love the purity of a chaste life, because Christ is the Son of a virgin. "Abstain from fleshly lusts which war against the soul ," as the blessed Apostle, present in his words as we read, exhorts us, "In malice be ye children ," because the Lord of glory conformed Himself to the infancy of mortals. Follow after humility which the Son of God deigned to teach His disciples. Put on the power of patience, in which ye may be able to gain your souls; seeing that He who is the Redemption of all, is also the Strength of all. "Set your minds on the things which are above, not on the things which are on the earth ." Walk firmly along the path of truth and life: let not earthly things hinder you for whom are prepared heavenly things through our Lord Jesus Christ, who with the Father and the Holy Ghost liveth and reigneth for ever and ever. Amen.

SERMON XXXIII. ON THE FEAST OF THE EPIPHANY, III.

I. When We Were Yet Sinners, Christ Came to Save.

Although I know, dearly-beloved, that you are fully aware of the purpose of to-day's festival, and that the words of the Gospel have according to use unfolded it to you, yet that nothing may be omitted on our part, I shall venture to say on the subject what the Lord has put in my mouth: so that in our common joy the devotion of our hearts may be so much the more sincere as the reason of our keeping the feast is better understood. The providential Mercy of God, having determined to succour the perishing world in these latter times, fore-ordained the salvation of all nations in the Person of Christ; in order that, because all nations had long been turned aside from the worship of the true God by wicked error, and even God's peculiar people Israel had well-nigh entirely fallen away from the enactments of the Law, now that all were shut up under sin , He might have mercy upon all.

For as justice was everywhere failing and the whole world was given over to vanity and wickedness, if the Divine Power had not deferred its judgment, the whole of mankind would have received the sentence of damnation. But wrath was changed to forgiveness, and, that the greatness of the Grace to be displayed might be the more conspicuous, it pleased God, to apply the mystery of remission to the abolishing of men's sins at a time when. no one could boast of his own merits.

II. The Wise Men from the East are Typical Fulfilments of God's Promise to Abraham.

Now the manifestation of this unspeakable mercy, dearly-beloved, came to pass when Herod held the royal power in Judea, where the legitimate succession of Kings having failed and the power of the High-priests having been overthrown, an alien-born had gained the sovereignty: that the rising of the true King might be attested by the voice of prophecy, which had said: "a prince shall not fail from Juda, nor a leader from his loins, until He come for whom it is reserved , and He shall be the expectation of the nations." Concerning which an innumerable succession was once promised to the most blessed patriarch Abraham to be begotten not by fleshly seed but by fertile faith; and therefore it was compared to the stars in multitude that as father of all the nations he might hope not for an earthly but for a heavenly progeny. And therefore, for the creating of the promised posterity, the heirs designated under the figure of the stars are awakened by the rising of a new star, that the ministrations of the heaven might do service in that wherein the witness of the heaven had been adduced. A star more brilliant than the other stars arouses wise men that dwell in the far East, and from the brightness of the wondrous light these men, not unskilled in observing such things, appreciate the importance of the sign: this doubtless being brought about in their hearts by Divine inspiration, in order that the mystery of so great a sight might not be hid from them, and, what was an unusual appearance to their eyes, might not be obscure to their minds. In a word they scrupulously set about their duty and provide themselves with such gifts that in worshipping the One they may at the same time show their belief in His threefold function: with gold they honour the Person of a King, with myrrh that of Man, with incense that of God .

III. The Chosen Race is No Longer the Jews, But Believers of Every Nation.

And so they enter the chief city of the Kingdom of Judaea, and in the royal city ask that He should be shown them Whom they had learnt was begotten to be King.

Herod is perturbed: he fears for his safety, he trembles for his power, he asks of the priests and teachers of the Law what the Scripture has predicted about the birth of Christ, he ascertains what had been prophesied: truth enlightens the wise men, unbelief blinds the experts: carnal Israel understands not what it reads, sees not what it points out; refers to the pages, whose utterances it does not believe. Where is thy boasting, O Jew? where thy noble birth drawn from the stem of Abraham? is not thy circumcision become uncircumcision ? Behold thou, the greater servest the less , and by the reading of that covenant which thou keepest in the letter only, thou becomest the slave of strangers born, who enter into the lot of thy heritage. Let the fulness of the nations enter into the family of the patriarchs, yea let it enter, and let the sons of promise receive in Abraham's seed the blessing which his sons, according to the flesh, renounce their claim to. In the three Magi let all people worship the Author of the universe: and let God be known not in Judaea alone, but in all the world, so that everywhere "His name" may be "great in Israel ." For while the dignity of the chosen race is proved to be degenerate by unbelief in its descend ants, it is made common to all alike by our belief.

IV. The Massacre of the Innocents Through the Consequent Flight of Christ, Brings the Truth into Egypt.

Now when the wise men had worshipped the Lord and finished all their devotions, according to the warning of a dream, they return not by the same route by which they had come. For it behoved them now that they believed in Christ not to walk in the paths of their old line of life, but having entered on a new way to keep away from the errors they had left: and it was also to baffle Herod's design, who, under the cloke of homage, was planning a wicked plot against the Infant Jesus. Hence when his crafty hopes were overthrown, the king's wrath rose to a greater fury. For reckoning up the time which the wise men had indicated, he poured out his cruel rage on all the men-children of Bethlehem, and in a general massacre of the whole of that city slew the infants, who thus passed to their eternal glory, thinking that, if every single babe was slain there, Christ too would be slain. But He Who was postponing the shedding of His blood for the world's redemption till another time, was carried and brought into Egypt by his parents' aid, and thus sought the ancient cradle of the Hebrew race, and in the power of a greater providence dispensing the princely office of the true Joseph, in that He, the Bread of Life and the Food of reason that came down from heaven, removed that worse than all famines under which the Egyptians' minds were labouring, the lack of truth , nor without that sojourn would the symbolism of that One Victim have been complete ; for there first by the slaying of the lamb was fore-shadowed the health-bringing sign of the Cross and the Lord's Passover.

V. We Must Keep This Festival as Thankful Sons of Light.

Taught then, dearly-beloved, by these mysteries of Divine grace, let us with reasonable joy celebrate the day of our first-fruits and the commencement of the nations' calling: "giving thanks to" the merciful God "who made us worthy," as the Apostle says, "to be partakers of the lot of the saints in light: who delivered us from the power of darkness and translated us into the kingdom of the Son of His love :" since as Isaiah prophesied, "the people of the nations that sat in darkness, have seen a great light, and they that dwelt in the land of the shadow of death, upon them hath the light shined ." Of whom he also said to the Lord, "nations which knew not thee, shall call on thee: and peoples which were ignorant of thee, shall run together unto thee ." This day "Abraham saw and was glad ," when he understood that the sons of his faith would be blessed in his seed that is in Christ, and foresaw that by believing he should be the father of all nations, "giving glory to God and being fully assured that What He had promised, He was able also to perform ." This day David sang of in the psalms saying: "all nations that thou hast made shall come and worship before Thee, O Lord: and they shall glorify Thy name ;" and again: "The Lord hath made known His salvation: His righteousness hath He openly showed in the sight of the nations ." This in good truth we know to have taken place ever since the three wise men aroused in their far-off land were led by a star to recognize and worship the King of heaven and earth,[which to those who gaze aright ceases not daily to appear. And if it could make Christ known when concealed in infancy, how much more able was it to reveal Him when reigning in majesty] . And surely their worship of Him exhorts us to imitation; that, as far as we can, we should serve our gracious God who invites us all to Christ. For whosoever lives religiously and chastely in the Church and "sets his mind on the, things which are above, not on the things that are upon the earth ," is in some measure like the heavenly light: and whilst he himself keeps the brightness of a holy life, he points out to many the way to the Lord like a star. In which regard, dearly-beloved, ye ought all to help one another in turn, that in the kingdom of God, which is reached by right faith and good works, ye may shine as the sons of light: through our Lord Jesus Christ, Who with God the Father and the Holy Spirit lives and reigns for ever and ever. Amen.

SERMON XXXIV. ON THE FEAST OF THE EPIPHANY, IV.

I. The Yearly Observance of the Epiphany is Profitable to Christians.

It is the right and reasonable duty of true piety, dearly-beloved, on the days which bear witness to the works of Divine mercy, to rejoice with the whole heart and to celebrate with all honour the things which have been wrought for our salvation: for the very law of recurring seasons calls us to such devout observance, and has now brought before us the feast of the Epiphany, consecrated by the Lord's appearance soon after the clay on which the Son of God co-eternal with the Father was born of a Virgin. And herein the providence. of God has established a great safeguard to our faith, so that, whilst the worship of the Saviour's earliest infancy is repeated year by year, the production of true man's nature in Him might be proved by the original verifications themselves. For this it is that justifies the ungodly, this it is that makes sinners saints, to wit the belief in the true Godhead and the true Manhood of the one Jesus Christ, our Lord: the Godhead, whereby being before all ages "in the form of God" He is equal with the Father: the Manhood whereby in the last days He is united to Man in the "form of a slave." For the confirmation therefore of this Faith which was to be fore-armed against all errors, it was a wondrous loving provision of the Divine plan that a nation which dwelt in the far-off country of the East and was cunning in the art of reading the stars, should receive the sign of the infant's birth who was to reign over all Israel. For the unwonted splendour of a bright new star appeared to the wise men and filled their mind with such wonder, as they gazed upon its brilliance, that they could not think they ought to neglect what was announced to them with such distinctness. And, as the event showed, the grace of God was the disposing cause of this wondrous thing: who when the whole of Bethlehem itself was still unaware of Christ's birth, brought it to the knowledge of the nations who would believe, and declared that which human words could not yet explain, through the preaching of the heavens.

II. Both Herod and the Wise Men Originally Had an Earthly Conception of the Kingdom Signified; But the Latter Learnt the Truth, the Former Did Not.

But although it was the office of the Divine condescension to make the Saviour's Nativity recognizable to the nations, yet for the under standing of the wondrous sign the wise men could have had intimation even from the ancient prophecies of Balaam, knowing that it was predicted of old and by constant repetition spread abroad: "A star shall rise out of Jacob, and a man shall rise out of Israel, and shall rule the nations ." And so the three men aroused by God through the shining of a strange star, follow the guidance of its twinkling light, thinking they will find the babe designated at Jerusalem in the royal city. But finding themselves mistaken in this opinion, through the scribes and teachers of the Jews they learnt what the Holy Scripture had foretold of the birth of Christ; so that confirmed by a twofold witness, they sought with still more eager faith Him whom both the brightness of the star and the sure word of prophecy revealed. And when the Divine oracle was proclaimed through the chief priests' answers and the Spirit's voice declared, which says: "And thou, Bethlehem, the land of Judah, art not least among the princes of Judah; for out of thee shall come a leader to rule My people Israel ," how easy and how natural it was that the leading men among the Hebrews should believe what they taught! But it appears that they held material notions with Herod, and reckoned Christ's kingdom as on the same level as the powers of this world: so that they hoped for a temporal leader while he dreaded an earthly rival. The fear that racks thee, Herod, is wasted; in vain dost thou try to vent thy rage on the infant thou suspectest. Thy realm cannot hold Christ; the Lord of the world is not satisfied with the narrow limits of thy sway. He, whom thou dost not wish to reign in Judaea, reigns everywhere: and thou wouldst rule more happily thyself, if thou wert to submit to His command. Why dost thou not do with sincerity what in treacherous falseness thou dost promise? Come with the wise men, and in suppliant adoration worship the true King. But thou, from too great fondness for Jewish blindness, wilt not imitate the nations' faith, and directest thy stubborn heart to cruel wiles, though thou art doomed neither to stay Him whom thou fearest nor to harm them whom thou slayest.

III. The Perseverance of the Magi Has Led to the Most Important Results.

Led then, dearly beloved, into Bethlehem by obeying the guidance of the star, the wise men "rejoiced with very great joy," as the evangelist has told us: "and entering the house, found the child with Mary, His mother; and falling down they worshipped Him; and opening their treasures they presented to Him gifts, gold, frankincense and myrrh ." What wondrous faith of perfect knowledge, which was taught them not by earthly wisdom, but by the instruction of the Holy Spirit! Whence came it that these men, who had quitted their country without having seen Jesus, and had not noticed anything in His looks to enforce such systematic adoration, observed this method in offering their gifts? unless it were that besides the appearance of the star, which attracted their bodily eyes, the more refulgent rays of truth taught their hearts that before they started on their toilsome road, they must understand that He was signified to Whom was owed in gold royal honour, in incense Divine adoration, in myrrh the acknowledgment of mortality. Such a belief and understanding no doubt, as far as the enlightenment of their faith went, might have been sufficient in themselves and have prevented their using their bodily eyes in inquiring into that which they had beheld with their mind's fullest gaze. But their sagacious diligence, persevering till they found the child, did good service for future peoples and for the men of our own time: so that, as it profited us all that the apostle Thomas, after the Lord's resurrection, handled the traces of the wounds in His flesh, so it was of advantage to us that His infancy should be attested by the visit of the wise men. And so the wise men saw and adored the Child of the tribe of Judah, "of the seed of David according to the flesh ," "made from a woman, made under the law ," which He had come "not to destroy but to fulfil ." They saw and adored the Child, small in size, powerless to help others , incapable of speech, and in nought different to the generality of human children. Because, as the testimonies were trustworthy which asserted in Him the majesty of invisible Godhead, so it ought to be impossible to doubt that "the Word became flesh," and the eter- nal essence of the Son of God took man's true nature: lest either the inexpressible marvels of his acts which were to follow or the infliction of sufferings which He had to bear should overthrow the mystery of our Faith by their inconsistency: seeing that no one at all can be justified save those who believe the Lord Jesus to be both true God and true Man.

IV. The Manichoean Heresy Corrupts the Scriptures in Order to Disprove the Truth.

This peerless Faith, dearly-beloved, this Truth proclaimed throughout all ages, is opposed by the devilish blasphemies of the Manichaeans: who to murder the souls of the deceived have woven a deadly tissue of wicked doctrine out of impious and forged lies, and over the ruins of their mad opinions men have fallen headlong to such depths as to imagine a Christ with a fictitious body, who presented nothing solid, nothing real to the eyes and touch of men , but displayed an empty shape of fancy-flesh. For they wish it to be thought unworthy of belief that God the Son of God placed Himself within a woman's body and subjected His majesty to such a degradation as to be joined to our fleshly nature and be born in the true body of human substance although this is entirely the outcome of His power, not of His ill-treatment, and it is His glorious condescension, not His being polluted that should be believed in. For if yonder visible light is not marred by any of the uncleannesses with which it is encompassed, and the brightness of the sun's rays, which is doubtless a material creature, is not contaminated by any of the dirty or muddy places to which it penetrates, is there anything whatever its quality which could pollute the essence of that eternal and immaterial Light? seeing that by allying Himself to that creature which He had made after His own image He furnished it with purification and received no stain, and healed the wounds of its weakness without suffering loss of power. And because this great and unspeakable mystery of divine Godliness was announced by all the testimonies of the Holy Scriptures, those opponents of the Truth of which we speak have rejected the law that was given through Moses and the divinely inspired utterances of the prophets, and have tampered with the very pages of the gospels and apostles, by removing or inserting certain things: forging for themselves under the Apostles' names and under the words of the Saviour Himself many volumes of falsehood, whereby to fortify their lying errors and instil deadly poison into the minds of those to be deceived. For they saw that everything contradicted and made against them and that not only by the New but also by the Old Testament their blasphemous and treacherous folly was confuted. And yet persisting in their mad lies they cease not to disturb the Church of God with their deceits, persuading those miserable creatures whom they can ensnare to deny that man's nature was truly taken by the Lord Jesus Christ; to deny that He was truly crucified for the world's salvation: to deny that from His side wounded by the spear flowed the blood of Redemption and the water of baptism : to deny that He was buried and raised again the third day: to deny that in sight of the disciples He was lifted above all the heights of the skies to take His seat on the right hand of the Father; and in order that when all the truth of the Apostles' Creed was destroyed, there may be nothing to frighten the wicked or inspire the saints with hope, to deny that the living and the dead must be judged by Christ; so that those whom they have robbed of the power of these great mysteries may learn to worship Christ in the sun and moon, and under the name of the Holy Spirit to adore Manichaeus himself, the inventor of all these blasphemies.

V. Avoid All Dealings with the Heretics, But Intercede with God For Them.

To confirm your hearts therefore, dearly-beloved, in the Faith and Truth, let to-day's festival help you all, and let the catholic confession be fortified by the testimony of the manifestation of the Saviour's infancy, while we anathematize the blasphemy of those who deny the flesh of our nature in Christ: about which the blessed Apostle John has forewarned us in no doubtful utterance, saying, "every spirit which confesses Christ Jesus to have come in the flesh is of God: and every spirit which destroys Jesus is not of God, and this is Antichrist ." Consequently let no Christian have aught in common with men of this kind, let him have no alliance or intercourse with such. Let it advantage the whole Church that many of them in the mercy of God have been discovered, and that their own confession has disclosed how sacrilegious their lives were. Let no one be deceived by their discriminations between food and food, by their soiled raiment, by their pale faces. Fasts are not holy which proceed not on the principle of abstinence but with deceitful de sign. Let this be the end of their harming the unwary, and deluding the ignorant; henceforth no one's fall shall be excusable: no longer must he be held simple but extremely worthless and perverse who hereafter shall be found entangled in detestable error. A practice countenanced by the Church and Divinely instituted, not only do we not forbid, we even incite you to, that you should supplicate the Lord even for such: since we also with tears and mourning feel pity for the ruins of cheated souls, carrying out the Apostles' example of loving-kindness , so as to be weak with those that are weak and to "weep with those that weep ." For we hope that God's mercy can be won by the many tears and due amendment of the fallen: because so long as life remains in the body no man's restoration must be despaired of, but the reform of all desired with the Lord's help, "who raiseth up them that are crushed, looseth them that are chained, giveth light to the blind :" to whom is honour and glory for ever and ever. Amen.

SERMON XXXVI. ON THE FEAST OF THE EPIPHANY, VI.

I. The Story of the Magi Not Only a Byegone Fact in History, But of Everyday Application to Ourselves.

The day, dearly-beloved, on which Christ the Saviour of the world first appeared to the nations must be venerated by us with holy worship: and to-day those joys must be entertained in our hearts which existed in the breasts of the three magi, when, aroused by the sign and leading of a new star, which they believed to have been promised, they fell down in presence of the King of heaven and earth. For that day has not so passed away that the mighty work, which was then revealed, has passed away with it, and that nothing but the report of the thing has come down to us for faith to receive and memory to celebrate; seeing that, by the oft-repeated gift of God, our times daily enjoy the fruit of what the first age possessed. And therefore, although the narrative which is read to us from the Gospel properly records those days on which the three men, who had neither been taught by the prophets' predictions nor instructed by the testimony of the law, came to acknowledge God from the furthest parts of the East, yet we behold this same thing more clearly and abundantly carried on now in the enlightenment of all those who are called, since the prophecy of Isaiah is fulfilled when he says, "the Lord has laid bare His holy arm in the sight of all the nations, and all the nations upon earth have seen the salvation which is from the Lord our God ;" and again, "and those to whom it has not been announced about Him shall see, and they who have not heard, shall understand ." Hence when we see men devoted to worldly wisdom and far from belief in Jesus Christ brought out of the depth of their error and called to an acknowledgment of the true Light, it is undoubtedly the brightness of the Divine grace that is at work: and whatever of new light illumines the darkness of their hearts, comes from the rays of the same star: so that it should both move with wonder, and going before lead to the adoration of God the minds which it visited with its splendour. But if with careful thought we wish to see how their threefold kind of gift is also offered by all who come to Christ with the foot of faith, is not the same offering repeated in the hearts of true believers? For he that acknowledges Christ the King of the universe brings gold from the treasure of his heart: he that believes the Only-begotten of God to have united man's true nature to Himself, offers myrrh; and he that confesses Him in no wise inferior to the Father's majesty, worships Him in a manner with incense.

II. Satan Still Carries on the Wiles of Herod, And, as It Were, Personates Him in His Opposition to Christ.

These comparisons, dearly-beloved, being thoughtfully considered, we find Herod's character also not to be wanting, of which the devil himself is now an unwearied imitator, just as he was then a secret instigator. For he is tortured at the calling of all the nations, and racked at the daily destruction of his power, grieving at his being everywhere deserted, and the true King adored in all places. He prepares devices, he hatches plots, he bursts out into murders, and that he may make use of the remnants of those whom he still deceives, is consumed with envy in the persons of the Jews, lies treacherously in wait in the persons of heretics, blazes out into cruelty in the persons of the heathen. For he sees that the power of the eternal King is invincible Whose death has extinguished the power of death itself; and therefore he has armed himself with all his skill of injury against those who serve the true King;

hardening some by the pride that knowledge of the law engenders, debasing others by the lies of false belief, and inciting others to the madness of persecution. Yet the madness of this "Herod" is vanquished, and brought to nought by Him who has crowned even infants with the glory of martyrdom, and has endued His faithful ones with so unconquerable a love that in the Apostle's words they dare to say, "who shall separate us from the love of Christ? shall tribulation, or want, or persecution, Or hunger, or nakedness, or peril, or the sword? as it is written, For thy sake are we killed all the day long, we are counted as sheep for the slaughter. But in all these things we overcome on account of Him who loved us ."

III. The Cessation of Active Persecution Does Not Do Away with the Need of Continued Vigilance : Satan Has Only Changed His Tactics.

Such courage as this, dearly-beloved, we do not believe to have been needful only at those times in which the kings of the world and all the powers of the age were raging against God's people in an outburst of wickedness, thinking it to redound to their greatest glory if they removed the Christian name from the earth, but not knowing that God's Church grows through the frenzy of their cruelty, since in the tortures and deaths of the martyrs, those whose number was reckoned to be diminished were augmented through the force of example . In fine, so much strength has our Faith gained by the attacks of persecutors that royal princedoms have no greater ornament than that the lords of the world are members of Christ; and their boast is not so much that they were born in the purple as that they have been re-born in baptism. But because the stress of former blasts has lulled, and with a cessation of fightings a measure of tranquillity has long seemed to smile upon us, those divergences are carefully to be guarded against which arise from the very reign of peace. For the adversary having been proved ineffective in open persecutions now exercises a hidden skill in doing cruel hurt, in order to overthrow by the stumbling-block of pleasure those whom he could not strike with the blow of affliction. And so seeing the faith of princes opposed to him and the indivisible Trinity of the one Godhead as devoutly worshipped in palaces as in churches, he grieves at the shedding of Christian blood being forbidden, and attacks the mode of life of those whose death he cannot compass. The terror of confiscations he changes into the fire of avarice, and corrupts with covetousness those whose spirit he could not break by losses. For the malicious haughtiness which long use has ingrained into his very nature has not laid aside its hatred, but changed its character in order to subjugate the minds of the faithful by blandishments. He inflames those with covetous desires whom he cannot distress with tortures: he sows strifes, kindles passions, sets tongues a-wagging, and, lest more cautious hearts should draw back from his lawless wiles, facilitates opportunities for accomplishing crimes: because this is the only fruit of all his devices that he who is not worshipped with the sacrifice of cattle and goats, and the burning of incense, should be paid the homage of divers wicked deeds .

IV. Timely Repentance Gains God's Merciful Consideration.

Our state of peace , therefore, dearly-beloved, has its dangers, and it is vain for those who do not withstand vicious desires to feel secure of the liberty which is the privilege of their Faith. Men's hearts are shown by the character of their works, and the fashion of their minds is betrayed by the nature of their actions. For there are some, as the Apostle says, "who profess that they know God, but deny Him by their deeds ." For the charge of denial is truly incurred when the good which is heard in the sound of the voice is not present in the conscience. Indeed, the frailty of man's nature easily glides into faults: and because no sin is without its attractiveness, deceptive pleasure is quickly acquiesced in. But we should run for spiritual succour from the desires of the flesh: and the mind that has knowledge of its God should turn away from the evil suggestion of the enemy. Avail thyself of the long-suffering of God, and persist not in cherishing thy sin, because its punishment is put off. The sinner must not feel secure of his impunity, because if he loses the time for repentance he will find no place for mercy, as the prophet says, "in death no one remembers thee; and in the realms below who will confess to thee ?" But let him who experiences the difficulty of self-amendment and restoration betake himself to the mercy of a befriending God, and ask that the chains of evil habit may be broken off by Him "who lifts up those that fall and raises all the crushed ." The prayer of one that confesses will not be in vain since the merciful God "will grant the desire of those that fear Him ," and will give what is asked, as He gave the Source from Which to ask. Through our Lend Jesus Christ, Who liveth and reigneth with the Father and the Holy Ghost for ever and ever. Amen.

SERMON XXXIX. ON LENT, I.

I. The Benefits of Abstinence Shown by the Example of the Hebrews.

In former days, when the people of the Hebrews and all the tribes of Israel were oppressed for their scandalous sins by the grievous tyranny of the Philistines, in order that they might be able to overcome their enemies, as the sacred story declares, they restored their powers of mind and body by the injunction of a fast. For they understood that they had deserved that hard and wretched subjection for their neglect of God's commands, and evil ways, and that it was in vain for them to strive with arms unless they had first withstood their sin. Therefore abstaining from food and drink, they applied the discipline of strict correction to themselves, and in order to conquer their foes, first conquered the allurements of the palate in themselves. And thus it came about that their fierce enemies and cruel taskmasters yielded to them when fasting, whom they had held in subjection when full. And so we too, dearly beloved, who are set in the midst of many oppositions and conflicts, may be cured by a little carefulness, if only we will use the same means. For our case is almost the same as theirs, seeing that, as they were attacked by foes in the flesh so are we chiefly by spiritual enemies. And if we can conquer them by God's grace enabling us to correct our ways, the strength of our bodily enemies also will give way before us, and by our self-amendment we shall weaken those who were rendered formidable to us, not by their own merits but by our shortcomings.

II. Use Lent to Vanquish the Enemy, and Be Thus Preparing for Eastertide.

Accordingly, dearly-beloved, that we may be able to overcome all our enemies, let us seek Divine aid by the observance of the heavenly bidding, knowing that we cannot otherwise prevail against our adversaries, unless we prevail against our own selves. For we have many encounters with our own selves: the flesh desires one thing against the spirit, and the spirit another thing against the flesh . And in this disagreement, if the desires of the body be stronger, the mind will disgracefully lose its proper dignity, and it will be most disastrous for that to serve which ought to have ruled. But if the mind, being subject to its Ruler, and delighting in gifts from above, shall have trampled under foot the allurements of earthly pleasure, and shall not have allowed sin to reign in its mortal body , reason will maintain a well-ordered supremacy, and its strongholds no strategy of spiritual wickednesses will cast down: because man has then only true peace and true freedom when the flesh is ruled by the judgment of the mind, and the mind is directed by the will of God. And although this state of preparedness, dearly-beloved, should always be maintained that our ever-watchful foes may be overcome by unceasing diligence, yet now it must be the more anxiously sought for and the more zealously cultivated when the designs of our subtle foes themselves are conducted with keener craft than ever. For knowing that the most hollowed days of Lent are now at hand, in the keeping of which all past slothfulnesses are chastised, all negligences alerted for, they direct all the force of their spite on this one thing, that they who intend to celebrate the Lord's holy Passover may be found unclean in some matter, and that cause of offence may arise where propitiation ought to have been obtained.

III. Fights are Necessary to Prove Our Faith.

As we approach then, dearly-beloved, the beginning of Lent, which is a time for the more careful serving of the Lord, because we are, as it were, entering on a kind of contest in good works, let us prepare our souls for fighting with temptations, and understand that the more zealous we are for our salvation, the more determined must be the assaults of our opponents. But "stronger is He that is in us than He that is against us ," and through Him are we powerful in whose strength we rely: because it was for this that the Lord allowed Himself to be tempted by the tempter, that we might be taught by His example as well as fortified by His aid. For He conquered the adversary, as ye have heard , by quotations from the law, not by actual strength, that by this very thing He might do greater honour to man, and inflict a greater punishment on the adversary by conquering the enemy of the human race not now as God but as Man. He fought then, therefore, that we too might fight thereafter: He conquered that we too might likewise conquer. For there are no works of power, dearly-beloved, without the trials of temptations, there is no faith without proof, no contest without a foe, no victory without conflict. This life of ours is in the midst of snares, in the midst of battles; if we do not wish to be deceived, we must watch: if we want to overcome, we must fight. And therefore the most wise Solomon says, "My son in approaching the service of God prepare thy soul for temptation ." For He being a man full of the wisdom of God, and knowing that the pursuit of religion involves laborious struggles, foreseeing too the danger of the fight, forewarned the intending combatant; lest haply, if the tempter came upon him in his ignorance, he might find him unready and wound him unawares.

IV. The Christian's Armour is Both for Defence and for Attack.

So, dearly-beloved, let us who instructed in Divine learning come wittingly to the present contest and strife, hear the Apostle when he says, "for our struggle is not against flesh and blood, but against principalities and powers, against the rulers of this dark world, against spiritual wickedness in heavenly things ," and let us not forget that these our enemies feel it is against them all is done that we strive to do for our salvation, and that by the very fact of our seeking after some good thing we are challenging our foes. For this is an old-standing quarrel between us and them fostered by the devil's ill-will, so that they are tortured by our being justified, because they have fallen from those good things to which we, God helping us, are advancing.

If, therefore, we are raised, they are prostrated: if we are strengthened, they are weakened. Our cures are their blows, because they are wounded by our wounds' cure. "Stand, therefore," dearly-beloved, as the Apostle says, "having the loins of your mind girt in truth, and your feet shod in the preparation of the gospel of peace, in all things taking the shield of faith in which ye may be able to extinguish all the fiery darts of the evil one, and put on the helmet of salvation and the sword of the Spirit, which is the Word of God ." See, dearly-beloved, with what mighty weapons, with what impregnable defences we are armed by our Leader, who is famous for His many triumphs, the unconquered Master of the Christian warfare. He has girt our loins with the belt of chastity, He has shod our feet with the bonds of peace: because the unbelted soldier is quickly vanquished by the suggester of immodesty, and he that is unshod is easily bitten by the serpent. He has given the shield of faith for the protection of our whole body; on our head has He set the helmet of salvation; our right hand has He furnished with a sword, that is with the word of Truth: that the spiritual warrior may not only be safe from wounds, but also may have strength to wound his assailant.

V. Abstinence Not Only from Food But from Other Evil Desires, Especially from Wrath, is Required in Lent.

Relying, therefore, dearly-beloved, on these arms, let us enter actively and fearlessly on the contest set before us: so that in this fasting struggle we may not rest satisfied with only this end, that we should think abstinence from food alone desirable. For it is not enough that the substance of our flesh should be reduced, if the strength of the soul be not also developed. When the outer man is somewhat subdued, let the inner man be somewhat refreshed; and when bodily excess is denied to our flesh, let our mind be invigorated by spiritual delights. Let every Christian scrutinise himself, and earth severely into his inmost heart: let him see that no discord cling there, no wrong desire be harboured. Let chasteness drive incontinence far away; let the light of truth dispel the shades of deception; let the swellings of pride subside; let wrath yield to reason; let the darts of ill-treatment be shattered, and the chidings of the tongue be bridled; let thoughts of revenge fall through, and injuries be given over to oblivion. In fine, let "every plant which the heavenly Father hath not planted be removed by the roots ." For then only are the seeds of virtue well nourished in us, when every foreign germ is uprooted from the field of wheat. If any one, therefore, has been fired by the desire for vengeance against another, so that he has given him up to prison or bound him with chains, let him make haste to forgive not only the innocent, but also one who seems worthy of punishment, that he may with confidence make use of the clause in the Lord's prayer and say, "Forgive us our debts, as we also forgive our debtors ." Which petition the Lord marks with peculiar emphasis, as if the efficacy of the whole rested on this condition, by saying, "For if ye forgive men their sins, your Father which is in heaven also will forgive you: but if ye forgive not men, neither will your Father forgive you your Sins ."

VI. The Right Use of Lent Will Lead to a Happy Participation in Easter.

Accordingly, dearly-beloved, being mindful of our weakness, because we easily fall into all kinds of faults, let us by no means neglect this special remedy and most effectual healing of our wounds. Let us remit, that we may have remission: let us grant the pardon which we crave: let us not be eager to be revenged when we pray to be forgiven. Let us not pass over the groans of the poor with deaf ear, but with prompt kindness bestow our mercy on the needy, that we may deserve to find mercy in the judgment. And he that, aided by God's grace, shall strain every nerve after this perfection, will keep this holy fast faithfully; free from the leaven of the old wickedness, in the unleavened bread of sincerity and truth , he will reach the blessed Passover, and by newness of life will worthily rejoice in the mystery of man's reformation through Christ our Lord Who with the Father and the Holy Spirit lives and reigns for ever and ever. Amen.

SERMON XL. ON LENT, II.

I. Progress and Improvement Always Possible.

Although, dearly-beloved, as the Easter festival approaches, the very recurrence of the season points out to us the Lenten fast, yet our words also must add their exhortations which, the Lord helping us, may be not useless to the active nor irksome to the devout. For since the idea of these days demands the increase of all our religious performances, there is no one, I am sure, that does not feel glad at being incited to good works. For though our nature which, so long as we are mortal, will be changeable, is advancing to the highest pursuits of virtue, yet always has the possibility of filling back, so has it always the possibility of advancing. And this is the true justness of the perfect that they should never assume themselves to be perfect, lest flagging in the purpose of their yet unfinished journey,they should fall into the danger of failure, through giving up the desire for progress.

And, therefore, because none of us, dearly beloved, is so perfect and holy as not to be able to be more perfect and more holy, let us all together, without difference of rank, without distinction of desert, with pious eagerness pursue our race from what we have attained to what we yet aspire to, and make some needful additions to our regular devotions. For he that is not more attentive than usual to religion in these days, is shown at other times to be not attentive enough.

II. Satan Seeks to Subtly His Numerous Lasses by Fresh Gains.

Hence the reading of the Apostle's proclamation has sounded opportunely in our ears, saying, "Behold now is the accepted time, behold now is the day of salvation ." For what is more accepted than this time, what more suitable to salvation than these days, in which war is proclaimed against vices and progress is made in all virtues? Thou hadst indeed always to keep watch, O Christian soul, against the enemy of thy salvation, lest any spot should be exposed to the tempter's snares: but now greater wariness and keener prudence must be employed by thee when that same foe of thine rages with fiercer hatred. For now in all the world the power of his ancient sway is taken from him, and the countless vessels of captivity are rescued from his grasp. The people of all nations and of all tongues are breaking away from their cruel plunderer, and now no race of men is found that does not struggle against the tyrant's laws, while through all the borders of the earth many thousands of thousands are being prepared to be reborn in Christ : and as the birth of a new creature draws near, spiritual wickedness is being driven out by those who were possessed by it. The blasphemous fury of the despoiled foe frets, therefore, and seeks new gains because it has lost its ancient right. Unwearied and ever wakeful, he snatches at any sheep he finds straying carelessly from the sacred folds, intent on leading them over the steeps of treasure anti down the slopes of luxury into the abodes of death. And so he inflames their wrath, feeds their hatreds, whets their desires, mocks at their continence, arouses their gluttony.

III. The Twofold Nature of Christ Shown at the Temptation.

For whom would he not dare to try, who did not keep from his treacherous attempts even on our Lord Jesus Christ? For, as the story of the Gospel has disclosed , when our Saviour, Who was true God, that He might show Himself true Man also, and banish all wicked and erroneous opinions, after the fast of 40 days and nights, had experienced the hunger of human weakness, the devil, rejoicing at having found in Him a sign of possible and mortal nature, in order to test the power which he feared, said, "If Thou art the Son of God, command that these stones become bread ." Doubtless the Almighty could do this, and it was easy that at the Creator's command a creature of any kind should change into the form that it was commanded: just as when He willed it, in the marriage feast, He changed the water into wine: but here it better agreed with His purposes of salvation that His haughty foe's cunning should be vanquished by the Lord, not in the power of His Godhead, but by the mystery of His humiliation. At length, when the devil had been put to flight and the tempter baffled in all his arts, angels came to the Lord and ministered to Him, that He being true Man and true God, His Manhood might be unsullied by those crafty questions, and His Godhead displayed by those holy ministrations. And so let the sons and disciples of the devil be confounded, who, being filled with the poison of vipers, deceive the simple, denying in Christ the presence of both true natures, whilst they rob either His Godhead of Manhood, or His Manhood of Godhead, although both falsehoods are destroyed by a twofold and simultaneous proof: for by His bodily hunger His perfect Manhood was shown, and by the attendant angels His perfect Godhead.

IV. The Fast Should Not End with Abstinence Front Food, But Lead to Good Deeds.

Therefore, dearly-beloved, seeing that, as we are taught by our Redeemer's precept, "man lives not in bread alone, but in every word of God ," and it is right that Christian people, whatever the amount of their abstinence, should rather desire to satisfy themselves with the "Word of God" than with bodily food, let us with ready devotion and eager faith enter upon the celebration of the solemn fast, not with barren abstinence flora food, which is often imposed on us by weakliness of body, or the disease of avarice, but in bountiful benevolence: that in truth we may be of those of whom the very Truth speaks, "blessed are they which hunger and thirst after righteousness, for they shall be filled ." Let works of piety, therefore, be our delight, and let us be filled with those kinds of food which feed us for eternity. Let us rejoice in the replenishment of the poor, whom our bounty has satisfied. Let us delight in the clothing of those whose nakedness we have covered with needful raiment. Let our humaneness be felt by the sick in their illnesses, by the weakly in their infirmities, by the exiles in their hardships, by the orphans in their destitution, and by solitary widows in their sadness: in the helping of whom there is no one that cannot carry out some amount of benevolence. For no one's income is small, whose heart is big: and the measure of one's mercy and goodness does not depend on the size of one's means. Wealth of goodwill is never rightly lacking, even in a slender purse. Doubtless the expenditure of the rich is greater, and that of the poor smaller, but there is no difference in the fruit of their works, where the purpose of the workers is the same.

V. And Still Further It Should Lead to Personal Amendment and Domestic Harmony.

But, beloved, in this opportunity for the virtues' exercise there are also other notablecrowns, to be won by no dispersing abroad of granaries, by no disbursement of money, if wantonness is repelled, if drunkenness is abandoned, and the lusts of the flesh tamed by the laws of chastity: if hatreds pass into affection, if enmities be turned into peace, if meekness extinguishes wrath, if gentleness forgives wrongs, if in fine the conduct of master and of slaves is so well ordered that the rule of the one is milder, and the discipline of the other is more complete. It is by such observances then, dearly-beloved, that God's mercy will be gained, the charge of sin wiped out, and the adorable Easter festival devoutly kept. And this the pious Emperors of the Roman world have long guarded with holy observance; for in honour of the Lord's Passion and Resurrection they bend their lofty power, and relaxing the severity of their decrees set free many of their prisoners: so that on the clays when the world is saved by the Divine mercy, their clemency, which is modelled on the Heavenly goodness, may be zealously followed by us. Let Christian peoples then imitate their princes, and be incited to forbearance in their homes by these royal examples. For it is not right that private laws should be severer than public. Let faults be forgiven, let bonds be loosed offences wiped out, designs of vengeance fall through, that the holy festival through the Divine and human grace may find all happy, all innocent: through our Lord Jesus Christ Who with the Father and the Holy Spirit liveth and reigneth God for endless ages of ages. Amen.

SERMON XLII. ON LENT, IV.

I. The Lenten Fast an Opportunity for Restoring Our Purely.

In proposing to preach this most holy and important fast to you, dearly beloved, how shall I begin more fitly than by quoting the words of the Apostle, in whom Christ Himself was speaking, and by reminding you of what we have read : "behold, now is the acceptable time, behold now is the day of salvation." For though there are no seasons which are not full of Divine blessings, and though access is ever open to us to God's mercy through His grace, yet now all men's minds should be moved with greater zeal to spiritual progress, and animated by larger confidence, when the return of the day, on which we were redeemed, invites us to all the duties of godliness: that we may keep the super-excellent mystery of the Lord's passion with bodies and hearts purified. These great mysteries do indeed require from us such unflagging devotion and unwearied reverence that we should remain in God's sight always the same, as we ought to be found on the Easter feast itself. But because few have this constancy, and, because so long as the stricter observance is relaxed in consideration of the frailty of the flesh, and so long as one's interests extend over all the various actions of this life, even pious hearts must get some soils from the dust of the world, the Divine Providence has with great beneficence taken care that the discipline of the forty days should heal us and restore the purity of our minds, during which the faults of other times might be redeemed by pious acts and removed by chaste fasting.

II. Lent Must Be Used For Removing All Our Defilements, and of Good Works There Must Be No Stint.

As we are therefore, dearly-beloved, about to enter on those mystic days which are dedicated to the benefits of fasting, let us take care to obey the Apostle's precepts, cleansing "ourselves from every defilement of flesh and spirit :" that by controlling the struggles that go on between our two natures, the spirit which, if it is under the guidance of God, should be the governor of the body, may uphold the dignity of its rule: so that we may give no offence to any, nor be subject to the chidings of reprovers. For we shall be rightly attacked with rebukes, and through our fault ungodly tongues will arm themselves to do harm to religion, if the conduct of those that fast is at variance with the standard of perfect purity. For our fast does not consist chiefly of mere abstinence from food, nor are dainties withdrawn from our bodily appetites with profit, unless the mind is recalled from wrong-doing and the tongue restrained from slandering. This is a time of gentleness and long-suffering, of peace and tranquillity: when all the pollutions of vice are to be eradicated and continuance of virtue is to be attained by us. Now let godly minds boldly accustom themselves to forgive faults, to pass over insults, and to forget wrongs. Now let the faithful spirit train himself with the armour of righteousness on the right hand and on the left, that through honour and dishonour, through ill repute and good repute, the conscience may be undisturbed in unwavering uprightness, not puffed up by praise and not wearied out by revilings. The self-restraint of the religious should not be gloomy, but sincere; no murmurs of complaint should be heard from those who are never without the consolation of holy joys. The decrease of worldly means should not be feared in the practice of works of mercy. Christian poverty is always rich, because what it has is more than what it has not. Nor does the poor man fear to labour in this world, to whom it is given to possess all things in the Lord of all things. Therefore those who do the things which are good must have no manner of fear lest the power of doing should fail them; since in the gospel the widow's devotion is extolled in the case of her two mites, and voluntary bounty gets its reward for a cup of cold water . For the measure of our charitableness is fixed by the sincerity of our feelings, and he that shows mercy on others will never want for mercy himself. The holy widow of Sarepta discovered this, who offered the blessed Elias in the time of famine one day's food, which was all she had, and putting the prophet's hunger before her own needs, ungrudgingly gave up a handful of corn and a little oil . But she did not lose what she gave in all faith, and in the vessels emptied by her godly bounty a source of new plenty arose, that the fulness of her substance might not be diminished by the holy purpose to which she had put it, because she had never dreaded being brought to want.

III. As with the Saviour, So with Us, the Devil Tries to Make Our Very Piety Its Own Snare.

But, dearly-beloved, doubt not that the devil, who is the opponent of all virtues, is jealous of these good desires, to which we are confident you are prompted of your own selves, and that to this end he is arming the force of his malice in order to make your very piety its own snare, and endeavouring to overcome by boastfulness those whom he could not defeat by distrustfulness. For the vice of pride is a near neighbour to good deeds, and arrogance ever lies in wait hard by virtue: because it is hard for him that lives praise-worthily not to be caught by man's praise unless, as it is written, "he that glorieth, glorieth in the Lord ." Whose intentions would that most naughty enemy not dare to attack? whose fasting would he not seek to break down? seeing that, as has been shown in the reading of the Gospel , he did not restrain his wiles even against the Saviour of the world Himself. For being exceedingly afraid of His fast, which lasted 40 days and nights, he wished most cunningly to discover whether this power of abstinence was given Him or His very own: for he need not fear the defeat of all his treacherous designs, if Christ were throughout subject to the same conditions as He is in body . And so he first craftily examined whether He were Himself the Creator of all things, such that He could change the natures of material things as He pleased: secondly, whether under the form of human flesh the Godhead lay concealed, to Whom it was easy to make the air His chariot, and convey His earthly limbs through space. But when the Lord preferred to resist him by the uprightness of His true Manhood, than to display the power of His Godhead, to this he turns the craftiness of his third design, that he might tempt by the lust of empire Him in Whom the signs of Divine power had failed, and entice Him to the worship of himself by promising the kingdoms of the world. But the devil's cleverness was rendered foolish by God's wisdom, so that the proud foe was bound by that which he had formerly bound, and did not fear to assail Him Whom it behoved to be slain for the world.

IV. The Perverse Turn Even Their Fasting into Sin.

This adversary's wiles then let us beware of, not only in the enticements of the palate, but also in our purpose of abstinence. For he who knew how to bring death upon mankind by means of food, knows also how to harm us through our very fasting, and using the Manichaeans as his tools, as he once drove men to take what was forbidden, so in the opposite direction he prompts them to avoid what is allowed. It is indeed a helpful observance, which accustoms one to scanty diet, and checks the appetite for dainties: but woe to the dogmatizing of those whose very fasting is turned to sin. For they condemn the creature's nature to the Creator's injury, and maintain that they are defiled by eating those things of which they contend the devil, not God, is the author: although absolutely nothing that exists is evil, nor is anything in nature included in the actually bad. For the good Creator made all things good and the Maker of the universe is one, "Who made the heaven and the earth, the sea and all that is in them ." Of which whatever is granted to man for food and drink,' is holy and clean after its kind. But if it is taken with immoderate greed, it is the excess that disgraces the eaters and drinkers, not the nature of the food or drink that defiles them. "For all things," as the Apostle says, "are clean to the clean. But to the defiled and unbelieving nothing is clean, but their mind and conscience is defiled ."

V. Be Reasonable and Seasonable in Your Fasting.

But ye, dearly-beloved, the holy offspring of the catholic Mother, who have been taught in the school of Truth by God's Spirit, moderate your liberty with due reasonableness, knowing that it is good to abstain even from things lawful, and at seasons of greater strictness to distinguish one food from another with a view to giving up the use of some kinds, not to condemning their nature. And so be not infected with the error of those who are corrupted merely by their own ordinances, "serving the creature rather than the Creator ," and offering a foolish abstinence to the service of the lights of heaven: seeing that they have chosen to fast on the first and second days of the week in honour of the sun and moon, proving themselves in this one instance of their perverseness twice disloyal to God, twice blasphemous, by setting up their fast not only in worship of the stars but also in contempt of the Lord's Resurrection. For they reject the mystery of man's salvation and refuse to believe that Christ our Lord in the true flesh of our nature was truly born, truly suffered, was truly buried and was truly raised. And in consequence, condemn the day of our rejoicing by the gloom of their fasting. And since to conceal their infidelity they dare to be present at our meetings, at the Communion of the Mysteries they bring themselves sometimes, in order to ensure their concealment, to receive Christ's Body with unworthy lips, though they altogether refuse to drink the Blood of our Redemption. And this we make known to you, holy brethren, that men of this sort may be detected by you by these signs, and that they whose impious pretences have been discovered may be driven from the society of the saints by priestly authority. For of such the blessed Apostle Paul in his foresight warns God's Church, saying: "but we beseech you, brethren, that ye observe those who make discussions and offences contrary to the doctrine which ye learnt and turn away from them. For such persons serve not Christ the Lord but their own belly, and by sweet words and fair speeches beguile the hearts of the innocent ."

VI. Make Your Fasting a Reality by Amendment in Your Lives.

Being therefore, dearly-beloved, fully instructed by these admonitions of ours, which we have often repeated in your ears in protest against abominable error, enter upon the holy days of Lent with Godly devoutness, and prepare yourselves to win God's mercy by your own works of mercy. Quench your anger, wipe out enmities, cherish unity, and vie with one another in the offices of true humility. Rule your slaves and those who are put under you with fairness, let none of them be tortured by imprisonment or chains. Forego vengeance, forgive offences: exchange severity for gentleness, indignation for meekness, discord for peace. Let all men find us self-restrained, peaceable, kind: that our fastings may be acceptable to God. For in a word to Him we offer the sacrifice of true abstinence and true Godliness, when we keep ourselves from all evil: the Almighty God helping us through all, to Whom with the Son and Holy Spirit belongs one Godhead and one Majesty, for ever and ever. Amen:

SERMON XLVI. ON LENT, VIII.

I. Lent Must Be Kept Not Only by Avoiding Bodily Impurity But Also by Avoiding Errors of Thought and Faith.

We know indeed, dearly-beloved, your devotion to be so warm that in the fasting, which is the forerunner of the Lord's Easter, many of you will have forestalled our exhortations. But because the right practice of abstinence is needful not only to the mortification of the flesh but also to the purification of the mind, we desire your observance to be so complete that, as you cut down the pleasures that be long to the lusts of the flesh, so you should banish the errors that proceed from the imaginations of the heart. For he whose heart is polluted with no misbelief prepares himself with true and reasonable purification for the Paschal Feast, in which all the mysteries of our religion meet together. For, as the Apostle says, that "all that is not of faith is sin ," the fasting of those will be unprofitable and vain, whom the father of lying deceives with his delusions, and who are not fed by Christ's true flesh. As then we must with the whole heart obey the Divine commands and sound doctrine, so we must use all foresight in abstaining from wicked imaginations. For the mind then only keeps holy and spiritual fast when it rejects the food of error and the poison of falsehood, which our crafty and wily foe plies us with more treacherously now, when by the very return of the venerable Festival, the whole church generally is admonished to understand the mysteries of its salvation. For he is the true confessor and worshipper of Christ's resurrection, who is not confused about His passion, nor deceived about His bodily nativity. For some are so ashamed of the Gospel of the Cross of Christ, as to impudently nullify the punishment which He underwent for the world's redemption, and have denied the very nature of true flesh in the Lord, not understanding how the impossible and unchangeable Deity of God's Word could have so far condescended for man's salvation, as by His power not to lose His own properties, and in His mercy to take on Him ours. And so in Christ, there is a twofold form but one person, and the Son of God, who is at the same time Son of Man, is one Lord, accepting the condition of a slave by the design of loving-kindness, not by the law of necessity, because by His power He became humble, by His power passible, by His power mortal; that for the destruction of the tyranny of sin and death, the weak nature in Him might be capable of punishment, and the strong nature not lose aught of its glory.

II. All the Actions of Christ Reveal the Presence of the Twofold Nature.

And so, dearly-beloved, when in reading or hearing the Gospel you find certain things in our Lord Jesus Christ subjected to injuries and certain things illumined by miracles, in such a way that in the same Person now the Humanity appears, and now the Divinity shines out, do not put down any of these things to a delusion, as if in Christ there is either Manhood alone or Godhead alone, but believe both faithfully, worship both right humbly; so that in the union of the Word and the Flesh there may be no separation, and the bodily proofs may not seem delusive, because the divine signs were evident in Jesus. The attestations to both natures in Him are true and abundant, and by the depth of the Divine purpose all concur to this end, that the inviolable Word not being separated from the passible flesh, the Godhead may be understood as in all things partaker with the flesh and flesh with the Godhead. And, therefore, must the Christian mind that would eschew lies and be the disciple of truth, use the Gospel-story confidently, and, as if still in company with the Apostles themselves, distinguish what is visibly done by the Lord, now by the spiritual understanding and now by the bodily organs of sight. Assign to the man that He is born a boy of a woman: assign to God that His mother's virginity is not harmed, either by conception or by bearing. Recognize "the form of a slave" enwrapped in swaddling clothes, lying in a manger, but acknowledge that it was the Lord's form that was announced by angels, "proclaimed by the elements ," adored by the wise men. Understand it of His humanity that he did not avoid the marriage feast confess it Divine that he turned water into wine. Let your own feelings explain to you why He shed tears over a dead friend: let His Divine power be realized, when that same friend, after mouldering in the grave four days, is brought to life and raised only by the command of His voice. To make clay with spittle and earth was a work of the body: but to anoint therewith and enlighten the eyes of the blind is an undoubted mark of that power which had reserved for the revelation of its glory that which it had not allowed to the early part of His natural life. It is truly human to relieve bodily fatigue with rest in sleep: but it is truly Divine to quell the violence of raging storms by a rebuking command. To set food before the hungry denotes human kindness and a philanthropic spirit: but with five loaves and two fishes to satisfy 5,000 men, besides women and children, who would dare deny that to be the work of Deity? a Deity which, by the co-operation of the functions of true flesh, showed not only itself in Manhood, but also Manhood in itself; for the old, original wounds in man's nature could not be healed, except by the Word of God taking to Himself flesh from the Virgin's womb, whereby in one and the same Person flesh and the Word co-existed.

III. Hold Fast to the Statements of the Creed.

This belief in the Lord's Incarnation, dearly-beloved, through which the whole Church is Christ's body , hold firm with heart unshaken and abstain from all the lies of heretics, and remember that your works of mercy will only then profit you, and your strict continence only then bear fruit, when your minds are unsoiled by any defilement from wrong opinions. Cast away the arguments of this world's wisdom, for God hates them, and none can arrive by them at the knowledge of the Truth, and keep fixed in your mind that which you say in the Creed. Believe the Son of God to be co-eternal with the Father by Whom all things were made and without Whom nothing was made, born also according to the flesh at the end of the times. Believe Him to have been in the body crucified, dead, raised up, · and lifted above the heights of heavenly powers, set on the Father's right hand, about to come in the same flesh in which He ascended, to judge the living and the dead. For this is what the Apostle proclaims to all the faithful, saying: "if ye be risen with Christ seek the things which are above, where Christ is sitting on the right hand of God. Set your mind on the things that are above, not on the things that are upon the earth. For ye are dead, and your life is hid with Christ in God. For when Christ, our life, shall appear, then shall ye also appear with Him in glory ."

IV. Use Lent for General Improvement in the Whole Round of Christian Duties.

Relying, therefore, dearly-beloved, on so great a promise, be heavenly not only in hope, but also in conduct And though our minds must at all times be set on holiness of mind and body, yet now during these 40 days of fasting bestir yourselves to yet more active works of piety, not only in the distribution of alms, which are very effectual in attesting reform, but also in forgiving offences, and in being merciful to those accused of wrongdoing, that the condition which God has laid down between Himself and us may not be against us when we pray. For when we say, in accordance with the Lord's teaching, "Forgive us our debts, as we also forgive our debtors ," we ought with the whole heart to carry out what we say. For then only will what we ask in the next clause come to pass, that we be not led into temptation and freed from all evils : through our Lord Jesus Christ, Who with the Father and the Holy Spirit lives and reigns for ever and ever. Amen.

SERMON XLIX. ON LENT, XI.

I. The Lenten Fast is Incumbent on All Alike.

On all days and seasons, indeed, dearly-beloved, some marks of the Divine goodness are set, and no part of the year is destitute of sacred mysteries, in order that, so long as proofs of our salvation meet us on all sides, we may the more eagerly accept the never-ceasing calls of God's mercy. But all that is bestowed on the restoration of human souls in the divers works and gifts of grace is put before us more clearly and abundantly now, when no isolated portions of the Faith are to be celebrated, but the whole together. For as the Easter festival approaches, the greatest and most binding of fasts is kept, and its observance is imposed on all the faithful without exception; because no one is so holy that he ought not to be holier, nor so devout that he might not be devouter. For who, that is set in the uncertainty of this life, can be found either exempt from temptation, or free from fault? Who is there who would not wish for additions to his virtue, or removal of his vice? seeing that adversity does us harm, and prosperity spoils us, and it is equally dangerous not to have what we want at all, and to have it in the fullest measure. There is a trap in the fulness of riches, a trap in the straits of poverty. The one lifts us up in pride, the other incites us to complaint. Health tries us, sickness tries us, so long as the one fosters carelessness and the other sadness. There is a snare in security, a snare in fear; and it matters not whether the mind which is given over to earthly thoughts, is taken up with pleasures or with cares; for it is equally unhealthy to languish under empty delights, or to labour under racking anxiety.

II. The Broad Road is Crowded the Narrow Way of Salvation Nearly Empty.

And thus is perfectly fulfilled that assurance of the Truth, by which we learn that "narrow and steep is the way that leads to life ;" and whilst the breadth of the way that leads to death is crowded with a large company, the steps are few of those that tread the path of safety. And wherefore is the left road more thronged than the right, save that the multitude is prone to wordly joys and carnal goods? And although that which it desires is short-lived and uncertain, yet men endure toil more willingly for the lust of pleasure than for love of virtue. Thus while those who crave things visible are unnumbered, those who prefer the eternal to the temporal are hardly to be found. And, therefore, seeing that the blessed Apostle Paul says, "the things which are seen are temporal, but the things which are not seen are eternal ," the path of virtue lies hid and in concealment, to a certain extent, since "by hope we were saved ," and true faith loves that above all things, which it attains to without any intervention of the flesh. A great work and toil it is then to keep our wayward heart from all sin, and, with the numberless allurements of pleasure to ensnare it on all sides, not to let the vigour of the mind give way to any attack. Who "toucheth pitch, and is not defiled thereby ?" who is not weakened by the flesh? who is not begrimed by the dust? who, lastly, is of such purity as not to be polluted by those things without which one cannot live? For the Divine teaching commands by the Apostle's mouth that "they who have wives" should "be as though they had none: and those that weep as though they wept not; and those that rejoice as though they rejoiced not; and those that buy as though they possessed not; and those that use this world as though they used it not; for the fashion of this world passeth away ." Blessed, therefore, is the mind that passes the time of its pilgrimage in chaste sobriety, and loiters not in the things through which it has to walk, so that, as a stranger rather than the possessor of its earthly abode, it may not be wanting in human affections, and yet rest on the Divine promises.

III. Satan is Incited to Fresh Efforts at This Season of the Year.

And, dearly-beloved, no season requires and bestows this fortitude more than the present, when by the observance of a special strictness a habit is acquired which must be persevered in. For it is well known to you that this is the time when throughout the world the devil waxes furious, and the Christian army has to combat him, and any that have grown lukewarm and slothful, or that are absorbed in worldly cares, must now be furnished with spiritual armour and their ardour kindled for the fray by the heavenly trumpet, inasmuch as he, through whose envy death came into the world , is now consumed with the strongest jealousy and now tortured with the greatest vexation. For he sees whole tribes of the human race brought in afresh to the adoption of God's sons and the offspring of the New Birth multiplied through the virgin fertility of the Church. He sees himself robbed of all his tyrannic power, and driven from the hearts of those he once possessed, while from either sex thousands of the old, the young, the middle-aged are snatched away from him, and no one is debarred by sin either of his own or original, where justification is not paid for deserts, but simply given as a free gift. He sees, too, those that have lapsed, and have been deceived by his treacherous snares, washed in the tears of penitence and, by the Apostle's key unlocking the gates of mercy, admitted to the benefit of reconciliation . He feels, moreover, that the day of the Lord's Passion is at hand, and that he is crushed by the power of that cross which in Christ, Who was free from all debt of sin, was the world's ransom and not the penalty of sin.

IV. self-Examination by the Standard of God's Commands the Right Occupation in Lent.

And so, tha the malice of the fretting foe may effect nothing by its rage, a keener devotion must be awaked to the performance of the Divine commands, in order that we may enter on the season, when all the mysteries of the Divine mercy meet together, with preparedness both of mind and body, invoking the guidance and help of God, that we may be strong to fulfil all things through Him, without Whom we can do nothing. For the injunction is laid on us, in order that we may seek the aid of Him Who lays it Nor must any one excuse himself by reason of his weakness, since He Who has granted the will, also gives the power, as the blessed Apostle James says, "If any of you lack wisdom, let him ask of God, Who giveth to all liberally and upbraideth not, and it shall be given him ." Which of the faithful does not know what virtues he ought to cultivate, and what vices to fight against? Who is so partial or so unskilled a judge of his own conscience as not to know what ought to be removed, and what ought to be developed? Surely no one is so devoid of reason as not to understand the character of his mode of life, or not to know the secrets of his heart. Let him not then please himself in everything, nor judge himself according to the delights of the flesh, but place his every habit in the scale of the Divine commands, where, some things being ordered to be done and others forbidden, he can examine himself in a true balance by weighing the actions of his life according to this standard. For the designing mercy of God has set up the brightest mirror in His commandments, wherein a man may see his mind's face and realize its conformity or dissimilarity to God's image: with the specific purpose that, at least, during the days of our Redemption and Restoration, we may throw off awhile our carnal cares and restless occupations, and betake ourselves from earthly matters to heavenly.

V. Forgiveness of Our Own Sins Requires that We Should Forgive Others.

But because, as it is written, "in many things we all stumble ," let the feeling of mercy be first aroused and the faults of others against us be forgotten; that we may not violate by any love of revenge that most holy compact, to which we bind ourselves in the Lord's prayer, and when we say "forgive us our debts as we also forgive our debtors," let us not be hard in forgiving, because we must be possessed either with the desire for revenge, or with the leniency of gentleness, and for man, who is ever exposed to the dangers of temptations, it is more to be desired that his own faults should not need punishment than that he should get the faults of others punished. And what is more suitable to the Christian faith than that not only in the Church, but also in all men's homes, there should be forgiveness of sins? Let threats be laid aside; let bonds be loosed, for he who will not loose them will bind himself with them much more disastrously. For whatsoever one man resolves upon against another, he decrees against himself by his own terms. Whereas "blessed are the merciful, for God shall have mercy on them :" and He is just and kind in His judgments, allowing some to be in the power of others to this end, that under fair government may be preserved both the profitableness of discipline and the kindliness of clemency, and that no one should dare to refuse that pardon to another's shortcomings, which he wishes to receive for his own.

VI. Reconciliation Between Enemies and Alms-Giving are Also Lenten Duties.

Furthermore, as the Lord says, that "the peacemakers are blessed, because they shall be called sons of God ," let all discords and enmities be laid aside, and let no one think to have a share in the Paschal feast that has neglected to restore brotherly peace. For with the Father on high, he that is not in charity with the brethren, will not be reckoned in the number of His sons. Furthermore, in the distribution of alms and care of the poor, let our Christian fast-times be fat and abound; and let each bestow on the weak and destitute those dainties which he denies himself. Let pains be taken that all may bless God with one mouth, and let him that gives some portion of substance understand that he is a minister of the Divine mercy; for God has placed the cause of the poor in the hand of the liberal man; that the sins which are washed away either by the waters of baptism, or the tears of repentance, may be also blotted out by alms-giving; for the Scripture says, "As water extinguisheth fire, so alms extinguisheth sin ." Through our Lord Jesus Christ, &c.

SERMON LI. A HOMILY DELIVERED ON THE SATURDAY BEFORE THE SECOND SUNDAY IN LENT—ON THE TRANSFIGURATION, *S. MATT.* XVII. 1–13.

I. Peter's Confession Shown to Lead Up to the Transfiguration.

The Gospel lesson, dearly-beloved, which has reached the inner hearing of our minds through our bodily ears, calls us to the understanding of a great mystery, to which we shall by the help of God's grace the better attain, if we turn our attention to what is narrated just before.

The Saviour of mankind, Jesus Christ, in founding that faith, which recalls the wicked to righteousness and the dead to life, used to instruct His disciples by admonitory teaching and by miraculous acts to the end that He, the Christ, might be believed to be at once the Only-begotten of God and the Son of Man. For the one without the other was of no avail to salvation, and it was equally dangerous to have believed the Lord Jesus Christ to be either only God without manhood, or only man without Godhead , since both had equally to be confessed, because just as true manhood existed in His Godhead, so true Godhead existed in His Manhood. To strengthen, therefore, their most wholesome knowledge of this belief, the Lord had asked His disciples, among the various opinions of others, what they themselves believed, or thought about Him: whereat the Apostle Peter, by the revelation of the most High Father passing beyond things corporeal and surmounting things human by the eyes of his mind, saw Him to be Son of the living God, and acknowledged the glory of the Godhead, because he looked not at the substance of His flesh and blood alone; and with this lofty faith Christ was so well pleased that he received the fulness of blessing, and was endued with the holy firmness of the inviolable Rock on which the Church should be built and conquer the gates of hell and the laws of death, so that, in loosing or binding the petitions of any whatsoever, only that should be ratified in heaven which had been settled by the judgment of Peter.

II. The Same Continued.

But this exalted and highly-praised understanding, dearly-beloved, had also to be instructed on the mystery of Christ's lower substance, lest the Apostle's faith, being raised to the glory of confessing the Deity in Christ, should deem the reception of our weakness unworthy of the impassible God, and incongruous, and should believe the human nature to be so glorified in Him as to be incapable of suffering punishment, or being dissolved in death. And, therefore, when the Lord said that He must go to Jerusalem, and suffer many things from the elders and scribes and chief of the priests, and the third day rise again, the blessed Peter who, being illumined with light from above, was burning with the heat of his confession, rejected their mocking insults and the disgrace of the most cruel death, with, as he thought, a loyal and outspoken contempt, but was checked by a kindly rebuke from Jesus and animated with the desire to share His suffering. For the Saviour's exhortation that followed, instilled and taught this, that they who wished to follow Him should deny themselves. and count the loss of temporal flyings as light in the hope of things eternal; because he alone could save his soul that did not fear to lose it for Christ. In order, therefore, that the Apostles might entertain this happy, constant courage with their whole heart, and have no tremblings about the harshness of taking up the cross, and that they might not be ashamed of the punishment of Christ, nor think what He endured disgraceful for themselves (for the bitterness of suffering was to be displayed without despite to His; glorious power), Jesus took Peter and James and his brother John, and ascending a very high mountain with them apart, showed them the brightness of His glory; because, although they had recognised the majesty of God in Him, yet the power of His body, wherein His Deity was contained, they did not know. And, therefore, rightly and significantly, had He promised that certain of the disciples standing by should not taste death till they saw "the Son of Man coming in His Kingdom ," that is, in the kingly brilliance which, as specially belonging to the nature of His assumed Manhood, He wished to be conspicuous to these three men. For the unspeakable and unapproachable vision of the Godhead Itself which is reserved tilt eternal life for the pure in heart, they could in no wise look upon and see while still surrounded with mortal flesh. The Lord displays His glory, therefore, before chosen witnesses, and invests that bodily shape which He shared with others with such splendour, that His face was like the sun's brightness and His garments equalled the whiteness of snow.

III.the Object and the Meaning of the Transfiguration.

And in this Transfiguration the foremost object was to remove the offence of the cross from the disciple's heart, and to prevent their faith being disturbed by the humiliation of His voluntary Passion by revealing to them the excellence of His hidden dignity. But with no less foresight, the foundation was laid of the Holy Church's hope, that the whole body of Christ might realize the character of the change which it would have to receive, and that the members might promise themselves a share in that honour which had already shone forth in their Head. About which the Lord bad Himself said, when He spoke of the majesty of His coming, "Then shall the righteous shine as the sun in their Father's Kingdom ," whilst the blessed Apostle Paul bears witness to the self-same thing, and says: "for I reckon that the sufferings of this thee are not worthy to be compared with the future glory which shall be revealed in us :" and again, "for ye are dead, and your life is hid with Christ in God. For when Christ our life shall appear, then shall ye also appear with Him in glory ." But to confirm the Apostles and assist them to all knowledge, still further instruction was conveyed by that miracle.

IV. The Significance of the Appearance of Moses and Elias.

For Moses and Elias, that is the Law and the Prophets, appeared talking with the Lord; that in the presence of those five men might most truly be fulfilled what was said: "In two or three witnesses stands every word ." What more stable, what more steadfast than this word, in the proclamation of which the trumpet of the Old and of the New Testament joins, and the documentary evidence of the ancient witnesses combine with the teaching of the Gospel?For the pages of both covenants corroborate each other, and He Whom under the veil of mysteries the types that went before had promised, is displayed clearly and conspicuously by the splendour of the present glory. Because, as says the blessed John, "the law was given through Moses: but grace and truth came through Jesus Christ ," in Whom is fulfilled both the promise of prophetic figures and the purpose of the legal ordinances: for He both teaches the truth of prophecy by His presence, and renders the commands possible through grace.

V. S Peter's Suggestion Contrary to the Divine Order.

The Apostle Peter, therefore, being excited by the revelation of these mysteries, despising things mundane and scorning things earthly, was seized with a sort of frenzied craving for the things eternal, and being filled with rapture at the whole vision, desired to make his abode with Jesus in the place where he had been blessed with the manifestation of His glory. Whence also he says, "Lord, it is good for us to be here: if thou wilt let us make three tabernacles , one for Thee, one for Moses, and one for Elias." But to this proposal the Lord made no answer, signifying that what he wanted was not indeed; wicked, but contrary to the Divine order: since the world could not be saved, except; by Christ's death, and by the Lord's example the faithful were called upon to believe that, although there ought not to be any doubt about the promises of happiness, yet we should understand that amidst the trials of this life we must ask for the power of endurance rather than the glory, because the joyousness of reigning cannot precede the times of suffering.

VI. The Import of the Father's Voice from the Cloud.

And so while He was yet speaking, behold a bright cloud overshadowed them, and behold a voice out of the cloud, saying, "This is My beloved Son, in whom I am well pleased; hear ye Him." The Father was indeed present in the Son, and in the Lord's brightness, which He had tempered to the disciples' sight, the Father's Essence was not separated from the Only-begotten: but, in order to emphasize the two-fold personality, as the effulgence of the Son's body displayed the Son to their sight, so the Father's voice from out the cloud announced the Father to their hearing. And when this voice was heard, "the disciples fell upon their faces, and were sore afraid," trembling at the majesty, not only of the Father, but also of the Son: for they now had a deeper insight into the undivided Deity of Both: and in their fear they did not separate the One from the Other, because they doubted not in their faith . That was a wide and manifold testimony, therefore, and contained a fuller meaning than struck the ear. For when the Father said, "This is My beloved Son, in Whom, &c.," was it not clearly meant, "This is My Son," Whose it is to be eternally from Me and with Me? because the Begetter is not anterior to the Begotten, nor the Begotten posterior to the Begetter. "This is My Son," Who is separated from Me, neither by Godhead, nor by power, nor by eternity. "This is My Son," not adopted, but true-born, not created from another source, but begotten of Me: nor yet made like Me from another nature, but born equal to Me of My nature. "This is My Son," "through Whom all things were made, and without Whom was nothing made " because all things that I do He doth in like manner: and whatever I perform, He performs with Me inseparably and without difference: for the Son is in the Father and the Father in the Son , and Our Unity is never divided: and though I am One Who begot, and He the Other Whom I begot, yet is it wrong for you to think anything of Him which is not possible of Me. "This is My Son," Who sought not by grasping, and seized not in greediness , that equality with Me which He has, but remaining in the form of My glory, that He might carry out Our common plan for the restoration of mankind, He lowered the unchangeable Godhead even to the form of a slave.

VII. Who It is We Have to Hear.

"Here ye Him," therefore, unhesitatingly, in Whom I am throughout well pleased, and by Whose preaching I am manifested, by Whose humiliation I am glorified; because He is "the Truth and the Life ," He is My "Power and Wisdom ." "Hear ye Him," Whom the mysteries of the Law have foretold, Whom the mouths of prophets have sung. "Hear ye Him," Who redeems the world by His blood, Who binds the devil, and carries off his chattels, Who destroys the bond of sin, and the compact of the transgression. Hear ye Him, Who opens the way to heaven, and by the punishment of the cross prepares for you the steps of ascent to the Kingdom? Why tremble ye at being redeemed? why fear ye to be healed of your wounds?Let that happen which Christ wills and I will. Cast away all fleshly fear, and arm yourselves with faithful constancy; for it is unworthy that ye should fear in the Saviour's Passion what by His good gift ye shall not have to fear even at your own end.

VIII. The Father's Words Have a Universal Application to the Whole Church.

These things, dearly-beloved, were said not for their profit only, who heard them with their own ears, but in these three Apostles the whole Church has learnt all that their eyes saw and their ears heard. Let all men's faith then be established, according to the preaching of the most holy Gospel, and let no one be ashamed of Christ's cross, through which the world was redeemed. And let not any one fear to suffer for righteousness' sake, or doubt of the fulfilment of the promises, for this reason, that through toil we pass to rest and through death to life; since all the weakness of our humility was assumed by Him, in Whom, if we abide in the acknowledgment and love of Him, we conquer as He conquered, and receive what he promised, because, whether to the performance of His commands or to the endurance of adversities, I the Father's fore-announcing voice should always be sounding in our ears, saying, "This is My beloved Son, in Whom I am well pleased; hear ye Him:" Who liveth and reigneth, with the Father and the Holy Ghost, for ever and ever. Amen.

SERMON LIV. ON THE PASSION, III.; DELIVERED ON THE SUNDAY BEFORE EASTER.

I. The Two-Fold Nature of Christ Set Forth.

Among all the works of God's mercy, dearly-beloved, which from the beginning have been bestowed upon men's salvation, none is more wondrous, and none more sublime, than that Christ was crucified for the world. For to this mystery all the mysteries of the ages preceding led up, and every variation which the will of God ordained in sacrifices, in prophetic signs, and in the observances of the Law, foretold that this was fixed, and promised its fulfilment: so that now types and figures are at an end, and we find our profit in believing that accomplished which before we found our profit in looking forward to. In all things, therefore, dearly-beloved, which pertain to the Passion of our Lord Jesus Christ, the Catholic Faith maintains and demands that we acknowledge the two Natures to have met in our Redeemer, and while their properties remained, such a union of both Natures to have been effected that, from the thee when, as the cause of mankind required, in the blessed Virgin's womb, "the Word became flesh," we may not think of Him asGod without that which is man, nor as man without that which is God. Each Nature does indeed express its real existence by actions that distinguish it, but neither separatesitself from connexion with the other. Nothing is wanting there on either side; in the majesty the humility is complete, in the humility themajesty is complete: and the unity does not introduce confusion, nor does the distinctiveness destroy the unity. The one is passible,the other inviolable; and yet the degradation belongs to the same Person, as does the glory. He is present at once in weakness and in power; at once capable of death and the vanquisher of it. Therefore, God took on Him whole Manhood, and so blended the two Natures together by means of His mercy and power, that each Nature was present in the other, and neither passed out of its own properties into the other.

II. The Two Natures Acted Conjointly, and the Human Sufferings Were Not Compulsory, But in Accordance with the Divine Will.

But because the design of that mystery which was ordained for our restoration before the eternal ages, was not to be carried out without human weakness and without Divine power , both "form" does that which is proper to it in common with the other, the Word, that is, performing that which is the Word's and the flesh that which is of the flesh. One of them gleams bright with miracles, the other i succumbs to injuries. The one departs not from equality with the Father's glory, the other leaves not the nature of our race. But nevertheless even His very endurance of sufferings does not so far expose Him to a participation in our humility as to separate Him from the power of the Godhead. All the mockery and insults, all the persecution and pain which the madness of the wicked inflicted on the Lord, was not endured of necessity, but undertaken of free-will: "for the Son of Man came to seek and to save that which had perished :" and He used the wickedness of His persecutors for the redemption of all men in such a way that in the mystery of His Death and Resurrection even His murderers could have been saved, if they had believed.

III Judas' Infamy Has Never Been Exceeded.

And hence, Judas, thou art proved more criminal and unhappier than all; for when repentance should have called thee back to the Lord, despair dragged thee to the halter. Thou shouldest have awaited the completion of thy crime, and have put off thy ghastly death by hanging, until Christ's Blood was shed for all sinners. And among the many miracles and gifts of the Lords which might have aroused thy conscience, those holy mysteries, at least, might have rescued thee from thy headlong fall, which at the Paschal supper thou hadst received, being even then detected in thy treachery by the sign of Divine knowledge. Why dost thou distrust the goodness of Him, Who did not repel thee from the communion of His body and blood, Who did not deny thee the kiss of peace when thou camest with crowds and a band of armed men to seize Him. But O man that nothing could convert, O "spirit going and not returning ," thou didst follow thy heart's rage, and, the devil standing at thy right hand, didst turn the wickedness, which thou hadst prepared against the life of all the saints, to thine own destruction, so that, because thy crime had exceeded all measure of punishment, thy wickedness might make thee thine own judge, thy punishment allow thee to be thine own hangman.

IV. Christ Voluntarily Bartered His Glory for Our Weakness.

When, therefore, "God was in Christ reconciling the world to Himself ," and the Creator Himself was wearing the creature which was to be restored to the image of its Creator; and after the Divinely-miraculous works had been performed, the performance of which the spirit of prophecy had once predicted, "then shall the eyes of the blind be opened and the ears of the deaf shall hear; then shall the lame man leap as a hart, and the tongue of the dumb shall be plain ;" Jesus knowing that the thee was now come for the fulfilment of His glorious Passion, said, "My soul is sorrowful even unto death ;" and again, "Father, if it be possible, let this cup pass from Me ." And these words, expressing a certain fear, show His desire to heal the affection of our weakness by sharing them, and to check our fear of enduring pain by undergoing it. In our Nature, therefore, the Lord trembled with our fear, that He might fully clothe our weakness and our frailty with the completeness of His own strength. For He had come into this world a rich and merciful Merchant from the skies, and by a wondrous exchange had entered into a bargain of salvation with us, receiving ours and giving His, honour for insults, salvation for pain, life for death: and He Whom more than 12,000 of the angel-hosts might have served for the annihilation of His persecutors, preferred to entertain our fears, rather than employ His own power.

V. S. Peter Was the First To' Benefit by His Master's Humiliation.

And how much this humiliation conferred upon all the faithful, the most blessed Apostle Peter was the first to prove, who, after the fierce blast of threatening cruelty had dismayed him, quickly changed, and was restored to vigour, finding remedy from the great Pattern, so that the suddenly-shaken member returned to the firmness of the Head. For the bond-servant could not be "greater than the Lord, nor the disciple greater than the master ," and he could not have vanquished the trembling of human frailty had not the Vanquisher of Death first feared. The Lord, therefore, "looked back upon Peter ," and amid the calumnies of priests, the falsehoods of witnesses, the injuries of those that scourged and spat upon Him, met His dismayed disciple with those eyes wherewith He had foreseen his dismay: and the gaze of the Truth entered into him, on whose heart correction must be wrought, as if the Lord's voice were making itself heard there, and saying, Whither goest thou, Peter? why retirest thou upon thyself? turn thou to Me, put thy trust in Me, follow Me: this is the thee of My Passion, the hour of thy suffering is not yet come. Why dost thou fear what thou, too, shalt overcome?Let not the weakness, in which I share, confound thee. I was fearful for thee; do thou be confident of Me.

VI. The Mad Counsel of the Jews Was Turned to Their Own Destruction.

"And when morning was come all the chief priests and elders of the people took counsel against Jesus to put him to death ." This morning, O ye Jews, was for you not the rising, but the setting of the sun, nor did the wonted daylight visit your eyes, but a night of blackest darkness brooded on your naughty hearts. This morning overthrew for you the temple and its altars, did away with the Law and the Prophets, destroyed the Kingdom and the priesthood, turned all your feasts into eternal mourning. For ye resolved on a mad and bloody counsel, ye "fat bulls," ye "many oxen," ye "roaring" wild beasts, ye rabid "dogs ," to give up to death the Author of life and the Lord of glory; and, as if the enormity of your fury could be palliated by employing the verdict of him, who ruled your province, you lead Jesus bound to Pilate's judgment, that the terror-stricken judge being overcome by your persistent shouts, you might choose a man that was a murderer for pardon, and demand the crucifixion of the Saviour of the world. After this condemnation of Christ, brought about more by the cowardice than the power of Pilate, who with washed hands but polluted mouth sent Jesus to the cross with the very lips that had pronounced Him innocent, the licence of the people, obedient to the looks of the priests, heaped many insults on the Lord, and the frenzied mob wreaked its rage on Him, Who meekly and voluntarily endured it all. But because, dearly-beloved, the whole story is too long to go through to-day, let us put off the rest till Wednesday, when the reading of the Lord's Passion will be repeated . For the Lord will grant to your prayers, that of His own free gift we may fulfil our promise: through our Lord Jesus Christ, Who liveth and reigneth for ever and ever. Amen.

SERMON LV. ON THE LORD'S PASSION IV., DELIVERED ON WEDNESDAY IN HOLY WEEK.

I. The Difference Between the Penitence and Blasphemy of the Two Robbers is a Type of the Human Race.

That which we owe to your expectations, dearly-beloved, must be paid through the Lord's bountiful answer to your prayers that He Who has made you eager in the demanding would make us fit for the performing.

In speaking but lately of the Lord's Passion we reached the point in the Gospel story, where Pilate is said to have yielded to the Jews' wicked shouts that Jesus should be crucified. And so when all things had been accomplished, which the Godhead veiled in frail flesh permitted, Jesus Christ the Son of God was fixed to the cross which He had also been carrying, two robbers being similarly crucified, one on His right hand, and the other on the left: so that even in the incidentsof the cross might be displayed that difference which in His judgment must be made in the case of all men; for the believing robber's faith was a type of those who are to be saved, and the blasphemer's wickedness prefigured those who are to be damned. Christ's Passion, therefore, contains the mystery of our salvation, and of the instrument which the iniquity of the Jews prepared for His punishment, the Redeemer's power has made for us the stepping-stone to glory : and that Passion the Lord Jesus so underwent for the salvation of all men that, while hanging there nailed to the wood, He entreated the Father's mercy for His murderers, and said, "Father, forgive them, for they know' not what they do ."

II. The Chief Priests Showed Utter Ignorance of Scripture in Their Taunts.

But the chief priests, for whom the Saviour sought forgiveness, rendered the torture of the cross yet worse by the barbs of railery; and at Him, on Whom they could vent no more fury with their hands, they hurled the weapons of their tongues, saying, "He saved others; Himself he cannot save. If He is the King of Israel, let Him now come down from the cross, and we believe Him ." From what spring of error, from what pool of hatred, O ye Jews, do ye drink such poisonous blasphemies? What master informed you, what teaching convinced you that you ought to believe Him to be King of Israel and Son Of God, who should either not allow Himself to be crucified, or should shake Himself free from the binding nails. The mysteries of the Law, the sacred observances of the Passover, the mouths of the Prophets never told you this: whereas you did find truly and oft-times written that which applies to your abominable wicked-doing and to the Lord's voluntary suffering. For He Himself says by Isaiah, "I gave My back to the scourges, My cheeks to the palms of the hand, I turned not My face from the shame of spitting ." He Himself says by David, "They gave Me gall for My food, and in My thirst they supplied Me with vinegar ." and again, "Many dogs came about Me, the council of evil-doers beset Me. They pierced My hands and My feet, they counted all My bones. But they themselves watched and gazed on Me, they parted My raiment among them, and for My robe they cast lots ." And lest the course of your own evil doings should seem to have been foretold, and no power in the Crucified predicted, ye read not, indeed, that the Lord descended from the cross, but ye did read, "The Lord reigned on the tree ."

III. The Triumph of the Cross is Immediate and Effective.

The Cross of Christ, therefore, symbolizes the true altar of prophecy, on which the oblation of man's nature should be celebrated by means of a salvation-bringing Victim. There the blood of the spotless Lamb blotted out the consequences of the ancient trespass: there the whole tyranny of the devil's hatred was crushed, and humiliation triumphed gloriously over the lifting up of pride: for so swift was the effect of Faith that of the robbers crucified with Christ, the one who believed in Christ as the Son of God entered paradise justified. Who can unfold the mystery of so great a boon? who can state the power of so wondrous a change? In a moment of thee the guilt of long evil-doing is done away; clinging to the cross, amid the cruel tortures of his struggling soul, he passes over to Christ; and to him, on whom his own wickedness had brought punishment, Christ's grace now gives a crown.

IV. When the Last Act in the Tragedy Was Over How Must the Jews Have Felt?

And then, having now tasted the vinegar, the produce of that vineyard which had degenerated in spite of its Divine Planter, and had turned to the sourness of a foreign vine , the Lord says, "it is finished;" that is, the Scriptures are fulfilled: there is no more for Me to abide from the fury of the raging people: I have endured all that I foretold I should suffer. The mysteries of weakness are completed, let the proofs of power be produced. And so He bowed the head and yielded up His Spirit and gave that Body, Which should be raised again on the third day, the rest of peaceful slumber. And when the Author of Life was undergoing this mysterious phase, and at so great a condescension of God's Majesty, the foundations of the whole world were shaken, when all creation condemned their wicked crime by its upheaval, and the very elements of the world delivered a plain verdict against the criminals, what thoughts, what heart-searchings had ye, O Jews, when the judgment of the universe went against you, and your wickedness could not be recalled, the crime having been done? what confusion covered you? what torment seized your hearts?

V. Chastity, and Charity are the Two Things Most Needful in Preparing for Easter Communion.

Seeing therefore, dearly-beloved, that God's Mercy is so great, that He has deigned to justify. by faith many even from among such a nation, and had adopted into the company of the patriarchs and into the number of the chosen people us who were once perishing in the deep darkness of our old ignorance, let us mount to the summit of our hopes not sluggishly nor in sloth; but prudently and faithfully reflecting from what captivity and from how miserable a bondage, with what ransom we were purchased, by how strong an arm led out, let us glorify God in our body: that we may show Him dwelling in us, even by the uprightness of our manner of life: And because no virtues are worthier or more excellent than merciful loving-kindness and unblemished chastity, let us more especially equip ourselves with these weapons, so that, raised from the earth, as it were on the two wings of active charity and shining purity, we may win a place in heaven. And whosoever, aided by God's grace, is filled with this desire and glories not in himself, but in the Lord, over his progress, pays due honour to the Easter mystery. His threshold the angel of destruction does not cross, for it is marked with the Lamb's blood and the sign of the cross . He fears not the plagues of Egypt, and leaves his foes overwhelmed by the same waters by which he himself was saved. And so, dearly-beloved, with minds and bodies purified let us embrace the wondrous mystery of our salvation, and, cleansed from all "the leaven of our old wickedness, let us keep " the Lord's Passover with due observance: so that, the Holy Spirit guiding us, we may be "separated" by no temptations "from the love of Christ ," Who bringing peace by His blood to all things, has returned to the loftiness of the Father's glory, and yet not forsaken the lowliness of those who serve Him to Whom is the honour and the glory for ever and ever. Amen.

SERMON LVIII. (ON THE PASSION, VII.)

I. The Reason of Christ Suffering at the Paschal Feast.

I know indeed, dearly-beloved, that the Easter festival partakes of so sublime a mystery as to surpass not only the slender perceptions of my humility, but even the powers of great intellects. But I must not consider the greatness of the Divine work in such a way as to distrust or to feel ashamed of the service which I owe; for we may not hold our peace upon the mystery of man's salvation, even if it cannot be explained. But, your prayers aiding us, we believe God's Grace will be granted, to sprinkle the barrenness of our heart with the dew of His inspira- tion: that by the pastor's mouth things may be proclaimed which are useful to the ears of his holy flock. For when the Lord, the Giver of all good things, says: "open thy mouth, and I will fill it ," we dare likewise to reply in the prophet's words: "Lord, Thou shale open my lips, and my mouth shall shew forth Thy praise ." Therefore beginning, dearly-beloved, to handle once more the Gospel-story of the Lord's Passion, we understand it was part of the Divine plan that the profane chiefs of the Jews and the unholy priests, who had often sought occasion of venting their rage on Christ, should receive the power of exercising their fury at no other time than the Paschal festival. For the things which had long been promised under mysterious figures had to be fulfilled in all clearness; for instance, the True Sheep had to supersede the sheep which was its antitype, and the One Sacrifice to bring to an end the multitude of different sacrifices. For all those things which had been divinely ordained through Moses about the sacrifice of the lamb had prophesied of Christ and truly announced the slaying of Christ. In order, therefore, that the shadows should yield to the substance and types cease in the presence of the Reality, the ancient observance is removed by a new Sacrament, victim passes into Victim, blood is wiped away by Blood, and the law-ordained Feast is fulfilled by being changed.

II. The Leading Jews Broke Their Own Law, as Well as Failed to Apprehend the New Dispensation in Destroying Christ.

And hence, when the chief priests gathered the scribes and elders of the people together to their council, and the minds of all the priests were occupied with the purpose of doing wrong to Jesus, the teachers of the law put themselves without the law, and by their own voluntary failure in duty abolished their ancestral ceremonies. For when the Paschal feast began, those who ought to have adorned the temple, cleansed the vessels, provided the victims, and employed a holier zeal in the purifications that the law enjoined, seized with the fury of traitorous hate, give themselves upto one work, and with uniform cruelty conspire for one crime, though they were doomed togain nothing by the punishment of innocence and the condemnation of righteousness, except the failure to apprehend the new mysteries and the violation of the old. The chiefs, therefore, in providing against a tumult arising on a holy day , showed zeal not for the festival, but for a heinous crime; and their anxiety served not the cause of religion, but their own incrimination. For these careful pontiffs and anxious priests feared the occurrence of seditious riots on the principal feast-day, not lest the people should do wrong, but lest Christ should escape.

III. Jesus Instituting the Blessed Sacrament Showed Mercy to Thetraitor Judas to the Last.

But Jesus, sure of His purpose and undaunted in carrying out His Father's will, fulfilled the New Testament and founded a new Passover. For while the disciples were lying down with Him at the mystic Supper, and when discussion was proceeding in the hall of Caiaphas how Christ might be put to death, He, ordaining the Sacrament of His Body and Blood, was teaching them what kind of Victim must be offered up to God, and not even from this mystery was the betrayer kept away, in order to show that he was exasperated by no personal wrong, but had determined beforehand of his own free-will upon his treachery. For he was his own source of ruin and cause of perfidy, following the guidance of the devil and refusing to have Christ as director. And so when the Lord said, "Verily I say to you that one of you is about to betray Me," He showed that His betrayer's conscience was well known to

Him, not confounding the traitor by harsh or open rebukes, but meeting him with mild and silent warnings that he who had never been sent astray by rejection, might the easier be set right by repentance. Why, unhappy Judas, dose thou not make use of so great long-suffering? Behold, the Lord spares thy wicked attempts; Christ betrays thee to none save thyself. Neither thy name nor thy person is discovered, but only the secrets of thy heart are touched by the word of truth and mercy. The honour of the apostolic rank is not denied thee, nor yet a share in the Sacraments. Return to thy right mind; lay aside thy madness and be wise. Mercy invites thee, Salvation knocks at the door, Life recalls thee to life. Lo, thy stainless and guiltless fellow-disciples shudder at the hint of thy crime, and all tremble for themselves till the author of the treachery is declared. For they are saddened not by the accusations of conscience, but by the uncertainty of man's changeableness; fearing lest what each knew against himself be less true than what the Truth Himself foresaw. But thou abusest the Lord's patience in this panic of the saints, and believest that thy bold front hides thee. Thou addest impudence to guilt, and art not frightened by so clear a test And when the others refrain from the food in which the Lord had set His judgment, thou dost not withdraw thy band from the dish, because thy mind is not turned aside from the crime.

IV. Various Incidents of the Passion .further Explained and the Reality of Christ's Sufferings Asserted.

And thus it followed, dearly-beloved, that as John the Evangelist has narrated, when the Lord offered the bread which He had dipped to His betrayer, more clearly to point him out, the devil entirely seized Judas, and now, by his veritable act of wickedness, took possession of one whom he had already bound down by his evil designs.For only in body was he lying there with those at meat: in mind he was arming the hatred of the priests, the falseness of the witnesses, and the fury of the ignorant mob, At last the Lord, seeing on what a gross crime bent says, "What thou doest do Judas was quickly ." This is the voice not of command but of permission, and not of fear but of readiness: He, that has power over all times, shows that He puts no hindrance in the way of the traitor, and carries out the Father's will for the redemption of the world in such a way as neither to promote nor to fear the crime which His persecutors were preparing. When Judas, therefore, at the devil's persuasion, departed from Christ, and cut himself off from the unityof the Apostolic body, the Lord, without bring disturbed by any fear, but anxious only for the salvation of those He came to redeem, spent all the time that was free from His persecutors' attack on mystic conversation and holy teaching, as is declared in St. John's gospel: raising His eyes to heaven and beseeching the Father for the whole Church that all whom the Father had and would give the Son might become one and remain undivided to the Redeemer's glory, and adding lastly that prayer in which He says, "Father, if it be possible, let this cup pass from Me ." Wherein it is not to be thought that the Lord Jesus wished to escape the Passion and the Death, the sacraments of which He had already committed to His disciples' keeping, seeing that He Himself forbids Peter, when he was burning with devoted faith and love, to use the sword, saying, "The cup which the Father hath given Me, shall I not drink it ?" and seeing that that is certain which the Lord also says, according to John's Gospel, "For God so loved the world that He gave His only begotten Son, that everyone who believes in Him may not perish, but have eternal life ;" as also what the Apostle Paul says, "Christ loved us and gave Himself for us, a victim to God for a sweet-smelling savour ." For the saving of all through the Cross of Christ was the common will and the common plan of the Father and the Son; nor could that by any means be disturbed which before eternal ages had been mercifully determined and unchangeably fore-ordained. Therefore in assuming true and entire manhood He took the true sensations of the body and the true feelings of the mind. And it does not follow because everything in Him was full of sacraments, full of miracles, that therefore He either shed false tears or took food from pretended hunger or reigned slumber. It was in our humility that He was despised, with our grief that He was saddened, with our pain that He was racked on the cross. For His compassion underwent the sufferings of our mortality with the purpose of healing them, and His power encountered them with the purpose of conquering them. And this Isaiah has most plainly prophesied, saying, "He carries our sins and is pained for us, and we thought Him to be in pain and in stripes and in vexation. But He was wounded for our sins, and was stricken for our offences, and with His braises we are healed ."

V. The Resignation of Christ is an Undying Lesson to the Church

And so, dearly beloved, when the Son of God says, "Father, if it be possible, let this cup pass from Me ," He uses the outcry of our nature, and pleads the cause of human frailty and trembling: that our patience may be strengthened and our fears driven away in the things which we have to bear. At length, ceasing even to ask this now that He had in a measure palliated our weak fears, though it is not expedient for us to retain them, He passes into another mood, and says, "Nevertheless, not as I will but as Thou;" and again, "If this cup can not pass from Me, except I drink it, Thy will be done ." These words of the Head are the salvation of the whole Body: these words have instructed all the faithful, kindled the zeal of all the confessors, crowned all the martyrs. For who could overcome the world's hatred, the blasts of temptations, the terr onsf persecutors, had not Christ, in the name of all and for all, said, to the Father, "Thy will be done?" Then let the words be learnt by all the Church's sons who have been purchased at so great a price, so freely justified: and when the shock of some violent temptation has fallen on them, let them use the aid of this potent prayer, that they may conquer their fear and trembling, and learn to suffer patiently. From this point, dearly-beloved, our sermon must pass to the consideration of the details of the Lord's Passion, and lest we should burden you with prolixity, we will divide our common task, and put off the rest till the fourth day of the week. God's grace will be vouchsafed to you if you pray Him to give me the power of carrying out my duty: through our Lord Jesus Christ, &c.

SERMON LIX. (ON THE PASSION, VIII.: ON WEDNESDAY IN HOLY WEEK.)

I. Christ's Arrest Fulfils His Own Eternal Purpose.

Having discoursed, dearly beloved, in our last sermon, on the events which preceded the Lord's arrest, it now remains, by the help of God's grace, to discuss, as we promised, the details of the Passion itself. When the Lord had made it clear by the words of His sacred prayer that the Divine and the Human Nature was most truly and fully present in Him, showing that the unwillingness to suffer proceeded from the one, and from the other the determination to suffer by the expulsion of all frail fears and the strengthening of His lofty power, then did He return to His eternal purpose, and "in the form of a" sinless "slave" encounter the devil who was savagely attacking Him by the hands of the Jews: that He in Whom alone was all men's nature without fault, might undertake the cause of all. The sins of darkness, therefore, assailed the true Light, and, for all their torches and lanterns, could not escape the night of their own unbelief, because they did not recognize the Fount of Light. They arrest Him, and He is ready to be seized; they lead Him away, and He is willing to be led; for though, if He had willed to resist, their wicked hands could have done Him no harm, yet thereby the world's redemption would have been impeded, and He, who was to die for all men's salvation, would have saved none at all.

II. How Great Was Pilate's Crime in Allowing Himself to Be Led Astray & the Jews.

Accordingly, permitting the infliction on Himself of all that the people's fury inflamed by the priests dared do, He is brought to Annas, father-in-law to Caiaphas, and thence Annas passes Him on to Caiaphas: and after the calumniators' mad accusations, after the lying falsehoods of suborned witnesses, He is transferred to Pilate's hearing by the delegation of the two high-priests, who in neglecting the Divine law, and exclaiming that they had "no king but Caesar," as if they were devoted to the Roman laws, and had left the whole judgment in the hands of the governor, really sought for an accomplisher of their cruelty rather than an umpire of the case. For they gave up Jesus, bound in hard bonds, bruised by many buffets and blows, spat upon, already condemned by their shouts: so that amidst so many signs of their own verdict Pilate might not dare to acquit One Whom all desired to perish. In fact, the very inquiry shows both that he found in the Accused no fault and that in his judgment he did not adhere to his purpose: for as judge he condemns One Whom he pronounces guiltless, invoking on the unrighteous people the blood of the Righteous Man with Whom he felt by his own conviction, and knew from his wife's dream, he must have nothing to do. That stained soul is not cleansed by the washing of hands, there is no expiation in water-besprinkled fingers for the crime abetted by that wicked mind. Pilate's fault is indeed, less than the Jews' crime; for it was they that terrified him with Caesar's name, chode him with hateful words, and drove him to perpetrate his wickedness. But he also did not escape incrimination for playing into the hands of those that made the uproar, for abandoning his own judgment, and for acquiescing in the charges of others.

III. Yet the Jews' Guilt Was Infinitely Greater.

In bowing, therefore, dearly-beloved, to the madness of the impacable people, in permitting Jesus to be dishonoured by much mocking, and harassed with excessive insults, and in displaying Him to the eyes of His persecutors lacerated with scourges, crowned with thorns, and clothed in a robe of scorn, Pilate doubtless thought to appease the enemies' minds, so that when they had glutted their cruel hate, they might cease further to persecute One Whom they beheld subjected to such a variety of afflictions. But their wrath was still in full blaze, and they cried out to him to release Barabbas and thus, Jesus bear the penalty of the cross, and thus, when with consenting murmur the crowd said "His blood be on us and on our sons ," those wicked folk gained, to their own damnation what they had persistently demanded, "whose teeth," as the prophet bore witness, "were arms and arrows, and their tongue a sharp sword ." For in vain did they keep their own hands from crucifying the Lord of glory when they had hurled at Him the tongue's deadly darts and the poisoned weapons of words. On you, on you, false Jews and unholy leaders of the people, falls the full weight of that crime: and although the enormity of the guilt involves the governor and the soldiers also, yet you are the primary and chief offenders. And in Christ's condemnation, whatsoever wrong was done either by Pilate's judgment or by the cohorts carrying out of his commands, makes you only the more deserving of the hatred of mankind, because the impulse of your fury would not let even those be free from guilt who were displeased at your unrighteous acts.

IV. Christ Bearing His Own Cross is an Eternal Lesson to the Church.

And so the Lord was handed over to their savage wishes, and in mockery of His kingly state, ordered to be the bearer of His own instrument of death, that what Isaiah the prophet foresaw might be fulfilled, saying, "Behold a Child is born, and a Son is given to us whose government is upon His shoulders ." When, therefore, the Lord carried the wood of the cross which should turn for Him into the sceptre of power, it was indeed in the eyes of the wicked a mighty mockery, but to the faithful a mighty mystery was set forth, seeing that He, the glorious vanquisher of the Devil, and the strong defeater of the powers that were against Him, was carrying in noble sort the trophy of His triumph, and on the shoulders of His unconquered patience bore into all realms the adorable sign of salvation: as if even then to confirm all His followers by this mere symbol of His work, and say, "He that taketh not his cross and followeth Me, is not worthy of Me ."

V. The Transference of the Cross from the Lord To Simon of Cyrene Signifies the Participation of the Gentiles in His Sufferings.

But as the multitudes went with Jesus to the place of punishment, a certain Simon of Cyrene was found on whom to lay the wood of the cross instead of the Lord; that even by this act might be pre-signified the Gentiles' faith, to whom the cross of Christ was to be not shame but glory. It was not accidental, therefore, but symbolical and mystical, that while the Jews were raging against Christ, a foreigner was found to share His sufferings, as the Apostle says, "if we suffer with Him, we shall also reign with Him "; so that no Hebrew nor Israelite, but a stranger, was substituted for the Saviour in His most holy degradation. For by this transference the propitiation of the spotless Lamb and the fulfilment of all mysteries passed from the circumcision to the uncircumcision, from the sons according to the flesh to the sons according to the spirit: since as the Apostle says, "Christ our Passover is sacrificed for us ," Who offering Himself to the Father a new and true sacrifice of reconciliation, was crucified not in the temple, whose worship was now at an end, and not within the confines of the city which for its sin was doomed to be destroyed, but outside, "without the camp ," that, on the cessation of the old symbolic victims, a new Victim might be placed on a new altar, and the cross of Christ might be the altar not of the temple but of the world.

VI. We are to See Not Only the Cross But the Meaning of It.

Accordingly, dearly-beloved, Christ being lifted up upon the cross, let the eyes of your mind not dwell only on that sight which those wicked sinners saw, to whom it was said by the mouth of Moses, "And thy life shall be hanging before thine eyes, and thou shalt fear day and night, and shalt not be assured of thy life ." For in the crucified Lord they could think of nothing but their wicked deed, having not the fear, by which true faith is justified, but that by which an evil conscience is racked. But let our understandings, illumined by the Spirit of Truth, foster with pure and free heart the glory of the cross which irradiates heaven and earth, and see with the inner sight what the Lord meant when He spoke of His coming Passion: "The hour is come that the Son of man may be glorified :" and below He says, "Now is My spirit troubled. And what shall I say? Father, save Me from this hour, but for this cause came I unto this hour. Father, glorify Thy Son." And when the Father's voice came from heaven, saying, "I have both glorified it and will glorify it again," Jesus in reply said to those that stood by, "This voice came not for Me but for you. Now is the world's judgment, now shall the prince of this world be cast out. And I, if I be lifted up from the earth, will draw all things unto Me ."

VII. The Power of the Crass is Universally Attractive.

O wondrous power of the Cross! O in effable glory of the Passion, in which is contained the Lord's tribunal, the world's judgment, and the power of the Crucified! For thou didst draw all things unto Thee, Lord and when Thou hadst stretched out Thy hands all the day, long to an unbelieving people that gainsaid Thee , the whole world at last was brought to confess Thy majesty. Thou didst draw all things unto Thee, Lord, when all the elements combined to pronounce judgment in execration of the Jews' crime, when the lights of heaven were darkened, and the day turned into night, and the earth also was shaken with unwonted shocks, and all creation refused to serve those wicked men. Thou didst draw all things unto Thee, Lord. for the veil of the temple was rent, and the Holy of Holies existed no more for those unworthy high-priests: so that type was turned into Truth, prophecy into Revelation law into Gospel. Thou didst draw all things unto Thee, Lord, so that what before was done in the one temple of the Jews in dark signs, was now to be celebrated everywhere by the piety of all the nations in full and open rite. For now there is a nobler rank of Levites, there are elders of greater dignity and priests of holier anointing: because Thy cross is the fount of all blessings, the source of all graces, and through it the believers receive strength for weakness, glory for shame, life for death. Now, too, the variety of fleshly sacrifices has ceased, and the one offering of Thy Body and Blood fulfils all those different victims: for Thou art the true "Lamb of God, that takest away the sins of the world ," and in Thyself so accomplishest all mysteries, that as there is but one sacrifice instead of many victims, so there is but one kingdom instead of many nations.

VIII. We Must Live Not for Ourselves But for Christ, Who Died for Us.

Let us, then, dearly-beloved, confess what the blessed teacher of the nations, the Apostle Paul, confessed, saying, "Faithful is the saying, and worthy of all acceptation, that Christ Jesus came into the world to save sinners ." For God's mercy towards us is the more wonderful that Christ died not for the righteous nor for the holy, but for the unrighteous and wicked; and though the nature of the Godhead could not sustain the sting of death, yet at His birth He took from us that which He might offer for us. For of old He threatened our death with the power of His death, saying. by the mouth of Hosea the prophet, "O death, I will be thy death, and I will be thy destruction, O hell ." For by dying He underwent the laws of hell, but by rising again He broke them, and so destroyed the continuity of death as to make it temporal instead of eternal. "For as in Adam all die, even so in Christ shall all be made alive ." And so, dearly-beloved, let that come to pass of which S. Paul speaks, "that they that live, should henceforth not live to themselves but to Him who died for all and rose again ." And because the old things have passed away and all things are become new, let none remain in his old carnal life, but let us all be renewed by daily progress and growth in piety. For however much a man be justified, yet so long as he remains in this life, he can always be more approved and better. And he that is not advancing is going back, and he that is gaining nothing is losing something. Let us run, then, with the steps of faith, by the works of mercy, in the love of righteousness, that keeping the day of our redemption spiritually, "not in the old leaven of malice and wickedness, but in the unleavened bread of sincerity and truth ," we may deserve to be partakers of Christ's resurrection, Who with the Father and the Holy Ghost liveth and reigneth for ever and ever. Amen.

SERMON LXII. (ON THE PASSION, XI.)

I. The Mystery of the Passion Passes Man's Comprehension.

The Feast of the Lord's Passion that we have longed for and that the whole world may well desire, has come, and suffers us not to keep silence in the tumult of our spiritual joys: because though it is difficult to speak often on the same thing worthily and appropriately, yet the priest is not free to withhold from the people's ears instruction by sermon on this great mystery of God's mercy, inasmuch as the subject itself, being unspeakable, gives him ease of utterance, and what is said cannot altogether fail where what is said can never be enough. Let human frailty, then, succumb to God's glory, and ever acknowledge itself unequal to the unfolding of His works of mercy. Let us toil in thought, fail in insight, falter in utterance: it is good that even our right thoughts about the Lord's Majesty should be insufficient. For, remembering what the prophet says, "Seek ye the Lord and be strengthened: seek His face always ," no one must assume that he has found all he seeks, lest he fail of coming near, if he cease his endeavours. And amidst all the works of God which weary out man's wondering contemplation, what so delights and so baffles our mind's gaze as the Saviour's Passion? Ponder as we may upon His omnipotence, which is of one and equal substance with the Father, the humility in God is more stupendous than the power, and it is harder to grasp the complete emptying of the Divine Majesty than the infinite uplifting of the "slave's form" in Him. But we are much aided in our understanding of it by the remembrance that though the Creator and the creature, the Inviolable God and the possible flesh, are absolutely different, yet the properties of both substances meet together in Christ's one Person in such a way that alike in His acts of weakness and of power the degradation belongs to the same Person as the glory.

II. The Creed Takes Up S. Peter's Confession as the Fundamental Doctrine of the Church.

In that rule of Faith, dearly-beloved, which we have received in the very beginning of the Creed, on the authority of apostolic teaching, we acknowledge our Lord Jesus Christ, whom we call the only Son of God the Father Almighty, to be also born of the Virgin Mary by the Holy Ghost. Nor do we reject His Majesty when we express our belief in His crucifixion, death, and resurrection on the third day. For all that is God's and all that is Man's are simultaneously fulfilled by His Manhood and His Godhead, so that in virtue of the union of the Possible with the Impossible, His power cannot be affected by His weakness, nor His weakness overcome by His power. And rightly was the blessed Apostle Peter praised for confessing this union, who when the Lord was inquiring what the disciples knew of Him, quickly anticipated the rest and said, "Thou art Christ, the Son of the living God ." And this assuredly he saw, not by the revelation of flesh or blood, which might have hindered his inner sight, but by the very Spirit of the Father working in his believing heart, that in preparation for ruling the whole Church he might first learn what he would have to teach, and for the solidification of the Faith, which he was destined to preach, might receive the assurance, "Thou art Peter, and upon this rock I will build My Church, and the gates of hell shall not prevail against it ." The strength, therefore, of the Christian Faith, which, built upon an impregnable rock, fears not the gates of death, acknowledges the one Lord Jesus Christ to be both true God and true Man, believing Him likewise to be the Virgin's Son, Who is His Mother's Creator: born also at the end of the ages, though He is the Creator of time: Lord of all power, and yet one of mortal stock: ignorant of sin, and yet sacrificed for sinners after the likeness of sinful flesh.

III. The Devil's Devices Were Turned Against Himself.

And in order that He might set the human race free from the bonds of deadly transgression, He hid the power of His majesty from the raging devil, and opposed him with our frail and humble nature. For if the cruel and proud foe could have known the counsel of God's mercy, he would have aimed at soothing the Jews' minds into gentleness rather than at firing them with unrighteous hatred, lest be should lose the thraldom of all his captives in assailing the liberty of One Who owed him nought. Thus he was foiled by his malice: he inflicted a punishment on the Son of God, which was turned to the healing of all the sons of men. He shed righteous Blood, which became the ransom and the drink for the world's atonement. The Lord undertook that which He chose according to the purpose of His own will. He permitted madmen to lay their wicked hands upon Him: hands which, in ministering to their own doom, were of service to the Redeemer's work. And yet so great was His loving compassion for even His murderers, that He prayed to the Father on the cross, and begged not for His own vengeance but for their forgiveness, saying, "Father, forgive them, for they know not what they do ." And such was the power of that prayer, that the hearts of many of those who had said, "His blood be on us and on our sons ," were turned to penitence by the Apostle Peter's preaching, and on one day there were baptized about 3,000 Jews: and they all were "of one heart and of one soul ," being ready now to die for Him, Whose crucifixion they had demanded.

IV. Why Judas Could Not Obtain Forgiveness Through Christ.

To this forgiveness the traitor Judas could not attain: for he, the son of perdition, at whose right the devil stood , gave himself up to despair before Christ accomplished the mystery of universal redemption. For in that the Lord died for sinners, perchance even he might have found salvation if he had not hastened to hang himself. But that evil heart, which was now given up to thievish frauds, and now busied with treacherous designs, had never entertained aught of the proofs of the Saviour's mercy. Those wicked ears had heard the Lord's words, when He said, "I same not to call the righteous but sinners ," and "The Son of man came to seek and to save that which was lost ," but they conveyed not to his understanding the clemency of Christ, which not only healed bodily infirmities, but also cured the wounds of sick souls, saying to the paralytic man, "Son, be of good cheer,thy sins are forgiven thee ;" saying also to the adulteress that was brought to Him, "neither will I condemn thee; go and sin no more ," to show in all His works that He had come as the Saviour, not the Judge of the world. But the wicked traitor refused to understand this, and took measures against himself, not in the self-condemnation of repentance, but in the madness of perdition, and thus he who had sold the Author of life to His murderers, even in dying increased the amount of sin which condemned him.

V. The Cruelty of Christ's Crucifixion is Lost in Its Wondrous Power.

Accordingly that which false witnesses, cruel leaders of the people, wicked priests did against the Lord Jesus Christ, through the agency of a coward governor and an ignorant band of soldiers, has been at once the abhorrence and the rejoicing of all ages. For though the Lord's cross was part of the cruel purpose of the Jews, yet is it of wondrous power through Him they crucified. The people's fury was directed against One, and the mercy of Christ is for all mankind. That which their cruelty inflicts He voluntarily undergoes. in order that the work of His eternal will may be carried out through their unhindered crime. And hence the whole order of events which is most fully narrated in the Gospels must be received by the faithful in such a way that by implicit belief in the occurrences which happened at the time of the Lord's Passion, we should understand that not only was the remission of sins accomplished by Christ, but also the standard of justice satisfied. But that this may be more thoroughly discussed by the Lord's help, let us reserve this portion of the subject till the fourth day of the week God's grace, we hope, will be vouchsafed at your entreaties to help us to fulfil our promise: through Jesus Christ our Lord, &c. Amen.

SERMON LXIII. (ON THE PASSION, XII.: PREACHED ON WEDNESDAY.)

I. God Those to Save Man by Strength Made Perfect in Weakness.

The glory, dearly-beloved, of the Lord's Passion, on which we promised to speak again to-day, is chiefly wonderful for its mystery of humility, which has both ransomed and instructed us all, that He, Who paid the price, might also impart His righteousness to us. For the Omnipotence of the Son of God, whereby He is by the same Essence equal to the Father, might have rescued mankind from the dominion of the devil by the mere exercise of Its will, had it not better suited the Divine working to conquer the opposition of the foe's wickedness by that which had been conquered, and to restore our nature's liberty by that very nature by which bondage had come upon the whole race. But, when the evangelist says, "The Word became flesh and dwelt in us ," and the Apostle, "God was in Christ reconciling the world to Himself ," it was shown that the Only-begotten of the Most High Father entered on such a union with human humility, that, when He took the substance of oar flesh and soul, He remained one and the same Son of God by exalting our properties, not His own: because it was the weakness, not the power that had to be reinforced, so that upon the union of the creature with the Creator there should be nothing wanting of the Divine to the assumed, nor of the human to the Assuming.

II. God's Plan Was Always Partially Understood, and is Now of Universal Application.

This plan of God's mercy and justice, though in the ages past it was in a measure enshrouded in darkness, was yet not so completely hidden that the saints, who have most merited praise from the beginning till the coming of the Lord, were precluded from understanding it: seeing that the salvation, which was to come through Christ, was promised both by the words of prophecy and by the significance of events, and this salvation not only they attained who foretold it, but all they also who believed their predictions. For the one Faith justifies the saints of all ages, and to the self-same hope of the faithful pertains all that by Jesus Christ, the Mediator between God and man, we acknowledge done, or our fathers reverently accepted as to be done. And between Jew and Gentile there is no distinction, since, as the Apostle says, "Circumcision is nothing, and uncircumcision is nothing, but the keeping of God's commands ," and if they be kept in entirety of faith, they make Christians the true sons of Abraham, that is perfect, for the same Apostle says, "For whosoever of you were baptized in Christ Jesus, have put on Christ. There is neither Jew nor Greek: there is neither slave nor free: there is neither male nor female. For ye are all one in Christ. But if ye are Christ's, then are ye Abraham's seed, heirs according to promise ."

III. The Union of the Divine Head with Its Members Inseparable.

There is no doubt therefore, dearly-beloved, that man's nature has been received by the Son of Go/3 into such a union that not only in that Man Who is the first-begotten of all creatures, but also in all His saints there is one and the self-same Christ, and as the Head cannot be separated from the members, so the members cannot be separated from the Head. For although it is not in this life, but in eternity that God is to be "all in all ," yet even now He is the inseparable Inhabitant of His temple, which is the Church, according as He Himself promised, saying, "Lo! I am with you all the days till the en of the age ." And agreeably therewith the Apostle says, "He is the head of the body, the Church, which is the beginning, the first-begotten from the dead, that in all things He may have the pre-eminence, because in Him it was pleasing that all fulness (of the Godhead) should dwell, and that through Him all things should be reconciled in Himself ."

IV. Christ's Passion Provided a Saving Mystery and an Example for Us to Follow.

And what is suggested to our hearts by these and many other references, save that we should in all things be renewed in His image Who, remaining "in the form of God ," deigned to "take the form" of sinful flesh? For all our weaknesses, which come from sin, He took on Him without sharing in sin, so that He felt the sensation of hunger and thirst and sleep and fatigue, and grief and weeping, and suffered the fiercest pangs up to the extremity of death, because no one could be loosed from the snares of death, unless He in Whom alone all men's nature was guileless allowed Himself to be slain by the hands of wicked men. And hence our Saviour the Son of God provided for all that believe in Him both a mystery and an example , that they might apprehend the one by being born again, and follow the other by imitation. For the blessed Apostle Peter teaches this, saying, "Christ suffered for us, leaving you an example that ye should follow His steps. Who did no sin, neither was guile found in His mouth. Who when He was reviled, reviled not: when He suffered, threatened not, but gave Himself up to His unjust judge. Who Himself bare our sins in His body on the tree, that being dead to sins, we may live to righteousness ."

V. Christ Not Destroyed, But Fulfilled and Elevated the Law.

As therefore there is no believer, dearly-beloved, to whom the gifts of grace are denied, so there is no one who is not a debtor in the matter of Christian discipline; because, although the severity of the mystic Law is done away, yet the benefits of its voluntary observance have increased, as the evangelist John says, "Because the Law was given through Moses, but grace and truth came through Jesus Christ ." For all things that, according to the Law, went before, whether in the circumcision of the flesh, or in the multitude of victims, or in the keeping of the Sabbath, testified of Christ, and foretold the grace of Christ. And He is "the end of the Law ," not by annulling, but by fulfilling its meanings. For although He is at once the Author of the old and of the new, yet He changed the symbolic rites connected with the promises, because He accomplished the promises and put an end to the announcement by the coming of the Announced. But in the matter of moral precepts, no decrees of the earlier Testament are rejected, but many of them are amplified by the Gospel teaching: so that the things which give salvation are more perfect and clearer than those which promise a Saviour.

VI. The Present Effect of Christ's Passion is Daily Realized by Christians, Especially in Hall, Baptism.

All therefore that the Son of God did and taught for the world's reconciliation, we not only know as a matter of past history, but appreciate in the power of its present effect. It is He Who, born of the Virgin Mother by the Holy Ghost, fertilizes His unpolluted Church with the same blessed Spirit, that the birth of Baptism an innumerable multitude of sons may be born to God, of Whom it is said, "who were born not of blood, nor of the will of the flesh, nor of the will of man, but of God ." It is He, in Whom the seed of Abraham is blessed by the adoption of the whole world , and the patriarch becomes the father of nations by the birth. through faith not flesh, of the sons of promise. It is He Who, without excluding any nation, makes one flock of holy sheep froth every nation under heaven, and daily fulfils what He promised, saying, "Other sheep also I have which are not of this fold; them also I must bring, and they shall hear My: voice, and there shall be one flock and one shepherd ." For though to the blessed Peter first and foremost He says, "Feed My sheep ;" yet the one Lord directs the charge of all the shepherds, and feeds those that come to the rock with such glad and well-watered pastures, that countless sheep are nourished by the richness of His love, and hesitate not to perish for the Shepherd's sake, even as the good Shepherd Himself was content to lay down His life for His sheep. It is He whose sufferings are shared not only by the martyrs' glorious courage, but also in the very act of regeneration by the faith of all the new-born. For the renunciation of the devil and belief in God , the passing from the old state into newness of life, the casting off of the earthly image, and the putting on of the heavenly form—all this is a sort of dying and rising again, whereby he that is received by Christ and receives Christ is not the same after as he was before he came to the font, for the body of the regenerate becomes the flesh of the Crucified .

VII. The Good Works of Christians are Only Part of Christ's Good Works.

This change, dearly-beloved, is the handiwork of the Most High , Who "worketh all things in all," so that by the good manner of life observed in each one of the faithful, we know Him to be the Author of all just works, and give thanks to God's mercy, Who so adorns the whole body of the Church with countless gracious gifts, that through the many rays of the one Light the same brightness is everywhere diffused, and that which is well done by any Christian whatsoever cannot but be part the glory of Christ. This is that true which justifies and enlightens every man. This it is that rescues from the power of darkness and transfers us into the Kingdom of the Son of God. This it is that by newness of life exalts the desires of the mind and quenches the lusts of the flesh. This it is whereby the Lord's Passover is duly kept "With the unleavened bread of sincerity and truth" by the casting away of "the old leaven of wickedness " and the inebriating and feeding of the new creature with the very Lord. For naught else is brought about by the partaking of the and Blood of Christ than that we pass into that which we then take , and both in spirit and in body carry everywhere Him, in and with Whom we were dead, buried, and rose again, as the Apostle says, "For ye are dead, and your life is hid with Christ in God. For when Christ, your life, shall appear, then shall ye also appear with Him in glory ." Who with the Father, &c.

SERMON LXVII. (ON THE PASSION, XVI.: DELIVERED ON THE SUNDAY.)

I. The Contemplation of the Prophecies of Christ's Suffering are a Great Source of Pious Delight.

The minds of the faithful, beloved, ought indeed always to be occupied with wonder atGod's works and their reasoning faculties devoted particularly to those reflexions by which they may gain increase of faith. For so long as the pious heart's attention is directed either to the benefits which all enjoy, or to special gifts of His grace, it keeps aloof from many vanities and retires from bodily cares into a spiritual seclusion. But this must be the more eagerly and thoroughly done at the season of the Lord Passion, that what is then read in the sacred lections may surely be received with the ears of understanding, and that the themes which are great in word may be seen to be yet greater from the mysterious realities which underlie them. For the first reason for our lifting up our hearts is that the voices of the prophets have sung of the things which the truth of the Gospel has also narrated, not as destined to happen, but as having happened, and that what man's ears had not yet learnt was to be accomplished, was already being proclaimed as fulfilled by the (Holy) Spirit. For King David, whose seed according to the flesh is Christ, completed his lifetime more than 1,100 years before the day of the Lord's Crucifixion, and endured none of those punishments which he relates as inflicted upon himself. But because by his mouth One spoke Who was to take suffering flesh of his stock, the story of the cross is tightly anticipated in the person of him who was the bodily ancestor of the Saviour. For David truly suffered in Christ, because Jesus was truly crucified in the flesh which He had from David.

II. The Divine Foreknowledge Does Not Account for the Jews' wickedness So as to Excuse Them.

Since then all things which Jewish ungodliness committed against the Lord of Majesty were foretold so long before , and the language of the prophets is concerned not so much with things to come as with things last, what else is thereby revealed to us but the unchangeable order of God's eternal decrees, with Whom the things which are to be decided are already determined, and what will be is already accomplished? For since both the character of our actions and the fulfilment of all our wishes are fore-known to God,. how much better known to Him are His own works? And He was rightly pleased that things should be recorded as if done which nothing could hinder from being done. And hence when the Apostles also, being full of the Holy Ghost, suffered the threats and cruelty of Christ's enemies, they said to God with one consent, "For truly in this city against Thy holy Servant Jesus, Whom Thou hast anointed, Herod and Pontius Pilate, with the Gentiles and the peoples of Israel were gathered together to do what Thy hand and Thy counsel ordained to come to pass ." Did then the wickedness of Christ's persecutors spring from God's plan, and was that unsurpassable crime prefaced and set in motion by the hand of God? Clearly we must not think this of the highest Justice: that which was fore-known in respect of the Jews' malice is far different, indeed quite contrary to what was ordained in respect of Christ's Passion. Their desire to slay Him did not proceed from the same source as His to die: nor were their atrocious crime and the Redeemer's endurance the offspring of One Spirit. The Lord did not incite but permit those madmen's naughty hands: nor in His foreknowledge of what must be accomplished did He compel its accomplishment, even though it was in order to its accomplishment that He had taken flesh.

III. Christ Was in No Sense the Author of His Murderer's Guilt.

In fact, the case of the Crucified is so different from that of His crucifiers that what Christ undertook could not be reversed, while what they did could be wiped out. For He Who came to save sinners did not refuse mercy even to His murderers, but changed the evil of the wicked into the goodness of the believing, that God's grace might be the more wonderful, being mercifully put in force, not according to men's merits, but according to the multitude of the riches of God's wisdom anti knowledge, seeing that they also who had shed the Saviour's blood were received into the baptismal flood. For, as says the Scripture, which contains the Apostles' acts when the preaching of the blessed Apostle Peter pierced the hearts of the Jews, and they acknowledged the iniquity of their crime, saying, "what shall we do, brethren?" the same Apostle said, "Repent and be baptized, each one of you, in the name of Jesus Christ for the remission of your sins, and ye shall receive the gift of the Holy Ghost. For to you is the promise, and to your sons, and to all that are afar off, whomsoever our Lord God has called," and soon after the Scripture goes on to say: "they therefore that received his word were baptized, and there were added on that day about 3,000 souls ." And so, in being willing to suffer their furious rage, the Lord Jesus Christ was in no way the Author of their crimes; nor did He force them to desire this, but permitted them to be able, and used the madness of the blinded people just as He did also the treachery of His betrayer, whom by kindly acts and words He vouchsafed to recall from the awful crime he had conceived, by taking him for a disciple, by promoting him to be an apostle, by warning him with signs, by admitting him to the revelation of holy mysteries , that one who had lacked no degree of kindness to correct him, might have no pretext for his crime at all.

IV. The Enormity Of Judas' Crime is Set Forth.

But O ungodliest of men, "thou seed of Chanaan and not of Juda ," and no longer "a vessel of election," but "a son of perdition" and death, thou didst think the devil's instigations would profit thee better, so that, inflamed with the torch of greed, thou wert ablaze to gain 30 pieces of silver and sawest not what riches thou wouldst lose. For even if thou didst not think the Lord's promises were to be believed, what reason was there for preferring so small a sum of money to what thou hadst already received? Thou wast wont to command the evil spirits, to heal the sick, to receive honour with the rest of the apostles, and that thou mightest satisfy thy thirst for gain, it was open to thee to steal from the box that was in thy charge. But thy mind, which lusted after forbidden things, was more strongly stimulated by that which was less allowed: and the amount of the price pleased thee not so much as the enormity of the sin. Wherefore thy wicked bargain is not so detestable merely because thou countedst the Lord sO cheap, but because thou didst sell Him Who was the Redeemer, yea, even thieve, and badst no pity on thyself. And justly was thy punishment put into thine own hands because none could be found more cruelly bent on thy destruction than thyself.

V. Christ's Passion Was for Our Redemption by Mystery and Example.

The fact, therefore, that at the time appointed, according to the purpose of His will, jesus Christ was crucified, dead, and buried was not the doom necessary to His own condition, but the method of redeeming us from captivity. For "the Word became flesh" in order that from the Virgin's womb He might take our suffering nature, and that what could not be inflicted on the Son of God might be inflicted on the Son of Man. For although at His very birth the signs of Godhead shone forth in Him, and the whole course of His bodily growth was full of wonders, yet had He truly assumed our weaknesses, and without share in sin had spared Himself no human frailty, that He might impart what was His to us and heal what was ours in Himself. For He, the Almighty Physician, had prepared a two-fold remedy for us in our misery, of which the one part consists of mystery and the other of example, that by the one Divine powers may be bestowed, by the other human weaknesses driven out. Because as God is the Author of our justification, so man is a debtor to pay Him devotion.

VI. we Can Only Attain to Christ's Perfection by Following in His Steps.

Therefore, dearly-beloved, by this unspeakable restoration of our health no place is left us for pride or for idleness: because we have nothing which we did not receive , and we are expressly warned not to treat the gifts of God's grace with negligence . For He that comes so timely to our aid justly urges us with precept, and He that leads us to glory mercifully incites us to obedience. Wherefore the Lord Himself is rightly made our way, because save through Christ there is no coming to Christ. But through Him and to Him does he take his way who treads the path of His endurance and humiliation, and on that road you may be sure there are not wanting the heats of toil, the clouds of sadness, the storms of fear. The snares of the wicked, the persecutions of the unbelieving, the threats of the powerful, the insults of the proud are I there; and all these things the Lord of hosts and King of glory passed through in the form of our weakness and in the likeness of sinful flesh, to the end that amid the danger of this present life we might desire not so much to avoid and escape them as to endure and overcome them.

VII. Christ Cry of "Forsaken" On the Cross Was to Teach Us the Insufficiency of the Human Nature Without the Divine.

Hence it is that the Lord Jesus Christ, our Head, representing all the members of His body in Himself, and speaking for those whom He was redeeming in the punishment of the cross, uttered that cry which He had once uttered in the psalm, "O God, My God, look upon Me: why hast Thou forsaken Me?" That cry, dearly-beloved, is a lesson, not a complaint. For since in Christ there is oneperson of God and man, and He could not have been forsaken by Him, from Whom He could not be separated, it is on behalf of us, trembling and weak ones, that He asks why the flesh that is afraid to suffer has not been heard. For when the Passion was beginning, to cure anti correct our weak fear He had said, "Father, if it be possible, let this cup pass from Me: nevertheless not as I will but as Thou;" and again, "Father, if this cup cannot pass except I drink it, Thy will be done ." As therefore He had conquered the tremblings of the flesh, and had now accepted the Father's will, and trampling all dread of death under foot, was then carrying out the work of His design, wily at the very time of His triumph over such a victory does He seek the cause and reason of His being forsaken, that is, not heard, save to show that the feeling which He entertained in excuse of His human fears is quite different from the deliberate choice which, in accordance with the Father's eternal decree, He had made for the reconciliation of the world? And thus the very cry of "Unheard" is the exposition of a mighty Mystery, because the Redeemer's power would have conferred nothing on mankind if our weakness in Him had obtained what it sought. Let these words dearly-beloved, suffice to-day, lest we burden you by the length of our discourse: let us put off the rest till Wednesday. The Lord shall hear you if you pray that we may keep our promise through the bounty of Him Who lives and reigns for ever and ever. Amen.

SERMON LXVIII. (ON THE PASSION, XVII.: DELIVERED ON THE WEDNESDAY.)

I. Christ's Godhead Never Forsook Him in His Passion.

The last discourse, dearly-beloved, of which we desire now to give the promised portion, had reached that point in the argument where we were speaking of that cry which the crucified Lord uttered to the Father: we bade the simple and unthinking hearer not take the words "My Con, &c.," in a sense as if, when Jesus was fixed upon the wood of the cross, the Omnipotence of the Father's Deity had gone away from Him; seeing that God's and Man's Nature were so completely joined in Him that the union could not be destroyed by punishment nor by death. For while each substance retained its own properties, God neither held aloof from the suffering of His body nor was made passible by the flesh, because the Godhead which was in the Sufferer did not actually suffer. And hence, in accordance with the Nature of the Word made Man, He Who was made in the midst of all is the same as He through Whom all things were made. He Who is arrested by the hands of wicked men is the same as He Who is bound by no limits. He Who is pierced with nails is the same as He Whom no wound can affect. Finally, He Who underwent death is the same as He Who never ceased to be eternal, so that both facts are established by indubitable signs, namely, the truth of the humiliation in Christ and the truth of the majesty; because Divine power joined itself to human frailty to this end, that God, while making what was ours His, might at the same time make what was His ours. The Son, therefore, was not separated from the Father, nor the Father from the Son; and the unchangeable Godhead and the inseparable Trinity did not admit of any division. For although the task of undergoing Incarnation belonged peculiarly to the Only-begotten Son of God, yet the Father was not separated from the Son any more than the flesh was separated from the Word .

II. Christ's Death Was Voluntary an His Part, and Yet in Saving Others He Could Not Save Himself.

Jesus, therefore, cried with a loud voice, saying, "Why hast Thou forsaken Me?" in order to notify to all how it behoved Him not to be rescued, not to be defended, but to be given up into the hands of cruel men, that is to become the Saviour of the world and the Redeemer of all men, not by misery but by mercy; and not by the failure of succour but by the determination to die. But what must we feel to be the intercessory power of His life Who died and rose again by His own inherent power For the blessed Apostle saysthe Father "spared not His own Son, but gave Him up for us all ;" and again, he says, "For Christ loved the Church, and gave Himself up for her, that He might sanctify it ." And hence the giving up of the Lord to His Passion was as much of the Father's as of His own will, so that not only did the Father "forsake" Him, but He also abandoned Himself in a certain sense, not in hasty flight, but in voluntary withdrawal. For the might of the Crucified restrained itself from those wicked men, and in order to avail Himself of a secret design, He refused to avail Himself of His open power. For how would He who had come to destroy death and the author of death by His Passion have saved sinners, if he had resisted His persecutors? This, then, had been the Jews' belief, that Jesus had been forsaken by God, against Whom they had been able to commit such unholy cruelty; for not understanding the mystery of His wondrous endurance, they said in blasphemous mockery: "He saved others, Himself He cannot save. If He be the King of Israel, let Him now come down from the cross, and we believe Him ." Not at your blind will, O foolish scribes and wicked priests, was the Saviour's power to be displayed, nor in obedience to blasphemers' evil tongues was the Redemption of mankind to be delayed; for if you had wished to recognize the Godhead of the Son of God, you would have observed His numberless works, and they must have confirmed you in that faith, which you so deceitfully promise. But if, as you yourselves acknowledge, it is true that He saved others, why have those many, great miracles, which have been done under the public gaze, done nothing to soften the hardness of your hearts, unless it be because you have always so resisted the Holy Ghost as to turn all God's benefits towards you into your destruction? For even though Christ should descend from the cross, youwould yet remain in your crime.

III. A Transition Was Then Being Effect from the Old to the New Dispensation.

Therefore the insults of empty exultation were scorned, and the Lord's mercy in restoring the lost and the fallen was not turned from the path of its purpose by contumely or reviling. For a peerless victim was being offered to God for the world's salvation, and the slaying of Christ the true Lamb, predicted through so many, ages, was transferring the sons of promise into the liberty of the Faith. The New Testament also was being ratified, and in the blood of Christ the heirs of the eternal Kingdom were being enrolled; the High Pontiff was entering the Holy of Holies, and to intercede with God the spotless Priest was passing in through the veil of His flesh . In fine, so evident a transition was being effected fromthe Law to the Gospel, from the from the synagogue to Sc the Church, from many sacrifices to the One Victim , that, when the Lord gave up the ghost, that mystic veil which hung before and shut out the inner part of the Temple and its holy recess was by sudden force torn from top to bottom , for the reason that Truth was displacing figures, and forerunners were needless in the presence of Him they announced. Tothis was added a terrible confusion of all the elements, and nature herself withdrew her support from Christ's crucifiers. And although the centurion in charge of the crucifixion, in fright at what he had seen, said "truly this man was the Son of God ," yet the wicked hearts of the Jews, which were harder than all tombs and rocks, is not reported to have been pierced by any compunction: so that it seems the Roman soldiers were then readier to recognize the Son of God than the priests of Israel.

IV. Let Us Profit by Fasting and Good Works at This Sacred Season of the Year.

Because, then, the Jews, deprived of all the sanctification imparted by these mysteries, turned their light into darkness and their "feasts into mourning ," let us, dearly-beloved, prostrate our bodies and our souls and worship God's Grace, which has been poured out upon all nations, beseeching the merciful Father and the rich Redeemer from day to day to give us His aid and enable us to escape all the dangers of this life. For the crafty tempter is present everywhere, and leaves nothing free from his snares. Whom, God's mercy helping us, which is stretched out to us amid all dangers, we must ever with stedfast faith resist so that, though he never ceases to asail, he may never succeed in carrying the assault. Let all, dearly-beloved, religiously keep and profit by the fast, and let no excesses mar the benefits of such self-restraint as we have proved convenient both for soul and body. For the things which pertain to sobriety and temperance must be the more diligently observed at this season, that a lasting habit may be contracted from a brief zeal; and whether in works of mercy or in strict self-denial, no hours may be left idle by the faithful, seeing that, as years increase and time glides by, we are bound to increase our store of works, and not squander our opportunities. And to devout wills and religious souls God's Mercy will be granted, that He may enable us to obtain that which He enabled us to desire, Who liveth and reigneth with our Lord Jesus Christ His Son, and with the Holy Ghost, for ever and ever. Amen.

SERMON LXXI. (ON THE LORD'S RESURRECTION, I.; DELIVERED ON HOLY SATURDAY IN THE VIGIL OF EASTER .)

I. We Must All Be Partakers in Christ's Resurrection Life.

In my last sermon , dearly-beloved, not in- appropriately, as I think, we explained to you our participation in the cross of Christ, whereby the life of believers contains in itself the mystery of Easter, and thus what is honoured at the feast is celebrated by our practice. And how useful this is you yourselves have proved, and by your devotion have learnt, how greatly benefited souls and bodies are by longer fasts, more frequent prayers, and more liberal alms. For there can be hardly any one who has not profited by this exercise, and who has not stored up in the recesses of his conscience something over which he may rightly rejoice. But these advantages must be retained with persistent care, lest our efforts fall away into idleness, and the devil's malice steal what God's grace gave. Since, therefore, by our forty days' observance we have wished to bring about this effect, that we should feel something of the Cross at the time of the Lord's Passion, we must strive to be found partakers also of Christ's Resurrection, and "pass from death unto life ," while we are in this body. For when a man is changed by some process from one thing into another, not to be what he was is to him an ending, and to be what he was not is a beginning. But the question is, to what a man either dies or lives: because there is a death, which is the cause of living, and there is a life, which is the cause of dying. And nowhere else but in this transitory world are both sought after, so that upon the character of our temporal actions depend the differences of the eternal retributions. We must die, therefore, to the devil and live to God: we must perish to iniquity that we may rise to righteousness.Let the old sink, that the new may rise; and since, as says the Truth, "no one can serve two masters ," let not him be Lord who has caused the overthrow of those that stood, but Him Who has raised the fallen to victory.

II. God Did Not Leave His Soul in Hell, Nor Suffer His Flesh to See Corruption.

Accordingly, since the Apostle says, "the first man is of the earth earthy, the second man is from heaven heavenly. As is the earthy, such also are they that are earthy; and as is the heavenly, such also are they that are heavenly. As we have borne the image of the earthy, so let us also bear the image of Him Who is from heaven ," we must greatly rejoice over this change, whereby we are translated from earthly degradation to heavenly dignity through His unspeakable mercy, Who descended into our estate that He might promote us to His, by assuming not only the substance but also the conditions of sinful nature, and by allowing the impossibility of Godhead to be affected by all the miseries which are the lot of mortal manhood. And hence that the disturbed minds of the disciples might not be racked by prolonged grief, He with such wondrous speed shortened the three days' delay which He had announced, that by joining the last part of the first and the first part of the third day to the whole of the second, He cut off a considerable portion of the period, and yet did not lessen the number of days. The Saviour's Resurrection therefore did not long keep His soul in Hades, nor His flesh in the tomb; and so speedy was the quickening of His uncorrupted flesh that it bore a closer resemblance to slumber than to death, seeing that the Godhead, Which quitted not either part of the Human Nature which He had assumed, reunited by Its power that which Its power had separated .

III. Christ's Manifestation After the Resurrection Showed that His Person Was Essentially the Same as Before.

And then there followed many proofs, whereon the authority of the Faith to be preached through the whole world might be based. And although the rolling away of the stone, the empty tomb, the arrangement of the linen cloths, and the angels who narrated the whole deed by themselves fully built up the truth of the Lord's Resurrection, yet did He often appear plainly to the eyes both of the women and of the Apostles not only talking with them, but also remaining and eating with them, and allowing Himself to be handled by the eager and curious hands of those whom doubt assailed. For to this end He entered when the doors were closed upon the disciples, and gave them the Holy Spirit by breathing on them, and after giving them the light of understanding opened the secrets of the Holy Scriptures, and again Himself showed them the wound in the side, the prints of the nails, and all the marks of His most recent Passion, whereby it might be acknowledged that in Him the properties of the Divine and Human Nature remained undivided, and we might in such sort know that the Word was not what the flesh is, as to confess God's only Son to be both Word and Flesh.

IV. But Though It is the Same, It is Also Glorified.

The Apostle of the Gentiles, Paul, dearly. beloved, does not disagree with this belief, when he says, "even though we have known Christ after the flesh, yet now we know Him so no more ." For the Lord's Resurrection was not the ending, but the changing of the flesh, and His substance was not destroyed by His increase of power. The quality altered, but the nature did not cease to exist: the body was made impassible, which it had been possible to crucify: it was made incorruptible, though it had been possible to wound it. And properly is Christ's flesh said not to be known in that state in which it had been known, because nothing remained passible in it, nothing weak, so that it was both the same in essence and not the same in glory. But what wonder if S. Paul maintains this about Christ's body, when he says of all spiritual Christians "wherefore henceforth we know no one after the flesh." Henceforth, he says, we begin to experience the resurrection in Christ, since the time when in Him, Who died for all, all our hopes were guaranteed to us. We do not hesitate in diffidence, we are not under the suspense of uncertainty, but having received an earnest of the promise, we now with the eye of faith see the things which will be, and rejoicing in the uplifting of our nature, we already possess what we believe.

V. Being Saved by Hope, We Must Not Fulfil the Lasts of the Flesh.

Let us not then be taken up with the appearances of temporal matters, neither let our contemplations be diverted from heavenly to earthly things. Things which as yet have for the most part not come to pass must be reckoned as accomplished: and the mind intent on what is permanent must fix its desires there, where what is offered is eternal. For although "by hope we were saved ," and still bear about with us a flesh that is corruptible and mortal, yet we are rightly said not to be in the flesh, if the fleshly affections do not dominate us, and are justified in ceasing to be named after that, the will of which we do not follow. And so, when the Apostle says, "make not provision for the flesh in the lusts thereof ," we understand that those things are not forbidden us, which conduce to health and which human weakness demands, but because we may not satisfy all our desires nor indulge in all that the flesh lusts after, we recognizethat we are warned to exercise such self-restraint as not to permit what is excessive nor refuse what is necessary to the flesh, which is placed under the mind's control . And hence the same Apostle says in another place, "For no one ever hated his own flesh, but nourisheth and cherisheth it ;" in so far, of course, as it must be nourished and cherished not in vices and luxury, but with a view to its proper functions, so that nature may recover herself and maintain due order, the lower parts not prevailing wrongfully and debasingly over the higher, nor the higher yielding to the lower, lest if vices overpower the mind, slavery ensues where there should be supremacy.

VI. Our Godly Resolutions Must Continue All the Year Round, Not Be Confined to Easier Only.

Let God's people then recognize that they are a new creation in Christ, and with all vigilance understand by Whom they have been adopted and Whom they have adopted . let not the things, which have been made new, return to their ancient instability; and let not him who has "put his hand to the plough " forsake his work, but rather attend to that which he sows than look back to that which he has left behind. Let no one fall back into that from which he has risen, but, even though from bodily weakness he still languishes under certain maladies, let him urgently desire to be healed and raised up. For this is the path of health through imitation of the Resurrection begun in Christ, whereby, notwithstanding the many accidents and falls to which in this slippery life the traveller is liable, his feet may be guided from the quagmire on to solid ground, for, as it is written, "the steps of a man are directed by the Lord, and He will delight in his way. When the just man falls he shall not be overthrown, because the Lord will stretch out His hand ." These thoughts, dearly-beloved, must be kept in mind not only for the Easter festival, but also for the sanctification of the whole life, and to this our present exercise ought to be directed, that what has delighted the souls of the faithful by the experience of a short observance may pass into a habit and remain unalterably, and if any fault creep in, it may be destroyed by speedy repentance. And because the cure of old-standing diseases is slow and difficult, remedies should be applied early, when the wounds are fresh, so that rising ever anew from all downfalls, we may deserve to attain to the incorruptible Resurrection of our glorified flesh in Christ Jesus our Lord, Who lives and reigns with the Father and the Holy Ghost for ever and ever. Amen.

SERMON LXXII. (ON THE LORD'S RESURRECTION, II.)

I. The Cross is Not Only the Mystery of Salvation, But an Example to Follow.

The whole of the Easter mystery, dearly-beloved, has been brought before us in the Gospel narrative, and the ears of the mind have been so reached through the ear of flesh that none of you can fail to have a picture of the events: for the text of the Divinely-inspired story has clearly shown the treachery of the Lord Jesus Christ's betrayal, the judgment by which He was condemned, the barbarity of His crucifixion, and glory of His resurrection. But a sermon is still required of us, that the priests' exhortation may be added to the solemn reading of Holy Writ, as I am sure you are with pious expectation demanding of us as your accustomed due. Because therefore there is no place for ignorance in faithful ears, the seed of the Word which consists of the preaching of the Gospel, ought to grow in the soil of your heart, so that, when choking thorns and thistles have been removed, the plants of holy thoughts and the buds of right desires may spring up freely into fruit. For the cross of Christ, which was set up for the salvation of mortals, is both a mystery and an example : a sacrament where by the Divine power takes effect, an example whereby man's devotion is excited: for to those who are rescued from the prisoner's yoke Redemption further procures the power of following the way of the cross by imitation. For if the world's wisdom so prides itself in its error that every one follows the opinions and habits and whole manner of life of him whom he has chosen as his leader, how shall we share in the name of Christ save by being inseparably united to Him, Who is, as He Himself asserted, "the Way, the Truth, and the Life ?" the Way that is of holy living, the Truth of Divine doctrine, and the Life of eternal happiness.

II. Christ Look Our Nature Upon Him for Our Salvation.

For when the whole body of mankind had fallen in our first parents, the merciful God purposed so to succour, through His only-begotten Jesus Christ, His creatures made after His image, that the restoration of our nature should not be effected apart from it, and that our new estate should be an advance upon our original position. Happy, if we had not fallen from that which God made us; but happier, if we remain that which He has re-made us. It was much to have received form from Christ; it is more to have a substance in Christ . For we were taken up into its own proper self by that Nature (which condescended to those limitations which loving kindness dictated and which yet incurred no sort of change. We were taken up by that Nature

, which destroyed not what was His in what was ours, nor what was ours in what was His; which made the person of the Godhead and of the Manhood so one in Itself that by co-ordination of weakness and power, the flesh could not be rendered inviolable through the Godhead, nor the Godhead passible through the flesh. We were taken up by that Nature, which did not break off the Branch from the common stock of our race, and yet excluded all taint of the sin which has passed upon all men. That is to say, weakness and mortality, which were not sin, but the penalty of sin, were undergone by the Redeemer of the World in the way of punishment, that they might be reckoned as the price of redemption. What therefore in all of us is the heritage of condemnation, is in Christ "the mystery of godliness ." For being free from debt, He gave Himself up to that most cruel creditor, and suffered the hands of Jews to be the devil's agents in torturing His spotless flesh. Which flesh He willed to be subject to death, even up to His (speedy) resurrection, to this end, that believers in Him might find neither perse- cution intolerable, nor death terrible, by the remembrance that there was no more doubt about their sharing His glory than there was about His sharing their nature.

III. The Presence of the Risen and Ascended Lord Is Still with Us.

And so, dearly-beloved, if we unhesitatingly believe with the heart what we profess with the mouth, in Christ we are crucified, we are dead, we are buried; on the very third day, too, we are raised. Hence the Apostle says, "If ye have risen with Christ, seek those things which are above, where Christ is, sitting on God's right hand: set your affections on things above, not on things on the earth For ye are dead, and your life is hid with Christ in God. For when Christ, your life, shall have appeared, then shall ye also appear with Him in glory ." But that the hearts of the faithful may know that they have that whereby to spurn the lusts of the world and be lifted to the wisdom that is above, the Lord promises us His presence, saying, "Lo! I am with you all the days, even till the end of the age ." For not in vain had the Holy Ghost said by Isaiah: "Behold! a virgin shall conceive and shall bear a Son, and they shall call His name Emmanuel, which is, being interpreted, God wire us ." Jesus, therefore, fulfils the proper meaning of His name, and in ascending into the heavens does not forsake His adopted brethren, though "He sitteth at the right hand of the Father," yet dwells in the whole body, and Himself from above strengthens them for patient waiting while He summons them upwards to His glory.

IV. We Must Have the Same Mind as Was in Christ Jesus.

We must not, therefore, indulge in folly amid vain pursuits, nor give way to fear in the midst of adversities. On the one side, no doubt, we are flattered by deceits, and on the other weighed down by troubles; but because "the earth is full of the mercy of the Lord ," Christ's victory is assuredly ours, that what He says may be fulfilled, "Fear not, for I have overcome the world ." Whether, then, we fight against the ambition of the world, or against the lusts of the flesh, or against the darts of heresy, let us arm ourselves always with the Lord's Cross. For our Paschal feast will never end, if we abstain from the leaven of the old wickedness (in the sincerity of truth . For amid all the changes of this life which is full of various afflictions, we ought to remember the Apostle's exhortation; whereby he instructs us, saying, "Let this mind be in you which was also in Christ Jesus: Who being in the form of God counted it not robbery to be equal with God, but emptied Himself, taking the form of a bond-servant, being made in the likeness of men and found in fashion as a man.

Wherefore God also exalted Him, and gave Him a name which is above every name, that in the name of Jesus every knee should bow of things in heaven, of things on earth, and of things below, and that every tongue should confess that the Lord Jesus Christ is in the glory of God the Father ." If, he says, you understand "the mystery of great godliness," and remember what the Only-begotten Son of God did for the salvation of mankind, "have that mind in you which was also in Christ Jesus," Whose humility is not to be scorned by any of the rich, not to be thought shame of by any of the high-born. For no human happiness whatever can reach so great a height as to reckon it a source of shame to himself that God, abiding in the form of Coy, thought it not unworthy of Himself to take the form of a slave.

V. Only He Who Holds T/re Truth on the Incarnation Can Keep Easter Properly.

Imitate what He wrought: love what He loved, and finding in you the Grace of God, love in Him your nature in return, since as He was not dispossessed of riches in poverty, lessened not glory in humility, lost not eternity in death, so do ye, too, treading in His footsteps, despise earthly things that ye may gain heavenly: for the taking up of the cross means the slaying of lusts, the killing of vices, the turning away from vanity, and the renunciation of all error. For, though the Lord's Passover can be kept by no immodest, self-indulgent, proud, or miserly person, yet none are held so far aloof from this festival as heretics, and especially those who have wrong views on the Incarnation of the Word, either disparaging what belongs to the Godhead or treating what is of the flesh as unreal. For the Son of God is true God, having from the Father all that the Father is, with no beginning in time, subject to no sort of change, undivided from the One God, not different from the Almighty, the eternal Only-begotten of the eternal Father; so that the faithful intellect believing in the Father and the Son and the Holy Ghost in the same essence of the one Godhead, neither divides the Unity by suggesting degrees of dignity, nor confounds the Trinity by merging the Persons in one. But it is not enough to know the Son of God in the Father's nature only, unless we acknowledge Him in what is ours without withdrawal of what is His own. For that self-emptying, which He underwent for man's restoration, was the dispensation of compassion, not the loss of power . For, though by the eternal purpose of God there was "no other name under heaven given to men whereby they must be saved ," the Invisible made His substance visible. the Intemporal temporal, the Impassible passible: not that power might sink into weakness, but that weakness might pass into indestructible power.

VI. A Mystical Application of the Term "Passover" Is Given.

For which reason the very feast which by us is named *Pascha*, among the Hebrews is called *Phase*, that is Pass-over , as the evangelist attests, saying, "Before the feast of Pascha, Jesus knowing that His hour was come that He should pass out of this world unto the Father ." But what was the nature in which He thus passed out unless it was ours, since the Father was in the Son and the Son in the Father inseparably? But because the Word and the Flesh is one Person, the Assumed is not separated from the Assuming nature, and the honour of being promoted is spoken of as accruing to Him that promotes, as the Apostle says in a passage we have already quoted, "Wherefore also God exalted Him and gave Him a name which is above every name." Where the exaltation of His assumed Manhood is no doubt spoken of, so that He in Whose sufferings the Godheard remains indivisible is likewise coeternal in the glory of the Godhead. And to share in this unspeakable gift the Lord Himself was preparing a blessed "passing over" for His faithful ones, when on the very threshhold of His Passion he interceded not only for His Apostles and disciples but also for the whole Church, saying, "But not for these only I pray, but for those also who shall believe on Me through their word, that they all may be one, as Thou also, Father, art in Me, and I in Thee, that they also may be one in us ."

VII. Only True Believers Can Keep the Easter Festival.

In this union they can have no share who deny that in the Son of God, Himself true God, man's nature abides, assailing the health-giving mystery and shutting themselves out from the Easter festival. For, as they dissent from the Gospel and gainsay the creed, they cannot keep it with us, because although they dare to take to themselves the Christian name, yet they are repelled by every creature who has Christ for his Head: for you rightly exult and devoutly rejoice in this sacred season as those who, admitting no falsehood into the Truth, have no doubt about Christ's Birth according to the flesh, His Passion and Death, and the Resurrection of His body: inasmuch as without any separation of the Godhead you acknowledge a Christ, Who was truly born of a Virgin's womb, truly hung on the wood of the cross, truly laid in an earthly tomb, truly raised in glory, truly set on the right hand of the Father's majesty; "whence also," as the Apostle says, "we look for a Saviour our Lord Jesus Christ. Who shall refashion the body of our humility to become conformed to the body of His glory ." Who liveth and reigneth, &c.

SERMON LXXIII. (ON THE LORD'S ASCENSION, I.)

I.the Events Recorded as Happening After the Resurrection Were Intended to Convince Its Truth.

Since the blessed and glorious Resurrection of our Lord Jesus Christ, whereby the Divine power in three days raised the true Temple of God, which the wickedness of the Jews had overthrown, the sacred forty days, dearly-beloved are to-day ended, which by most holy appointment were devoted to our most profitable instruction, so that, during the period that the Lord thus protracted the lingering of His bodily presence, our faith in the Resurrection might be fortified by needful proofs. For Christ's Death had much disturbed the disciples' hearts, and a kind of torpor of distrust had crept over their grief-laden minds at His torture on the cross, at His giving up the ghost, at His lifeless body's burial. For, when the holy women, as the Gospel-story has revealed,brought word of tile stone rolled away from the tomb, the sepulchre emptied of the body, and the angels bearing witness to the living Lord, their words seemed like ravings to the Apostles and other disciples. Which doubtfulness, the result of human weakness, the Spirit of Truth would most assuredly not have permitted to exist in His own preacher's breasts, had not their trembling anxiety and careful hesitation laid the foundations of our faith. It was our perplexities and our dangers that were provided for in the Apostles: it was ourselves who in these men were taught how to meet the cavillings of the ungodly and the arguments of earthly wisdom. *We* are instructed by their lookings, *we* are taught by their hearings, *we* are convinced by their handlings. Let us give thanks to the Divine management and the holy Fathers' necessary slowness of belief. Others doubted, that we might not doubt.

II. And Therefore They are in the Highest Degree Instructive.

Those days, therefore, dearly-beloved, which intervened between the Lord's Resurrection and Ascension did not pass by in uneventful leisure, but great mysteries were ratified in them, deep truths revealed. In them the fear of awful death was removed, and the immortality not only of the soul but also of the flesh established. In them, through the Lord's breathing upon them, the Holy Ghost is poured upon all the Apostles, and to the blessed Apostle Peter beyond the rest the care of the Lord's flock is entrusted, in addition to the keys of the kingdom. Then it was that the Lord joined the two disciples as a companion on the way, and, to the sweeping away of all the clouds of our uncertainty, upbraided them with the slowness of their timorous hearts. Their enlightened hearts catch the flame of faith, and lukewarm as they have been, are made to burn while the Lord unfolds the Scriptures. In the breaking of bread also their eyes are opened as they eat with Him: how far more blessed is the opening of their eyes, to whom the glorification of their nature is revealed than that of our first parents, on whom fell the disastrous consequences of their transgression.

III. The Prove the Resurrection of the Flesh.

And in the course of these and other miracles, when the disciples were harassed by bewildering thoughts, and the Lord had appeared in their midst and said, "Peace be unto you ," that what was passing through their hearts might not be their fixed opinion (for they thought they saw a spirit not flesh), He refutes their thoughts so discordant with the Truth, offers to the doubters' eyes the marks of the cross that remained in His hands and feet, and invites them to handle Him with careful scrutiny, because the traces of the nails and spear had been retained to heal the wounds of unbelieving hearts, so that not with wavering faith, but with most stedfast knowledge they might comprehend that the Nature which had been lain in the sepulchre was to sit on God the Father's throne.

IV. Christ's Ascension Has Given Us Greater Privileges and Joys Than the Devil Had Taken from Us.

Accordingly, dearly-beloved, throughout this time which elapsed between the Lord's Resurrection and Ascension, God's Providence had this in view, to teach and impress upon both the eyes and hearts of His own people that the Lord Jesus Christ might be acknowledged to have as truly risen, as He was truly born, suffered, and died. And hence the most blessed Apostles and all the disciples, who had been both bewildered at His death on the cross and backward in believing His Resurrection, were so strengthened by the clearness of the truth that when the Lord entered the heights of heaven, not only were they affected with no sadness, but were even filled with great joy. And truly great and unspeakable was their cause for joy, when in the sight of the holy multitude, above the dignity of all heavenly creatures, the Nature of mankind went up, to pass above the angels' ranks and to rise beyond the archangels' heights, and to have Its uplifting limited by no elevation until, received to sit with the Eternal Father, It should be associated on the throne with His glory, to Whose Nature It was united in the Son. Since then Christ's Ascension is our uplifting, and the hope of the Body is raised, whither the glory of the Head has gone before, let us exult, dearly-beloved, with worthy joy and delight in the loyal paying of thanks. For to-day not only are we confirmed as possessors of paradise, but have also in Christ penetrated the heights of heaven, and have gained still greater things through Christ's unspeakable grace than we had lost through the devil's malice. For us, whom our virulent enemy had driven out from the bliss of our first abode, the Son of God has made members of Himself and placed at the right hand of the Father, with Whom He lives and reigns in the unity of the Holy Spirit, God for ever and ever. Amen.

SERMON LXXIV. (ON THE LORD'S ASCENSION, II.)

I. The Ascension Completes Our Faith in Him, Who Was God As Well as Man.

The mystery of our salvation, dearly-beloved, which the Creator of the universe valued at the price of His blood, has now been carried out under conditions of humiliation from the day of His bodily birth to the end of His Passion. And although even in "the form of a slave" many signs of Divinity have beamed out, yet the events of all that period served particularly to show the reality of His assumed Manhood. But after the Passion, when the chains of death were broken, which had exposed its own strength by attacking Him, Who was ignorant of sin, weakness was turned into power, mortality into eternity, contumely into glory, which the Lord Jesus Christ showed by many clear proofs in the sight of many, until He carried even into heaven the triumphant victory which He had won over the dead. As therefore at the Easter commemoration, the Lord's Resurrection was the cause of our rejoicing; so the subject of our present gladness is His Ascension, as we commemorate and duly venerate that day on which the Nature of our humility in Christ was raised above all the host of heaven, over all the ranks of angels, beyond the height of all powers, to sit with God the Father. On which Providential order of events we are founded and built up, that God's Grace might become more wondrous, when, notwithstanding the removal from men's sight of what was rightly felt to command their awe, faith did not fail, hope did not waver, love did not grow cold. For it is the strength of great minds and the light of firmly-faithful souls, unhesitatingly to believe what is not seen with the bodily sight, and there to fix one's affections whither you cannot direct your gaze. And whence should this Godliness spring up in our hearts, or how should a man be justified by faith, if our salvation rested on those things only which lie beneath our eyes? Hence our Lord said to him who seemed to doubt of Christ's Resurrection, until he had tested by sight and touch the traces of His Passion in His very Flesh, "because thou hast seen Me, thou hast believed: blessed are, they who have not seen and yet have believed ."

II. The Ascension Renders Our Faith More Excellent and Stronger.

In order, therefore, dearly-beloved, that we may be capable of this blessedness, when all things were fulfilled which concerned the Gospel preaching and the mysteries of the New Testament, our Lord Jesus Christ, on the fortieth day after the Resurrection in the presence of the disciples, was raised into heaven, and terminated His presence with us in the body, to abide on the Father's right hand until the times Divinely fore-ordained for multiplying the sons of the Church are accomplished, and He comes to judge the living and the dead in the same flesh in which He ascended. And so that which till then was visible of our Redeemer was changed into a sacramental presence , and that faith might be more excellent and stronger, sight gave way to doctrine, the authority of which was to be accepted by believing hearts enlightened with rays from above.

III. The Marvellous Effects of This Faith on All.

This Faith, increased by the Lord's Ascension and established by the gift of the Holy Ghost, was not terrified by bonds, imprisonments, banishments, hunger, fire, attacks by wild beasts, refined torments of cruel persecutors. For this Faith throughout the world not only men, but even women, not only beardless boys, but even tender maids, fought to the shedding of their blood. This Faith cast out spirits, drove off sicknesses, raised the dead: and through it the blessed Apostles themselves also, who after being confirmed by so many miracles and instructed by so many discourses, had yet been panic-stricken by the horrors of the Lord's Passion and had not accepted the truth of His resurrection without hesitation, made such progress after the Lord's Ascension that everything which had previously filled them with fear was turned into joy. For they had lifted the whole contemplation of their mind to the Godhead of Him that sat at the Father's right hand, and were no longer hindered by the barrier of corporeal sight from directing their minds' gaze to That Which had never quitted the Father's side in descending to earth, and had not forsaken the disciples in ascending to heaven.

IV. His Ascension Refines Our Faith : the Ministering of Angels to Hint Shows the Extent of His Authority.

The Son of Man and Son of God, therefore, dearly-beloved, then attained a more excellent and holier fame, when He betook Himself back to the glory of the Father's Majesty, and in an ineffable manner began to be nearer to the Father in respect of His Godhead, after having become farther away in respect of His manhood. A better instructed faith then began to draw closer to a conception of the Son's equality with the Father without the necessity of handling the corporeal substance in Christ, whereby He is less than the Father, since, while the Nature of the glorified Body still remained the faith of believers was called upon to touch not with the hand of flesh, but with the spiritual understanding the Only-begotten, Who was equal with the Father. Hence comes that which the Lord said after His Resurrection, when Mary Magdalene, representing the Church, hastened to approach and touch Him: "Touch Me not, for I have not yet ascended to My Father :" that is, I would not have you come to Me as to a human body, nor yet recognize Me by fleshly perceptions: I put thee off for higher things, I prepare greater things for thee: when I have ascended to My Father, then thou shall handle Me more perfectly and truly, for thou shall grasp what thou canst not touch and believe what thou canst not see. But when the disciples' eyes followed the ascending Lord tO heaven with upward gaze of earnest wonder, two angels stood by them in raiment shining with wondrous brightness, who also said, "Ye men of Galilee, why stand ye gazing into heaven? This Jesus Who was taken up from you into heaven shall so come as ye saw Him going into heaven ." By which words all the sons of the Church were taught to believe that Jesus Christ will come visibly in the same Flesh wherewith He ascended, and not to doubt that all things are subjected to Him on Whom the ministry of angels had waited from the first beginning of His Birth. For, as an angel announced to the blessed Virgin that Christ should be conceived by the Holy Ghost, so the voice of heavenly beings sang of His being born of the Virgin also to the shepherds. As messengers from above were the first to attest His having risen from the dead, so the service of angels was employed to foretell His coming in very Flesh to judge the world, that we might understand what great powers will come with Him as Judge, when such great ones ministered to Him even in being judged.

V. We Must Despise Earthly Things and Rise to Things Above, Especially by Active Works of Mercy and Love.

And so, dearly-beloved, let us rejoice with spiritual joy, and let us with gladness pay God worthy thanks and raise our hearts' eyes unimpeded to those heights where Christ is. Minds that have heard the call to be uplifted must not be pressed down by earthly affections, they that are fore-ordained to things eternal must not be taken up with the things that perish; they that have entered on the way of Truth must not be entangled in treacherous snares, and the faithful must so take their course through these temporal things as to remember that they are sojourning in the vale of this world, in which, even though they meet with some attractions, they must not sinfully embrace them, but bravely pass through them. For to this devotion the blessed Apostle Peter arouses us, and entreating us with that loving eagerness which he conceived for feeding Christ's sheep by the threefold profession of love for the Lord, says, "dearly-beloved, I beseech you, as strangers and pilgrims, abstain from fleshly lusts which war against the soul ." But for whom do fleshly pleasures wage war, if not for the devil, whose delight it is to fetter souls that strive after things above, with the enticements of corruptible good things, and to draw them away from those abodes from which he himself has been banished? Against his plots every believer must keep careful watch that he may crush his foe on the side whence the attack is made. And there is no more powerful weapon, dearly-beloved, against the devil's wiles than kindly mercy and bounteous charity, by which every sin is either escaped or vanquished. But this lofty power is not attained until that which is opposed to it be overthrown. And what so hostile to mercy and works of charity as avarice from the root of which spring all evils ? And unless it be destroyed by lack of nourishment, there must needs grow in the ground of that heart in which this evil weed has taken root, the thorns and briars of vices rather than any seed of true goodness. Let us then, dearly-beloved, resist this pestilential evil and "follow after charity ," without which no virtue can flourish, that by this path of love whereby Christ came down to us, we too may mount up to Him, to Whom with God the Father and the Holy Spirit is honour and glory for ever and ever. Amen.

SERMON LXXV. (ON WHITSUNTIDE, I.)

I. The Giving of the Law by Moses Prepared the Way for the Outpouring of the Holy Ghost.

The hearts of all catholics, beloved, realize that to-day's solemnity is to be honoured as one of the chief feasts, nor is there any doubt that great respect is due to this day, which the Holy Spirit has hallowed by the miracle of His most excellent gift. For from the day on which the Lord ascended up above all heavenly heights to sit down at God the Father's right hand, this is the tenth which has shone, and the fiftieth from His Resurrection, being the very day on which it began , and containing in itself great revelations of mysteries both new and old, by which it is most manifestly revealed that Grace was fore-announced through the Law and the Law fulfilled through Grace. For as of old, when the Hebrew nation were released from the Egyptians, on the fiftieth day after the sacrificing of the lamb the Law was given on Mount Sinai, so after the suffering of Christ, wherein the true Lamb of God was slain on the fiftieth day from His Resurrection, the Holy Ghost came down upon the

Apostles and the multitude of believers, so that the earnest Christian may easily perceive that the beginnings of the Old Testament were preparatory to the beginnings of the Gospel, and that the second covenant was rounded by the same Spirit that had instituted the first.

II. How Marvellous Was the Gift of "Divers Tongues."

For as the Apostles' story testifies: "while the days of Pentecost were fulfilled and all the disciples were together in the same place, there occurred suddenly from heaven a sound as of a violent wind coming, and filled the whole house where they were sitting. And there appeared to them divided tongues as of fire and it sat upon each of them. And they were all filled with the Holy Spirit, and began to speak with other tongues, as the Holy Spirit gave them utterance ." Oh! how swift are the words of wisdom. and where God is the Master, how quickly is what is taught, learnt. No interpretation is required for understanding, no practice for using, no time for studying, but the Spirit of Truth blowing where He wills , the languages peculiar to each nation become common property in the mouth of the Church. And therefore from that day the trumpet of the Gospel-preaching has sounded loud: from that day the showers of gracious gifts, the rivers of blessings, have watered every desert and all the dry land, since to renew the face of the earth the Spirit of God "moved over the waters ," and to drive away the old darkness flashes of new light shone forth, when by the blaze of those busy tongues was kindled the Lord's bright Word and fervent eloquence, in which to arouse the understanding, and to consume sin there lay both a capacity of enlightenment and a power of burning.

III. The Three Persons in the Trinity are Perfectly Equal in All Things.

But although, dearly-beloved, the actual form of the thing done was exceeding wonderful, and undoubtedly in that exultant chorus of all human languages the Majesty of the Holy Spirit was present, yet no one must think that His Divine substance appeared in what was seen with bodily eyes. For His Nature, which is invisible and shared in common with the Father and the Son, showed the character of His gift and work by the outward sign that pleased Him, but kept His essential property within His own Godhead: because human sight can no more perceive the Holy Ghost than it can the Father or the Son. For in the Divine Trinity nothing is unlike or unequal, and all that can be thought concerning Its substance admits of no diversity either in power or glory or eternity. And while in the property of each Person the Father is one, the Son is another, and the Holy Ghost is another, yet the Godhead is not distinct and different; for whilst the Son is the Only begotten of the Father, the Holy Spirit is the Spirit of the Father and the Son, not in the way that every creature is the creature of the Father and the Son, but as living and having power with Both, and eternally subsisting of That Which is the Father and the Son . And hence when the Lord before the day of His Passion promised the coming of the Holy Spirit to His disciples, He said, "I have yet many things to say to you, but ye cannot bear them now. But when He, the Spirit of Truth shall have come, He shall guide you into all the Truth. For He shall not speak from Himself, but whatsoever He shall have heard, He shall speak and shall announce things to come unto you. All things that the Father hath are Mine: therefore said I that He shall take of Mine, and shall announce it to you ." Accordingly, there are not some things that are the Father's, and other the Son's, and other the Holy Spirit's. but all things whatsoever the Father has, the Son also has, and the Holy Spirit also has: nor was there ever a time when this communion did not exist, because with Them to have all things is to always exist. In them let no times, no grades, no differences be imagined, and, if no one can explain that which is true concerning God, let no one dare to assert what is not true. For it is more excusable not to make a full statement concerning His ineffable Nature than to frame an actually wrong definition. And so whatever loyal hearts can conceive of the Father's eternal and unchangeable Glory, let them at the same time understand it of the Son and of the Holy Ghost without any separation or difference. For we confess this blessed Trinity to be One God for this reason, because in these three Persons there is no diversity either of substance, or of power, or of will, or of operation.

IV. The Macedonian Heresy is as Blasphemous as the Arian.

As therefore we abhor the Arians, who maintain a difference between the Father and the Son, so also we abhor the Macedonians, who, although they ascribe equality to the Father and the Son, yet think the Holy Ghost to be of a lower nature, not considering that they thus fall into that blasphemy, which is not to be forgiven either in the present age or in the judgment to come, as the Lord says: "whosoever shall have spoken a word against the Son of Man, it shall be forgiven him, but he that shall have spoken against the Holy Ghost, it shall not be forgiven him either in this age or in the age to come ." And so to persist in this impiety is unpardonable, because it cuts him off from Him, by Whom he could confess: nor will he ever attain to healing pardon, who has no Advocate to plead for him. For from Him comes the invocation of the Father, from Him come the tears of penitents, from Him come the groans of suppliants, and "no one can call Jesus the Lord save in the Holy Ghost ," Whose Omnipotence as equal and Whose Godhead as one, with the Father and the Son, the Apostle most clearly proclaims, saying, "there are divisions of graces but the same Spirit; and the divisions of ministrations but the same Lord; and there are divisions of operations but the same God, Who worketh all things in all ."

V. The Spirit's Work is Still Continued in Thechurch.

By these and other numberless proofs, dearly-beloved, with which the authority of the Divine utterances is ablaze, let us with one mind be incited to pay reverence to Whitsuntide, exulting in honour of the Holy Ghost, through Whom the whole catholic Church is sanctified, and every rational soul quickened; Who is the Inspirer of the Faith, the Teacher of Knowledge, the Fount of Love, the Seal of Chastity, and the Cause of all Power. Let the minds of the faithful rejoice, that throughout the world One God, Father, Son, and Holy Ghost, is praised by the confession of all tongues, and that that sign of His Presence, which appeared in the likeness of fire, is still perpetuated in His work and gift. For the Spirit of Truth Himself makes the house of His glory shine with the brightness of His light, and will have nothing dark nor lukewarm in His temple. And it is through His aid and teaching also that the purification of fasts and alms has been established among us. For this venerable day is followed by a most wholesome practice, which all the saints have ever found most profitable to them, and to the diligent observance of which we exhort you with a shepherd's care, to the end that if any blemish has been contracted in the days just passed through heedless negligence, it may be atoned for by the discipline of fasting and corrected by pious devotion. On Wednesday and Friday, therefore, let us fast, and on Saturday for this very purpose keep vigil with accustomed devotion, through

Jesus Christ our Lord, Who with the Father and the Holy Ghost lives and reigns for ever and ever. Amen.

SERMON LXXVII. (ON WHITSUNTIDE, III.)

I. The Holy Ghost's Work Did Not Begin at Pentecost, But Was Continued Because the Holy Trinity is One in Action and in Will.

To-day's festival, dearly-beloved, which is held in reverence by the whole world, has been hallowed by that advent of the Holy Ghost, which on the fiftieth day after the Lord's Resurrection, descended on the Apostles and the multitude of believers, even as it was hoped. And there was this hope, because the Lord Jesus had promised that He should come, not then first to be the Indweller of the saints, but to kindle to a greater heat, and to fill with larger abundance the hearts that were dedicated to Him, increasing, not commencing His gifts, not fresh in operation because richer in bounty. For the Majesty of the Holy Ghost is never separate from the Omnipotence of the Father and the Son, and whatever the Divine government accomplishes in the ordering of all things, proceeds from the Providence of the whole Trinity. Therein exists unity of mercy and loving-kindness, unity of judgment and justice: nor is there any division in action where there is no divergence of will. What, therefore, the Father enlightens, the Son enlightens, and the Holy Ghost enlightens: and while there is one Person of the Sent, another of the Sender, and another of the Promiser both the Unity and the Trinity are at the same time revealed to us, so that the Essence which possesses equality and does not admit of solitariness is understood to belong to the same Substance but not the same Person.

II. Each Person in the Trinity Look Part in Our Redemption.

The fact, therefore, that, with the co-operation of the inseparable Godhead still perfect, certain things are performed by the Father, certain by the Son, and certain by the Holy Spirit, in particular belongs to the ordering of our Redemption and the method of our salvation. For if man, made after the image and likeness of God, had retained the dignity of his own nature, and had not been deceived by the devil's wiles into transgressing through lust the law laid down for him, the Creator of the world would not have become a Creature, the Eternal would not have entered the sphere of time, nor God the Son, Who is equal with God the Father, have assumed the form of a slave and the likeness of sinful flesh. But because "by the devil's malice death entered into the world ," and captive humanity could not otherwise be set free without His undertaking our cause, Who without loss of His majesty should both become true Man, and alone have no taint of sin, the mercy of the Trinity divided for Itself the work of our restoration in such a way that the Father should be propitiated, the Son should propitiate , and the Holy Ghost enkindle. For it was necessary that those who are to be saved should also do something on their part, and by the turning of their hearts to the Redeemer should quit the dominion of the enemy, even as the Apostle says, "God sent the Spirit of His Son into our hearts, crying Abba, Father ," "And where the Spirit of the Lord is, there is liberty ," and "no one can call Jesus Lord except in the Holy Spirit ."

III. But This Apportionment of Functions Does Not Mar the Unity of the Trinity.

If, therefore, under guiding grace, dearly-beloved, we faithfully and wisely understand what is the particular work of the Father, of the Son, and of the Holy Ghost, and what is common to the Three in our restoration, we shall without doubt so accept what has been wrought for us by humiliation and in the body as to think nothing unworthy about the One and Selfsame Glory of the Trinity. For although no mind is competent to think, no tongue to speak about God, yet whatever that is which the human intellect apprehends about the essence of the Father's Godhead, unless one and the selfsame truth is held concerning His Only-begotten or the Holy Spirit, our meditations are disloyal, and beclouded by the intrusions of the flesh, and even that is lost, which seemed a right conclusion concerning the Father, because the whole Trinity is forsaken, if the Unity therein is not maintained; and That Which is different by any inequality can in no true sense be One.

IV. In Thinking Upon God, We Must Put Aside All Material Notions.

When, therefore, we fix our minds on confessing the Father and the Son and the Holy Ghost, let us keep far from our thoughts the forms of things visible, the ages of beings born in time, and all material bodies and places. Let that which is extended in space, that which is enclosed by limit, and whatever is not always everywhere and entire be banished from the heart. The conception of the Triune Godhead must put aside the idea of interval or of grade , and if a man has attained any worthy thought of God, let him not dare to withhold it from any Person therein, as if to ascribe with more honour to the Father that which he does not ascribe to the Son and Spirit. It is not true Godliness to put the Father before the Only-begotten: insult to the Son is insult to the Father: what is detracted from the One is detracted from Both. For since Their Eternity and Godhead are alike common, the Father is not accounted either Almighty and Unchangeable, if He begot One less than Himself or gained by having One Whom before He had not .

V. Christ as Man is Less Than the Father, as God Co-Equal.

The Lord Jesus does, indeed, say to His disciples, as was read in the Gospel lection, "if ye loved Me, ye would assuredly rejoice, because I go to the Father, because the Father is greater than I ;" but those ears, which have often heard the words, "I and the Father are One ," and "He that sees Me, sees the Father also ," accept the saying without supposing a difference of Godhead or understanding it of that Essence which they know to be co-eternal and of the same nature with the Father. Man's uplifting, therefore, in the Incarnation of the Word, is commended to the holy Apostles also, and they, who were distressed at the announcement of the Lord's departure from them, are incited to eternal joy over the increase in their dignity; "If ye loved Me," He says, "ye would assuredly rejoice, because I go to the Father:" that is, if, with complete knowledge ye saw what glory is bestowed on you by the fact that, being begotten of God the Father, I have been born of a human mother also, that being invisible I have made Myself visible, that being eternal "in the form of God" I accepted the "form of a slave," "ye would rejoice because I go to the Father." For to you is offered this ascension, and your humility is in Me raised to a place above all heavens at the Father's right hand. But I, Who am with the Father that which the Father is, abide undivided with My Father, and in coming from Him to you I do not leave Him, even as in returning to Him from you I do not forsake you. Rejoice, therefore, "because I go to the Father, because the Father is greater than I." For I have united you with Myself, and am become Son of Man that you might have power to be sons of God. And hence, though I am One in both forms, yet in that whereby I am conformed to you I am less than the Father, whereas in that whereby I am not divided from the Father I am greater even than Myself. And so let the Nature, which is less than the Father, go to the Father, that the Flesh may be where the Word always is, and that the one Faith of the catholic Church may believe that He Whom as Man it does not deny to be less, is equal as God with the Father.

VI. And This Equality Which the Son Has with the Father, the Holy Ghost Also Has.

Accordingly, dearly-beloved, let us despise the vain and blind cunning of ungodly heretics, which flatters itself over its crooked interpretation of this sentence, and when the Lord says, "All things that the Father hath are Mine ," does not understand that it takes away from the Father whatever it dares to deny to the Son, and is so foolish in matters even which are human as to think, that what is His Father's has ceased to belong to His Only-begotten, because He has taken on Him what is ours. Mercy in the case of God does not lessen power, nor is the reconciliation of the creature whom He loves a falling off of Eternal glory. What the Father has the Son also has, and what the Father and the Son have, the Holy Ghost also has, because the whole Trinity together is One God. But this Faith is not the discovery of earthly wisdom nor the conviction of man's opinion: the Only-begotten Son has taught it Himself, and the Holy Ghost has established it Himself, concerning Whom no other conception must be formed than is formed concerning the Father and the Son. Because albeit He is not the Father nor the Son, yet He is not separable from the Father and the Son: and as He has His own personality in the Trinity, so has He One substance in Godhead with the Father and the Son, filling all things, containing all things, and with the Father and the Son controlling all things, to Whom is the honour and glory for ever and ever. Amen.

SERMON LXXVIII. (ON THE WHIDSUNTIDE FAST, I.)

I. Since the Apostles' Day Till Now Self-Restraint is the Best Defence Against the Devil's Assaults.

To-day's festival, dearly-beloved, hallowed by the descent of the Holy Ghost, is followed, as you know by a solemn fast, which being a salutary institution for the healing of soul and body, we must keep with devout observance. For when the Apostles had been filled with the promised power, and the Spirit of Truth had entered their hearts, we doubt not that among the other mysteries of heavenly doctrine this discipline of spiritual self-restraint was first thought of at the prompting of the Paraclete in order that minds sanctified by fasting might be fitter for the chrism to be bestowed on them . The disciples of Christ had the protection of the Almighty aid, and the chiefs of the infant Church were guarded by the whole Godhead of the Father and the Son through the presence of the Holy Ghost. But against the threatened attacks of persecutors, against the terrifying shouts of the ungodly, they could not fight with bodily strength or pampered flesh, since that which delights the outer does most harm to the inner man, and the more one's fleshly substance is kept in subjection, the more purified is the reasoning soul.

II. The Templer is Foiled in Attacks Upon Those Who Have Learnt These Tactics.

And so those teachers, who have instructed all the Church's sons by their examples and their traditions, began the rudiments of the Christian warfare with holy fasts, that, having to fight against spiritual wickednesses, they might take the armour of abstinence, wherewith to slay the incentives to vice. For invisible foes and incorporeal enemies will have no strength against us, if we be not entangled in any lusts of the flesh. The desire to hurt us is indeed ever active in the tempter, but he will be disarmed and powerless, if he find no vantage around within us from which to attack us. But who, encompassed with this frail flesh, and placed in this body of death, even one who has made much decided progress, can be so sure of his safety now, as to believe himself free from the peril of all allurements? Although Divine Grace gives daily victory to His saints , yet He does not remove the occasion for fighting, because this very fact is part of our Protector's Mercy, Who has always designed that something should remain for our ever-changing nature to win, lest it should boast itself on the ending of the battle.

III. And So This Fast Comes Very Opportunely After the Feast of Whitsuntide.

Therefore, after the days of holy gladness, which we have devoted to the honour of the Lord rising from the dead and then ascending into heaven, and after receiving the gift of the Holy Ghost, a fast is ordained as a wholesome and needful practice, so that, if perchance through neglect or disorder even amid the joys of the festival any undue licence has broken out, it may be corrected by the remedy of strict abstinence, which must be the more scrupulously carried out in order that what was on this day Divinely bestowed on the Church may abide in us. For being made the Temple of the Holy Ghost, and watered with a greater supply than ever of the Divine Stream, we ought not to be conquered by any lusts nor held in possession by any vices in order that the habitation of Divine power may be stained with no pollution.

IV. And by Proper Use of It We Shall Win God's Favour.

And this assuredly it is possible for all to obtain, God helping and guiding us, if by the purification of fasting and by merciful liberality, we take pains to be set free from the filth of sins, and to be rich in the fruits of love. For whatever is spent in feeling the poor, in healing the sick, in ransoming prisoners, or in any other deeds of piety, is not lessened but increased, nor will that ever be lost in the sight of God which the loving-kindness of the faithful has expended, seeing that whatever a man gives in relief, he lays up for his own reward. For "blessed are the merciful, since God shall have mercy on them ;" nor wilt shortcomings be remembered, where the presence of true religion has been attested. On Wednesday and Friday, therefore, let us fast, and on Saturday let us keep vigil in the presence of the most blessed Apostle, Peter, by whose prayers we surely trust to be set free both from spiritual foes and bodily enemies; through our Lord Jesus Christ, who with the Father and the Holy Ghost, lives and reigns for ever and ever. Amen.

SERMON LXXXII. ON THE FEAST OF THE APOSTLES PETER AND PAUL (JUNE 29).

I. Rome Owes Its High Position to These Apostles.

The whole world, dearly-beloved, does indeed take part in all holy anniversaries, and loyalty to the one Faith demands that whatever is recorded as done for all men's salvation should be everywhere celebrated with common rejoicings. But, besides that reverence which to-day's festival has gained from all the world, it is to be honoured with special and peculiar exultation in our city, that there may be a predominance of gladness on the day of their martyrdom in the place where the chief of the Apostles met their glorious end . For these are the men, through whom the light of Christ's gospel shone on thee, O Rome, and through whom thou, who wast the teacher of error, wast made the disciple of Truth. These are thy holy Fathers and true shepherds, who gave thee claims to be numbered among the heavenly kingdoms, and built thee under much better and happier auspices than they, by whose zeal the first foundations of thy walls were laid: and of whom the one that gave thee thy name defiled thee with his brother's blood . These are they who promoted thee to such glory, that being made a holy nation, a chosen people, a priestly and royal state , and the head of the world through the blessed Peter's holy See thou didst attain a wider sway. by the worship of God than by earthly government. For although thou weft increased by many victories, and didst extend thy rule on land and sea, yet what thy toils in war subdued is less than what the peace of Christ has conquered.

II. The Extension of the Roman Empire Was Part of the Divine Scheme.

For the good, just, and Almighty God, Who has never withheld His mercy from mankind, and has ever instructed all men alike in the knowledge of Himself by the most abundant benefits, has by a more secret counsel and a deeper love shown pity upon the wanderers' voluntary blindness and proclivities to evil, by sending His co-equal and co-eternal Word. Which becoming flesh so united the Divine Nature with the human that He by lowering His Nature to the uttermost has raised our nature to the highest. But that the result of this unspeakable Grace might be spread abroad throughout the world, God's Providence made ready the Roman empire, whose growth has reached such limits that the whole multitude of nations are brought into close connexion. For the Divinely-planned work particularly required that many kingdoms should be leagued together under one empire, so that the preaching of the world might quickly reach to all people, when they were held beneath the rule of one state. And yet that state, in ignorance of the Author of its aggrandisement though it rule almost all nations, was enthralled by the errors of them all, and seemed to itself to have fostered religion greatly, because it rejected no falsehood. And hence its emancipation through Christ was the more wondrous that it had been so fast bound by Satan.

III. On the Dispersing of the Twelve, St. Peter Was Sent to Rome.

For when the twelve Apostles, after receiving through the Holy Ghost the power of speaking with all tongues, had distributed the world into parts among themselves, and undertaken to instruct it in the Gospel, the most blessed Peter, chief of the Apostolic band, was appointed to the citadel of the Roman empire, that the light of Truth which was being displayed for the salvation of all the nations, might spread itself more effectively throughout the body of the world from the head itself. What nation had not representatives then living in this city; or what peoples did not know what Rome had learnt? Here it was that the tenets of philosophy must be crushed, here that the follies of earthly wisdom must be dispelled, here that the cult of demons must be refuted, here that theblasphemy of all idolatries must be rooted out, here where the most persistent superstition had gathered together all the various errors which had anywhere been devised.

IV. St. Peter's Love Conquered His Fears in Coming to Rome.

To this city then, most blessed Apostle Peter, thou dost not fear to come, and when the Apostle Paul, the partner of thy glory, was still busied with regulating other churches, didst enter this forest of roaring beasts, this deep, stormy ocean with greater boldness than when thou didst walk upon the sea. And thou who hadst been frightened by the high priest's maid in the house of Caiaphas, hadst no fear of Rome the mistress of the world. Was there any less power in Claudius, any less cruelty in Nero than in the judgment of Pilate or the Jews' savage rage? So then it was the force of love that conquered the reasons for fear: and thou didst not think those to be feared whom thou hadst undertaken to love. But this feeling of fearless affection thou hadst even then surely conceived when the profession of thy love for the Lord was confirmed by the mystery of the thrice-repeated question. And nothing else was demanded of this thy earnest purpose than that thou shouldst bestow the food wherewith thou hadst thyself been enriched, on feeding His sheep whom thou didst love.

V. S. Peter Was Providentially Prepared for His Great Mission.

Thy confidence also was increased by many miraculous signs, by many gifts of grace, by many proofs of power. Thou hadst already taught the people, who from the number of the circumcised had believed: thou hadst already founded the Church at Antioch, where first the dignity of the Christian name arose: thou hadst already instructed Pontus, Galatia, Cappadocia, Asia, and Bithynia, in the laws of the Gospel-message: and, without doubt as to the success of the work, with full knowledge of the short span of thy life didst carry the trophy of Christ's cross into the citadel of Rome, whither by the Divine fore-ordaining there accompanied thee the honour of great power and the glory of much suffering.

VI. Many Noble Martyrs Have Sprung from the Blood of Ss. Peter and Paul.

Thither came also thy blessed brother-Apostle Paul, "the vessel of election ," and the special teacher of the Gentiles, and was associated with thee at a time when all innocence, all modesty, all freedom was into jeopardy under Nero's rule. Whose fury, inflamed by excess of all vices, hurled him headlong into such a fiery furnace of madness that he was the first to assail the Christian name with a general persecution, as if God's Grace could be quenched by the death of saints, whose greatest gain it was to win eternal happiness by contempt of this fleeting life. "Precious," therefore, "in the eyes of the Lord is the death of His saints :" nor can any degree of cruelty destroy the religion which is founded on the mystery of Christ's cross. Persecution does not diminish but increase the church, and the Lord's field is clothed with an ever richer crop, while the grains, which fall singly, spring up and are multiplied a hundred-fold . Hence how large a progeny have sprung from these two Heaven-sown seeds is shown by the thousands of blessed martyrs, who, rivalling the Apostles' triumphs, have traversed the city far and wide in purple-clad and ruddy-gleaming throngs, and crowned it, as it were with a single diadem of countless gems.

VII. No Distinction Must Be Drawn Between the Merits of the Two.

And over this band, dearly-beloved, whom God has set forth for our example in patience and for our confirmation in the Faith, there must be rejoicing everywhere in the commemoration of all the saints, but of these two Fathers' excellence we must rightly make our boast in louder joy, for God's Grace has raised them to so high a place among the members of the Church, that He has set them like the twin light of the eyes in the body, whose Head is Christ. About their merits and virtues, which pass all power of speech, we must not make distinctions, because they were equal in their election, alike in their toils, undivided in their death. But as we have proved for Ourselves, and our forefathers maintained, we believe, and are sure that, amid all the toils of this life, we must always be assisted in obtaining God's Mercy by the prayers of special interceders, that we may be raised by the Apostles' merits in proportion as we are weighed down by our own sins. Through our Lord Jesus Christ, &c.

SERMON LXXXIV. CONCERNING THE NEGLECT OF THE COMMEMORATION.

I. The Churchmen of Rome are in Danger of Forgetting Past Judgments and Mercies, and Becoming Ungrateful to God.

The fewness of those who were present has of itself shown, dearly-beloved, that the religious devotion wherewith, in commemoration of the day of our chastisement and release, the whole body of the faithful used to flock together in order to give God thanks, has on this last occasion been almost entirely neglected: and this has caused me much sadness of heart and great fear. For there is much danger of men becoming ungrateful to God, and through forgetfulness of His benefits not feeling sorrow for the chastisement, nor joy for the liberation. Accordingly I fear, dearly-beloved, lest that utterance of the Prophet be addressed in rebuke to such men, which says, "thou hast scourged them and they have not grieved: thou hast chastised them, and they have refused to receive correction " For what amendment is shown by them in whom such aversion to God's service is found? One is ashamed to say it, but one must not keep silence: more is spent upon demons than upon the Apostles, and mad spectacles draw greater crowds than blessed martyrdoms. Who was it that restored this city to safety? that rescued it from captivity? the games of the circus-goers or the care of the saints? surely it was by the saints' prayers that the sentence of Divine displeasure was diverted, so that we who deserved wrath, were reserved for pardon.

II. Let Them Avail Themselves Betimes of God's Long-Suffering and Return to Him.

I entreat you, beloved, let those words of the Saviour touch your hearts, Who, when by the power of His mercy He had cleansed ten lepers, said that only one of them all had returned to give thanks : meaning without doubt that, though the ungrateful ones had gained soundness of body, yet their failure in this godly duty arose from ungodliness of heart. And therefore, dearly-beloved, that this brand of ingratitude may not be applied to you, return to the Lord, remembering the marvels which He has deigned to perform among us; and ascribing. our release not, as the ungodly suppose, to the influences of the stars, but to the unspeakable mercy of Almighty God, Who has deigned to soften the hearts of raging barbarians, betake yourselves to the commemoration of so great a benefit with all the vigour of faith. Grave neglect must be atoned for by yet greater tokens of repentance. Let us use the Mercy of Him, Who has spared us, to our own amendment, that the blessed Peter and all the saints, who have always been near us in many afflictions, may deign to aid our entreaties for you to the merciful God, through Jesus Christ our Lord. Amen.

SERMON LXXXV. ON THE FEAST OF S. LAURENCE THE MARTYR (AUG. 10).

I. The Example of the Martyrs is Most Valuable

Whilst the height of all virtues, dearly-beloved, and the fulness of all righteousness is born of that love, wherewith God and one's neighbour is loved, surely in none is this love found more conspicuous and brighter than in the blessed martyrs; who are as near to our Lord Jesus, Who died for all men, in the imitation of His love, as in the likeness of their suffering. For, although that Love, wherewith the Lord has redeemed us, cannot be equalled by any man's kindness, because it is one thing that a man who is doomed to die one day should die for a righteous man, and another that One Who is free from the debt of sin should lay down His life for the wicked : yet the martyrs also have done great service to all men, in that the Lord Who gave them boldness, has used it to show that the penalty of death and the pain of the cross need not be terrible to any of His followers, but might be imitated by many of them. If therefore no good man is good for himself alone, and no wise man's wisdom befriends himself only, and the nature of true virtue is such that it leads many away from the dark error on which its light is shed, no model is more useful in teaching God's people than that of the martyrs. Eloquence may make intercession easy, reasoning may effectually persuade; but yet examples are stronger than words, and there is more teaching in practice than in precept.

II. The Saint's Martyrdom Described.

And how gloriously strong in this most excellent manner of doctrine the blessed martyr Laurentius is, by whose sufferings to-day is marked, even his persecutors were able to feel, when they found that his wondrous courage, born principally of love for Christ, not only did not yield itself, but also strengthened others by the example of his endurance. For when the fury of the gentile potentates was raging against Christ's most chosen members, and attacked those especially who were of priestly rank, the wicked persecutor's wrath was vented on Laurentius the deacon, who was pre-eminent not only in the performance of the sacred rites, but also in the management of the church's property , promising himself double spoil from one man's capture: for if he forced him to surrender the sacred treasures, he would also drive him out of the pale of true religion. And so this man, so greedy of money and such a foe to the truth, arms himself with double weapon: with avarice to plunder the gold; with impiety to carry off Christ. He demands of the guileless guardian of the sanctuary that the church wealth on which his greedy mind was set should be brought to him. But the holy deacon showed him where he had them stored, by pointing to the many troops of poor saints, in the feeding and clothing of whom he had a store of riches which he could hot lose, and which were the more entirely safe that the money had been spent on so holy a cause.

III.the Description of His Sufferings Continued.

The baffled plunderer, therefore, frets, and blazing out into hatred of a religion, which had put riches to such a use, determines to pillage a still greater treasure by carrying off that sacred deposit , wherewith he was enriched, as he could find no solid hoard of money in his possession. He orders Laurentius to renounce Christ, and prepares to ply the deacon's stout courage with frightful tortures. and, when the first elicit nothing, fiercer follow. His limbs, torn and mangled by many cutting blows, are commanded to be broiled upon the fire in an iron framework, which was of itself already hot enough to burn him, and on which his limbs were turned from time to time, to make the torment fiercer, and the death more lingering.

IV. Laurentius Has Conquered His Persecutor.

Thou gainest nothing, thou prevailest nothing, O savage cruelty. His mortal frame is released from thy devices, and, when Laurentius departs to heaven, thou art vanquished. The flame of Christ's love could not be overcome by thy flames, and the fire which burnt outside was less keen than that which blazed within. Thou didst but serve the martyr in thy rage, O persecutor: thou didst but swell the reward in adding to the pain. For what did thy cunning devise, which did not redound to the conqueror's glory, when even the instruments of torture were counted as part of the triumph? Let us rejoice, then, dearly-beloved, with spiritual joy, and make our boast over the happy end of this illustrious man in the Lord, Who is "wonderful in His saints," in whom He has given us a support and an example, and has so spread abroad his glory throughout the world, that, from the rising of the sun to its going down, the brightness of his deacon's light doth shine, and Rome is become as famous in Laurentius as Jerusalem was ennobled by Stephen. By his prayer and intercession we trust at all times to be assisted; that, because all, as the Apostle says, "who wish to live holily in Christ, suffer persecution," we may be strengthened with the spirit of love, and be fortified to overcome all temptations by the perseverance of steadfast faith. Through our Lord Jesus Christ, &c.

SERMON LXXXVIII. ON THE FAST OF THE SEVENTH MONTH, III.

I. The Fasts, Which the Ancient Prophets Proclaimed, are Still Necessary.

Of what avail, dearly-beloved, are religious fasts in winning the mercy of God, and in renewing the fortunes of human frailty, we know from the statements of the holy Prophets, who proclaim that justice of God, Whose vengeance the people of Israel had again and again incurred through their iniquities, cannot be appeased save by fasting. Thus it is that the Prophet Joel warns them, saying, "thus saith the Lord your God, turn ye to Me with all your heart, with fasting and weeping and mourning, and rend your hearts and not your garments, and turn ye to the Lord your God, for He is merciful and patient, and of great kindness, and very merciful," and again, "sanctify a fast, proclaim a healing, assemble the people, sanctify the church." And this exhortation must in our days also be obeyed, because these healing remedies must of necessity be proclaimed by us too, in order that in the observance of the ancient sanctification Christian devotion may gain what Jewish transgression lost.

II. Public Services are of a Higher Character Than Private.

But the respect that is paid to the Divine decrees always brings a special blessing, whatever may be the extent of our voluntary services, so that publicly proclaimed celebrations are of a higher character than those which rest on private institution. For the exercise of self-restraint, which each individual imposes on himself at his own discretion, concerns thebenefit of a certain portion only of the Church, but the fast which the whole Church undergoes leaves out no one from the general purification, and God's people' then become strongest, when the hearts of all the faithful meet together in one common act of holy obedience, when in the camp of the Christian army there is on all sides the same making ready for the fight and for defence. Though the cruel enemy rage in restless fury, and spread all round his hidden snares, yet he will be able to catch no one and wound no one, if he find no one off his guard, no one given up to sloth, nO one inactive in works of piety.

III. The September Fast Calls Us in This Public Way to Self-Amendment.

To this unconquerable strength of unity, therefore, dearly-beloved, we are even now invited by the solemn Fast of the Seventh Month, that we may lift our souls to the Lord free from worldly cares and earthly concerns. And because, always needful as this endeavour is, we cannot all adhere to it perpetually, and often through human frailty we fall back from higher things to the things of earth, let us at least on these days, which are most healthfully ordained for our correction, withdraw ourselves from worldly occupations, and steal a little time for promoting our eternal welfare. "For in many things," as it is written, "we all stumble ." And though by the daily gift of God we be cleansed from divers pollutions, yet there cling to unwary souls for the most part darker stains, which need a greater care to wash them out, a stronger effort to destroy them. And the fullest abolition of sins is obtained when the whole Church offers up one prayer and one confession. For if the Lord has promised fulfilment of all they shall ask, to the holy and devout agreement of two or three, what shall be denied to many thousands of the people who unite in one act of worship, and with one breath make their common supplications ?

IV. Community of Goods and of Actions is Most Precious in God's Sight.

It is a great and very precious thing, beloved, in the Lord's sight, when Christ's whole people engage together in the same duties, and all ranks and degrees of either sex co-operate with the same intent: when one purpose animates all alike of declining from evil and doing good; when God is glorified in the works of His slaves, and the Author of all godliness is blessed in unstinted giving of thanks. The hungry are nourished, the naked are clothed, thesick are visited, and men seek not their own but "that which is another's ," so long as in relieving the misery of others each one makes the most of his own means; and it is easy to find "a cheerful giver ," where a man's performances are only limited by the extent of his power. By this grace of God, "which worketh all in all ," the benefit: and the deserts of the faithful are both enjoyed in common. For they, whose income is not like, can yet think alike, and when one rejoices over another's bounty his feelings put him on the same level with him whose powers of spending are on a different level. In such a community there is no disorder nor diversity, for all the members of the whole body agree in one strong purpose of godliness, and he who glories in the wealth of others is not put to shame at his own poverty. For the excellence of each portion is the glory of the whole body, and when we are all led by God's Spirit, not only are the things we do ourselves our own but those of others also over the doing of which we rejoice.

V. Let Us Then Make the Best Use Possible of the Opportunity.

Let us then, dearly-beloved, lay hold upon this most sacred unity in all its blessed integrity and engage in the solemn fast with the concordant purpose of a good will. Nothing hard, nothing harsh is asked of anyone, nor is anything imposed beyond our strength, whether in the discipline of abstinence or in the amount of alms. Each knows what he can and what he cannot do: let every one pay his quota, assessing himself at a just and reasonable rate, that the sacrifice of mercy be not offered sadly nor reckoned among losses. Let so much be expended on pious work, as will justify the heart, wash the conscience, and in a word profit both giver and receiver. Happy indeed is that soul and truly to be admired which in its love of doing good fears not the failing of the means, and has no distrust that He will give him money still to spend, from Whom he had what he spent in the past. But because few possess this greatness of heart, and yet it is truly a pious thing for each one not to forsake the care of his own, we, without prejudice to the more perfect sort, lay down for you this general rule and exhort you to perform God's bidding according to the measure of your ability. For cheerfulness becomes the benevolent man, who should so manage his liberality that while the poor rejoice over the help supplied, home needs may not suffer. "And He that ministers seed to the sower, shall both provide bread to be eaten and multiply your seed and increase the fruits of your righteousness ." On Wednesday and Friday therefore let us fast; and on Saturday keep vigil all together in the presence of the most blessed Apostle Peter, by whose merits and prayers we are sure God's mercy will be vouchsafed to us in all things through our Lord Jesus Christ, Who lives and reigns for ever and ever. Amen.

SERMON XC. (ON THE FAST OF SEVENTH MONTH, V.)

I. we Must Always Be Seeking Pardon, Because We are Always Liable to Sin.

We proclaim the holy Fast of the Seventh Month, dearly-beloved, for the exercise of common devotions, confidently inciting you with fatherly exhortations to make Christian by your observance that which was formerly Jewish . For it is at all times suitable and in agreement with both the New and Old Testament, that the Divine Mercy should be sought with chastisement both of mind and body, because nothing is more effectual in prevailing with God than that a man should judge himself and never cease from asking pardon, knowing that he is never without fault For human nature has this flaw in itself, not planted there by the Creator but contracted by the transgressor , and transmitted to his posterity by the law of generation , so that from the corruptible body springs that which may corrupt the soul also. Hence although the inner man be now reborn in Christ and rescued from the bonds of captivity, it has unceasing conflicts with the flesh, and has to endure resistance in seeking to restrain vain desires. And in this strife such perfect victory is not easily obtained that even those habits which must be broken off do not still encumber us, and those vices which must be slain do not wound. However wisely and prudently the mind presides as judge over the outer senses, yet even amid the pains it takes to rule and the limits it imposes on the appetites of the flesh, the temptation is always too close at hand. For who so abstracts himself from pleasure or pain of body that his mind is not affected by that which delights or racks it from without? Joy and sorrow are inseparable from a man: no part of him is free from the kindlings of wrath, the overpowerings of delight, the castings down of affliction. And what turning away from sin can there be, where ruler and ruled alike are liable to the same passions? Rightly does the Lord exclaim that "the spirit indeed is willing but the flesh is weak ."

II. Christ is Himself the Way, Which He Bids Us Tread.

And lest we should be led by despair into sheer inaction, He promises that the Divine power shall make those things possible which are to man impossible from his own lack of power: "for narrow and strait is the way which leadeth unto life ," and no one couldset foot on it, no one could advance one step, unless Christ by making

Himself the Way unbarred the difficulties of approach: and thus the Ordainer of the journey becomes the Means whereby we are able to accomplish it, because not only does He impose the labour, but also brings us to the haven of rest. In Him therefore we find our Model of patience, in Whom we have our Hope of life eternal; for "if we suffer with Him, we shall also reign with Him ," since, as the Apostle says, "he that saith he abideth in Christ ought himself also to walk as He walked ." Otherwise we make a vain presence and show, if we follow not His steps, Whose name we glory in, and assuredly they would not be irksome to us, but would free us from all dangers, if we loved nothing but what He commanded us to love.

III. The Love of God Contrasted with the Love of the World.

For there are two loves from which proceed all wishes, as different in quality as they are different in their sources. For the reasonable soul, which cannot exist without love, is the lover either of God or the world. In the love of God there is no excess, but in the love of the world all is hurtful. And therefore we must cling inseparably to eternal treasures, but things temporal we must use like passers-by, that as we are sojourners hastening to return to our own land, all the good things of this world which meet us may be as aids on the way, not snares to detain us. Therefore the blessed Apostle makes this proclamation, "the time is short: it remains that those who have wives be as though they had none; and those who weep, as though they wept not; and those who rejoice, as though they rejoiced not; and those who buy, as though they possessed not; and those that use this world, as though they used it not. For the fashion of this world passes away ." But as the world attracts us with its appearance, and abundance and variety, it is not easy to turn away from it unless in the beauty of things visible the Creator rather than the creature is loved; for, when He says, "thou shale love the Lord Shy God from all thy heart, and from all thy mind, and from all shy strength ," He wishes us in noticing to loosen ourselves from the bonds of His love. And when He links the love of our neighbour also to this command, He enjoins on us the imitation of His own goodness, that we should love what He loves and do what He does. For although we be "God's husbandry and God's building," and "neither is he that planteth anything, nor he that watereth, but God that giveth the increase ," yet in all things He requires our ministry and service, and wishes us to be the stewards of His gifts, that he who bears God's image may do God's will. For this reason, in the Lord's prayer we say most devoutly, "Thy Kingdom come, Thy will be done as in heaven, so also on earth." For what else do we ask for in these words but that God may subdue those whom He has not yet subdued, and as in heaven He makes the angels ministers of His will, so also on earth He may make men? And in seeking this we love God, we love also our neighbour: and the love within us has but one Object, since we desire the bond-servant to serve and the Lord to have rule.

IV. The Love of God Is Fostered by Good Works.

This state of mind, therefore, beloved, from which earthly love is excluded, is strengthened by the habit of well-doing, because the conscience must needs be delighted at good deeds, and do willingly what it rejoices to have done. Thus it is that fasts are kept, alms freely given, justice maintained, frequent prayer resorted to, and the desires of individuals become the common wish of all. Labour fosters patience, gentleness extinguishes anger, loving-kindness treads down hatred, unclean desires are slain by holy, aspirations, avarice is east out by liberality, and burdensome wealth becomes the means of virtuous acts . But because the snares of the devil are not at rest even in such a state of things, most rightly at certain seasons of the year the renewal of our vigour is provided for: and now in particular, when one who is greedy of present good might boast himself over the clemency of the weather and the fertility of the land, and having stored his crops in great barns, might say to his soul, "thou hast much goods, eat and drink," let him take heed to the rebuke of the Divine voice, and hear it saying, "Thou fool, this night they require thy soul of thee, and the things which thou hast prepared, whose shall they be ?" This should be the wise man's most anxious consideration, in order that, as the days of this life are short and its span uncertain, death may never come upon him unawares, and that knowing himself mortal he may meet his end fully prepared. And so, that this may avail both for the sanctification of out bodies and the renewal of our souls, on Wednesday and Friday let us fast, and on Saturday let us keep vigil with the most blessed Apostle Peter, whose prayers will help us to obtain fulfilment of our holy desires through Christ our Lord, Who with the Father and the Holy Ghost lives and reigns for ever and ever. Amen.

SERMON XCI ON THE FAST OF THE SEVENTH MONTH, .VI.

I. Abstinence Must Include Discipline of the Soul as Well Asof the Body.

There is nothing, dearly-beloved, in which the Divine Providence does not assist the devotions of the faithful. For the very elements of the world also minister to the exercise of mind and body in holiness, seeing that the distinctly varied revolution of days and months opens for us the different pages of the commands, and thus the seasons also in some sense speak to us of that which the sacred institutions enjoin. And hence, since the year's course has brought back the seventh month to us, I feel certain that your minds are spiritually aroused to keep the solemn fast; since you have learnt by experience how well this preparation purifies both the outer and the inner parts of men, so that by abstaining from the lawful, resistance becomes easier to the unlawful. But do not limit your plan of abstinence, dearly-beloved, to the mortifying of the body, or to the lessening of food alone. For the greater advantages of this virtue belong to that chastity of the soul, which not only crushes the lusts of the flesh, but also despises the vanities of worldly wisdom, as the Apostle says, "take heed that no one deceive you through philosophy and empty deceit, according to the tradition of men ."

II. And in Particular We Must Abstain from Heresy, and that of Eutyches as Well as that of Nestorius.

We must restrain ourselves, therefore, from food, but much more must we fast from errors that the mind, given up to no carnal pleasure, may be taken captive by no falsehood: because as in past days, so also in our own, there are not wanting enemies of the Truth, who dare to stir up civil wars within the catholic Church , in order that by leading the ignorant into agreement with their ungodly doctrines they may boast of increase in numbers through those whom they have been able to sever from the Body of Christ. For what is so opposed to the Prophets, so repugnant to the Gospels, so at variance with the Apostles' teaching as to preach one single Nature in the Lord Jesus Christ born of Mary, and without respect to time co-eternal with the Eternal Father? If it is only man's nature which is to be acknowledged, where is the Godhead Which saves? if only God's, where is the humanity which is saved? But the catholic Faith, which withstands all errors, refutes these blasphemies also at the same time, condemning Nestorius, who divides the Divine from the human, and denouncing Eutyches, who nullifies the human in the Divine; seeing that the Son of True God, Himself True God, possessing unity and equality with the Father and with the Holy Ghost, has vouchsafed likewise to be true Man, and after the Virgin Mother's conception was not separated from her flesh and child-bearing, so uniting humanity to Himself as to remain immutably God; so imparting Godhead to man as not to destroy but enhance him by glorification. For He, Who became "the form of a slave," ceased not to be "the form of God," and He is not one joined with the other, but One in Both, so that ever since "the Word became Flesh" our faith is disturbed by no vicissitudes of circumstance, but whether in the miracles of power, or in the degradation of suffering, we believe Him to be both God, Who is Man, and Man, Who is God .

III. The Truth of the Incarnation is Proved Both by the Eucharistic Feast and by the Divine Institution of Almsgiving.

Dearly-beloved, utter this confession with all your heart and reject the wicked lies of heretics, that your fasting and almsgiving may not be polluted by any contagion with error: for then is our offering of the sacrifice clean and oar gifts of mercy holy, when those who perform them understand that which they do. For when the Lord says, "unless ye have eaten the flesh of the Son of Man, and drunk His blood, ye will not have life in you ," you ought so to be partakers at the Holy Table, as to have no doubt whatever concerning the reality of Christ's Body and Blood. For that is taken in the mouth which is believed in Faith, and it is vain for them to respond Amen who dispute that which is taken. But when the Prophet says, "Blessed is he, who considereth the poor and needy ," he is the praiseworthy distributor of clothes and food among the poor, who knows he is clothing and feeding Christ in the poor: for He Himself says, "as long as ye have done it to one of My brethren, ye have done it to Me ." And so Christ is One, True God and True Man, rich in what is His own, poor in what is ours, receiving gifts and distributing gifts, Partner with mortals, and the Quickener of the dead, so that in the "name of Jesus every knee should bow, of things in heaven, of things on earth, and of things under the earth, and that every tongue should confess that the Lord Jesus Christ is in the glory of God the Father ," living and reigning with the Holy Spirit for ever and ever. Amen.

SERMON XCV. A HOMILY ON THE BEATITUDES, ST. MATT. V. 1–9.

I. Introduction of the Subject.

When our Lord Jesus Christ, beloved, was preaching the gospel of the Kingdom, and was healing divers sicknesses through the whole of Galilee, the fame of His mighty works had spread into all Syria: large crowds too from all parts of Judaea were flocking to the heavenly Physician . For as human ignorance is slow in believing what it does not see, and in hoping for what it does not know, those who were to be instructed in the divine lore , needed to be aroused by bodily benefits and visible miracles: so that they might have no doubt as to the wholesomeness of His teaching when they actually experienced His benignant power. And therefore that the Lord might use outward healings as an introduction to inward remedies, and after healing bodies might work cures in the soul, He separated Himself from the surrounding crowd, ascended into the retirement of a neighbouring mountain, and called His apostles to Him there, that from the height of that mystic seat He might instruct them in the loftier doctrines, signifying from the very nature of the place and act that He it was who had once honoured Moses by speaking to him: then indeed with a more terrifying justice, but now with a holier mercifulness, that what had been promised might be fulfilled when the Prophet Jeremiah says: "behold the days come when I will complete a new covenant for the house of Israel and for the house of Judah. After those days, saith the Lord, I will put My laws in their minds , and in their heart will I write them ." He therefore who had spoken to Moses, spoke also to the apostles, and the swift hand of the Word wrote and deposited the secrets of the new covenant in the disciples' hearts: there were no thick clouds surrounding Him as of old, nor were the people frightened off from approaching the mountain by frightful sounds and lightning , but quietly and freely His discourse reached the ears of those who stood by: that the harshness of the law might give way before the gentleness of grace, and "the spirit of adoption" might dispel the terrors of bondage.

II. The Blessedness of Humility Discussed

The nature then of Christ's teaching is attested by His own holy statements: that they who wish to arrive at eternal blessedness may understand the steps of ascent to that high happiness. "Blessed," He saith, "are the poor in spirit, for theirs is the kingdom of heaven ." It would perhaps be doubtful what poor He was speaking of, if in saying "blessed are the poor" He had added nothing which would explain the sort of poor: and then that poverty by itself would appear sufficient to winthe kingdom of heaven which many suffer from hard and heavy necessity. But when He says "blessed are the poor *in spirit*," He shows that the kingdom of heaven must be assigned to those who are recommended by the humility of their spirits rather than by the smallness of their means. Yet it cannot be doubted that this possession of humility is more easily acquired by the poor than the rich: for submissiveness is the companion of those that want, while loftiness of mind dwells with riches . Notwithstanding, even in many of the rich is found that spirit which uses its abundance not for the increasing of its pride but on works of kindness, and counts that for the greatest gain which it expends in the relief of others' hardships. It is given to every kind and rank of men to share in this virtue, because men may be equal in will, though unequal in fortune: and it does not matter how different they are in earthly means, who are found equal in spiritual possessions. Blessed. therefore, is poverty which is not possessed with a love of temporal things, and does not seek to be increased with the riches of the world, but is eager to amass heavenly possessions.

III. Scriptural Examples of Humility.

Of this high-souled humility the Apostles first , after the Lord, have given us example, who, leaving all that they had without difference at the voice of the heavenly Master, were turned by a ready change from the catching of fish to be fishers of men, and made many like themselves through the imitation of their faith, when with those first-begotten sons of the Church, "the heart of all was one, and the spirit one, of those that believed :"for they, putting away the whole of their things and possessions, enriched themselves with eternal goods, through the most devoted poverty, and in accordance with the Apostles' preaching rejoiced to have nothing of the world and possess all things with Christ. Hence the blessed Apostle Peter, when he was going up into the temple, and was asked for alms by the lame man, said, "Silver and gold is not mine, but what I have that I give thee: in the Name of Jesus Christ of Nazareth, arise and walk ." What more sublime than this humility? what richer than this poverty? He hath not stores of money , but he hath gifts of nature. He whom his mother had brought forth lame from the womb, is made whole by Peter with a word; and he who gave not Caesar's image in a coin, restored Christ's image on the man. And by the riches of this treasure not he only was aided whose lower of walking was restored, but 5,000 men also, who then believed at the Apostle's exhortation on account of the wonder of this cure. And that poor man who had not what to give to the asker, bestowed so great a bounty of Divine Grace, that, as he had set one man straight on his feet, so he healed these many thousands of believers in their hearts, and made them "leap as an hart" in Christ whom he had found limping in Jewish unbelief.

IV. The Blessedness of Mourning Discussed.

After the assertion of this most happy humility, the Lord hath added, saying, "Blessed are they which mourn, for they shall be comforted ." This mourning, beloved, to which eternal comforting is promised, is not the same as the affliction of this world: nor do those laments which are poured out in the sorrowings of the whole human race make any one blessed. The reason for holy groanings, the cause of blessed tears, is very different. Religious grief mourns sin either that of others' or one's own: nor does it mourn for that which is wrought by God's justice, but it laments over that which is committed by man's iniquity, where he that does wrong is more to be deplored than he who suffers it, because the unjust man's wrongdoing plunges him into punishment, but the just man's endurance leads him on to glory.

V. The Blessedness of the Meek.

Next the Lord says: "blessed are the meek, for they shall possess the earth by inheritance ." To the meek and gentle, to the humble and modest, and to those who are prepared to endure all injuries, the earth is promised for their possession. And this is not to be reckoned a small or cheap inheritance, as if it were distinct from our heavenly dwelling, since it is no other than these who are understood to enter the kingdom of heaven. The earth, then, which is promised to the meek, and is to be given to the gentle in possession, is the flesh of the saints, which in reward for their humility will be changed in a happy resurrection, and clothed with the glory of immortality, in nothing now to act contrary to the spirit, and to be in complete unity and agreement with the will of the soul . For then the outer man will be the peaceful and unblemished possession of the inner man: then the mind, engrossed in beholding God, will be hampered by no obstacles of human weakness nor will it any more have to be said "The body which is corrupted, weigheth upon the soul, and its earthly house presseth down the sense which thinketh many things :" for the earth will not struggle against its tenant, and will not venture on any insubordination against the rule of its governor. For the meek shall possess it in perpetual peace, and nothing shall be taken from their rights, "when this corruptible shall have put on incorruption, and this mortal shall have put on immortality :" that their danger may turn into reward, and what was a burden become an honour .

VI. The Blessedness of Desiring Righteousness.

After this the Lord goes on to say: "blessed are they who hunger and thirst after righteousness, for they shall be satisfied ." It is nothing bodily, nothing earthly, that this hunger, thisthirst seeks for: but it desires to be satiated with the good food of righteousness, and wants to be admitted to all the deepest mysteries, and be filled with the Lord Himself. Happy the mind that craves this food and is eager for such drink: which it certainly would not seek for if it had never tasted of its sweetness. But hearing the Prophet's spirit saying to him: "taste and see that the Lord is sweet ;" it has received some portion of sweetness from on high, and blazed out into love of the purest pleasure, so that spurning all things temporal, it is seized with the utmost eagerness for eating and drinking righteousness, and grasps the truth of that first commandment which says: "Thou shalt love the Lord thy God out of all thy heart, and out of all thy mind, and out of all thy strength :" since to love God is nothing else but to love righteousness . In fine, as in that passage the care for one's neighbour is joined to the love of God, so, too, here the virtue of mercy is linked to the desire for righteousness, and it is said:

VII. The Blessedness of the Merciful:

"Blessed are the merciful, for God shall have mercy on them ." Recognize, Christian, the worth of thy wisdom, and understand to what rewards thou art called, and by what methods of discipline thou must attain thereto. Mercy wishes thee to be merciful, righteousness to be righteous, that the Creator may be seen in His creature, and the image of God may be reflected in the mirror of the human heart expressed by the lines of imitation. The faith of those who do good is free from anxiety: thou shalt have all thy desires, and shalt obtain without end what thou lovest. And since through thine alms-giving all things are pure to thee, to that blessedness also thou shalt attain which is promised in consequence where the Lord says:

VIII. The Blessedness of a Pure Heart.

"Blessed are the pure in heart, for they shall see God ." Great is the happiness, beloved, of him for whom so great a reward is prepared. What, then, is it to have the heart pure, but to strive after those virtues which are mentioned above? And how great the blessedness of seeing God, what mind can conceive, what tongue declare? And yet this shall ensue when man's nature is transformed, so that no longer "in a mirror," nor "in a riddle," but "face to face " it sees the very Godhead "as He is ," which no man could see ; and through the unspeakable joy of eternal contemplation obtains that "which eye has not seen, nor ear heard, neither has entered into the heart of man ." Rightly is this blessedness promised to purity of heart. For the brightness of the true light will not be able to be seen by the unclean sight: and that which will be happiness to minds that are bright and clean, will be a punishment to those that are stained. Therefore, let the mists of earth's vanities be shunned. and your inward eyes purged from all the filth of wickedness, that the sight may be free to feed on this great manifestation of God. For to the attainment of this we understand what follows to lead.

IX. The Blessedness of Peace-Making.

"Blessed are the peace-makers, for they shall be called the sons of God ." This blessedness, beloved, belongs not to any and every kind of agreement and harmony, but to that of which the Apostle speaks: "have peace towards God ;" and of which the Prophet David speaks: "Much peace have they that love Thy law, and they have no cause of offences ." This peace even the closest ties of friendship and the exactest likeness of mind do not really gain, if they do not agree with God's will. Similarity of bad desires, leagues in crimes, associations of vice, cannot merit this peace. The love of the world does not consort with the love of God, nor doth he enter the alliance of the sons of God who will not separate himself from the children of this generation Whereas they who are in mind always with God, "giving diligence to keep the unity of the Spirit in the bond of peace ," never dissent from the eternal law, uttering that prayer of faith, "Thy will be done as in heaven so on earth ." These are "the peacemakers," these are thoroughly of one mind, and fully harmonious, and are to be called sons "of God and joint-heirs with Christ ," because this shall be the record of the love of God and the love of our neighbour, that we shall suffer no calamities, be in fear of no offence, but all the strife of trial ended, rest in God's most perfect peace, through our Lord, Who, with the Father and the Holy Spirit, liveth and reigneth for ever and ever. Amen.

www.ingramcontent.com/pod-product-compliance
Lightning Source LLC
LaVergne TN
LVHW052340080426
835508LV00045B/2883